THE ORVIS® GUIDE TO STILLWATER TROUT FISHING

PHIL ROWLEY

FOREWORD BY TOM ROSENBAUER

Guilford, Connecticut

An imprint of The Rowman & Littlefield Publishing Group, Inc.
4501 Forbes Blvd., Ste. 200
Lanham, MD 20706
www.rowman.com

Distributed by NATIONAL BOOK NETWORK

British Library Cataloguing in Publication Information available

Library of Congress Cataloging-in-Publication Data
Names: Rowley, Phil (Fly fisher), author.
Title: The Orvis guide to stillwater trout fishing / Phil Rowley ; foreword by Tom Rosenbauer.
Description: Guilford, Connecticut : Lyons Press, [2021] | Includes index. | Summary: "A guide to everything the aspiring stillwater fly fisher needs to be successful and build a sound foundation that will last through a lifetime plying stillwater'— Provided by publisher.
Identifiers: LCCN 2020056029 (print) | LCCN 2020056030 (ebook) | ISBN 9781493040049 (paperback) | ISBN 9781493040056 (epub)
Subjects: LCSH: Trout fishing—Guidebooks.
Classification: LCC SH687 .R695 2021 (print) | LCC SH687 (ebook) | DDC 799.17/57—dc23
LC record available at https://lccn.loc.gov/2020056029
LC ebook record available at https://lccn.loc.gov/2020056030

∞™ The paper used in this publication meets the minimum requirements of American National Standard for Information Sciences—Permanence of Paper for Printed Library Materials, ANSI/NISO Z39.48-1992.

DEDICATION

To my wife, Patsy; my sons, Brandon and Sean; and the steadily growing number of dedicated stillwater fly fishers worldwide

"Because You Never Stop Learning!"

CONTENTS

Acknowledgments . . . vi

Foreword by Tom Rosenbauer . . . ix

Introduction: Why Lakes? . . . xi

1 Equipment: Rods, Reels, and Lines . . . 1

2 Equipment: Accessories . . . 15

3 Getting Around: Watercraft and Anchoring . . . 38

4 Leaders, Knots and Droppers . . . 62

5 How Lakes Work . . . 87

6 What Trout Eat: Stillwater Entomology . . . 105

7 How to Find Trout in Lakes . . . 166

8 Inducing a Take: Stillwater Presentation and Retrieves . . . 194

9 Floating Line Techniques: Strike Indicators and Long Leader Nymphing . . . 212

10 Floating Line Techniques: Dries, Emergers, and Targeting Sighted Fish . . . 239

11 Going Deep: Sinking Line Techniques . . . 259

12 The Power of Attraction: Attractor Techniques . . . 276

13 Introduction to Loch Style . . . 289

14 What's in Your Fly Box? Stillwater Flies . . . 305

Index . . . 333

ACKNOWLEDGMENTS

This book is the culmination of my thirty-five-plus-year fly-fishing journey, most of it focused on chasing trout and other species in lakes. The content within these pages has been pinballing around in my head for years. Getting the concepts and knowledge out of my brain proved challenging at times. The writing process took far longer than I expected, and none of it would have been possible without the assistance of my family, friends, and colleagues.

I must thank my mother, Phyllis, and my late father, Ted, for letting me go fishing with our neighbor Peter Hopley when I was six years old. Little did they know that this initial trip to chase coarse fish in Liverpool England's Sefton Park would ignite such a strong love of fishing.

When we emigrated in October of 1969, my love of fishing traveled with me. I carried on through my childhood fishing for anything that swam, in both fresh and salt water: trout, bullhead catfish, panfish, bass, sculpin, and pile perch, to name a few. In my early twenties, I met Richard Linden. Richard and I played hockey together. Knowing that I loved fishing, he was always asking me to go fly fishing with him and his father, Ted, but for some reason I never took him up on his offers.

Early in our marriage, my wife and I spent a frustrating weeklong trip fishing Vancouver Island's Cameron Lake. At the end of our trip, we had nothing to show for our efforts other than one tiny trout. One evening I watched a fly fisher, complete with wicker creel, wade into the lake, where he proceeded to catch several good-size trout. Looking back, he seemed to be the epitome of Roderick Haig Brown.

After that experience, I decided when I got home, I was going to take Richard up on his offer. After a couple of introductory casting lessons, I knew enough to be dangerous. I joined Richard and his dad on their next trip to the Skagit River, a few hours east of Vancouver. Here I caught my first trout on the fly. A dry fly no less! This experience fanned the flames of my fishing passion. I knew right there all I wanted to do was fly fish.

Thank you, Richard, for your persistence.

With my desire to learn more about fly fishing unleashed, I joined the Osprey Fly Fishers of British Columbia. I learned so much from my club experience through the club outings, method sessions, and the speakers that visited the club, further cultivating my love of fly fishing, particularly stillwaters. It was here that I first began to write about my fly-fishing experiences within the club newsletter, culminating with my first tying column, Phil's Fly Bench. Thank you to all the club members, past and present, who shared and supported my passion for fly fishing.

My club experience helped hone my writing skills to where I felt confident enough to solicit magazines for article assignments. Thankfully, after numerous rejection letters, my persistence paid off. Thanks to Art Scheck, then editor of *American Angler* magazine, for publishing my first article on chironomid larvae. With my first published article under my belt, I continued to write as other magazines published my thoughts on stillwater fly fishing and flies. Thank you to the many editors I have worked with along my writing journey.

My first book, *Fly Patterns for Stillwaters*, put me on the radar, receiving invitations to speak to fly clubs and present at fishing- and fly-fishing-specific shows. I loved these opportunities to pass along my knowledge and experience to others, a practice I still enjoy and continue today. These events led to stillwater-specific workshops, schools, guiding, and hosted trips, along with a few TV appearances.

With each talk, presentation, workshop, or school, I learned so much from the exchange of knowledge I had with other fly fishers and speakers. The lessons I learned rounded out my approach to fly fishing lakes, providing me with the versatility to develop and use a variety of different stillwater tricks and techniques, so I didn't become a "one-trick pony." Thanks to Chuck Furimsky for first allowing me to be the "stillwater guy" at his fly-fishing shows across America. My role as the stillwater guy continues today, thanks to Chuck's son, Ben Furimsky.

I owe a debt of thanks to the many other fly fishers and speakers I have met and exchanged knowledge with, many of whom have become great friends, including Gary Borger, Skip and Carol Morris, Denny Rickards, Jeff Currier, Pete Erickson, Kelly Galloup, Hal Janssen, Bill Forward, Lance Eagan, Devin Olsen, John Kent, Gareth Jones, John Randall, George Daniels, and Bill Scheiss.

Through my speaking trips and travels, I managed to spend some time fishing too. I consider myself fortunate to have been able to fish every western province and state in North America. Every time I venture out on the water, my knowledge and experience grow. Thank you to people such as Simon Gawesworth, Mike Andreassen, Ernie Gully, and the late Gord Honey, who let me join them on the water so I could learn even more. Besides your great company, many of the tricks, techniques, and presentation tactics you showed me formed part of my stillwater repertoire and are now woven within the pages of this book.

As with all projects, there are a few people who deserve special recognition for their help, their support, and perhaps most importantly, their friendship over the years.

A special thanks to Tom Rosenbauer, one of the true icons of fly fishing. Since first spending a week together to film an episode of *The New Fly Fisher* over ten years ago, Tom and I have gotten to know each other quite well. It was an initial discussion

Tom and I had while sitting at the authors' table at the Somerset Fly Fishing Show that led directly to this book. Tom felt there was a need for a comprehensive book on stillwater fly fishing and that I was the person to write it. Thank you, Tom, for your support, trust, and belief in me on this project.

Thanks to good friend, of over twenty-five years, and mentor Brian Chan. Brian and I have spent many enjoyable hours on the water together. Each time I learn something new. As a fisheries biologist, Brian's love and knowledge of trout and trout lakes are unmatched. We have worked together as presenters, hosted joint workshops, and become business partners through our online Stillwater Fly Fishing Store and Stillwater Fly Fishing app. Brian was gracious to review and provide feedback on the "How Lakes Work" chapter.

An enormous thanks to Rick Hafele. Like Brian Chan, Rick is a perfect blend of science and fishing. Rick has a master's degree in aquatic entomology and spent over twenty-five years as an aquatic biologist, specializing as an aquatic entomologist for the State of Oregon. Through the course of our friendship, Rick has become my sounding board for all things entomology. He is patient and understanding, and he tolerates my entomology-based questions and theories. His responses are always clear and concise, easy for the layperson to understand. If I headed down some entomological rabbit hole, Rick was there to guide me back, educating me along the way. I couldn't have written the "What Trout Eat" chapter without his assistance and proofreading.

Thank you to Dave Hughes for providing images for this book and for his support over the years. I had the good fortune to spend a day on some private Oregon trout ponds a few years ago, and managed to have a particularly good day on the water. This day made a positive impression on Dave, as I managed to dupe him into thinking I knew a thing or two about fly fishing stillwaters.

Thanks to Todd Oishi for his help, support, and willingness to pass along his years of knowledge and experience as a competitive fly fisher. Todd provided invaluable assistance and guidance with the "Introduction to Loch Style" chapter.

Thank you to Gerry McBride. I have enjoyed our conversations regarding specific fly pattern and presentation challenges. Gerry introduced me to a number of his innovative patterns and tying techniques, especially balanced flies. Balanced flies have had a huge impact on my personal pattern design.

And last but not least, I owe an enormous amount of thanks and love to my wife, Patsy, and my two sons, Brandon and Sean. Words can't say enough. They keep me humble and balanced, tolerate my obsession gone wild, and complain when I don't take them fishing enough. A special thanks to my younger son, Sean. His graphic talents are scattered throughout the pages of this book. Without my family's love, support, and belief, I would never have been able to pursue my passion for fly fishing or been able to complete this book.

FOREWORD BY TOM ROSENBAUER

I find myself periodically claiming to dislike stillwater trout fishing. There's no current to play in, you typically need some kind of watercraft, you often need to go to sinking lines. But, like most things we claim to have no interest in, it's more from a lack of familiarity and, honestly, a lack of knowledge that brings me to this conclusion. I suck at stillwater trout fishing. The times when I actually get on a lake or pond and conditions are right, whether it's fishing a Hex hatch on a northern lake for brook trout or sight-fishing to big browns cruising the shoreline, I love stillwater trout. Not having done it a lot, I've had some slow days and some amazing experiences. But I suppose it's a lot like taking a stillwater angler to moving water on a day when the river is too high, the water is too cold for decent hatches, and you never even see a fish. If that were my only experience with moving water fishing for trout, I wouldn't think much of it either. And I've had plenty of those days, but have also had many fine days on rivers and that's what keeps me coming back. I just need more days on the water with Phil Rowley to experience what is wonderful about lake fishing for trout.

Here's a great example of what makes Phil *Phil.* We were filming a TV show in a series I hosted and wanted to include a stillwater trout episode, but I was not comfortable hosting it or being the expert. Because I'm not. So I twisted Phil's arm to be the primary host, with me as a guest, because I don't know of a better teacher when it comes to this discipline. We started on an early morning on Henry's Lake in Idaho. The wind was blowing somewhere north of 20 mph, it was spitting snow, and we had a long boat ride across the lake. So there we were, me crumpled on the bow of the boat trying to draw as much rain jacket and Primaloft around me, pulling my wool hat down below my ears, and generally remembering why I don't like stillwater trout fishing. And there was Phil in the stern, running the tiller, no gloves, trying to squint through the sleet banging into his face. And all the while he's making cheerful conversation, as if we were sitting in a warm coffee shop with a big pile of doughnuts in front of us. How the fishing was going to be great, this is great weather for lake fishing, it's just a wonderful day. I'm telling you I was ready to turn around and bag the whole day of shooting right there.

But when we got to the spot Phil had scouted out the day before, he gave me an outfit with one of his special streamers on it, and I was almost immediately into big cutthroats. As long as I did exactly what Phil told me. And then he set me up with a long indicator rig and I caught fish that way. Suddenly my hands felt like they were again part of my body and my spirits were lifted. That's what Phil will do to you. He loves stillwater fishing and he adores teaching.

I don't want to pigeonhole Phil as just a stillwater angler, though. I spent a few days with him on some tough spring creeks fishing to Hex and PMD hatches, and he was every bit as knowledgeable (and cheerful) as he is on flat water. But the stillwater world is woefully short of good instructional material, and luckily Phil has concentrated his efforts in this realm.

A lot has happened in stillwater trout fishing over the past twenty years, and North America has a long way to catch up to European anglers. Just ask members of the US fly-fishing team about the first time they competed against European anglers. It was a humbling experience, and we North Americans, with our vast resources as compared to those of Europe, were so far behind in techniques that we had to learn fly fishing from scratch. It wasn't just Euro nymphing that they opened our eyes with. They were such better stillwater anglers because a lot of the trout fishing in Europe is on reservoirs, and they have developed extremely sophisticated techniques for catching them. But Phil has been quietly forging ahead with innovative techniques that match our North American waters even better than borrowed tactics from the other side of the Atlantic.

So when I realized that the Orvis series of instructional books was missing a thorough, modern guide to stillwater trout fishing to complement the podcasts and videos I've done with Phil over the years, it was pretty much a no-brainer to find the right author. If you've been searching for answers on finding trout in lakes and ponds, how to rig for them, what watercraft to buy, and how to pick the right fly, you need to go no further.

Just don't ask me these questions. I'd have to look them up in Phil's book.

INTRODUCTION: WHY LAKES?

As I look back, it seems ironic that I prefer to fly fish lakes. My first fly-fishing experience took place on the Skagit River just above Ross Lake in southwest British Columbia. During my first trip, I caught a couple of beautiful rainbow trout, and my fly-fishing addiction began. You might think that based on these initial experiences, I would be a devoted river and stream fly fisher. Although I thoroughly enjoy fly fishing rivers and streams, I love fly fishing lakes.

So why lakes? For many people, lakes can be intimidating. At first glance, they seem vast and featureless. You feel defeated before you even get a chance to wet a fly, especially anglers comfortable and accustomed to fishing rivers and streams. If you wish to learn or improve your stillwater skills, the quest can be tough. Most fly-fishing literature seems skewed toward moving waters. I can assure you lakes have just as much personality as a river and stream. You just have to learn how they work and how to approach them. Understanding how lakes work and the presentation skills needed to be successful is one of the guiding principles this book aims to clarify. Thankfully lakes offer numerous benefits.

At first glance, lakes seem vast, intimidating, and challenging to figure out. The riches lakes have to offer are well worth the investment.

NO ANNUAL RUNOFF

One of the annual challenges moving water fly fishers face on most rivers and streams is high water due to yearly runoff. Once annual runoff begins on a river, it can be a week or more before the water returns to a safe and fishable shape. Anglers must wait until runoff is complete or cram themselves onto runoff-resistant tailwater fisheries. At this time, crowded conditions are the norm. Many productive trout lakes are in prime condition when runoff is in full swing. Insects are hatching and trout are active, providing an excellent opportunity to give stillwater fly fishing a try. At the very least, getting out on a lake beats sitting at home waiting until runoff has finished.

Other than seasonal turnover, lakes are not subject to runoff.

The exception is turnover, which happens twice a year on productive lakes that ice over and once a year on lakes that don't ice over. Turnover lasts approximately five to seven days, and during that time fishing can be challenging. Unlike rivers, which may all be experiencing runoff in an area, if you choose a lake that is in turnover, you have the option of moving to a nearby lake that has yet to turn or one that has already turned.

FEWER CROWDS

Although there are always exceptions, lakes tend to be less crowded than rivers and streams. I often find when fishing moving water that if I come across another angler who has fished the water I was hoping to prospect, fishing can be challenging. An experienced fly fisher will probably have thoroughly explored the water, leaving little to catch. Conversely, if they are less experienced, they might have inadvertently put all of the fish down or at least on notice, making fishing more challenging. Some might argue, particularly competitive fly fishers, that these are opportunities to relish, as they undoubtedly improve your fly-fishing skills. Catching fish in tough, crowded conditions is a challenge that motivates many fly fishers.

Lakes offer plenty of space, so crowding is seldom an issue.

REDUCED PACE

For many, stillwaters offer a more relaxed experience. Moving waters are dynamic. There is lots of activity to keep you busy—walking, wading, casting, and mending. The pace of the day, especially if you end up wading against the current, can be tiring. Lakes offer a much more relaxed pace, often in a seated position in a boat, pontoon boat, or other watercraft. If the rigors of stream fishing are becoming too much, maybe lakes are the place for you.

The pace of a day on a lake is typically more relaxed than on moving water.

Be warned, if you are high energy and always on the move, the pace and patience required to fish lakes can be challenging. When I am on the water with run-and-gun streamer fly fishers, tempering their enthusiasm so they develop the necessary patience and touch to be consistently successful can be difficult.

MATCHING THE HATCH

Suggesting what fish are feeding on, or "matching the hatch," is one of the foundation pillars of fly fishing. Understanding and learning about all of the different food sources stillwater trout feed upon was one of the initial fascinations that drew me to fly fishing. It's an attraction that remains with me to this day.

Trout in productive lakes dine on myriad prey. Depending on the season and the biological makeup of a lake, trout have the option of feeding on a laundry list of food items including chironomids, scuds, leeches, damselflies, dragonflies, water boatmen, backswimmers, zooplankton, minnows, mayflies, caddisflies, terrestrials, snails, and crayfish. It is common for trout to shift their attention throughout any given day to two or more of these food items, adding another level of complexity to this hatch-matching matrix. The following day the plate may be wiped clean. The trout have switched their attention to something different despite conditions appearing the same as they were the day before.

For those who enjoy the challenge of matching the hatch, lakes offer a lifetime of challenges.

Another benefit when matching the hatch is that trout food in lakes tends to be larger than river and stream food sources. Rarely do I have to choose flies smaller than size 16. Although there are exceptions such as small scuds or chironomid pupae, the stillwater hatch matcher, depending on the food source of choice, can compete fishing a range of patterns from size 16 through 6.

Chironomids, arguably the most essential stillwater food source, particularly in productive western stillwaters, can be an all-consuming food to match. The pupal stage, in particular, offers an almost limitless supply of size and color options, so much so that many addicted chironomid fishers often affectionately reference their addiction as a cult.

Other localized food items could also end up on this list. This inventory of food offers more than enough to keep even the most ardent hatch matcher occupied for years. We will be discussing the most common prey items in detail through the entomology chapter in this book.

AVERAGE FISH SIZE

It's no secret that lakes, especially productive ones, offer the perfect combination of food and habitat to produce massive trout. A trout's head grows at a controlled rate each year, but their bodies expand as fast as they can feed. In ideal conditions, it is not unheard of for trout to pack on 2 pounds in a single season. It is common to see mutant trout featuring tiny heads and tails connected to a body that should belong to a fish four times their actual size.

Perhaps the best example of this is Argentina's Lago Strobel (Jurassic Lake). Lago Strobel trout frequently dine on calorie-rich scuds, resulting in an unbelievable average size. Rainbow trout of 20 pounds are commonplace. It is a destination that throws your entire concept of trout size out the window.

Granted, Lago Strobel is one of the world's exceptions, but ask any stillwater fly fisher how they did on any given day, and their catch statistics almost always refer to fish sizes in pounds, not inches—a scoring system I often use to tease my river- and stream-based fly-fishing friends. Although I freely admit to my bias, I believe if you want to catch a trout of a lifetime, lakes offer you the best chance to make that dream a reality.

It has been said, by some, that in addition to size, stillwater trout tend to be more gullible than their river and stream brethren. As with any fishery, many variables dictate the ease or difficulty of fishing, such as angling pressure. Some private lakes that don't see many anglers arguably offer the chance to catch large, less demanding trout. There are also times when supposedly easy-to-fish private lakes provide considerable challenges. Public lakes that see large numbers of fly fishers can offer some of the most perplexing fly-fishing situations I have ever encountered. After being caught and released more than once, stillwater trout can be just as wary

Under the right conditions, trout in productive lakes can reach gargantuan sizes.

and challenging to deceive as a river or stream trout—conditions that are as challenging or, at times, more challenging than any blue-ribbon trout stream.

DIVERSITY OF SPECIES

Lakes, as with rivers, are often home to a variety of different species. Besides trout, lakes offer the opportunity to dupe several different species on the fly. Once you have a good understanding of how lakes work, learn how fish react to environmental changes, develop the presentation skills to suggest the various food sources, and learn how to locate and target different stillwater structures, you can catch all manner of fish.

Stillwater fly fishing is not just a trout game. Many of the techniques and tactics discussed in this book work not only for trout but for other species too.

If you don't have any trout lakes nearby, don't worry. The strategies and tactics discussed in this book work on a variety of species, not just trout. I approach and fish all lakes the same regardless of species. With a few tweaks to compensate for various fish preferences, you can catch bass, pike, walleye, and lake whitefish consistently on the fly.

I subscribe to an underlying philosophy when it comes to fly fishing: "If it swims and eats, I believe I can catch it on the fly."

CHAPTER 1

EQUIPMENT: RODS, REELS, AND LINES

As with fly fishing rivers, streams, and oceans, the fly rod, reel, and line are the primary presentation tools for the stillwater fly fisher. You can certainly begin fly fishing lakes with the gear you already have on hand. For many river and stream anglers, this consists of a 5-weight, 9-foot or perhaps 9½-foot rod, reel, and floating line. This basic setup will work, but you will soon find out it has limitations if you want to fly fish lakes regularly. Lakes are different from moving waters. As a result, if you plan on spending more than a few trips per year fly fishing lakes, equipment best suited for the job will provide greater enjoyment and on-the-water success.

When it comes to these three core pieces of equipment, there is always a variety of opinions. Based on my stillwater experiences, here are my thoughts and preferences regarding fly rods, reels, and the diversity of lines available for the lake angler.

FLY RODS

Depending on wind and fish size, fly rods from 4-weight through 7-weight are best suited for stillwater trout fishing. A 4-weight rod would be the right choice for smaller trout and light winds, while a 7-weight would be a better choice for larger fish and strong winds. If you plan on fishing from a drifting boat, loch style, as many competition fly fishers do, a 6-weight or 7-weight rod would be the better choice due to the increased casting frequency associated with this technique. A 5-weight or 6-weight rod offers the best blend, enabling you to enjoy the fight without undue stress to the fish and helping you cope with wind.

Personal preference is always a factor when choosing a fly rod. For stillwaters, I recommend long rods, a minimum of 9½ feet, preferably 10 feet or longer, as they offer several presentation benefits.
BARRY ACTON

Although always open for debate, I believe rod length makes a difference. Casting distance, except for indicator presentations and targeting surface feeders, is a prime consideration. While some stillwater fly fishers prefer stiff, fast-action rods for distance and for casting heavy, fast-sinking lines, I have a definite preference for long rods, a minimum of 9½ feet, 10 feet preferred, with a moderate to moderate-fast action. To me, longer rods offer several benefits:

Long rods help facilitate the formation of wide, open loops. Open loops help reduce tangles when casting complex indicator rigs or floating lines coupled with long leaders and multiple flies.

1. Open loops: As the tip of a long, 9½- to 10-foot rod travels through a longer path than a shorter 9-foot rod over the same stroke distance, it forms a more open loop. When casting narrow-diameter indicator leaders and long leaders, an open loop is less likely to tangle
2. Roll casting: Roll casts are ideal when using strike indicator presentations featuring long, thin leaders, indicators, swivels, and multiple flies. As the flies only leave the water on the final push to a stop, the risk of tangles is minimal. Long casts are not required or desired when fishing strike indicators. For my casting style, a moderate-fast rod loads well into the blank, allowing for a great roll cast with barely a rod length of line out of the rod tip. In these situations, I find stiff, fast-action rods struggle trying to roll cast a short length of fly line, as there isn't enough line outside of the rod to effectively load it. Having a rod length that can roll cast a short length of line allows for longer presentations, as I can retrieve the line almost within a rod length of the tip.
3. Longer indicator sets: A longer rod allows for a greater set distance between indicator and fly. Once set, fixed position indicators don't slide on the leader,

Strike indicator leaders are complex and can be tangle-prone. A roll cast helps reduce tangles when using indicators, as your leader, indicator, and flies only come out of the water as you push the rod forward to complete the cast. Long, 9½ feet or greater, fly rods are ideal roll-casting tools. SEAN ROWLEY

limiting the presentation depth. Having your indicator set at a longer length than your rod can result in the indicator jamming against the rod tip and becoming a barrier when you attempt to land a fish.

4. Mending: Using the wind-induced current to help drift your flies with floating lines, with or without indicators, is an excellent presentation technique. Reach casts and mends are key presentation elements allowing you to control the downwind drift, fly speed, and presentation depth while covering water. Long rods provide superior mending and presentation control versus shorter rods.

BRIAN CHAN

5. Cushion hook-sets: The soft, forgiving tip of a long moderate- or moderate-fast-action rod protects tippets, especially when using strike indicators or floating lines with long leaders.
6. Improved hang: The hang is a controlled rod raise at the end of a cast intended to induce any fish following the fly to take it. A long rod offers a longer hang while keeping the flies farther away from the boat so you don't spook any fish following your fly should it see you in the background.
7. Steering and controlling fish: As the fight nears the boat, pontoon, or float tube, trout have an uncanny knack of wrapping line and leader around anchor ropes, motors, transducers, drogues, and anything else they can find. A long rod provides you with an added level of extension to reach out and steer fish away from or around potential obstructions.

An up-locking reel seat or fighting butt is an advantage when fighting a large trout. While fighting a fish, you should aim to keep the rod and reel within your body core. In this position, you are better able to respond to the fish, establish control, and reduce fight time, a practice that reduces stress on the fish. The up-lock seat or fighting butt keeps the reel away from your body just enough so that should a fish surge unexpectedly, the reel will not bind against your body, causing a break-off or the hook to pull free.

REELS

The majority of the time, a stillwater reel serves the same primary purpose as it does on rivers and streams: line storage. When fighting fish, the shock absorption and power of the fly rod coupled with pinching the line against the handle using the forefinger of the rod hand is often all that is needed to win the battle. An exposed rim

Look for reels featuring an exposed rim. Reels with exposed rims are less likely to pinch and potentially damage a line when changing a spool, and you can also use the palm of your hand to apply drag to help slow down a running fish.

is beneficial for palming a reel to help slow down an energetic fish and is less likely to pinch the fly line should you change spools. The need to drag a speeding trout into submission isn't usually called for. However, there are those special times when you hook a large trout and having a reel with a robust disc drag system is a definite asset. Large-arbor reels are also beneficial for gathering slack line, or should a fish turn and run at you.

Depending on angler preference and presentation needs, a variety of fly lines are available for the stillwater fly fisher. Having a reel that offers additional spools to store your extra lines comes in handy. Another, less expensive option are reels that use plastic cartridges or cassettes. Often you can purchase a reel and two extra cartridges for less than a reel and spare spool. Cartridge-style reels are popular with competition stillwater anglers.

Most stillwater fly fishers store multiple lines on separate reels, spools, or cassettes. Cassette reels have become quite popular with many competition anglers.
STUART MCKIE

FLY LINES

The one item seasoned stillwater fly fishers usually have in abundance are fly lines. There is a wide variety of lines to choose from, each with different applications, some presentation based and others preference based. I admit to carrying lots of different stillwater lines. Having a variety of lines at my disposal allows me to tackle almost any presentation challenge thrown my way. On any given trip, I have three floating lines, two clear-tip lines, a hover line, two clear intermediate sinking lines of differing sink rates, and a range of sinking lines from type III through type VII sink rate. In recent years I have also been adding other fly lines, such as integrated sweep lines and lines initially intended for non-stillwater applications, with excellent results.

Line Cores

Today's stillwater lines offer a variety of core options. Each core option provides different pros and cons:

- Braided multifilament: Supple multifilament cores feature low memory and work across a range of conditions, including cool to cold water temperatures. They are a standard, widespread core option with many different line companies.
- Mono or braided mono: Clear intermediate lines feature mono or braided mono cores. These cores are low stretch and can help facilitate long casts, enabling you to cover more water. As these cores are primarily transparent, they also provide an element of stealth. When fishing a clear-water lake on a bright sunny day, a solid-color line may create a shadow that could alert or spook fish. As they aren't as supple as multifilament cores, mono or braided core lines can be more memory-prone when fishing in cold temperatures. A good line stretch typically cures this issue.
- Low stretch: An average multifilament core line can stretch up to 18 percent, but low-stretch lines only stretch 6 percent. I fish low-stretch lines most of the time, as I feel they offer many benefits:

    1. Enhanced strike detection: Low-stretch cores allow you to detect subtle grabs, as the take isn't absorbed by any elasticity in the line. There is a chance that a solid strike may cause a break-off due to a lack of line absorption. A rod with a forgiving tip helps with this potential shortfall.
    2. Improved casting performance: A low-stretch line won't expand, creating a possible loss of casting energy when you stop the rod on either the forward cast or backcast.
    3. Efficiently defeat fish: Once you hook a fish, a low-stretch line transfers the rod actions you use to subdue the fish proficiently, helping to land and release fish quickly.

Density Compensation

Almost all top-end sinking lines, type III or higher, are density compensated, while entry-level sinking lines usually are not. So, what does density compensation mean? Before density compensation, line manufacturers concentrated the tungsten powder coating used to weight sinking lines in the mid-portion, or belly, of the head section of the fly line. Due to its thin diameter, the thin coating of the running line behind the head section on a weight-forward sinking line also contained less tungsten. The belly area, within the head section of the sinking line, was the densest. As a result, it sank in a curved, or "hockey stick," profile. This profile made controlling line depth and strike detection difficult.

To address this profile, line manufacturers adjusted the line density by concentrating more tungsten powder toward the end of the line, combining different sink rates along the length of the line, or a combination of both. The result is a line that sinks tip first, providing superior bite detection and presentation control. Density compensation is a desirable feature all manufacturers promote, on both their line packaging and their websites.

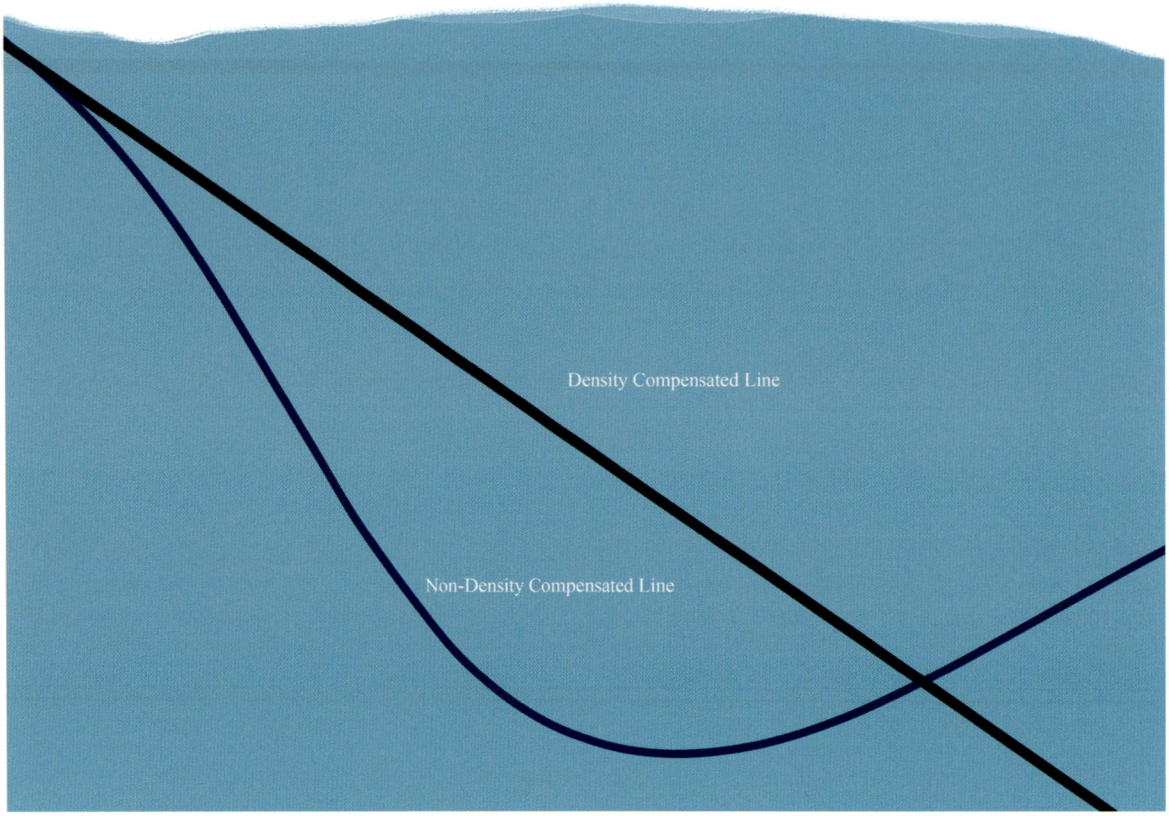

Density-compensated lines sink tip first, providing superior bite detection and presentation control. There is still a place, however, for lines that are not density compensated in your kit bag, such as slow-sinking lines like a hover or clear intermediate. These are two line types I would never venture out on the water without.

Floating Lines

The majority of stillwater floating line presentations are subsurface, either suspending flies beneath strike indicators or long-leader nymphing. Floating lines for lakes should feature a line profile capable of dealing with these two primary presentation options. Specific stillwater floating lines aren't commonplace. While any floating line can cast an indicator or long leader, fly lines designed to fish complex nymphing rigs and indicators on rivers, load fast-action rods, cast in windy conditions, or toss large, wind-resistant flies are best suited for strike indicator or long-leader presentations.

Check the manufacturer's line diagrams on the box art or website. Look for weight-forward lines featuring short, abrupt front tapers or large heads. These line profiles are well suited to push wind-resistant indicators, swivels, multiple flies, and long skinny leaders. Indicator lines designed for moving water also offer a larger surface area for mending. A line with a large surface area eases mending and provides increased friction and rod loading for roll casts. Lines featuring long front tapers dissipate casting energy to allow a delicate presentation. Presentation lines struggle when asked to cast indicator and long-leader setups.

A floating line is arguably the most versatile stillwater line—a line that all stillwater fly fishers should have with them at all times. The versatility of a floating line allows you to fish dry flies and emergers at the surface, suspend flies at various depths using strike indicators, and use long leaders and weighted flies to reach water over 20 feet deep.

Many floating lines feature color changes separating the head of the line from the running line. These color changes come in handy when trying to gauge casting distance when fishing indicators. Long casts aren't necessary when fishing indicators, and are actually a detriment. The farther you are away from your strike indicator, the less likely you will be able to recognize or react to subtle takes. Don't make casts any longer than the color change.

Despite my reliance on floating lines designed for subsurface presentations, I still save a space for a presentation line for fishing adult and emerger imitations. While you can use a floating line suited to cast indicators or long leaders to target surface-feeding fish, there is a high probability of landing a less-than-delicate cast among a pod of rising fish and having them scatter. You need to be able to make short, accurate casts for consistent success. If you expect to fish dries and emergers, a floating line featuring a long front taper designed with surface-feeding fish in mind is an asset. Depending on the manufacturer, floating lines are available on either multifilament or low-stretch cores.

Clear-Tip Lines

Clear-tip, or midge-tip, lines are one of the most underrated but versatile lines available to the stillwater angler. A clear-tip line is a subtle sink tip featuring a slow-sinking clear intermediate tip fused to a floating line. Depending on the manufacturer, the clear tip can be anywhere from 3 feet to 12 feet long. I have a preference for short tips, 6 feet or less. Longer clear-tip, shooting head lines intended for other, non-stillwater applications are also available and are a worthwhile addition. These longer lines are ideal choices for baitfish, leech, and scud patterns. I rarely, if ever, use a traditional 10-foot fast-sinking sink-tip line in lakes. Except for a clear-tip line, I believe I get a better presentation using full-sinking lines of varying sink rates. I am also not a fan of the hinging action of a fast-sinking sink tip.

Clear-tip lines are ideal tools for shallow-water nymphing or when fish are feeding near the surface. These lines are a favorite choice when mayfly nymphs, damselfly nymphs, and caddis pupae are on the menu. Emerging caddis pupae and mayfly nymphs ascend on an acute angle to the surface, and a clear-tip line helps provide the same ascent angle as the naturals. There are times when fish become attuned to how some food sources move through the water. Having your flies move through the same angle can, at times, prove to be a critical presentation consideration.

I also love these lines when imitating chironomid larva and pupa patterns in deep water, over 15 feet, and especially in windy conditions. The clear tip slices through the surface chop, helping to maintain contact with your fly or flies and provide better presentation control than a floating line or floating line and indicator system. An aggressive wind-induced surface chop often wreaks havoc with floating line presentations, as it pitches and jerks the flies around. When using long-leader nymphing tactics, connection to the flies is also lost in the swells, impeding strike detection.

A clear-tip line is also an ideal option for fishing dries and emergers. See chapter 10, "Floating Line Techniques: Dries, Emergers, and Targeting Sighted Fish," for a full explanation of how to use clear-tip lines to target surface-feeding trout.

Versi or Poly Leaders are a clear-tip alternative. These reusable leaders are available in a range of densities, from floating to fast sinking. Depending on the brand, Versi or Poly leaders come in either 7-foot or 12-foot lengths with a loop on the butt end. To add a clear tip, attach the clear intermediate leader to a floating line via a loop-to-loop connection. Versi or Poly leaders don't cast as well as an integrated clear-tip line, but they are an inexpensive option and are an excellent travel option, as they don't take up any space or weight.

Hover Lines

As with a clear-tip line, a hover line is another one of my favorite stillwater lines. Hover lines have the slowest sink rate. Depending on the manufacturer, most sink at a paltry 1 inch per second and are available in regular- or low-stretch flavors. Hover lines are ideal for prospecting shallow shoal areas or working nymph or pupa patterns to surface-feeding fish.

During the fall, when trout are cruising the shallows stocking up for the long cold winter ahead, I have experienced some memorable days stripping beadhead scud patterns, using a short, choppy, 3- to 4-inch strip-pause, through shallow water, less than 6 feet deep. The pedestrian sink rate of the hover also allows for slow, controlled presentations when water temperatures are cold, as is often the case immediately after ice-out or in late fall and when environmental conditions have fish in a fickle state of mind. The slow sink rate won't overpower your retrieve, helping you keep your fly free from fouling in the bottom weeds and debris.

A hover line is also an excellent deep-water presentation option on windy days when trout are feeding on chironomid larvae and emerging pupae in particular. In these conditions, the surface chop can harm strike indicator or long-leader presentations. A hover line slices through the chop, allowing better presentation control. The shorter, 9- to 12-foot leaders associated with this technique are also less tangle-prone than the leaders used with subsurface floating line presentations. For a complete explanation of this technique, see chapter 11, "Going Deep."

Clear Intermediate Lines

Initially designed for warm tropical conditions, the clear intermediate is a primary stillwater line. The first-generation clear intermediate lines were challenging to fish. The monofilament core didn't react well with cold lake temperatures, causing frustrating line memory issues, as it behaved more like a clear Slinky. Thankfully those issues are a concern of the past, as most quality line manufacturers now feature cold-water cores.

Clear intermediate lines sink slightly faster than a hover line, anywhere from 1½ to 2 inches per second, depending on the brand. Some manufacturers also offer clear intermediate lines in two different sink rates, a slow rate of approximately 1½ inches per second and a faster 2-inch-per-second sink rate. A clear intermediate is an ideal trolling line when paddled behind a float tube or pontoon boat. Depending on the brand, clear intermediate lines feature either a supple monofilament or low-stretch core.

Due to their slow sink rates, you can use a clear intermediate in similar situations as a hover line, and at a somewhat higher retrieve pace due to the line's increased sink rate. Stealth is one of the primary advantages of the clear intermediate. Some clear intermediates are, as their name implies, transparent; others are opaque. Other lines feature a mottled camo finish that does an excellent job cloaking the line in clear-water lakes, where line shadow can alert or spook fish.

Full-Sinking Lines

There are four types of sinking lines common to all manufacturers: type III, type V, type VI, and type VII. In general, the line type, III, V, VI, or VII, corresponds approximately to the line's sink rate measured in inches per second, or ips. For example, a type III line sinks at approximately at 3 ips. Depending on the specific manufacturer, other sink rate lines are also available.

To determine the exact sink rate of a particular line, check the specifications listed on either the packaging or website. Knowing the sink rate of your line is essential so you can systematically explore different depths using a technique called the countdown.

Sinking lines are available in a variety of colors, depending on the brand. Darker colors are standard, such as gray, black, green, and blue. At depth, dark colors blend in with the surrounding water. Within a given line manufacturer, the darker the color, the faster the sink rate. Line diameter also decreases as the sink rate increases. Thin-diameter lines can tangle, but there are a few simple strategies you can use to reduce this frustration.

Sinking line cores can be multifilament, mono, braided mono, or low stretch. Low-stretch cores are an advantage at times, especially for fish that aren't aggressive or when fishing buoyant flies. Losing contact with a buoyant fly can result in a deeply hooked fish.

I have at least one of each sink rate with me when I am on the water. Line choice depends on a variety of factors including water depth, what I am trying to suggest, and perhaps most importantly, the activity level of the fish. For a complete explanation regarding sinking line selection and use, see chapter 11, "Going Deep."

Integrated Lines

One of the benefits a sinking line provides is the ability to explore water vertically. You can do this by varying the sink time, line type, and retrieve pace. In North America, some fly line designs have become more and more influenced by competition fishing. Competition anglers are not allowed to fish from an anchored position; casting and retrieving from a drifting boat or loch style is the only way you can fish. Many anglers prefer this technique, as you are always on the move and presenting your flies to fresh fish as you drift down to them. When competition fishing, you are fishing in a session governed by a set time. The goal is to catch and release as many fish as possible over the session. Covering as much water as possible, both horizontally and vertically, is a crucial component of success. Enter the sweep line.

The sweep line is the evolution of the non-density-compensated sink line. Lines that are not density compensated sink in an arc. When using slow retrieves, the fly follows, or sweeps, along this arc-shaped path. The sweep line has refined the curved retrieve path of a non-density-compensated line into a benefit.

Sweep lines integrate slower sink rate running and tip sections with a faster sink rate mid or belly section in a range of different combinations. For example, a 2-4-1.5 sweep line consists of a type II running line, a type IV belly section, and a tip section that sinks at 1½ inches per second. Each combination offers a different retrieve path and speed options depending on the conditions to match the mood of the fish. One day trout might be more responsive to a shallow sweep angle, and on another day they may respond to a steep retrieve angle.

Summary

Stillwater lines are always in a state of flux as new line options and combinations become available. Line manufacturers provide these options based on angler feedback and a genuine desire to improve our stillwater experience. However, it can become daunting and confusing.

To manage the presentation challenges of fly fishing lakes, you will need at least a floating, a clear intermediate, and a fast-sinking line. I usually have a minimum of two rods rigged with different lines, making it easy and efficient to change from one line or presentation technique to another.

Budget and your personal preferences temper the sometimes mind-boggling choices available today. Although I am a horrible golfer, I compare stillwater fly line options to golf clubs. Some golfers use a narrow range of clubs that match both their style and skill level. There are core clubs that will get you through most rounds. Stillwater lines are similar. There are three core lines that all stillwater fly fishers should carry. As your experience grows, you can add other lines as your budget, needs, and wants allow. The line types listed below cover the initial requirements of most stillwater fishers:

1. Floating line (not for fishing dries and emergers, but rather subsurface using either strike indicator or long-leader nymphing techniques)
2. Clear intermediate or "camo" line
3. Fast-sinking line, type V

If you are going to invest in a new line, it is imperative that you learn and understand the line's characteristics, how to use them to your advantage, and in which situations the line performs best. The best time to do this is when fishing is good.

After you have satisfied your initial appetite for catching fish, give the new line a try. Practice and learn the presentation methods and techniques it is known or recommended for.

This practice instills confidence in the line, and you gain value for your investment. When you are on the water and conditions seem against you and the fish aren't cooperating, you are more likely to try a new line and associated presentation techniques. But tough days are not the time to figure out something new. If all goes well, you will be like me, smothered in a variety of line types and options.

CHAPTER TAKEAWAYS

- I favor long rods, a minimum of 9½ feet, preferably 10 feet, for my stillwater fly fishing. Long rods offer several presentation benefits over shorter rods.
- Several fly line cores are available. Each core type option provides different pros and cons. A good cross section of stillwater lines will feature lines of each core type.
- Low-stretch core fly lines offer several casting and presentation benefits including enhanced strike detection, improved casting performance, and efficiently fighting fish.
- Density-compensated lines sink tip first, ensuring direct contact between you and your flies and providing superior bite detection and presentation control.
- The majority of stillwater floating line presentations are subsurface, either suspending flies beneath strike indicators or long-leader nymphing. Floating lines for lakes should feature a line profile capable of dealing with these two primary presentation options.
- Fly lines designed to fish complex nymphing rigs and indicators on rivers, load fast-action rods, cast in windy conditions, or toss large, wind-resistant flies are best suited for floating line strike indicator or long-leader presentations.
- A variety of sinking line types are available to the stillwater fly fisher. Within your kit bag you should have a cross section of sinking lines that sink anywhere from 1 inch to 7 inches per second.
- Sweep lines integrate slower sink rate running and tip sections with a faster sink rate mid or belly section in a range of different combinations.
- A floating line suited to casting indicators and long leaders, a clear intermediate line, and a fast-sinking type V full-sink line cover the initial fly line requirements of most stillwater fishers.
- If you are going to invest in a new line, it is imperative that you learn and understand the line's characteristics, how to use them to your advantage, and in which situations the line performs best. The ideal time to do this is when fishing is good. This way, you have a level of confidence and experience to use your new line when fishing is challenging.

CHAPTER 2

EQUIPMENT: ACCESSORIES

In addition to my rod, reel, and fly lines, there are several accessories that I always have on the water with me. Most of these accessories are small and easily stored in a boat bag or the storage compartments on a pontoon boat or float tube. These items are also relatively inexpensive but become priceless should they be forgotten or lost. These are my most important, don't leave home without them, accessories.

LANDING NET

A quality long-handled landing net is a stillwater essential. The long handle extends your reach, allowing you to land fish faster. I prefer wooden nets, as besides their aesthetic appeal, they offer two primary benefits: buoyancy and fish management.

I prefer to use a long-handled wood landing net. Wooden nets float, allowing you to use both hands to handle and release fish without worry about your net sinking. Plus, they look better in photos.

Metal nets sink and, as a result, often catch you in two minds when you are trying to land a fish. Your attention is split between worrying about the welfare of the trout and trying to make sure your grip on the net doesn't slip so you don't lose it. You can add supplemental floatation to almost any metal net, such as spraying foam insulation caulking into the net handle and hoop to add buoyancy. Attaching hot water tank foam insulation around the net hoop using plastic zip ties also adds floatation. These net additions provide a functional approach to net flotation, but not the look of a well-crafted wooden net.

You can add floatation to a metal net using spray insulation foam or hot water tank foam around the hoop. Both of these foam products are available at any home improvement store.
ERNIE GULLEY

A floating net allows you to use both hands to handle, support, and manage a fish without worrying about the net sinking into the depths. Once landed, let the fish rest and recover in the floating net. On the downwind side of any boat or pontoon boat, there is always a calm spot where you can place the net with minimal risk of it drifting away. Should the net drift, you can reach out and grab it. I have on occasion, when the net drifted out of reach, had to catch it by casting and hooking the net with my flies. It is always a good idea to get some casting practice in whenever you can!

No matter the net type, the type of mesh is essential when practicing catch-and-release to protect fish adequately so their slimy protective coating remains intact. Soft cotton or rubber mesh works best. Avoid hard nylon mesh, as it is particularly tough on fish.

STILLWATER KIT BAG

A quality stillwater kit bag is worth its weight in gold for the boat-based stillwater fly fisher, as it keeps all of your gear and accessories in one place, neat and organized. It is my equipment nerve center. For those using watercraft such as pontoon boats or float tubes, the various pockets and compartments serve a similar purpose as a dedicated kit bag. You can also carry a smaller kit bag on the rear deck of a pontoon boat or float tube to complement the gear you have stored in the side pockets.

My kit bag is my on-the-water nerve center, allowing me to keep all of my equipment and accessories neat and organized in one central location.

My kit bags have always been in a constant state of flux. So far, I have yet to find the perfect bag. No matter the kit bag type, I always look for a few constants. Waterproof construction is a primary consideration. It is crucial to have a kit bag that protects your gear from the elements. Separate, adjustable, internal compartments are also important. I like to keep my gear in different sections so items are easier to find and, at the end of a busy day, return to their various compartments.

As I carry lots of equipment and accessories, I use the largest kit bag I can manage so I have everything I need for an enjoyable day on the water. Within my kit bag I have my gear sorted into six basic categories:

1. Flies (I have small boxes within my kit bag along with a larger separate fly box. See chapter 14, "What's in Your Fly Box?")
2. Reels and spare spools
3. Medical (Band-Aids, aspirin, sunscreen, lip balm, etc.)
4. Tippet and leaders (see chapter 4, "Leaders, Knots, and Droppers")
5. Accessories (nippers, swivels, bobber stops, hemostats, strike indicators, throat pump vials, etc.)
6. Observation (binoculars, small camera, notepad, etc.)

POLARIZED SUNGLASSES

Polarized sunglasses are a must. So much so that, after forgetting my glasses on one trip, I now carry two pairs. The primary function of polarized sunglasses is to eliminate surface glare. As light strikes a horizontal surface such as water, it reflects horizontally, becoming polarized and creating glare. Polarized lenses reduce glare by filtering the horizontal light waves reflected off the surface. As only vertical light waves pass through a polarized lens, you can see through the surface glare into the water. Being able to see into the water provides an invaluable advantage, helping you see subsurface structure, aquatic invertebrates and other food sources, and the fish themselves. Being able to spot fish is crucial to sight-fishing success.

Polarized sunglasses are a must on any trip, stillwaters or otherwise. They protect your eyes from errant flies and penetrate surface glare, allowing you to see into the water and helping you locate structure, cruising fish, and potential trout food.

In addition to eliminating surface glare, polarized glasses protect your eyes from harmful UV rays, reduce eye strain on bright days, and shield your eyes from errant flies as a result of a wind gust or bad cast.

Several different lens colors are available, and each works best in different light conditions. Many fly fishers today carry a variety of different-colored polarized sunglasses so they can choose the best lens color for the conditions. Blue and green lenses work best on bright days, amber and copper on overcast days. Yellow is the best choice for low-light conditions. Silver or gray is an excellent overall choice, offering good visibility on both bright and cloudy days.

THROAT PUMP

A throat pump is one of my essential accessories. Although sold as a stomach pump, I refer to this small turkey baster–like tool, consisting of an opaque tube and rounded bulb, as a throat pump, as this is the region of the trout's digestive tract that is of the most interest. A throat pump allows you to sample what a trout is feeding upon, helping to guide pattern selection and determine feeding activity and presentation depth. See chapter 7, "How to Find Trout in Lakes," for a complete explanation on how to use this invaluable tool.

A throat pump is one of my essential, don't leave home without it, accessories. A throat pump samples what a trout is feeding upon, helping to guide pattern selection and determine feeding activity and presentation depth.

SAMPLING EQUIPMENT

I always have a small aquarium net with me. Aquarium nets can fit in a kit bag or a pontoon boat or float tube pocket, while larger pond nets are an excellent boat option. A baking sieve duct-taped to a pole is another cost-effective option that works. Aquarium nets are available at pet stores. If you don't have a pet store nearby, you can usually find small aquarium nets at your local dollar store.

Poking around the shallows before getting on the water should be standard practice to see what food sources are available. A net or sieve makes it easy and safe to sample potential food sources, allowing you to catch them if they are swimming around in the shallows. Swiping a sampling net through aquatic vegetation almost always reveals something to guide both presentation and pattern choice.

An aquarium net or baking sieve allows you to sample what food sources are living in any lake. Knowing what food sources might be available will save you time on the water by helping you choose the right pattern and presentation technique.

In addition to a sampling net, a white tray, a turkey baster, and an ice cube tray are worth having on hand to further focus your sampling efforts. All of these items are readily available at most dollar stores. The white tray provides contrast, making the various items in a sample easy to see and identify. The turkey baster serves as a handy vacuum to sample smaller organisms. Trying to catch a fast-moving scud or mayfly nymph is challenging and often ends up with you crushing the sample if you are quick enough to grab one. There are also a few lake critters, such as backswimmers, that are capable of a nasty bite. The turkey baster eliminates any handling risks. Once vacuumed up into the baster, squirt the sample into one of the compartments in the ice cube tray. Keeping your samples separated is often a good idea, as at times your samples may begin feeding on each other. The aquatic jungle is one tough neighborhood.

It is always a good idea to invest 10 or 15 minutes taking stock of the various food sources that live in a lake. A visit to any local dollar store will provide you with the necessary sampling equipment.

HEMOSTATS

Hemostats, or forceps, are a standard accessory for many fly fishers. I use them for removing deeply embedded flies or for reaching into the mouth of a toothy trout. Although I typically crush the barbs down on my flies before tying, there are a few that slip through this initial step; or if I use a commercially tied pattern, hemostats easily mash barbs.

A pair of hemostats also works as a removable weight by clipping it to a fly to set indicator depth, or when setting fly depth when presenting flies vertically using fast-sinking lines, a technique commonly referred to as dangling.

I prefer hemostats with cutters at the rear of the jaws. These cutters make short work of thicker-diameter nylon or fluorocarbon, and if you ever use wire leaders for pike or muskie, cutters are a must. Nippers simply won't sever wire bite tippet.

Hemostats help remove flies from fish. A cutter at the rear of the blades helps make short work of thicker-diameter material and braid.

NIPPERS AND CUTTERS

I am forever losing track of my nippers, so I always have several pairs on hand. In recent years I have been placing them on a lanyard around my neck so they are readily available. The lanyard makes a handy place to hang my depth locator as well.

Standard leader nippers are not suitable for cutting braid. You will need specific braid-cutting nippers or scissors when building low-stretch indicator leaders.

Braid cutters or scissors are essential for constructing low-stretch leaders. A traditional nipper does a feeble job cutting braid, resulting in frayed cuts. Specific cutters or scissors are a must for cutting braided leader material.

SECONDARY ACCESSORIES

I always have a variety of accessories with me when I am on the water. Many of these are unique. They form an essential niche in addition to more traditional fly-fishing accessories such as nippers and hemostats. It is a list of items I am always adding to and adjusting each season.

Headlamp

It's always a good idea to carry a flashlight with you, but the trouble with a flashlight is that it doesn't allow you to use both hands. A small portable headlamp enables you to safely navigate around the shoreline during early morning or evening hours, leaving your hands free to carry items or maneuver a boat or other watercraft. A headlamp also allows you to find things in your boat and within your kit bag without sacrificing your hands by holding a flashlight or other light source.

Clothes Peg

1. Changing lines on the water is challenging, as it can be tricky, even dangerous, to safely and efficiently thread a fly rod. When you are on the water, changing a fly line is best done from a seated position and using lines featuring a welded loop. A wooden clothes-peg helps keep a leader under control when changing fly lines loaded on either a spool or separate reel.

2. Begin by reeling the leader into the guides as far as possible. When using multiple flies, it may be necessary to remove the dropper flies so only the point fly remains. If the leader is longer than the rod, drop the point fly into the boat to avoid accidently hooking a fish and interrupting the changeover procedure. Use the clothes-peg to pinch and hold the leader against the rod blank. With the leader secured, cut it from the end of the welded loop.

3. Remove the spool or reel and replace it with the line you wish to change to. If there is a leader already on the replacement spool, remove it. You can reattach it later if needed once the transfer process is complete. Attach the leader held by the clothes-peg to the welded loop of the replacement line using a clinch knot. When using lighter leader material, be careful not to snug the leader so tight that it cuts into the welded loop.

BARRY ACTON

4. Remove the clothes-peg. Strip roughly two rod lengths of line from the spool. Make a few firm false casts to thread the fly line through the guides and out of the rod tip. Once the new line is through all the guides, the leader can be adjusted or removed to match the replacement line better. For example, a 20-foot leader from a floating line would not be the right choice on a fast-sinking line.

Depth Locator

Depth locators are an inexpensive heavy weight, fused to an alligator clip. They are my preferred weight for surgically setting indicator depth or fly depth when fishing fast-sinking lines vertically. For the serious stillwater indicator fly fisher, they are an essential tool, especially if you don't have a sounder to determine depth. They are an everyday accessory for many ice fishers too, so if you live in a region where ice fishing takes place, you should be able to find these at your local tackle shop. Depth locators are also available online.

A depth locator is my preferred weight for surgically setting indicator depth or fly depth when fishing fast-sinking lines vertically.

You can also fashion a heavy bell sinker into a suitable, inexpensive depth locator. One of the easiest methods involves forcing a foam earplug through the wire loop on the sinker. Stab your fly into the foam earplug when using it to set depth.

Permanent Markers

I always have a handful of permanent markers on hand, stored in a plastic bag to avoid any accidental leakage. Black, olive, and brown are my favorite colors, but you can certainly add other colors if you wish. I use double-ended markers featuring a wide tip at one end and a narrow tip at the other.

Brown and olive and combinations of these two colors are common to many invertebrates. I use either of these markers to give my flies an impromptu, on-the-water color change should I need to modify an existing pattern to match the naturals.

I use white beadhead, or "Ice Cream Cone" style, chironomid pupa patterns most often in murky stained water, as the white bead stands out among all of the surrounding clutter. In clear water conditions, the white bead may be too bright, causing fish to avoid the fly. If you don't have a version of the pattern available without a white bead, a black permanent marker allows you to blacken the white bead partially so it is not as overt.

I always have a variety of permanent markers in my kit bag. Use a black marker to darken a bright indicator so it silhouettes on the water. Other colors, such as olive or brown, allow you to change pattern colors on the fly to better match a preferred food source.

You can also use a black marker to darken a bright fluorescent indicator. Bright-colored indicators stand out best with a high sun or with the sun at your back. When fishing into glare, however, bright colors are difficult, if not impossible, to see. A dark indicator provides a visible silhouette. Dark, black indicators aren't readily available. The black marker allows you to turn a bright indicator black. On some lakes, such as Nevada's famous Pyramid Lake, the water appears a bright lime green due to the surrounding aquatic vegetation. This bright background makes it difficult to see hot-colored indicators. Blackening a bright indicator solves this problem.

Black Electrician's Tape

Black electrician's tape has many uses. It can be used for a variety of temporary repairs to hold something together that should be together, such as an oar on a pontoon boat.

Styrofoam-based Quick Release Indicators eventually wear out from having the plastic peg repeatedly pushed into the indicator. The worn indicator typically disguises a good problem, hooking numerous fish. When fishing is hot, nobody wants to waste time replacing an indicator.

You can replace it when things settle down. Wrapping a short, ¾-inch length of black tape around the plastic peg builds up its outer diameter, allowing you to repair the indicator so you can keep on fishing.

Black electrical tape is always good to have on hand. When the indicator bite is on and you don't have time to change your worn-out Quick Release Indicator, use a short length of tape to increase the peg diameter so it fits better into the worn indicator.

Clear Nail Polish and Brushable Superglue

Clear nail polish or brushable superglue helps extend Styrofoam indicator life. After prolonged use, the coatings on these indicators often chip, making them difficult to see. Before fishing, add a protective layer to your indicator by applying a liberal coat of clear nail polish or superglue all over it.

Nail polish or superglue helps reinforce flies, repairs tattered flies, or provides a protective coat to a strike indicator to reduce chipping.

Brushable superglue allows you to provide some on-the-water repairs to flies tattered by fish. Many chironomid larva and pupa patterns feature bodies tied out of shiny but fragile materials. Applying a quick coating of brushable superglue before using them provides added durability and shine. Brushable superglue is also handy for sealing small but often painful cuts.

Swivels

Swivels provide many benefits for both indicator and non-indicator presentations. I use a variety of swivel colors in size 12 and 14. Swivel sizing is not consistent. One supplier's size 14 may be the equivalent of a size 12 with another supplier. Pick one brand, if possible, for sizing consistency. Although swivels are inexpensive, don't scrimp on quality. Cheaper swivels may open up under pressure, or there may be gaps in the rings you tie your leader and tippet to. These gaps could cut your leader or tippet, or in some cases your leader and tippet may slide off the swivel. The benefits of a swivel, however, far outweigh any concerns. Here's what they can do:

- Add weight: Swivels add an in-line weight for both indicator and non-indicator presentations. I use either a clinch or improved clinch knot to tie the swivel

Small, size 12 to 16, barrel swivels provide several benefits when using indicators or when fishing vertically using fast-sinking lines. I also use them with boatman and backswimmer patterns featuring extended legs to prevent leader twist.

between the leader and the final tippet section. Once in place, swivels don't accidentally fly off, an often-irritating occurrence with split shot. When fishing vertically I like to keep my swivels 18 to 24 inches above the fly. For non-indicator presentations I place my swivel between 3 and 5 feet above the fly. The clearer the water, the greater the spacing. I still have split shot or tungsten putty on hand to augment a swivel when facing strong, wind-induced current. I favor a graduated approach when adding weight, and would first increase swivel size before adding any shot. A size 12 barrel swivel helps anchor the presentation while dampening any unnatural action transmitted down to the fly caused by the indicator being bounced around in the surface chop.

- Reduce tangles: Swivels rotate, so they reduce tangles created by any bad casting "English" you transmit to your leader. When using non-indicator cast and retrieve tactics with patterns that may spin, such as water boatman or backswimmer patterns, a swivel can eliminate any leader twist the legs on these flies might create.
- Eliminate leader and tippet incompatibility: Some anglers struggle with leader and tippet incompatibility issues when trying to knot stiffer, harder fluorocarbon to softer nylon leader or tippet material. The swivel serves as a junction between the two materials, eliminating any frustration due to the fluorocarbon biting into the nylon and causing what I call "separation anxiety."
- Reduce Quick Release Indicator loss: I prefer to place the plastic peg of a Quick Release Indicator on the fly side of the indicator. If a fish breaks off, the tippet will usually snap at the fly or the lower end of the swivel. The sharp tug caused by the break-off trips the indicator, and the peg and indicator slide off the leader. A swivel acts as a stopper, preventing the plastic peg from sliding off the leader, and the peg, in turn, stops the indicator from sliding off. You will have to replace the fly and perhaps some tippet, but the indicator remains along with the main portion of the leader.
- Add attraction: Swivels are available in three primary colors: black or black nickel, silver, and gold. During intense chironomid emergences, your flies are competing with hundreds, if not thousands, of shiny natural pupae. A silver

swivel catches the light and can draw fish to your flies. During the fall months, when sunlight is on more of an acute angle, I find gold swivels perform best.

- Help determine fly color, size, and depth: During a chironomid hatch, swivels can help you determine fly color and size or presentation depth. It is not uncommon for fish to take or sample your swivel. This action results in a puzzling pull down with no fish or, in extreme circumstances, foul hooking a fish as you strike by pulling the fly below up into the fish. If this happens consistently, trout could be attracted to the swivel's size, or perhaps the swivel color better matches the color of the natural pupae than your pattern. More often than not, swivel takes are an indication you are fishing too deep. A simple indicator adjustment so that your fly suspends at the depth the swivel was hanging should address the problem and catch more fish.

Bobber Stops

Conventional anglers use rubberized bobbers stops to set the depth a lure or jig suspends beneath a slip bobber, as spacers on specific rigging systems, and to prevent tungsten bullet weights used to plunge dense weeds from sliding up the leader. I use both rubberized and Dacron bobber stops for my stillwater fly fishing to ensure consistent fly depth when using indicators and as fly line markers.

Presenting your fly at the correct depth is a critical component of stillwater success, especially when using indicators. Some anglers use a pair of bobber stops, one on each side, to lock strike indicators in place on the leader. Rubberized bobber stops allow you to mark the position of a Quick Release Indicator before it releases. The rubberized bobber stop is transferred onto the leader before sliding on the Quick

I use two types of bobber stops: rubberized bobber stops as leader markers when indicator fishing, and Dacron bobber stops as hang or line markers on sinking lines.

Release Indicator. Once you have set your indicator, slide the bobber stop down to the indicator. After releasing the fish, move the indicator leader back up to the bobber stop and lock it in place. This simple practice eliminates the need for always having to remeasure your indicator depth.

Rubberized bobber stops are inexpensive. You can find them in most tackle shops selling slip bobbers. They come on a solid plastic ring, each mounted on individual wire loops. Transferring the stop to your leader is easy:

1. Isolate the bobber stop you wish to use. Slide 2 to 3 inches of leader material through the wire loop.

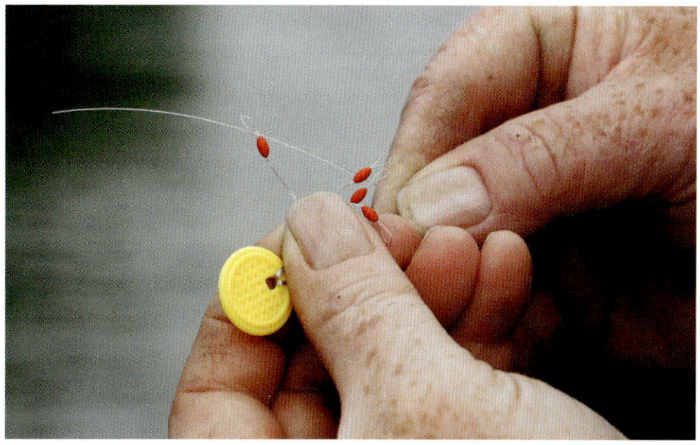

2. Gently pull on the bobber stop to slide it off the wire loop and onto the leader, folding the 2- to 3-inch tag end on top of the main leader.

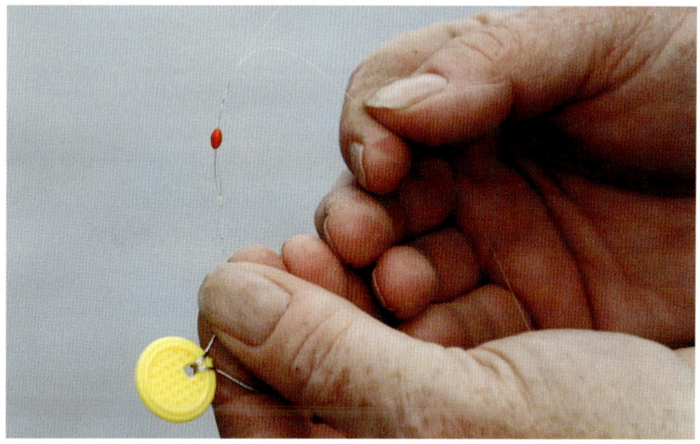

3. With the bobber stop now on the folded leader, moisten the leader material to lubricate it. Continue pulling on the bobber stop until the short, 2- to 3-inch tag end of the leader pops out of the bobber stop.

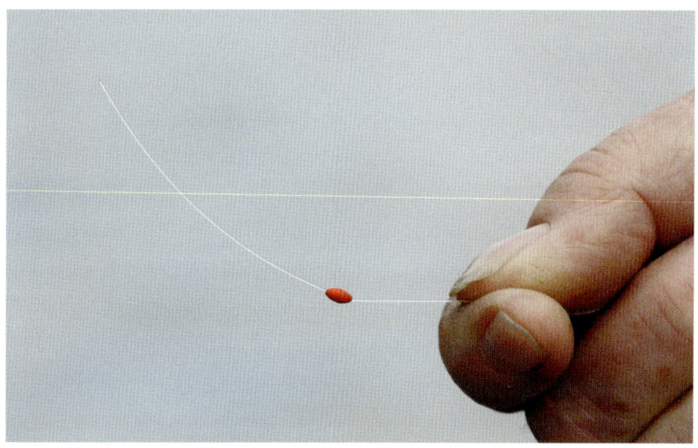

BARRY ACTON

You have now transferred the bobber stop onto your leader. Simply slide it up and down the leader as needed. Avoid brisk movements of the bobber stop, as this can cause heat through friction that might weaken the leader. I moisten the leader every time I move the bobber stop.

When using a bobber stop as a leader marker, place it on the leader first so it sits between the indicator and fly line.

I use Dacron bobber stops to mark a sinking line when fishing vertically, a technique referred to as "dangling." Dangling is discussed in detail in chapter 11, "Going Deep." You can also use Dacron bobber stops as hang markers on any fly line.

The braided or Dacron line bobber stops come nail knotted onto a small plastic tube. Attaching them to a fly line is simple:

1. Slide the fly line through the plastic tube.

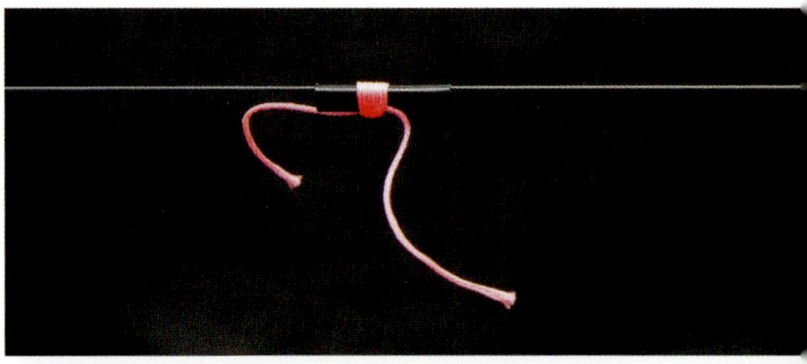

2. Work the braided stop off one end of the tube onto the fly line.

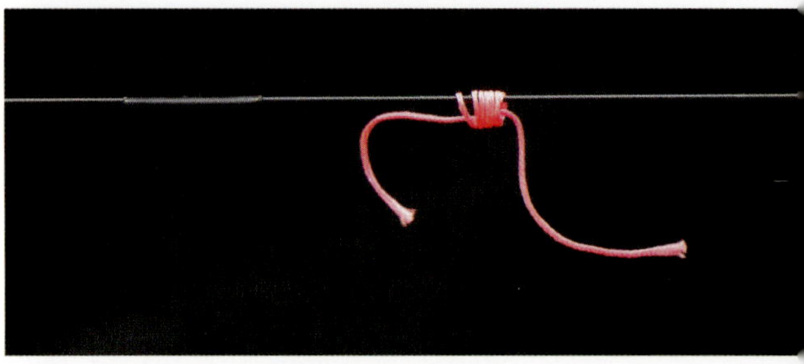

3. Pull the ends gently, so it snugs around the fly line. Use the thumb and forefinger to slide to any point on the fly line to mark a specific location. I typically place mine right at the reel.

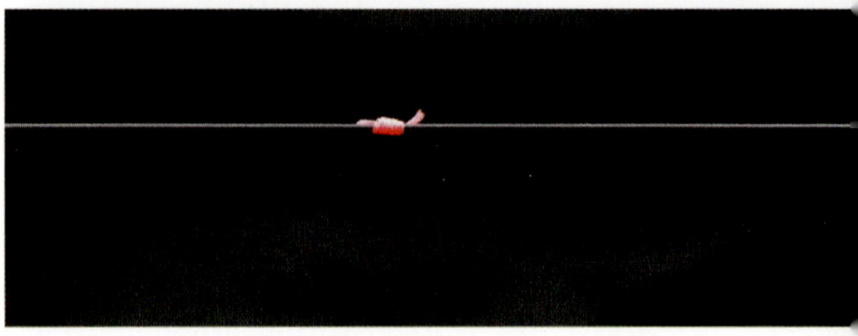

If you can't find or don't wish to use a braided or Dacron bobber stop but still wish to mark your line, you can also knot a section of braid or Dacron onto the fly line using a uni knot. See chapter 4, "Leaders, Knots, and Droppers," for step-by-step instructions on how to tie a uni knot.

Tippet Rings

Popular with river and stream anglers, particularly those who use European or tight-line nymphing techniques, tippet rings also belong in a stillwater kit bag. I use tippet rings as a junction between the leader and the tippet section, typically on sinking lines. Like a swivel, tippet rings serve as a junction preventing harder fluorocarbon tippet from biting into and damaging softer nylon leader and tippet material. Dropper tags can also be easily added to any tippet ring using several different knots. I prefer either a clinch, improved clinch, or uni knot to attach a tippet ring to a leader or tippet section. I also use tippet rings when connecting no-stretch braid to leader or tippet.

My primary reason for using tippet rings is to maintain leader length as, over time, a break-off or tippet change shortens the leader. A tippet ring contains any overall leader length adjustments to the tippet section only.

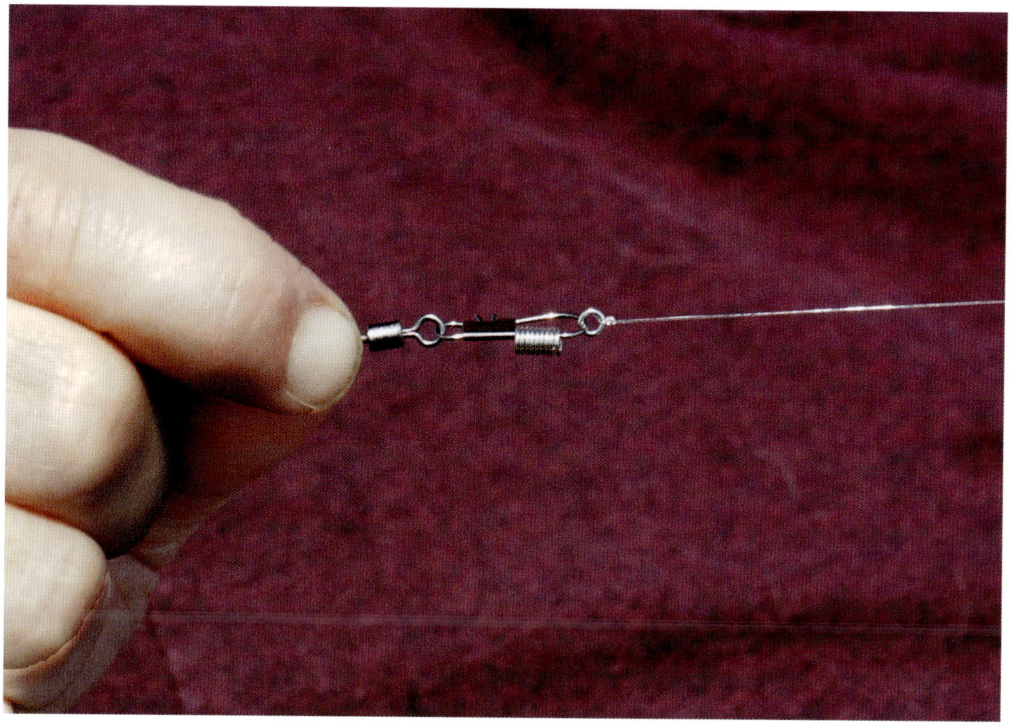

Never remove a tippet ring from the snap swivel. Always attach your leader or tippet to the ring before you remove it from the snap swivel.

Most suppliers dispense tippet rings on large snap swivels. Always tie on a tippet ring while it is still on the snap swivel. Isolate a tippet ring closest to where the snap swivel opens. Pass the leader or tippet material through the ring, and use a clinch or improved clinch knot to attach the tippet ring to the leader. Trim the tag end flush. Open the snap ring and slide the attached tippet ring off, then close the snap ring to avoid having the unused tippet rings slide off. Never remove a tippet ring before attaching it to the leader or tippet. Chances are you will drop it, and knotting leader or tippet to a loose ring is frustrating and almost impossible to do.

Knot-Tying Tool

I prefer to use fly lines that have welded loops at both ends. However, not all fly lines feature welded loops, so you must use a nail knot to connect either leader or backing to the fly line. A one-piece, Tie Fast–style knot-tying tool is my preferred tool for tying nail knots. There are other types of knot-tying tools available too. Choose one that works best for you.

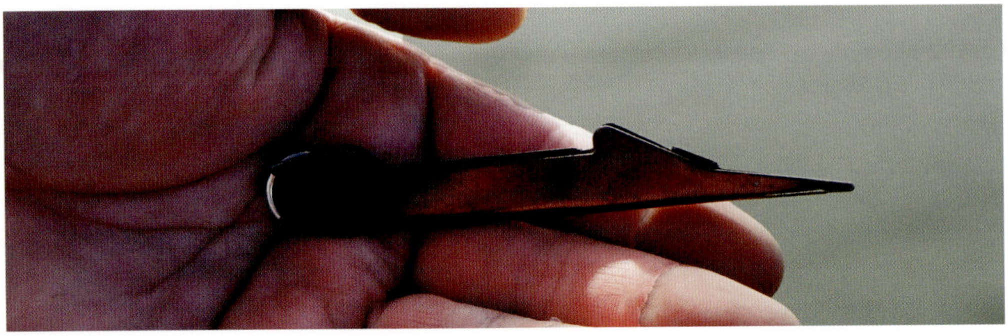

A Tie Fast–style knot-tying tool is my preferred tool for tying nail knots.

You can also use a Tie Fast tool to form a nail knot splice where two nail knots are tied back to back. This connection works well to join nylon and braided materials together when forming a hybrid low-stretch indicator leader.

Split Shot and Tungsten Putty

I always have a selection of small split shot and tungsten putty on hand when I want to augment the weight of a swivel. Strong winds often create significant circulation currents that behave similarly to river and stream currents and negatively affect a fly's sink rate. A small split shot pinched onto the leader, a foot above the fly, or at the top end of the swivel or a touch of tungsten putty massaged around the swivel provides the additional horsepower needed to combat the current.

Split shot or tungsten putty helps keep your flies down when wind-induced circulation currents are strong.

Leader Mud

Leader mud is a paste used to degrease nylon tippet so it breaks the surface when fishing dries and emergers. In bright, clear, calm conditions, nylon material casts a distinct shadow and causes surface disturbance that may alert fish. Although I use fluorocarbon tippet, I always have leader mud on hand just in case.

Floatant and Desiccant

Although the majority of stillwater presentations are subsurface in nature, always have floatant and desiccant on hand should fish feed at the surface. I use a team approach when using these products: Apply floatant before the first cast. If the fly becomes saturated with water or fish slime, give it a healthy squeeze to remove as much water or slime as possible. With the fly still attached to the tippet, drop it into the desiccant container to further dry the fly. Once dry, add a pinch of floatant as a finishing touch. The fly is ready for battle once again.

Floatant can also be used as a lubricant to quiet squeaky oarlocks or rubbed into the body of a dubbed nymph or pupa to trap air bubbles.

When fishing dries or emergers, floatant, powder, and at times leader mud are essential.

UV Knot Resin

A flexible UV-cure knot resin is good to have on hand to coat nail knots or provide on-the-water wader repairs. A smooth-coated nail knot passes through the guides with minimal risk of binding or jamming on a rod guide.

Thermometer and Deptherm

When heading out, water temperature is one of the first factors I always make a note of. Water temperature is critical to stillwater success, as it has a strong influence on both trout behavior and insect activity, including hatch timings. I always have a thermometer and a Deptherm on hand.

I use a traditional analogue-style streamside thermometer. These thermometers are relatively inexpensive, so if you accidentally break or lose one, it doesn't break the bank. You can also purchase electronic thermometers that you can dip into the water as with a streamside thermometer or shoot a narrow beam at the surface to record temperature. Electronic thermometers tend to be more expensive but arguably provide more accurate temperature readings. As I often use my sounder to display surface temperature, I prefer a traditional streamside thermometer because I can lower it into the water to record subsurface water temperatures and it serves as a backup should my sounder fail for some reason.

A Deptherm records both water temperature and depth at the same time. As you lower the unit, water enters the chamber through a small pressure valve. The deeper the Deptherm goes, the more water enters the chamber. A scale on one side of the unit records depth, and the scale on the opposite side records the corresponding water temperature.

No matter the tool, thermometer or Deptherm, it is important to let the unit suspend for a few minutes to capture the correct information. Just remember to bring

Although I use my sounder to keep track of surface temperature, a thermometer or Deptherm on a cord helps me determine water temperature in deep water and serves as a backup in case of a power failure.

the thermometer or Deptherm on board before moving. Untangling the cord from an electric motor prop is a learning experience you won't want to repeat.

A thermometer or Deptherm attached to a length of cord or an anchor rope allows you to sample water temperatures at various depths. Electronic sounders also display temperature readings, but due to the location of the transducer, they only provide the surface temperature. As water temperatures begin to warm, trout slide into deeper water. You can use a thermometer or Deptherm to systematically sample temperature at different depths along the slope of a drop-off to identify likely levels where fish may be. Water temperature provides valuable information that you can use as a guide to help determine line choice, retrieve speed, and sink time.

Binoculars

A good pair of binoculars is invaluable. They can be used to search other areas of a lake without wasting time, battery life, or fuel. Before making a move, it is always a good idea to check out other likely spots to see if a location change is worthwhile. I use binoculars to watch what other anglers are doing or investigate isolated focused bird activity that may signal a hatch.

First Aid and Comfort

Although I always carry a full first-aid kit in my boat, I still have a bag containing a few essentials for the bumps and bruises that can occur on the water. Within a small resealable Ziploc bag, I keep items such as antacid tablets, Band-Aids, medicated ointment, lip balm, ibuprofen, acetaminophen, and aspirin.

Aspirin is an essential component. In the event of a suspected heart attack, it is a recommended protocol in every first-aid course I have taken. It is important to remember to ask the person if they have an aspirin allergy before administering.

Don't forget the sunscreen. As I am fair-skinned, I always have lots on hand with a minimum SPF rating of 30. Whenever possible, I apply sunscreen before getting into my vehicle to ensure it has had ample time to absorb into the skin. This practice also allows me to ensure I cover all exposed skin. Missing an earlobe or sideburn can be painful and have potential long-term negative effects. Sun gloves and a Buff are also with me whenever I head out on the water.

Warming Accessories

Cold air temperatures or wet conditions cool hands quickly, a common occurrence during early spring and late fall. It is important to have two pairs of warm gloves, a small hand towel, nitrile gloves, and hand warmers on hand during these times.

I use one pair of regular gloves or mitts to keep my hands warm when traveling from one location to another. At times I will use a second, fingerless glove that is better suited for fishing on my rod hand, but I prefer not to wear any gloves, if possible, when fishing, as I feel they inhibit my ability to recognize takes and effectively fight fish.

When your hands get wet, evaporation cools them. A small hand towel allows you to dry your hands, mitigating this effect. When air temperatures are cold, I always dry my hands after releasing a fish.

While they offer little insulating value, nitrile gloves also keep your hands dry. In addition, due to their tighter fit than gloves or mitts, there is no loss of sensitivity for recognizing takes. You can also tie larger flies onto your leader or tippet while wearing nitrile gloves.

When conditions are severe, hand warmers and heaters come into place. Icy cold conditions are common at the end of the season as we try to squeeze as many days on the water as possible before winter sets in. Hand warmers activated before getting on the water offer welcome warmth either in a jacket pocket or placed on the back of the hand in a pair of gloves or mitts. Keeping the tops of your hands warm helps maintain blood flow to the fingertips. Sandwiching a hand warmer between the back of your neck and a Buff also helps keep you warm, taking the sting out of the cold.

In extreme conditions, I have brought a propane heater into the boat. Care must be taken not to place anything near the heater that may melt, including rain pants, waders, and fly lines. I only use the heater when fishing from an anchored position. When moving to another location, I always turn the heater off.

When temperatures drop, being prepared for the conditions is crucial. Make sure you dress for the elements, including a wool hat, hand warmers, nitrile gloves, and two pairs of gloves or mitts. If you are in a boat and temperatures become extreme, a portable heater can be worth its weight in gold.

CHAPTER TAKEAWAYS

- Use a landing net that floats. A floating net allows you to use both hands after you have landed a fish, reducing stress on both yourself and the trout.
- A quality kit bag keeps all of your gear and accessories in one place, neat and organized. My kit bag is my on-the-water equipment nerve center.
- Categorize how you store your equipment and accessories so these items are easy to find. I use six basic categories: flies, reels and spare spools, medical, tippet and leaders, accessories, and observation.
- Polarized sunglasses are a must-have stillwater accessory, allowing you to penetrate surface glare to see fish and underwater structure while protecting your eyes.
- A throat pump allows you to sample what a trout is feeding upon, helping to guide pattern selection and determine feeding activity and presentation depth.
- A simple sampling kit consisting of a white tray, turkey baster, aquarium net, baker's sieve, and ice cube tray works great for shoreline sampling. All of these items are readily available at any dollar store.
- Changing fly lines on the water is challenging and potentially dangerous. A wooden clothes-peg helps keep a leader under control when changing fly lines in a boat, float tube, or pontoon boat.
- Swivels offer a number of benefits. Always have a selection of colors on hand in sizes 12 through 16.
- Bobber stops are used to ensure consistent fly depth when using indicators and as fly line markers. I use two types of bobber stops depending on the purpose: rubberized and Dacron.
- Water temperature is critical to stillwater success, as it has a strong influence on both trout behavior and insect activity, including hatch timings. Always have either a thermometer or Deptherm on hand.
- When conditions are cold, such as early spring or late fall, make sure to bring accessories such as gloves and hand warmers so your hands don't get cold. Nothing puts a damper on a day quicker than when your hands are cold.

CHAPTER 3

GETTING AROUND: WATERCRAFT AND ANCHORING

I enjoy fishing from shore, especially small productive ponds. Unfortunately, bank fishing, in the regions I fish across North America, is the exception rather than the rule. To properly fish lakes, you must be able to move. Mobility is critical for you to locate and explore stillwater structures such as weed beds, large shoals, points, and drop-offs. In addition to limited movement, other factors limit fishing from the shore, including the following:

- Muddy bottoms: The most productive trout lakes are typically shallow with fertile muddy bottoms. Mud is not safe or fun to wade in. Most of the time, your first step finds you up to your knees, or deeper, in a single step.
- Private property: Not all of the shoreline surrounding a lake is public land. Some lakes have a public right-of-way that allows shoreline access to launch, but launch areas aren't always the best fishing spots and more often than not, you find yourself in the way, particularly at the beginning and end of a day, of other anglers trying to get in or out of the water.
- Shoreline vegetation: Dense shoreline weeds often clog the edges of productive trout lakes. The shallow shoreline area, bathed in light, stimulates abundant weed growth through photosynthesis. Shoreline weeds are challenging to fish both through and across to the deeper water on the other side. You don't get the benefit of a full retrieve, and if you catch a fish, you often lose it as you attempt to drag or navigate it through the weeds.
- Backcast room: Trees and bushes often surround the shoreline, and casting becomes challenging. If you aren't careful, your backcast ends up fouled behind

Although fishing from shore can be productive, there are several reasons fishing from some type of watercraft is more productive, including muddy bottoms, backcast room, working in and around shoreline weeds and debris, and private access issues.
DAVE HUGHES

you. Bushwhacking in waders and a rod can be challenging, frustrating, and potentially expensive if you break your rod or tear your waders. Rocks and high bluffs also make for challenging casts, often making a roll cast the only option.

- Targeting structure: Stillwater structures such as drop-offs, points, and shoals can cover a large area, and it is tough to cover all areas of a piece of structure to find these specific spots from the bank. In many instances, you can't physically get within reach either by wading or casting. I prefer to target structure from deeper water, if at all possible. Fish love to cruise adjacent to deep water, as it provides protection should something startle them. Deep water also masks my presence. Although there are exceptions, I would much rather cast onto a shoal than move through it. Some shoals stretch out from shore, and wading out so you can potentially reach the edge is often difficult or impossible.

I believe to fly fish lakes properly, you need to fish from some type of watercraft. I break down my watercraft options into three main categories: float tubes, pontoon boats, and boats. Over my years fly fishing lakes, I have used and accumulated all three types and have more than a few in each category. Compromise is a common factor with all watercraft. Unfortunately, no one type of craft is going to meet all of the needs and challenges lakes offer. There are advantages and disadvantages to each kind—I guess that's one of the reasons I have accumulated so many different watercraft throughout my stillwater career.

FLOAT TUBES

Float tubes, or belly boats, consist of an inner tube encased in a nylon shell. Depending on the design, the outer shell offers a variety of storage options in the form of pockets and compartments. First-generation versions used automotive inner tubes as bladders and, as a result, were circular. As float tube design evolved, so did their shape. No longer reliant on circular inner tubes, newer U-boat float tubes now feature urethane bladders, allowing manufacturers the ability to create tapered, wind-resistant, easy-to-paddle boats.

In the early eighties, when I was just starting to fly fish lakes, a float tube was my preferred stillwater platform. I have spent a lot of time and logged many great memories paddling around in a belly boat.

Portability and cost are arguably the float tube's primary strengths. Float tubes are lightweight, compact, and easy to carry, either by hand or through the use of specialized backpack straps. If you can walk to the lake, chances are you can take a float tube. Other kinds of watercraft such as larger pontoons and boats, in particular, are difficult, if not impossible, to transport off the beaten path. Float tubes are the perfect choice for small, remote lakes and ponds. Years ago, to reduce travel costs on long-distance day trips, we used to deflate our float tubes and stuff them into the trunk of our cars. Once we had arrived, we used an inexpensive 12-volt powered air pump to inflate our tubes and get fishing.

As your legs hang down below the waterline, float tubes are incredibly stable, safe, and comfortable fishing platforms, almost like sitting in a favorite chair. I recall when

Float tubes are portable and are the most affordable watercraft to fish lakes out of. As original float tubes used vehicle inner tubes for floatation, they were circular. Today's tubes feature urethane bladders, allowing manufacturers to create tapered, wind-resistant, easy-to-paddle boats.

fishing was slow, the rhythmic chop put me to sleep on more than a few occasions. Even in a substantial wind-induced swell, you bob around like a cork, enabling you to paddle safely back to shore if wind and weather conditions prove too much.

Getting into a float tube and walking into the water are often the only risks. Never walk forward with fins on and a float tube around your waist. Stepping forward is a recipe for a fall that may result in a broken rod or body part, or worse. When carrying an expensive fly rod, we tend to fall to protect the rod, not our body. If you trip or fall with a float tube in an inverted position, with your head underwater, you can be in serious trouble, as righting yourself without assistance can be extremely difficult.

There is an art to getting into a float tube without incident. Carry your fins, float tube, and rod down to the water, making separate trips if necessary. Place your fins at the water's edge, tips pointing away from the water. Place your float tube so the open portion is over the fins, then place your fly rod within easy reach of the tube. Many tubes now offer rod holders to stow your rod safely. Carefully step into the tube, and place your feet into the fins. Using the fins straps, secure your feet into the fins. Attach the safety straps to ensure you don't lose a fin should the main strap fail or loosen. With your fins on, pick the boat up to your waist. Using small steps, shuffle into the water until you are deep enough to sit down and kick. If you ever feel like you are going to lose your balance, stop moving. If you stumble over a rock or log, sit down to avoid an embarrassing or awkward fall.

Choose your launch points carefully. Soft bottoms are challenging launch areas. When you step into the mud, it creates a vacuum, sucking your feet and fins deep into the mud, making for a challenging walk into the lake. The mud-induced vacuum

To avoid a potentially embarrassing, dangerous fall or a broken fly rod, never walk forward when wearing fins. Always walk backward into the water when using a float tube or pontoon boat.
BARRY ACTON

can also pull off your fins. Getting out of the water can be even more challenging, as standing up from a seated position ranges from difficult to near impossible. In extreme circumstances, where finding a firm bottom isn't possible, lay a half sheet of plywood down to step on. The plywood distributes your weight, allowing you to launch and recover successfully.

Although I am not a fan of trolling because you travel through the water before your flies, float tubes make excellent trolling platforms. The kicking motion used to propel a float tube allows you to cover a lot of water. The intermittent kicks, pauses, and turns translate down to your fly as you troll, making it irresistible, at times, to fish. You can also blend in a combination of both trolling and casting for additional presentation flavor. Having the ability to paddle and troll is also a definite asset for neophytes who have yet to develop their casting skills.

The financial realities of some types of watercraft can be a barrier. Compared to other craft, float tubes offer the cheapest way to get onto the water. You can get into a quality float tube for under $250. In addition to your fishing gear, all you need is a pair of waders, wading boots or booties, and fins for propulsion.

As your legs power a float tube, mobility is a barrier. Large bodies of water take a lot of time and effort to cover. You have to be weather conscious. If the wind and weather worsen, it can be challenging and tiring to get back to shore. If the wind is too strong, you can be blown away uncontrollably from your initial launch point. In extreme circumstances, the best option may be to head for the nearest landfall and wait until conditions improve or get out and walk back to your vehicle if you can.

Having your legs continuously in the water can be problematic if water temperatures are low, negatively impacting your on-the-water experience. If you are using breathable waders, make a point of investing in the appropriate undergarments. Many dedicated tubers still use neoprene waders for cold, nasty days. Even then, it can be hard to keep warm and comfortable. Pay attention to your body's warning signs. I can recall days, when I was younger and not so smart, where my feet were so cold after a session that it was challenging to walk until the blood flow returned to my lower legs.

The low profile of a float tube is both a strength and a weakness. As long as you don't paddle aggressively or create wake when casting, you can get quite close to fish without disturbing or spooking them. As float tubes are designed to move backward, however, you risk paddling over fish before you have a chance to see them. Float tubers paddling among a cluster of anchored boats can lead to more than a few arguments and colorful exchanges.

Unfortunately, the low profile of a float tube doesn't offer the best perspective when it comes to seeing strikes when using subsurface floating line techniques. This disadvantage is especially true when using indicators. Often the surface chop periodically hides the indicator from view, resulting in missed strikes. A higher, elevated perspective is the main reason I prefer to fish out of a pontoon boat or boat. Several float tube manufacturers now offer raised seats, so only your lower legs, from your upper shins down, remain in the water. This design improvement helps improve your sight perspective while keeping you drier and warmer when both air and water temperatures are cold.

On large or crowded lakes, a low-profile float tube isn't always easy to see. If you are in a float tube, you have to be conscious of other boats, particularly powerboats. Float tube defensively—assume others can't see you. Operators of other watercraft such as jet skis and water-ski boats aren't used to watching out for float tubes. Do what you can to be as visible as possible. Always use a float tube with a hi-vis back. In low-light conditions, use a small flashing light or glow stick.

Take care when traveling with an inflated float tube or pontoon boat. Increasing altitude causes air to expand, especially on warm days, and in extreme circumstances could burst a bladder, causing irreparable damages. If you choose to visit a high-altitude lake or travel with a fully inflated pontoon boat on a warm day, be sure to let some air out to compensate for expansion.

PONTOON BOATS

Pontoon boats first began appearing on lakes in the mid-eighties. These boats formed a perfect bridge between traditional boats and float tubes. Most pontoon boats feature two pontoons that support a seat and a rowing frame and range, on average, between 8 and 10 feet long. Some of the larger, more expensive pontoon boats feature dual pontoons, one pair per side, to support the seat and rowing frame.

Inflatable pontoon boats have become incredibly popular and are the preferred mode of transport for many stillwater fly fishers. Pontoon boats blend a float tube's portability with the stability, elevated casting platform, and maneuverability of a boat.

Float tubes and pontoon boats share similar benefits. Pontoon boats are relatively lightweight and portable, and smaller boats can be broken down and stored in a vehicle. Larger pontoon boats can be a challenge to store in smaller cars and are best suited to larger vehicles and pickup trucks. With a framed pontoon boat, I prefer, if possible, to deflate the boat and fold the pontoons into the middle of the frame, where I tie them together by the D rings found at the tip of most pontoons. Once secured in this manner, I can easily pick the boat up as a compact unit and slide it into the bed of my pickup. Not having to reassemble the frame each trip saves time and frustration if the frame assembly and attachment to the pontoons is finicky.

In an attempt to reduce weight and make inflation easier, frameless pontoon boats are becoming popular. These "blow and go" boats are easy to pack and inflate. Deflated frameless boats can be easily rolled up and stored in a large duffle bag or plastic container. Many frameless boats are so lightweight and easy to stow that they can be taken on flights as checked baggage, as they meet the baggage criteria for both size and weight.

Once assembled, lightweight pontoon boats are easy to move. Usually, all you need to do is grab each pontoon and drag the boat to the shore. You can also add specialized or homemade pontoon boat wheels to improve onshore maneuverability. These wheels attach under the seat, allowing you to move your boat around like a wheelbarrow. Wheels can be purchased ready to install, or if you are handy, they can be fashioned at home using a wheelbarrow wheel or small bicycle tires and rims.

Frameless, "blow and go" pontoon boats are an excellent stillwater platform. They inflate in minutes, and, like a framed pontoon boat, you can also use them on moving water.

Pontoon boat pricing varies depending upon several factors, including overall size, frame design, pontoon material, and storage options. For the most part, pontoon pricing falls between the price of a float tube and a traditional boat. There are always exceptions. I know of a few pontoon boats that are more expensive than a standard 12-foot aluminum boat.

Depending on the brand and your preference, pontoon boats can be powered by foot using a pair of fins or rowed. Some models allow for the installation and use of an electric motor. I most often use a blend of fins and oars to get around, my oars for long-distance treks and my fins for short journeys or minor repositioning. On larger lakes or if there is a risk of wind, having the security of an electric motor provides an added level of mobility and confidence. The drawback to an electric motor and battery is the cost and the weight they add both to the boat and carrying them back and forth to your vehicle.

Electric motors mount behind the angler and push the boat forward. It takes a bit of getting used to maneuvering the boat, as you have to reach behind or turn in the seat to steer. I have to admit, the times I have used an electric motor on my larger pontoon boat, I did enjoy the ease and pace at which I was able to move. Be sure to check your local regulations, as adding an electric motor to a pontoon boat may require additional licensing and use permits.

For me, the primary advantage of a pontoon boat over a float tube is the elevated seat position. As only your lower legs and feet are in the water, you tend to remain warmer and drier. From a presentation perspective, sitting in a raised seat allows you to better see indicator strikes, floating line takes when using long leaders and weighted flies, and rises to dry or emerger patterns.

Another advantage is the increased storage most pontoon boats offer. Most feature zippered pouches and pockets capable of holding fly boxes, leaders, tippets, spare spools, accessories, and a wide range of other items. Many anglers mount plastic storage containers or coolers to the rear deck, providing additional, often water-tight, storage for valuable items such as a camera. Metal frames also allow for further customization that is only limited by the imagination of the owner. I recall seeing a pontoon boat that had additional brackets installed for a sounder, a portable GPS, and a camera so the angler could easily take pictures using the timer function while holding a fish with both hands.

Safe rod storage can be a challenge for both pontoon boats and float tubes. If you aren't careful, extra unsecured rods can slide quietly overboard. Be careful when releasing fish. I recall having a rod slide backward, silently, into the water while releasing one. Once the fish had swum off, my rod was gone. Thankfully the heavy reel sank first, so the rod tip pointed up. After a few frantic seconds of looking and spinning around, I was able to recover the rod, as I was fortunate to be in 9 feet of water. The last remaining foot of my 10-foot rod poking out of the water caught my eye. Another, not so obvious, argument for long stillwater fly rods.

A simple cure to prevent rod loss is a soft, flexible, plastic coil key chain. My friends and I refer to them as plastic umbilical cords. One end of the key chain is attached to the frame of the pontoon boat or a D ring on the float tube, and the other end is

A soft, flexible, plastic coil key chain, available at most home improvement or hardware stores, allows you to secure your rod in either a float tube or pontoon boat to eliminate the risk of it sliding into the water.
BARRY ACTON

clipped to the stripping guide of the spare rod or a rod that was put down to revive and release a fish. The key chain doesn't prevent a rod from falling into the water, but if it does, it can be recovered, as the key chain won't allow it to sink. Today most pontoon boats and some float tubes come with built-in rod holders, or accessory holders can be easily added. If you are both innovative and handy, you can manufacture a rod holder from materials such as ABS pipe, found at most home improvement stores.

BOATS

Boats are the original lake watercraft. When I first began stillwater fly fishing, they were my only option, as float tubes and pontoon boats had yet to make an impact. Since those first stillwater forays, boats remain my favorite way of getting around on lakes. I echo what the water rat said to the mole in Kenneth Grahame's classic book, *The Wind in the Willows*: "Believe me, my young friend, there is nothing—absolutely nothing—half so much worth doing as simply messing about in boats."

For many, boat ownership is a serious stillwater investment. Price is perhaps a boat's biggest drawback. Depending on its size, what it is made of, motor options, accessories such as oars, and other miscellaneous but necessary gear, boats are expensive, especially when compared to the cost of float tubes and most pontoon boats. Some boat prices run into thousands of dollars.

In British Columbia, where I began fly fishing lakes, some lodges still use heavy wooden boats. Fiberglass and aluminum boats between 10 and 18 feet long have replaced most wooden boats, however. On most smaller lakes, boats between 10 and

Boats are perhaps the ultimate watercraft investment, and as with all watercraft, they are all about compromise. Some boats are lightweight; flat-bottom prams are wide, roomy, and stable; and V-hull boats cut through surface chop, providing a safe and comfortable ride. If you are going to invest in a boat, make sure it meets your specific needs.

14 feet work best. If you plan on fishing with friends, a longer, wider, 12- to 14-foot boat would be a better choice. Smaller, 10- to 12-foot boats are easier to handle, both onshore and on the water, and work best for solo anglers.

Fiberglass boats are probably the least popular option with stillwater fly fishers, as they can be heavy, tough to drag around, and prone to scratches. Many smaller lakes feature rough informal launches riddled with rocks and gravel, two materials that are hard on fiberglass. On the positive side, fiberglass boats are quieter than their aluminum counterparts. There are some fiberglass boats specially designed for small lakes. I have fished out of these boats, and they are wonderful fishing platforms.

Lightweight, riveted, "car topper" style aluminum boats are the most popular due to their price, durability, and weight. Heavier-gauge, robust, welded boats are the most expensive type of aluminum boat. Compared to a riveted boat, welded boats are challenging to move around on land, and many require trailers.

Some stillwater fly fishers also fish out of canoes, kayaks, and inflatable boats. I have little to no experience using these types of watercraft. As with all boats, regional influences, regulations, lake size, and personal preference are the primary factors.

Although designed for use on moving water, drift boats also work reasonably well on lakes. The versatility of a drift boat is a bonus, as most stillwater-specific boats don't transfer over to moving waters well. Perhaps one of the drift boat's most significant benefits is its ability to be launched almost anywhere. Not all trout lakes feature

Drift boats work well on many lakes. As with all watercraft, they have their pros and cons. Drift boats are maneuverable, stable, and draw very little water, enabling you to move into extremely shallow water. They are expensive and require a trailer, but you can launch them from almost anywhere. Their low draft is also a liability when the wind is up, as they can spin, making it difficult to control your presentation.

pristine launch areas, but high banks, steep banks, and muddy shallows offer little to no resistance to a drift boat. If you can back a drift boat to the lakeshore, chances are you can launch it. The rollers of a drift boat trailer also mean you don't have to put the trailer wheels in the lake to launch. Keeping the wheels and hubs dry prolongs bearing life; bearings, warm from the drive and immersed into cold lake water without sufficient time to cool, suck in dirt and other contaminants, which shortens life expectancy.

When it comes to lakes, some of the best features of a drift boat can also be a liability. Most drift boats are made of fiberglass. Fiberglass drift boats are typically heavier than riveted aluminum boats and, coupled with their width, can be challenging to move around if the wind is up. Drift boats require trailers and, like heavier welded aluminum boats, require a suitable tow vehicle to use them. A heavy, wide drift boat, however, makes for an incredibly stable casting platform.

The drift boat's high sides can also be a blessing and a curse. The high sides add stability, making it easy for two anglers to lean to one side to land a fish, take a picture, or video a release. But a drift boat's shallow draft and high sides also make them challenging to control when the wind gets up. If you wish to fish loch style, multiple drogues or drift socks may be required to control the boat so you can drift and cast downwind. The shallow draft of a drift boat can also be an advantage, especially when sight fishing for trout in skinny, shallow water.

Some drift boats also need modifications to facilitate an outboard motor or the installation of a second anchor lock system to complement the main factory anchor so you can effectively double anchor.

The majority of aluminum boats I see on trout lakes are flat-bottomed jon boats. Wide, flat-bottom boats are stable and are ideal when fishing from an anchored position. Jon boats provide lots of legroom compared to a V-hull boat of similar size. In larger boats, 12 feet or longer, two anglers can move around or even stand with confidence when anchored. The bow section of a V-hull boat can be narrow and, without some sort of floorboard system, can prove to be uncomfortable to sit or stand in due to the angled hull.

Avoid narrow jon boats, as they can tip should you or someone in your boat move suddenly to one side, putting the boat out of balance. My advice for anyone purchasing a jon boat is to buy the widest model they can find. Jon boats are also not the best boats in rough water, as their flat bottom provides for a bumpy ride, especially for those sitting in the bow section. V-hull boats slice through surface chop, making for a much more comfortable ride. On large lakes known for rough water, such as Idaho's Henry's Lake, a V-hull boat is the best option.

Any final boat decision is about choosing a boat size and style that is best suited for the lakes you intend to fish most often. Sadly, there isn't one perfect boat. At least I haven't found it. Boats are all about compromise. One size and style of boat performs well in one situation but not as well in others. I guess that's why I have accumulated several boats over the years. Among my fleet, I have a 17-foot modified-V jon boat complete with a 40 hp for large lakes, a 14-foot flat-bottomed boat for smaller lakes with less-formal launches or outboard motor restrictions, and a 10-foot pram, also for smaller lakes and when I want to fish by myself.

Due to their weight, most welded aluminum boats require a trailer to move them around. Trailers add additional costs and challenges, including trailer tires, lights, and wheel bearings—components I have had more than my fair share of adventures and frustrations with. If you follow a disciplined regular maintenance schedule, however, you can avoid flat tires, faulty lights, and seized bearings. Once you arrive at a lake, a trailered

Flat-bottomed jon boats are popular with many stillwater fly fishers. They are relatively lightweight, portable, and stable and are my preferred stillwater boat.

boat is much easier to launch and recover, as it is ready to go, extending your day on the water. Getting a non-trailered boat assembled with seats, flooring, motor, anchors, and other accessories on every trip adds time, and as one ages, it soon becomes tiresome.

Most boats require a boat plug to make them watertight. A simple boat plug is another adjustment many first-time owners or users have to be aware of, as it is something you don't want to misplace. A lost or forgotten boat plug usually ends a trip before it starts or causes serious or embarrassing issues at the boat launch should you accidentally sink your boat. As part of the precautions and awareness surrounding aquatic invasive species, most jurisdictions today require boat plug removal when traveling. Always put the boat plug in the same place so you can find it. Boat plugs are inexpensive, so it pays to have a few on hand, not only for yourself but for others too.

No matter the size and style of the boat, one of the most enjoyable aspects is outfitting it so it meets your needs on the water. Almost all small lake boats need some sort of configuration before heading out on the water for the first time. An adequately outfitted boat provides an enjoyable day on the water and allows you to carry all of your gear and equipment so it doesn't interfere with fishing. For example, at a minimum, all of my boats have carpeted floorboards, bow and stern anchor locks, carpeted deck covers over the rear gas tank / battery compartment, and enough seats for the capacity of the boat.

Sitting on a padded cushion all day long is uncomfortable and often leads to lower back pain. A raised padded seat complete with seatback makes for a more enjoyable day on the water. To some people, cutting plywood to fit each compartment and then gluing indoor/outdoor or marine-grade carpet may seem like a lot of work, but it's worth it. Removable, carpeted floorboards offer several benefits:

- Carpeted floorboards muffle sound, as aluminum boats are not as quiet as fiberglass boats.
- They provide a stable platform to stand and move around on.
- They protect fly lines from damage, should you stand on them.

Carpeted floorboards are common to every aluminum boat I have owned. They offer several benefits, including protecting fly lines, muffling noise, preventing leaks, and extending overall boat life.

- When transporting a boat, you can remove the floorboards to reduce weight.
- Dirt, tippet remnants, and bits of food can be vacuumed right in the boat, or the floorboards can be removed and hosed off.
- If you drop something in your boat, it isn't going to roll or fall into an inaccessible spot.
- Should something get under the floorboard, it can be removed, allowing for easy recovery.
- Carpeted floorboards extend the life of a riveted boat by dissipating weight. Standing directly on the floor of a boat causes the aluminum to flex, or oilcan. Over time this stresses the rivets, causing leaks. My twenty-five-plus-year-old 10-foot pram has had a carpeted plywood floor in it from day one, and it has never leaked.

THE ART OF ANCHORING

Except for loch style or fishing from a drifting boat, almost all of the techniques and tactics discussed in this book work best from an anchored position. I believe that fishing from an anchored position provides you with complete presentation control, as you don't have the challenge of compensating for the movement of your watercraft. When using floating line indicator or long-leader nymphing techniques, for example, fishing from an anchored position is the only way to control your presentation for consistent success.

Anchor Locks

There is an art to proper anchoring. The first step involves the installation and use of bow- and stern-mounted anchor locks on a boat, or an anchor lock on the front frame area of a pontoon boat. Most pontoon boats come equipped with a stern anchor jam cleat / pulley system that works reasonably well. Mounting an anchor lock to the front frame area of a pontoon boat stops annoying sway due to the low draft of the pontoons, helping you stay in control of your presentation. Installing an anchor on a float tube is a little different; I will discuss how to do this in detail later on.

Composite anchor locks, such as those manufactured by Scotty, are ideal for stillwaters. They can be mounted to any boat using a variety of mounts, both permanent and removable. The movable cam locks against the anchor rope, allowing you to move around your anchors, ready to deploy. The anchor lock also allows you to pull an anchor one-handed, without the risk of the anchor falling back down to the bottom, if there is a danger of a fish wrapping around the rope.

An anchor lock allows you to quickly and quietly raise and lower anchors without losing control of the anchor and boat. Never toss an anchor into the water—the subsequent splash and disturbance scatters fish. Anchor locks allow you to lower your anchors quietly into the water without spooking fish. Some anchor locks can be permanently mounted, while others are removable. Removable locks are stored separately, allowing for easy boat or pontoon boat assembly and disassembly.

There are a few different types of anchor locks, both aluminum and durable plastic composite, but the basic operating principle is the same. Feed the anchor rope over the pulley and through the pivoting cam so the anchors hang outside of the boat or pontoon boat ready to deploy. To lower the anchor, simply lift the rope, freeing the pivoting cam that pinches the anchor rope against the anchor lock frame. Let the weight of the anchor pull the rope through your hands until it hits bottom. If you let go of the rope as the anchor is deploying, the cam will swing down, pinching the rope and stopping the anchor's decent. Abrupt anchor drops and stops can stress the mounting point, potentially damaging your boat or pontoon boat. To recover the anchor, simply raise the rope and using one or both hands, pull in the anchor rope until the anchor is hanging at the anchor lock.

There are several benefits to the anchor lock system versus lowering an anchor over the side and tying it off to a cleat or a pontoon boat D ring:

- As the anchors are ready to deploy once you select a spot to anchor, you stand a good chance of hitting your anchor target. Lowering anchors over the side and then securing them to a cleat takes time, and chances are you won't anchor where you wanted to.
- Raised cleats on a boat catch fly line and soon become annoying. Rods can accidentally slip under a cleat while you are preoccupied with releasing a fish or looking for something. If you aren't aware that your rod has moved under the cleat, you can break it when you go to pick it up. I speak from experience on this point, as I have broken a rod in this manner.
- During the fight, a fish may attempt to wrap itself around the anchor. A cam-style anchor lock allows you to raise an anchor one-handed while you continue to fight the fish. After pulling on the rope to raise the anchor, the cam will jam and lock the rope, allowing you to re grip and pull again. If you are using a non-locking system, it is difficult to impossible to pull up the anchor, as when you attempt to re-grip, the rope slips and slides, causing you to lose control, sending the anchor plummeting back down to the bottom.
- If you want to make a short-distance move, you don't need to pull the anchors all the way up. Just pull the anchors up so they suspend a few feet above the bottom. Once you choose a new spot, it takes seconds to lower both anchors. If you are making a long-distance move, always pull the anchors in to reduce drag and the risk of an accident should you strike a shallow hump, rock pile, log, or shoal or have an anchor rope swing into a motor prop.

Anchor Ropes and Anchors

I recommend investing in the best anchor rope possible. Good-quality rope is typically soft and easy on the hands. At the end of a day or multiday trip, after numerous location changes, your hands will thank you. You also want to use the largest diameter rope you can that will still fit through the anchor lock. I use a minimum of ⅜-inch-diameter rope, and I prefer ½-inch rope if possible. As most productive lakes are shallow, you don't need miles of rope: 50 feet per anchor is ample. Some lakes require deep anchoring. In those instances, bring along a longer rope. I keep my excess rope in small buckets to avoid having rope all over the place.

Always tie a simple overhand knot in the end of your anchor rope. The knot serves as a stopper should your anchor cleat slip or if you attempt to anchor in water deeper than your rope. Without a stopper, if your anchor slips, nothing is stopping it as it plunges to the bottom, taking the anchor rope with it—a lesson I learned the hard way from personal experience.

Your anchor rope can also help determine depth. Mark the rope using black spray paint or a permanent marker every 3 or 5 feet. As the rope descends into the lake, simply count the number of marks to determine your approximate depth. If you choose 3-foot markings and five marks go into the water, you are in 15 feet. Even though I now use sounders all the time, I still mark my anchor ropes as a backup in the event something happens to my sounder, such as a power failure or, worse, forgetting it.

If you don't have electronics or as a backup should your sounder fail, always mark your anchor rope using 3- or 5-foot increments to determine depth.

Fishing from an anchored position provides the ultimate presentation control. There are several anchor styles available. I have used many different types and find pyramid anchors work best for the soft muddy bottoms common to most productive lakes.

There are several different anchor styles, and over the years I have tried most, if not all, of them. Years ago, before fully realizing the dangers of melting lead, we used to make our own anchors. We would melt old vehicle wheel weights used to balance tires in an old coffee can for a boat anchor or a soup can for a float tube, pontoon boat, or supplementary anchor for a boat.

My favorite anchor is a lead pyramid. Pyramid anchors plunge and hold in soft mud bottoms common to most productive lakes. Once a pyramid anchor hits bottom, it tends to lay on its side. The flat face pushes against the mud, further locking the boat or pontoon boat in place. I am not a fan of metal mushroom anchors. I find they don't bite into the bottom consistently and often slide and shuffle along the bottom in windy conditions.

I recommend always choosing an anchor weight for the average conditions you will encounter. Don't opt for the heaviest anchor you can find, as raising and lowering heavy anchors soon becomes tiring. My 17-foot guide boat has a 30-pound main anchor and a 25-pound secondary anchor. For my 14-foot jon boat, I have two 20-pound anchors. One and a quarter pounds per foot is a good guide for most boats. A 10-pound anchor should be more than enough for a pontoon boat.

If the wind comes up and I need more weight to hold, I have a couple of smaller 5-pound anchors attached to a carabiner. With the main anchors deployed, I clip the smaller anchor onto the rope and let it slide to the bottom. My 15-pound anchor just became a 20-pound anchor and should hold. When the additional weight is no longer needed, simply unclip the secondary anchor and stow it.

When double anchoring, you will need one heavier primary anchor and a lighter secondary anchor. The primary anchor is used to lock the boat in place, and the

Use anchor weights that are sufficient for the majority of your fishing. When determining anchor weight for a boat, 1.25 pounds per foot is a good gauge. If conditions dictate a heavier anchor to stay in place, have a smaller, 5- or 10-pound anchor, attached to a carabineer, on hand that you can slide down the rope to increase your overall anchor weight.

secondary anchor is used to support the primary anchor and stop the boat or pontoon boat from swinging. Once again, the primary reason for double anchoring is to essentially turn the boat or pontoon boat into dry land for maximum presentation control. If you are constantly battling with a swinging, swaying boat, you won't be able to control your presentation. Frustration soon follows.

How to Anchor

When it comes to anchoring, I prefer to anchor into the wind if I am fishing solo or perpendicular when I am in a bigger boat with more than one other person. Perpendicular, crosswind anchoring allows anglers to safely prospect individual quadrants without too much worry or risk of being struck by an errant cast.

There is an art to anchoring. Wind direction, the number of anglers, and whether you want to anchor bow into the wind or broadside to the wind are all factors to consider. If the wind is a factor, try letting out more rope to provide additional scope to help hold the anchors in place.

How I intend to anchor affects placement of my heavier primary anchor and my lighter secondary anchor. When anchoring into the wind, place the primary anchor at your back, so when deployed it locks you in place. In my small pram, I put my primary anchor at the bow. When you are in a pram, jon boat, or traditional V-hull boat, always anchor with your bow into the wind. By anchoring bow into the wind, you are using the streamlined shape of the boat to your advantage to avoid slippage. The bow is narrower than the stern, offering less resistance than the wide, flat stern.

In my larger pontoon boat, I attach my primary anchor to the factory anchor pulley system it came with at the stern. You always want to fish with your feet downwind in a single-person pontoon boat. Due to its symmetrical profile, use the same anchoring process for a drift boat. Use the factory anchor to anchor stern into the wind and then use a lighter secondary anchor to lock the bow in place to prevent annoying sway.

To anchor into the wind, deploy the primary anchor first and allow it to settle. If the wind is blowing, you may have to let out some additional rope to provide scope to adjust for the wind-induced chop. If you anchor in windy conditions on a tight vertical rope, the chop and swells may lift the boat, causing the anchor to slip and slide along the bottom and, in some instances, let go. Anchors shuffle and slip most often along the shallow edge of a drop-off, a sloped edge, or the top of a sunken hump or island.

Pontoon boats draw little water. As a result, they can sway back and forth uncontrollably, which negatively influences your presentation. A removable anchor lock can be mounted to a pontoon boat's frame using a rail mount system to combat boat sway.

Once you are locked in place by the primary anchor, use your oars, electric motor, or in most instances the wind to swing the unanchored end of the boat straight downwind. Once downwind, lower the secondary anchor to prevent swaying or swinging.

The process for anchoring perpendicular to the wind is different. I have my heavy, primary anchor located at the stern of the boat. The stern is the widest and heaviest part of my jon boat and is home to my outboard, electric motor, batteries, and gas tank. As a result, I need my primary anchor to hold the stern in place. I place my lighter secondary anchor at the bow.

When anchoring broadside, place the heavier anchor at the stern, mounted on the upwind side, as this is the end of the boat most likely to move. Place the lighter anchor at the bow. Deploy the bow anchor first and then swing the boat's stern perpendicular to the wind. Drop the stern anchor to lock the boat into position.

To anchor perpendicular to the wind, I lower the lighter bow anchor first. Once the bow is locked in place, I use the wind or motor, gas or electric, to swing the stern perpendicular to the wind. Once in position, I lower the rear anchor to complete the anchoring process.

During the initial setup of my boat, I had to choose which side of the boat I wanted to fish out of, as this affected where I placed my stern anchor lock. I decided to fish out of the left, or port, side, so I mounted the removable anchor lock on the right, or starboard, corner of the stern. The stern anchor rope must trail behind the boat when anchored for two main reasons:

1. With the anchor trailing behind the boat upwind, there is less likelihood of a fish getting into the rope during a fight. The goal is to do your best to control the fish and keep the battle contained to the port side. Should a fish become entangled in an anchor rope, don't panic. Most times, it can be worked free; see chapter 11, "Going Deep," for a full explanation. Fish can get tangled in an anchor rope when fishing sinking lines vertically, or dangling.
2. When you are anchoring in windy conditions with the rope trailing behind the boat, the anchor is less prone to slipping. If you had the rope off the downwind side, the wind and the swells it creates push against the upwind side of the boat. This forces the downwind side of the boat against the rope, causing the anchor to slide and break loose.

Drift boats can also be anchored perpendicular to the wind. Once again, due to their symmetrical shape, location of the primary anchor doesn't matter. You can anchor either the primary or secondary anchor first and use the wind, oars, or motor to swing perpendicular before deploying the second anchor to lock it in place.

Anchoring a Float Tube

Although many people paddle around in a float tube, you can also anchor them. You should only use a single anchor in a float tube. Having two anchor ropes close to each other is potentially dangerous should your fins and legs become entangled in them, not to mention a fish wrapping itself in the ropes. A single rope is less tangle-prone and, therefore, safer. If a fish wraps itself around the rope, it is much easier to raise a single rope and hopefully untangle and land the fish.

For you to fish straight downwind, the anchor point needs to be right behind your back. If you tie off the anchor rope to a D ring on the side, the float tube will sit on an angle, requiring you to twist in your seat to fish downwind—a position that soon becomes uncomfortable. Thankfully the solution is simple:

1. For a round float tube, take a length of narrow-diameter rope or cord that is long enough to be tied or clipped to the D rings typically located on the rear sides.
2. Take a swivel clip, the kind used on most dog leashes, and slide it onto the rope so it goes through the ring portion of the clip.
3. Tie or clip the rope to the D rings on the rear sides of the float tube so it runs across the back of the tube.

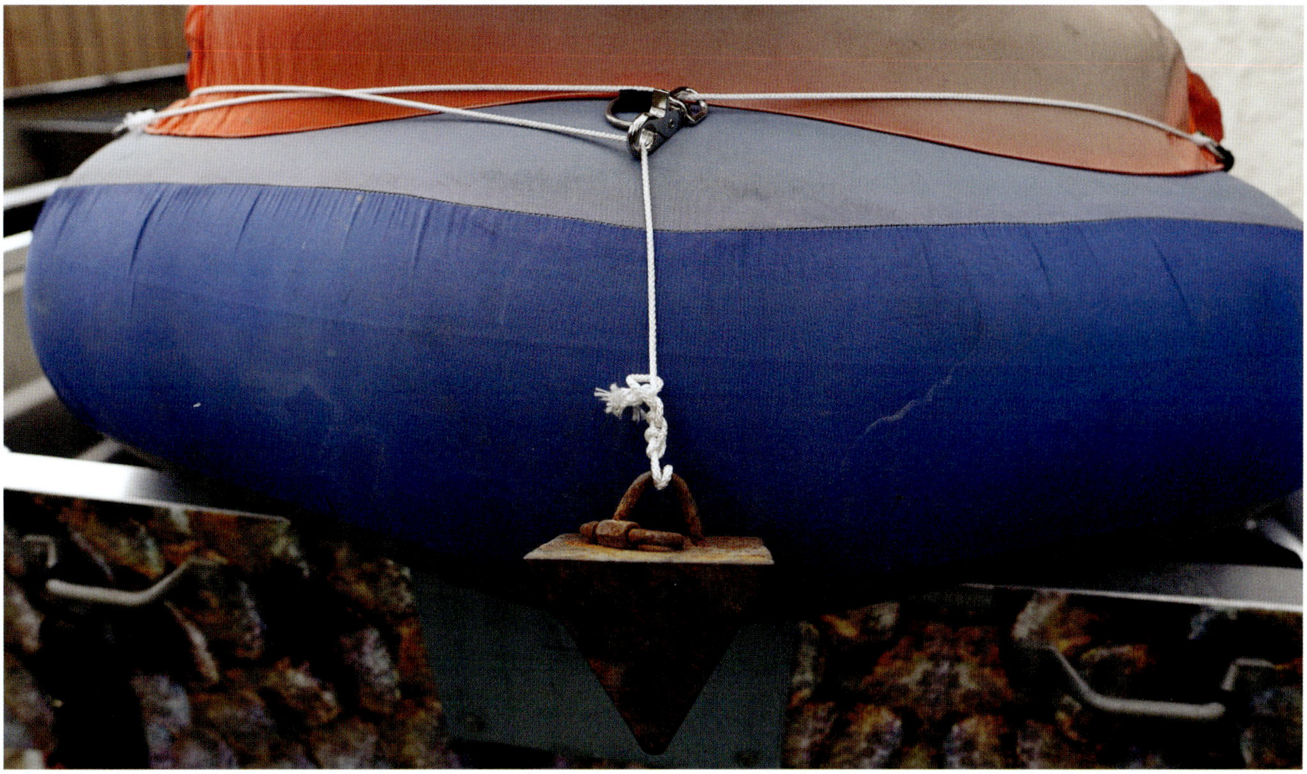

You can easily add an anchor to a float tube. Slide a swivel clip onto a short length of rope or cord. Attach the cord to the two rear D rings so it runs across the rear of the float tube. When deploying your anchor, place the rope through the swivel clip so it self-centers behind the float tube once the anchor lands on the bottom.

4. When you want to anchor, clip the anchor rope into the snap link portion of the swivel clip and lower the anchor.
5. Once the anchor hits bottom, let out a little more rope to ensure proper scope and to allow you to store the remaining rope in one of the float tube pockets.
6. As the swivel clip slides back on the rope between the right rear and left rear D rings of the float tube, you automatically self-center, enabling you to fish downwind.

U-Boat Anchoring

Anchoring a U-shaped float tube requires a different approach. You could pass a small anchor and rope through the small gap on the inside edge at the rear of a U-boat. Sliding an anchor through the hole requires tying it off. You don't want it to deploy accidentally. Having the rope rubbing against the tube could also damage the outer fabric.

The best option for U-boat tubes is to use a strap-on anchor system. Most strap-on anchors come with an anchor lock that allows you to raise and lower an anchor just like a larger pontoon boat or boat.

CHAPTER TAKEAWAYS

- There are several reasons fly fishing lakes from shore can be challenging. To fly fish lakes, you need to be able to move around. Mobility is critical for you to locate and explore stillwater structures such as weed beds, large shoals, points, and drop-offs.
- Boats, pontoon boats, and float tubes are the three most common types of watercraft. Compromise is a common factor with all watercraft. Unfortunately, no one type of craft is going to meet all of the needs and challenges lakes offer.
- Never walk forward with fins on and a float tube around your waist. Stepping forward is a recipe for a fall that may result in a broken rod or body part, or worse.
- The low profile of a float tube doesn't offer the best perspective when it comes to seeing strikes when using subsurface floating line techniques such as strike indicators, and long-leader weighted nymph tactics.
- Pontoon boats are an excellent compromise between a float tube and an often more expensive boat.
- To prevent accidental rod loss in a float tube or pontoon boat, clip your rod to a soft, flexible plastic coil key chain when releasing a fish, rowing, or any other scenario when you aren't holding your rod.
- Stable flat-bottom prams or jon boats are arguably the best stillwater boat option when fishing from an anchored position. Rivet or welded aluminum prams or jon boats are relatively inexpensive compared to other boat types.
- Drift boats can work well on lakes. Perhaps one of the drift boat's most significant benefits is its ability to be launched almost anywhere.
- As part of the precautions and awareness surrounding aquatic invasive species, most jurisdictions today require boat plug removal when traveling. Always put the boat plug in the same place so you can find it. Having spare boat plugs on hand is a good idea.
- Fishing from an anchored position provides you with complete presentation control, as you don't have the challenge of compensating for the movement of your watercraft.
- Avoid tying off an anchor rope to a cleat. Use cam-style anchor locks. Anchor locks allow for efficient anchor deployment. You can raise or lower your anchor single-handed without the risk of the anchor plummeting to the bottom. Anchor locks also enable you to partially raise an anchor and hold it in place when making short-distance moves.
- Never toss an anchor into the water. The subsequent splash and disturbance scatters fish. Anchor locks allow you to lower your anchors quietly into the water without spooking fish.
- Use a marked anchor rope to determine depth.
- Pyramid anchors are the best anchor type. Avoid metal mushroom-style anchors, as they often slip in windy, choppy conditions.

- When anchoring solo, place the heavier anchor on the upwind end. When in a small boat, put the heavier anchor at the bow. Lower the heavier primary anchor first to lock the boat in position. Allow the boat to swing downwind and then deploy the lighter secondary anchor to prevent annoying sway.
- To anchor perpendicular to the wind in a multi-person boat, place the lighter secondary anchor at the bow and the heavier primary anchor at the stern. Lower the secondary anchor first. Use the wind, oars, or motor to swing the boat perpendicular to the wind. Lower the primary anchor to lock the boat in place.
- When anchoring perpendicular to the wind, make sure the stern anchor and rope trail behind the boat on the upwind side. As you want to fight the fish on the downwind side of the boat, having the anchor upwind minimizes the risk of the fish becoming entangled in the rope. In windy conditions, the boat also won't push against the anchor rope and potentially dislodge the anchor, if deployed on the downwind side.
- Never double anchor in a float tube.
- A swivel, dog leash–style clip slid onto a short section of rope which you then attach to the rear D rings of a circular float tube allows you to anchor straight downwind, as the anchor rope self-centers directly behind you.
- A strap-on anchor system is the best option for a U-boat–style float tube. Most strap-on anchors come with an anchor lock that allows you to raise and lower an anchor just like you would with a larger pontoon boat or boat.

CHAPTER 4

LEADERS, KNOTS, AND DROPPERS

Fly-fishing leaders, knots, and dropper options garner an incredible amount of discussion and debate. There are so many different leader and dropper methods and systems available, each one possessing valid arguments for its use. I try to keep my approach to stillwater leaders, knots, and droppers simple.

LEADERS

When it comes to leaders, I try to blend in readily available "off the rack" options that are easy to find and, more importantly, figure out. Other fly fishers use different leader systems. Some fly fishers, especially competition anglers, prefer level leaders. Level leaders sink consistently along their length, and in the event of a tangle can be quickly rebuilt. Time is always a factor in competitions. Inexperienced stillwater fly fishers may find thin-diameter level leaders tangle-prone and, as a result, frustrating to use. My leader systems are a blend of tapered and level leaders.

In my experience, a leader serves two purposes:

1. Assist and augment the presentation. The leader works both with the fly and the fly line choice for the situation.
2. Practical to cast. The leader's construction and design aren't a source of frustration when casting due to poor turnover or frequent tangles.

I use tapered nylon leaders or level leaders for all of my leader systems. Level or predominantly level leaders work best for sinking line presentations, as they keep the fly or flies in the same proximity as the fly line. As a general rule, the faster the

A simple approach to leaders and tippet in lakes works best.

sink rate of the line, the shorter the leader. Long leaders are common to floating or midge-tip lines, anywhere from 9 feet to over 25 feet depending upon the presentation technique. Listed below is a breakdown of my preferred stillwater leader systems:

- I use long, 12- to 15-foot tapered leaders as the base for my long-leader nymphing or naked technique setup.
- Ten-foot indicator/nymphing leaders are the primary core for thin, level indicator leaders.
- For dry fly and emerger presentations, I use 9- to 14-foot tapered leaders. The calmer the water, the longer and finer my leader.
- I use short, 7½-foot tapered leaders as the foundation for all of my sinking lines from hover through type III. I then add equal or slightly lesser diameter tippet to complete the leader. Adding additional flies increases leader length to ensure the flies are working a reasonable distance from each other.
- For fast-sinking lines, type V sink rate or greater, my leaders range from 7 feet to as short as 4 feet. The faster the sink rate, the shorter the leader. As with all of my leader systems, additional flies result in longer leaders. This ensures my flies have enough space between them to work properly.

You can find the specific setups for my indicator, long-line nymphing, and a variety of sinking line leaders in the "Floating Lines: Strike Indicators and Long Leader Nymphing"; "Floating Lines: Dries, Emergers, and Targeting Sighted Fish"; and "Going Deep: Sinking Line Techniques" chapters.

Leader Storage

Organized leader storage within a kit bag can be challenging. Left loose, leaders soon end up everywhere. You want to find a specific leader quickly and efficiently without

Binder rings, available at most office supply stores, are ideal for storing and managing leaders.

having the contents of your kit bag scattered everywhere. Binder rings, found at most office supply stores, make an excellent storage solution, as they take advantage of how most leaders are packaged.

Placing leaders onto the binder ring is simple: Open a binder ring. Using the leader package holes, slide several leaders onto the binder ring. Close the ring. Using it is also simple: To find a leader, flip through the leaders on the binder ring until you locate the leader you want. Open the binder ring and remove the particular leader. Close the ring to keep the remaining leaders under control. Binder rings allow you to sort by leader length or type.

Tippet

I am a firm believer in fluorocarbon tippet for the same reasons many other fly fishers are: abrasion resistance and reduced visibility in the water. The terminal end of all of my leaders, including dries and emergers, is almost always fluorocarbon.

In addition to fluorocarbon, I also carry nylon tippet. I use nylon tippet to extend leader length between the main tapered leader and the final fluorocarbon tippet section. I also use nylon tippet when water clarity doesn't necessarily dictate the use of less-visible fluorocarbon. Having nylon tippet also provides a practical backup should you run out of or forget to bring fluorocarbon.

As a dedicated catch-and-release fly fisher, I use the heaviest tippet I can get away with so I can reduce stress to the fish by fighting it aggressively and getting it into the net as fast as possible. My average starting tippet size is 3X, approximately 8-pound breaking strain depending on the brand. For large fish, fishing in and around weed beds, or in murky water conditions, I often step up to 1X or 0X. In clear-water situations, I will go down to 4X or 5X in extreme circumstances.

PREFERRED KNOTS

When I was first learning to fly fish, I tried to master as many knots as I could. It seemed there were as many knots as fly fishers, and each knot had strong arguments for its use. At times it became overwhelming trying to keep all of the various knots and their specific applications in order. As my experience grew, I decided upon a simple suite of knots that I could tie quickly and proficiently.

Using a simple set of knots that you believe in and that perform consistently is a wise philosophy. Most people tend to shy away from things they don't like to do. This tendency is especially true with knots. If you are a proficient knot tier, you are more inclined to make a change, whether to adjust a leader, add a dropper, or change flies.

I break my suite of knots into two categories: primary and secondary. Primary knots I use every day on the water; secondary knots I use less frequently or as an alternative, at times, to one of my primary knots.

It seems, at times, that there are as many knots as there are fly fishers. Choose a simple suite of knots that are easy to tie and work best for you.

Primary knots:

- Nonslip loop knot
- Clinch knot
- Perfection loop
- Triple surgeon's knot

Secondary knots:

- Uni knot
- Blood knot
- Double surgeon's loop
- Nail knot
- Albright knot

Leader and tippet, along with flies, are among the least expensive pieces of equipment, yet this is where many fly fishers choose to cut corners. When it comes to leader and tippet, get the best materials you can, and use the necessary amount of material needed to tie the knot comfortably. If your knots are continually failing due to poor tying technique or inferior material, all the fancy rods, lines, and reels in the world won't make it better.

When tying any knot, it is important not to scrimp on the material and to make sure you can see. If you need glasses, use them. There is nothing more frustrating than trying to tie a knot in low-light conditions or if everything is blurred. If tying knots is unpleasant and frustrating, we naturally avoid it. Consequently, we won't make critical fly, leader, or dropper changes when they are required. As with fly casting, practice tying knots when you aren't fishing so they become second nature. Figuring things out on the water isn't always the best practice.

Don't be in a rush to draw a knot tight. A correctly formed knot shouldn't unravel. Pulling a knot tight too fast builds up heat due to friction that may weaken the knot, or the knot may not form properly. Moisten the knot and use gradual tension to draw it tight.

Primary Knots

Nonslip Loop Knot

The nonslip loop knot has a variety of names: Rapala knot, Lefty's loop knot, and 97% knot, to name a few. It is the primary knot I use to attach my fly to the end of the tippet or dropper. As the knot remains open, it allows the fly to move freely during the retrieve or hang if presented under an indicator. It is a strong knot, and one I have complete faith in.

The nonslip loop knot is easy to tie. The goal is to have the loop of the finished knot approximately twice the diameter of the hook eye. I accomplish this by adjusting the loop size after placing the fly onto the tag end and pulling both the tag and main line at the same time to shrink the loop to the desired size. If your first attempts result in an oversize loop, don't worry—the fly will still fish. The only concern would be that if the loop is too large, it may foul some flies, particularly long-tailed leech or minnow patterns.

How to Tie a Nonslip Loop Knot

1. Form an open overhand loop about 2 to 3 inches from the end of the leader or tippet. Slide the tag end through the hook eye. Bring the tag end back through the overhand loop.

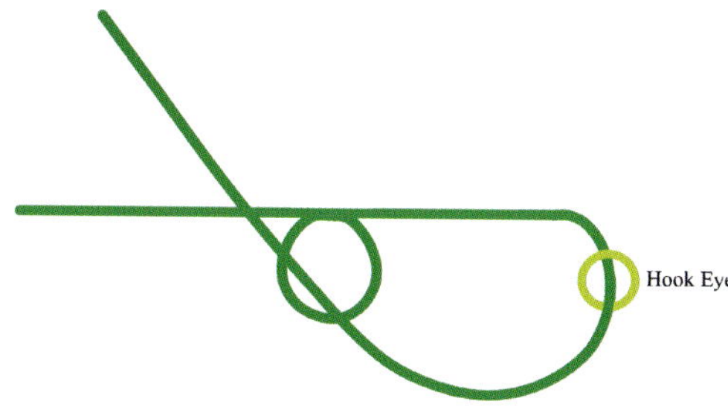

2. Pull both the main line and tag end to adjust the overhand loop size so it is twice the diameter of the hook eye.

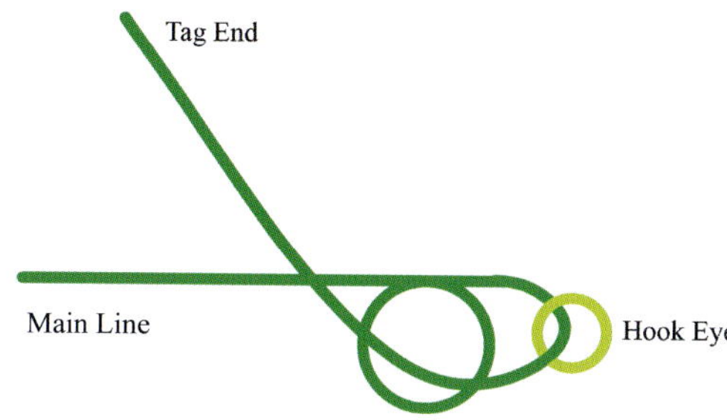

3. With the loop sized, pinch both the fly and tippet between your thumb and forefinger. Be careful not to accidentally pull on either the main line or the tag end, as this could accidentally close up the overhand loop. Wind the tag end around the main line directly above the overhand loop four times, as you would for a clinch or improved clinch knot.

4. Adjust your thumb and forefinger to expose the overhand loop. Push the tag end through the loop.

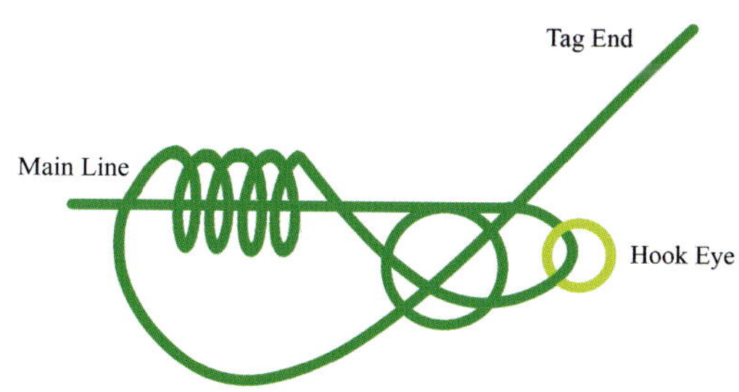

5. Using a small amount of saliva, moisten the knot. Tighten the knot using a slow, controlled pull. Avoid pulling too fast: This causes heat due to friction that could weaken the knot, or the wraps may not seat correctly. The tag end should protrude 90 degrees to the finished knot. Trim the tag end flush to complete the knot.

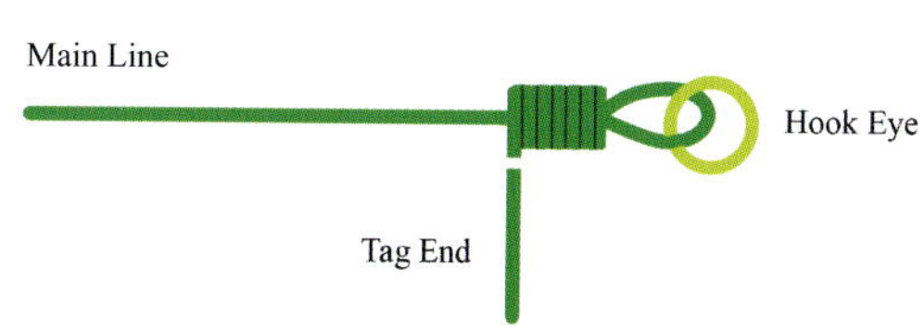

Clinch Knot

Although many use a clinch knot to attach a fly to the end of the tippet, I use it most often to attach barrel swivels or tippet rings, as well as for knotting the butt section of a leader to the welded loop of a fly line when doing an on-the-water fly line switch. See chapter 1, "Equipment: Rods, Reels, and Lines," for a complete explanation. You can also cinch a clinch knot tight against the hook eye of any fly tied on a jig hook to encourage it to sit horizontally when suspended under a strike indicator.

How to Tie a Clinch Knot

1. Slide 2 to 3 inches of tippet or leader material through the hook eye, tippet ring, or ring of a barrel swivel. Wrap the tag end around the main line five to seven times. The thinner the diameter, the more wraps.

2. Pass the tag end through the loop formed when it was doubled back against the main line just in front of the hook eye, tippet ring, or swivel.

3. Lubricate the knot. Pull the knot tight using smooth, even pressure. Trim the tag end to complete the knot.

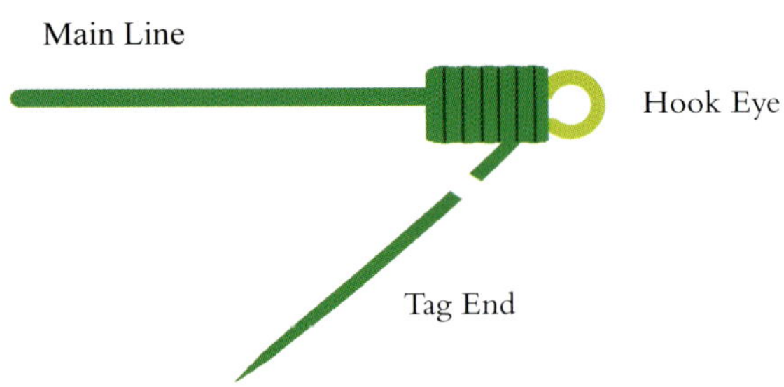

Perfection Loop

The perfection loop is my preferred loop knot. I find it easy to tie, and the loop always forms in line with the main line, never off-center, as can be the case with other loop knots. Adding a loop to a section of tippet for a sliding dropper is my primary use for the perfection loop. I also use the perfection loop for adding a loop to the end of the leader to facilitate a loop-to-loop connection with the welded loop of a fly line.

How to Tie a Perfection Loop

1. Starting with 3 to 4 inches of tippet or leader, form a loop by placing the tag end under the main line. The tag end should point away from you. Using your thumb and forefinger, pinch the base of the loop where the tag end passes under the tippet.

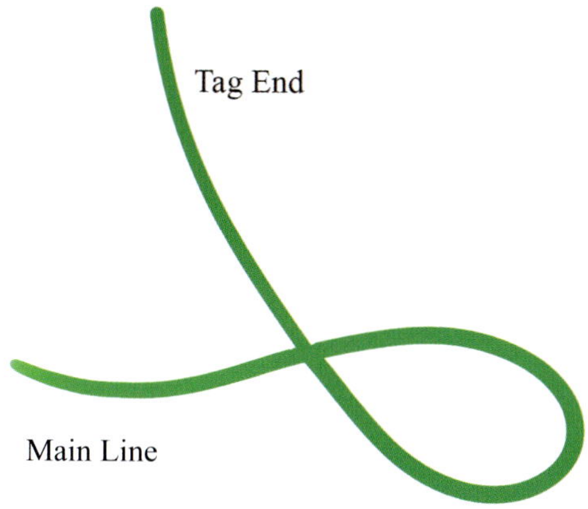

2. Form a second, smaller loop by bringing the tag end back over the top toward yourself and then under the main loop. Adjust your thumb and forefinger to pinch both loops. The smaller loop must lie on top of the larger loop.

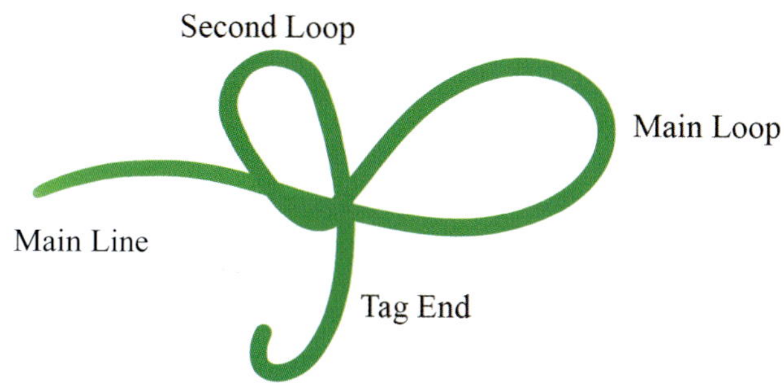

3. Bring the tag end back across and in between both loops toward you. Work the tag end down between your thumb and forefinger to hold everything in place.

4. While still holding the knot together with your thumb and forefinger, reach through the larger loop and pull the smaller loop with your other thumb and forefinger back through the main loop to form the knot. Moisten the knot before drawing the knot tight.

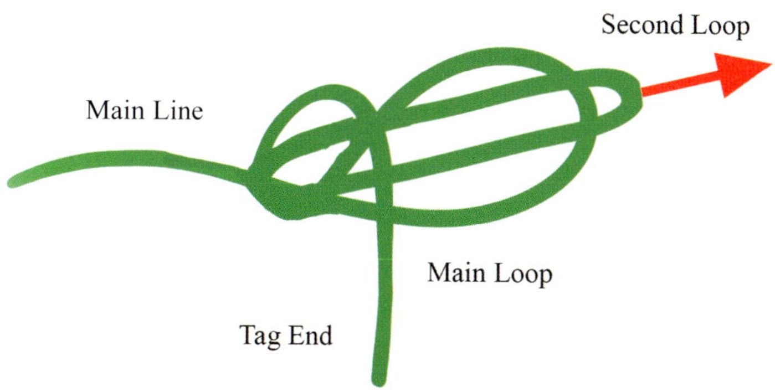

5. Trim the tag end to complete the knot.

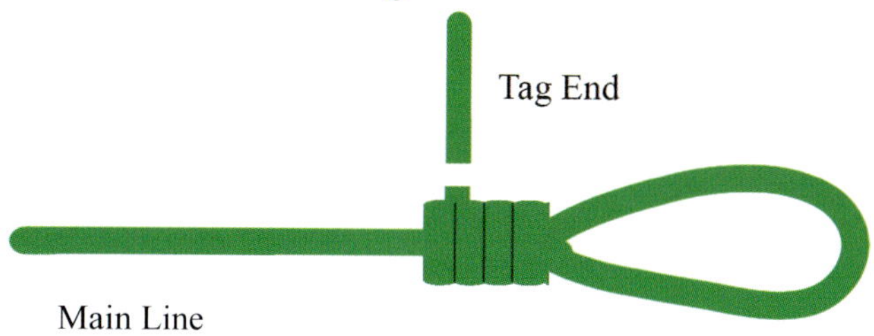

Triple Surgeon's Knot

The triple surgeon's knot is my go-to knot for connecting finer-diameter tippet and leader material. I find the triple surgeon's knot easier to tie than a blood knot, especially on cold, wet days when my dexterity isn't at peak levels. Like the blood knot, the triple surgeon's forms more laterally than the ball-like double surgeon's knot. As a result, a triple surgeon's knot passes through the guides easier, reducing the risk of a break-off should the knot jam against a guide. I also find when combining harder fluorocarbon and soft nylon material, which can bite into the nylon, that the triple surgeon's knot is less prone to breaking due to an aggressive take or the sudden surge of a fish than the two-turn double surgeon's knot.

The triple surgeon's knot is my preferred dropper tag knot, as the tag comes out of the end of the knot. Always use the tag end on the point fly side of the knot, opposite to the fly line side. When a fish takes the dropper, it pulls in the direction the knot was formed. If you use the tag from the fly line side, the fish is pulling against the knot, which stresses the knot and may cause breakage.

How to Tie a Triple Surgeon's Knot

1. Lay the two materials parallel to each other. If you are going to form a dropper, be sure to leave enough material to create a 4- to 6-inch tag on the *point fly side* of the knot. Moisten the two materials to keep them together. Form an overhand loop with both materials.

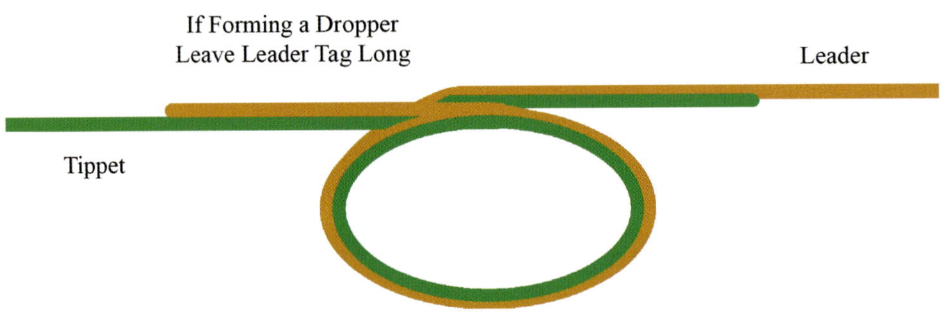

2. Pass both materials on the fly side of the knot through the overhand loop three times.

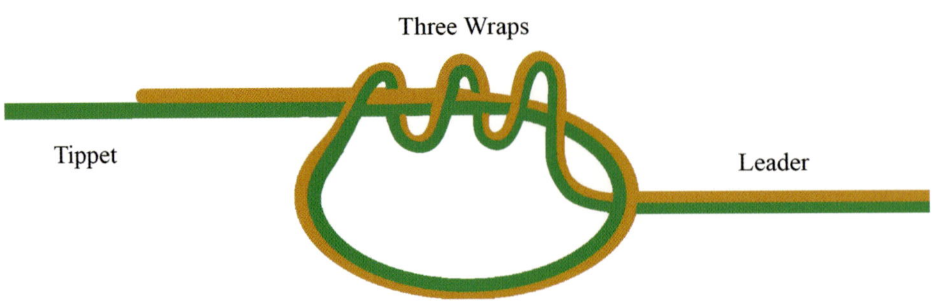

3. Using even, steady pressure, pull the knot tight. If you are forming a dropper tag, pinch the opposite side of the loop from the tag end. This technique draws the knot toward the pinch so you don't rob yourself of any tag length. If you aren't forming a dropper tag, trim both ends flush. If you are forming a dropper, trim the tag on the *fly line side* of the knot only.

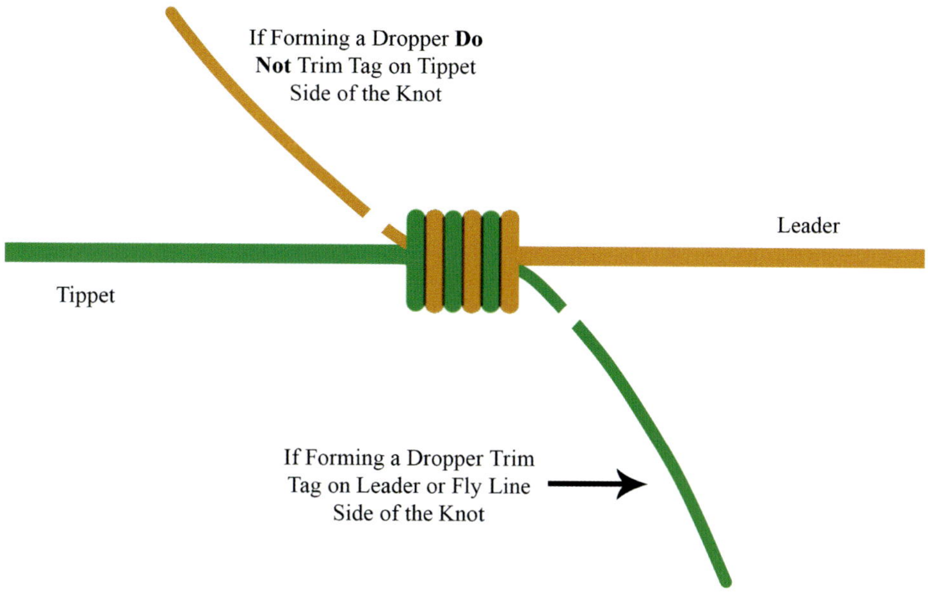

Secondary Knots

Uni Knot

The uni knot is a versatile knot. It can be used to attach a fly to the tippet, attach a dropper to the leader above a tippet-to-leader knot such as the triple surgeon's, attach a dropper to a hook bend, or to create a line marker on a sinking line. Dacron can be used to create hang markers or depth markers when fishing vertically using fast-sinking lines; see chapter 11, "Going Deep," for a complete explanation. Back-to-back uni knots can also be used to connect braided line to nylon leader and tippet.

I prefer the nonslip loop knot to attach a fly to the tippet, as it doesn't draw tight under pressure. Proponents of the uni knot argue all they have to do to is pinch the knot against their thumbnail as they pull and wiggle the fly to open it. I worry that the tippet could be nicked by the thumbnail, weakening it in the process.

One advantage of the uni knot drawing tight under tension when using multiple flies is that it can be used to identify which fly a fish took in the event of a missed take. If you miss a take, inspect your flies. If one of the uni knots is closed tight against the hook eye, you know that was the fly the fish took. You now have clues as to what fly type, size, and color, and probably most importantly, what presentation depth you should choose.

How to Tie a Fly onto a Leader or Tippet Using a Uni Knot

1. Slide approximately 3 to 4 inches of the leader or tippet through the hook eye. Double the tag end back, parallel against the main line.

2. Using the thumb and forefinger, pinch the main line and tag just in front of the hook eye. Make sure to have an ample amount of material in front of the pinch point to finish the knot. Using the tag end, form a large loop in front of the thumb and forefinger. Adjust the pinch to hold the loop in place parallel to the main leader.

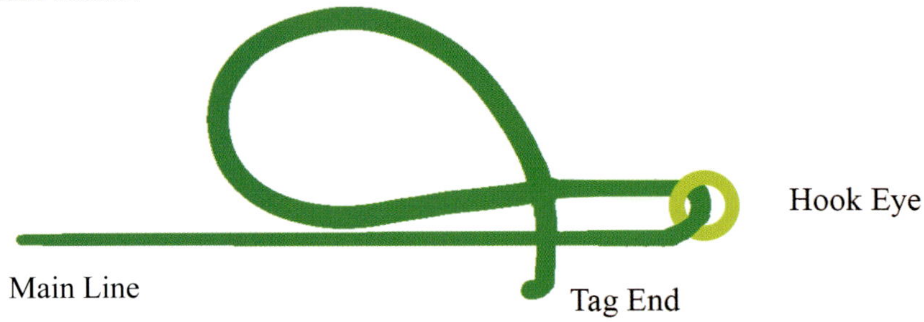

3. Pass the tag end through the loop and over the doubled main line and tippet five or six times.

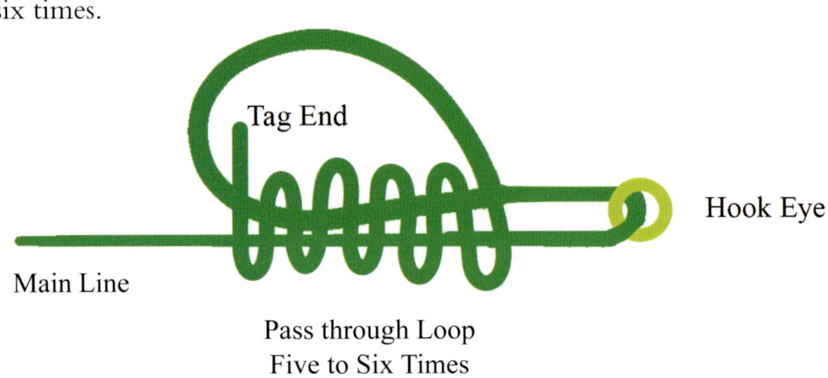

4. Moisten the knot. Using steady pressure, pull the knot tight. Trim the tag end. Pull the main line to adjust and shrink the loop size so it is twice the diameter of the hook eye.

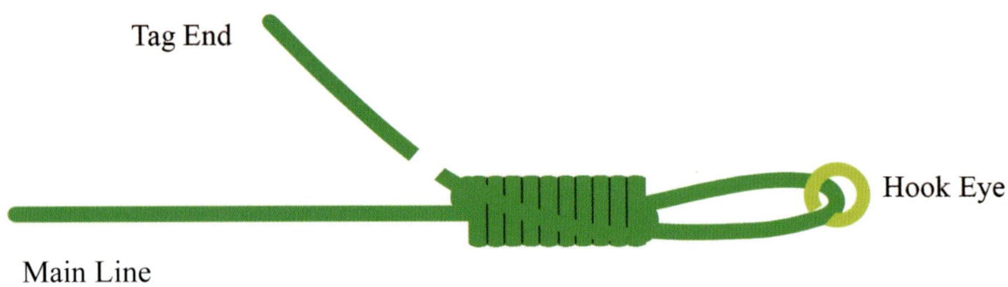

Blood Knot

Before the advent of welded loops, I attached a stiff butt section to the end of the fly line using a nail knot. I then attached a tapered leader to the butt section using a blood knot. Butt sections were a common component when building long, 15 feet or greater, nymphing leaders. The blood knot is my preferred connection whenever I am joining larger-diameter materials. A blood knot can also be used to tie smaller diameters together in place of a triple surgeon's knot. I find the triple surgeon's knot easier to join finer-diameter materials. The tag end of a blood knot can also be used to form a dropper. Honestly, I don't use a blood knot as much as I used to, but it is still a knot worth knowing how to tie.

How to Tie a Blood Knot

1. Take the two materials and cross them to form two 3- to 4-inch tags. Pinch the materials where they intersect.

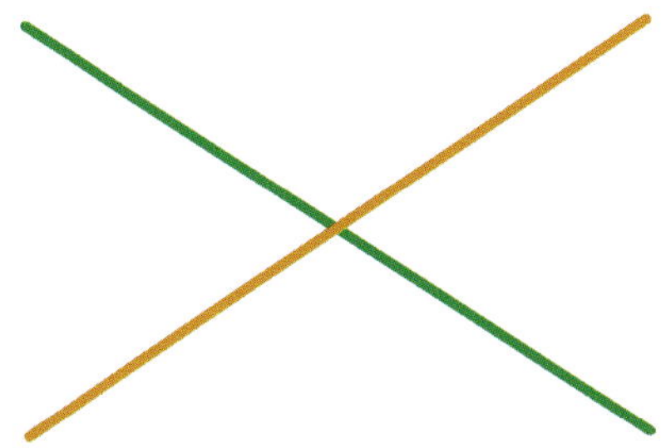

2. Wrap the tag end of one section of material around the main portion of the other three to five times. Thicker-diameter material requires fewer wraps.

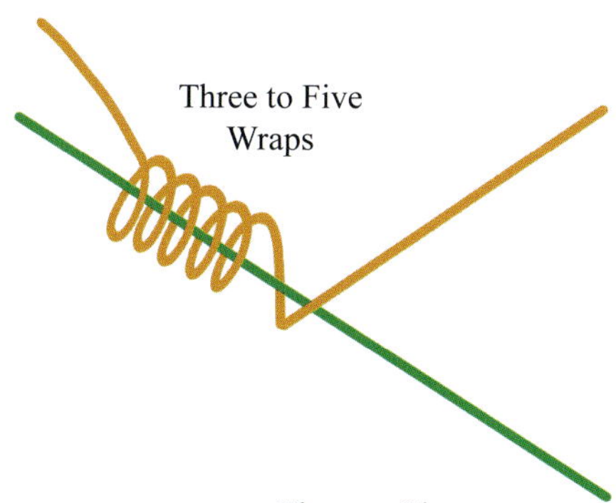

3. Repeat step 2 for the other side of the knot. It is crucial the tag end of the other side of the knot goes through the junction of the two materials in the opposite direction of the first tag. If the first tag went down through the junction, the second tag must go up.

4. Moisten the materials. Pull the main lines slowly and equally to draw the knot tight. Pulling too fast and aggressively may cause the knot to slip and unravel. The tag ends should point opposite to each other if the knot has been tied correctly.

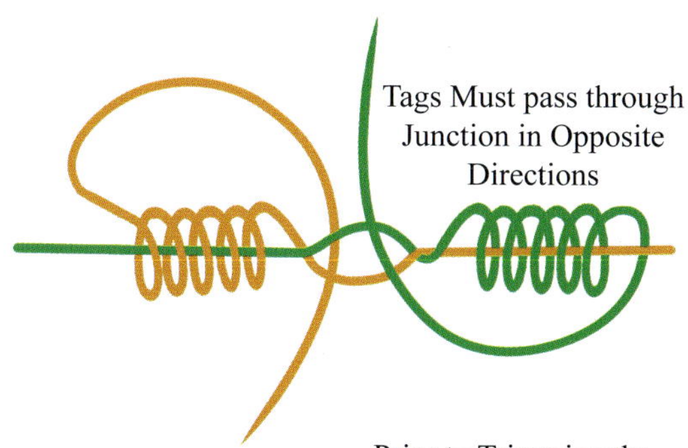

5. Once the knot is snug, trim the tag ends flush.

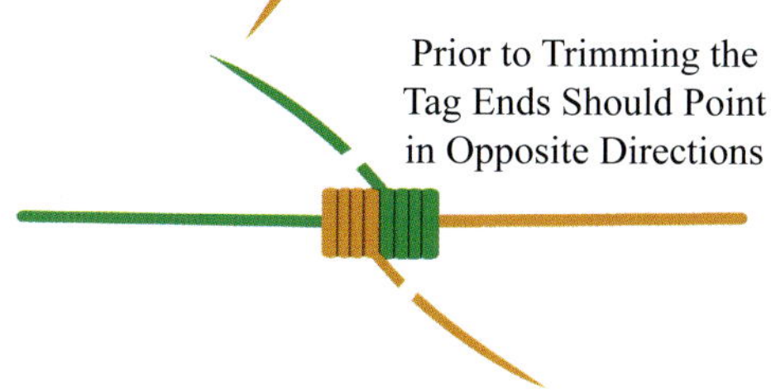

Double Surgeon's Loop

There are times when I swap lines on my reel spools. In these instances, a double surgeon's loop is my preferred loop-to-loop connection from the backing to the rear welded loop of the fly line. For added strength, I add a double surgeon's knot approximately an inch or two above the original double surgeon's loop. Make sure the finished loop is large enough for the spool or plastic line cartridge to pass through.

How to Tie a Double Surgeon's Loop

1. Double one end of the backing. To form a small loop, double a short length; for a large loop, double a longer length. I double 8 to 10 inches of material for a backing connection.

2. Pass the doubled end through the overhand loop twice.

3. Using smooth, even pressure, pull on the doubled and tag ends of the material to snug the knot tight.

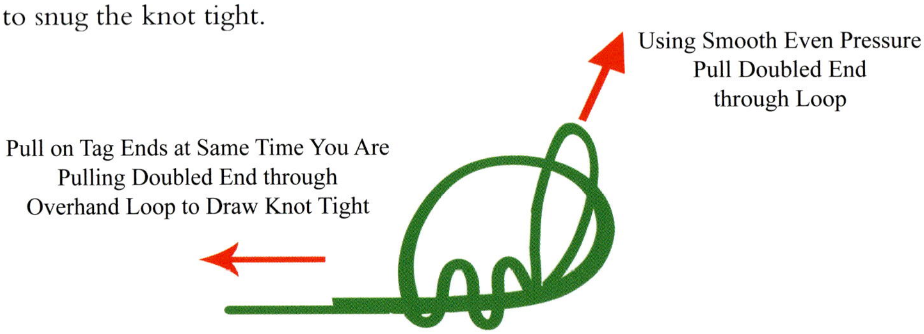

4. To complete a loop-to-loop backing connection, use the finished loop to form a double surgeon's knot an inch or so in front of the original double surgeon's loop for added security. Trim the tag end flush with the finished knot.

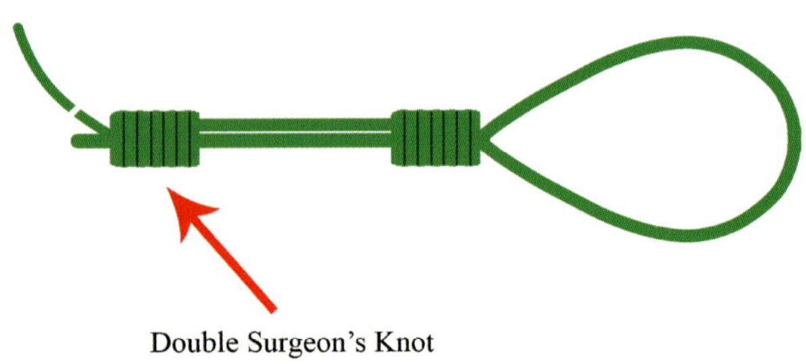

Nail Knot and Albright Knot

I prefer to attach my fly line to my backing via a loop-to-loop connection. However, not all fly lines come with a welded loop at the rear. As a result, the backing needs to be securely knotted to the end of the line. I use two fly line to backing knots: the nail knot and the Albright knot. Of these two, the Albright is a stronger knot but somewhat bulkier than the nail knot. The Albright is my preferred knot for smooth mono core lines. A nail knot doesn't always bite into some lines such as mono core lines, and under tension it can slide off the fly line. The Albright knot is much stronger than the nail knot, as it ties onto and around a small loop of fly line, hence its increased bulk.

Some stillwater fly fishers don't like connecting leaders to the fly line using loop-to-loop connections. They remove the welded loop, and nail knot a short nylon butt section to the end of the fly line. With the butt section in place, they attach the remainder of their leader.

Whenever I tie a nail knot, I prefer to use a Tie Rite–style knot-tying tool. This tool eases the knot-tying process and keeps the materials under control. I can't imagine trying to tie a nail knot without one.

How to Tie a Nail Knot Using a Tie Rite–Style Knot-Tying Tool

1. Place the knot-tying tool in the palm of your hand. Lay the backing or leader butt across the flat thumb pad and hold it in place with the thumb. Lay the tag end of the material into the V-notch of the tool. Make sure to have ample material sticking out in front of the tool.

2. Using firm thumb pressure on the flat pad to hold the backing or leader in place, wrap the tag end of the material around the tip of the tool five or six times. Use firm, controlled wraps, placing each wrap directly behind the previous wrap. Once the wraps are complete, hold them in place using the forefinger.

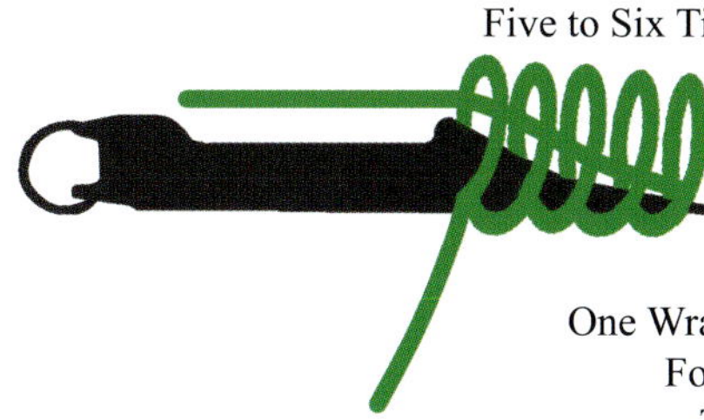

3. Slide the remaining tag end through the wraps from the back out through the front of the tool. Make sure there is enough material sticking out of the tool to get a firm grip so you can pull the knot tight.

4. Slide the end of the fly line into the tip of the tool and through the five or six loops of material. Push enough line in to ensure it doesn't slide out. About an inch is adequate.

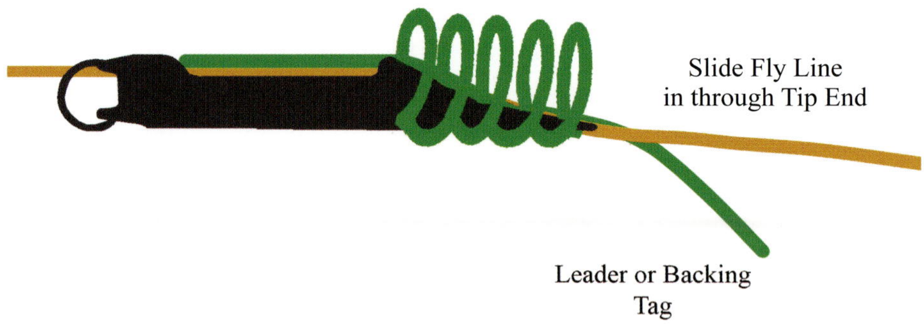

5. With the line in place, grip the tag end. Maintaining firm pressure on the thumb pad to hold the line in place, use a sharp, firm tug to pull the backing or leader material onto the fly line. A slow, lazy pull causes the backing or leader material to shift and bind on itself. Inspect the knot to make sure it has formed correctly. If necessary, use your thumb and forefinger to massage the knot. Massaging the knot neatly aligns the wraps, one behind the other. If possible, gently slide the knot toward the end of the line to avoid waste.

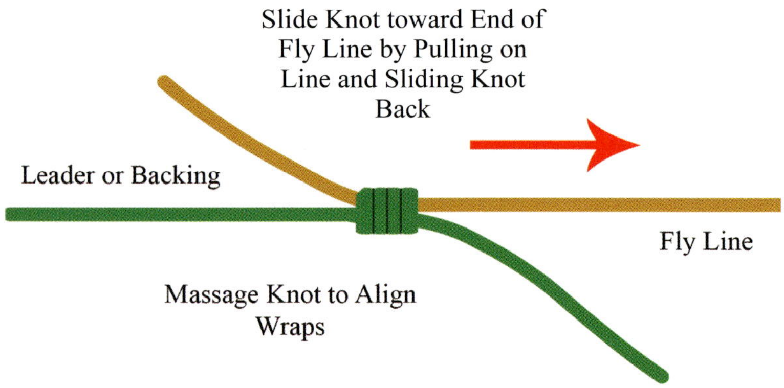

6. Once the knot is in position, pull on both the tag end and the main portion of the leader or backing material to snug the knot tight. Trim both ends flush on an angle. It is a good idea to coat the finished wraps with UV resin to protect and secure the knot while helping it travel through the rod guides.

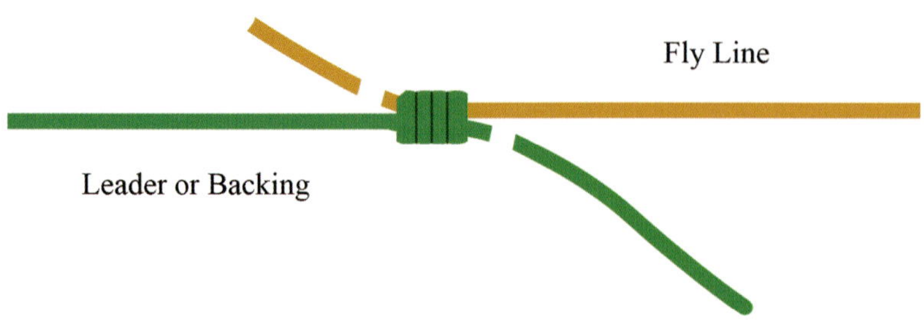

How to Tie a Albright Knot

1. Form a small loop in the end of the line. Hold the loop with your thumb and forefinger so approximately ½ inch of the looped line is exposed.

2. Push 7 to 8 inches of backing through the underside of the loop. Pinch the backing between your thumb and forefinger to hold it in place.

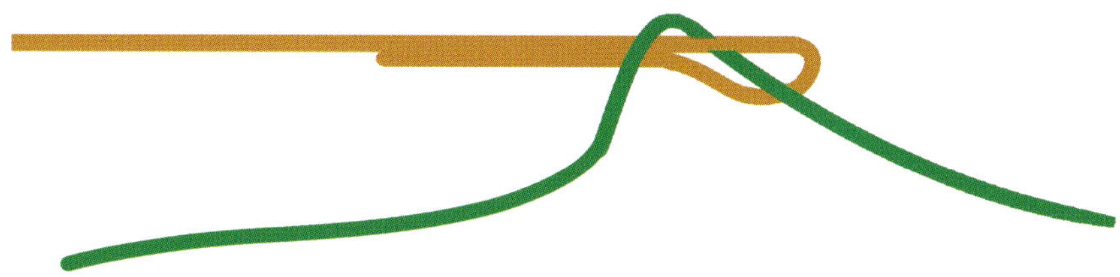

3. Using neat close-touching turns, wind the tag end of the backing toward the end of the looped fly line seven or eight times. Use your middle finger to hold the wraps in place. Pass the tag end of the backing back down through the top of the loop.

4. Pull on the main line of the backing to snug the knot tight.

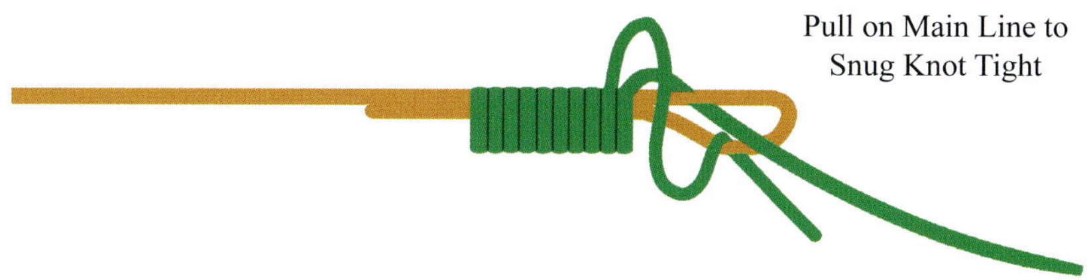

5. Reduce the fly line loop size by sliding the knot toward the end of the loop using a combination of your thumb and forefinger and strategic pulls on the main line of the backing. Tighten the knot by pulling on both the fly line and the backing. Once you are happy with the overall knot size, give a final tightening by pulling on the tag end of the knot using a pair of forceps.

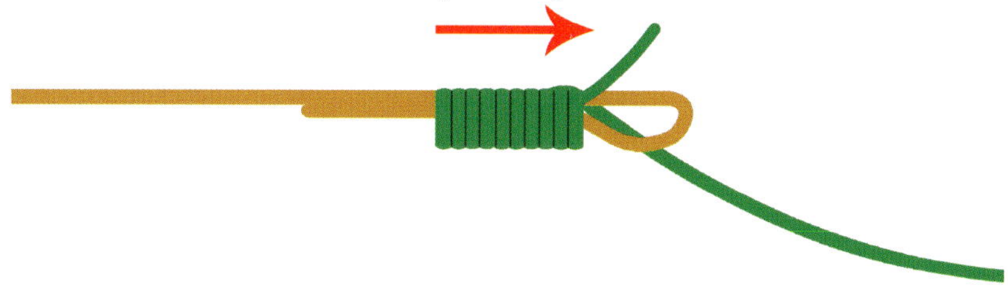

6. Trim the tag ends of both the backing and the fly to complete the knot. Coat the finished knot with UV resin to add a layer of protection and smoothness to the knot so it slides through the guides with minimal risk of a hang-up.

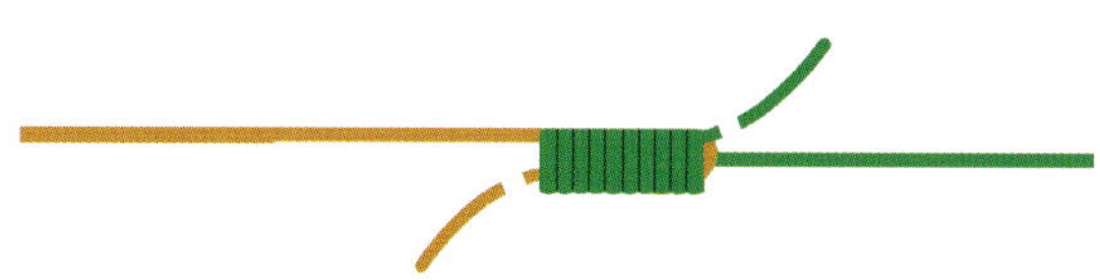

DROPPERS

When legal, I use two flies the majority of the time. If fish are proving difficult to catch and regulations allow, I will add a third fly. Be warned, the addition of the third fly significantly increases the risk of tangles.

Droppers offer several tactical presentation advantages over single-fly systems. Although hooking multiple fish at the same time can happen, it is the last thing you want. Having two or more large fish on at once is chaotic and exciting, but when they flee in different directions, you usually break one or more of them off, destroying your leader and in most instances costing you at least two flies and perhaps an indicator or other leader accessories.

Droppers offer a number of presentation benefits:

- They allow you to suggest a variety of prey items at once: different colors, sizes, and stages.
- You can use droppers to attract fish to a team of flies. A large mobile or gaudy pattern is easier for trout to see from a distance, calling them over to investigate. The trout may target the attractor pattern or take a smaller, perhaps more realistic-looking dropper fly on the leader.
- Droppers allow you to present flies at different depths. Trout can be selective as to the depth they wish to cruise and feed. Having flies working at different depths increases your odds, helping you determine the best presentation depth.
- A buoyant point fly, used in conjunction with the correct line type for the situation, can be used to suspend flies at a certain level or just above weed beds and other structure. This presentation technique is affectionately referred to as the "washing line," as the non-buoyant flies hang off the leader like clothes on a washing line.

The only time you won't find at least one dropper on my line is when:

- Regulations don't allow multiple flies.
- I'm targeting fish in shallow clear water where multiple flies landing around cruising trout may spook them.
- I'm fishing in and around dense weed beds where an additional fly or flies could become a liability after hooking a fish, as they are prone to snagging and fouling on the surrounding vegetation.
- I am using strike indicators in shallow water and there is not enough depth to allow more than one fly to work correctly.

Dropper Terminology

Depending on the number of flies in a team, each fly has a position reference. Here are the dropper position terms I use:

- Point fly: the fly farthest away from the fly line, tied on the end of the leader.
- Middle dropper: the middle fly in a three-fly setup.
- Top dropper or bob: the upper fly in either a two-fly or three-fly setup.

Dropper Spacing and Tag Length

Dropper tags shouldn't be excessively long, as longer tags are more tangle-prone. I keep my dropper tags between 4 and 8 inches long. A 6-inch dropper tag is a good average length. Short tags work best if you are experimenting with droppers for the first time.

How far apart should your flies be? Presentation technique influences my dropper spacing. Here are some guidelines:

- When fishing flies vertically, keep the flies 18 to 24 inches apart. The deeper the presentation, the greater the spacing.
- For subsurface cast and retrieve presentations using floating, clear-tip, or full-sinking lines, keep the flies 3 to 5 feet apart. The clearer the water, the greater the spacing. Keep in mind that once the retrieve begins, the flies no longer hang vertically as with an indicator but rather trail behind one another with only a short vertical distance between them. A brisk retrieve closes this vertical working distance even more.
- Use shorter 2- to 3-foot dropper spacing when using baitfish patterns to suggest individual baitfish trying to school after being split apart by marauding trout.
- When targeting surface-feeding trout with multiple flies, keep the flies approximately 3 feet apart. Short spacing improves casting accuracy while ensuring one or both of the flies fall within the narrow window of vision of a surface-feeding trout.
- Keep the distance between the upper fly and the other flies in the fly setup less than the rod length apart. If the fly spacing exceeds the rod length and the fish takes the point fly, the upper fly may catch the rod tip, causing a break-off or, worse, a broken tip section.

Dropper Rigging

There are several ways to rig droppers, and each method has its pros and cons. Often, it comes down to personal preference based on both skill and experience.

Simple Dropper

The simple dropper is one of the most straightforward systems and works well on level leaders. To form a simple dropper, attach a short, 6- to 8-inch tippet section at any point on the leader using both the main leader and tippet section to form a triple surgeon's knot. You can also use a uni knot to attach the tippet section. Using this method, a single length of material may be used to build the main leader. Individual sections don't have to be knotted together to form the leader. With the leader length established, you can add single droppers anywhere along its length.

There are pros and cons with the simple dropper. Pros: Flies are easy to change, and they work independently of each other. Cons: As the dropper comes off the leader at a fixed angle, it can wrap around the main leader and tangle, and once consumed, the dropper has to be replaced.

Tandem Method

The tandem method, where one fly is attached using a clinch or uni knot to the hook bend of another via a section of tippet, is arguably the least tangle-prone approach. If you are new to fishing droppers and concerned about tangles, tandem rigging is a good starting point, as the flies trail behind one another on the cast.

Tandem rigging is my least favorite dropper system. If you want to change the upper fly, you have to remove the lower tippet section and fly. I also have concerns that the upper fly's mobility is compromised by having another fly attached to it via the hook bend. If a fish takes the upper fly, the lower tippet section can slide off the bend or be chewed through during the fight, resulting in the loss of the point fly. The tippet attached to the hook eye and bend of the upper fly may inhibit a fish taking it, as the trout inadvertently pushes the fly away with its jaws or senses the leader above and below the fly.

Tippet Knot Dropper

A tippet knot dropper uses one of the remaining tag ends when attaching a tippet section to the main leader using either a triple surgeon's or blood knot. No matter the connection knot, always use the tag end opposite the fly line. When a fish takes the dropper, it pulls on the tag in the same direction as the knot was formed. Using the tag on the fly line side may stress the knot to its breaking point should a fish take the dropper fly.

Unlike the tandem system, flies are easily changed using this system, and they work independently of each other. I often start with a tippet knot dropper and then change to a sliding dropper once the tag is consumed through a number of fly changes.

As with the simple dropper, a tippet knot dropper tag can foul as it comes off the leader at a fixed angle. A new section of tippet also has to be added once the dropper tag becomes too short. Adding a new tippet section can negatively shorten or lengthen the leader, depending on the presentation tactic. For example, when using floating lines coupled with long leaders, correct leader length is crucial to success.

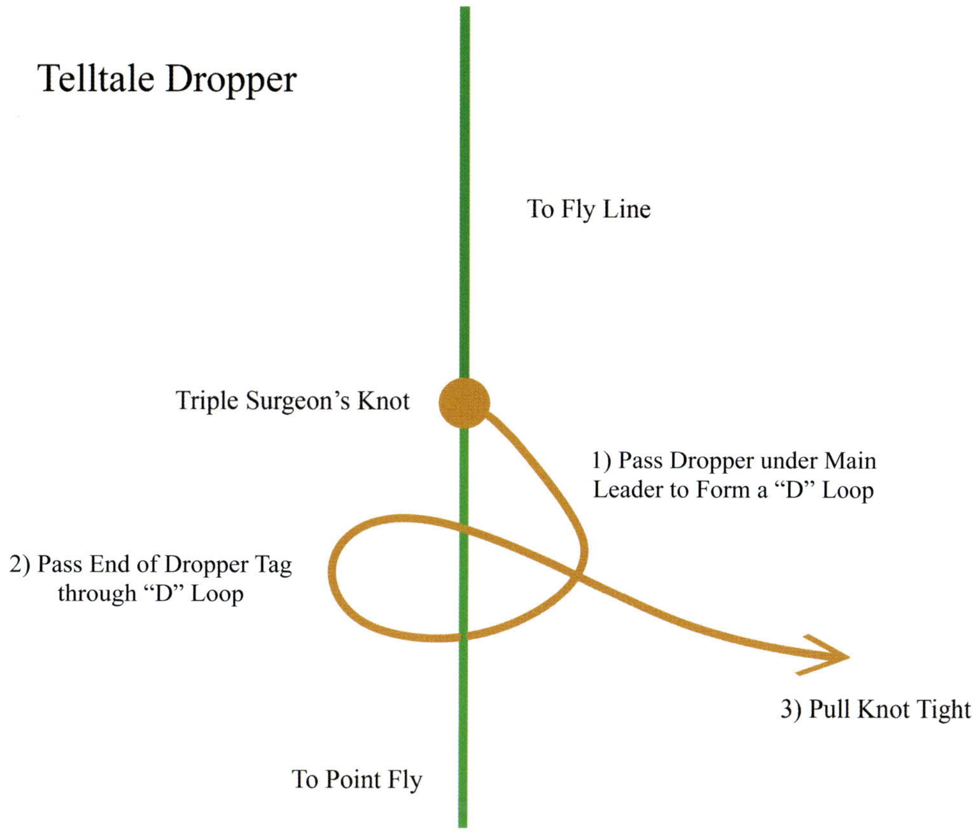

To help prevent the dropper tag from fouling, form a half hitch around the leader and snug it tight on the point fly side of the tippet knot. This practice causes the dropper to hang perpendicular to the leader so it is less likely to foul. Forming a half hitch also creates a bite detector or telltale dropper in the process. Should you miss a grab, the tension of the take causes the tippet knot dropper tag to droop down on an angle. If the half-hitched dropper tag isn't drooping down and still points perpendicular to the tippet knot, the fish took the point fly.

Sliding Dropper

The sliding dropper is my preferred dropper system, as it allows the dropper to spin or rotate around the leader, reducing dropper tangles. The sliding dropper consists of one or more dropper tags looped around the leader. As with all dropper systems, sliding droppers are not tangle-proof, as the dropper tags can tangle around the leader. Using stiffer tippet material helps reduce this risk.

Dropper tags can be easily added or subtracted without affecting overall leader length. As with both the simple dropper and the tippet knot dropper, flies can be easily changed and work independently of each other.

The leader must have a stopper of some sort so the dropper can't slide down the leader to the point fly. A stopper can be a tippet knot, tippet ring, or barrel swivel. As a swivel rotates, it also helps reduce tangles.

Forming a sliding dropper is simple:

1. Take approximately 8 inches of tippet material and form a perfection loop at one end.

Begin with 8 inches of Tippet Prior to Forming Perfection Loop to Allow for Fly Changes

2. Place the looped tippet section under the main leader on the fly side of a stopper such as a tippet knot, tippet ring, or barrel swivel.

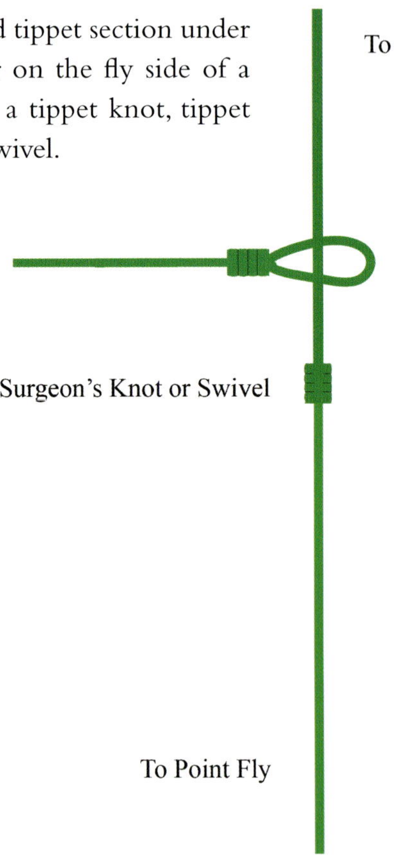

3. Pass the other end of the tippet section through the looped end.

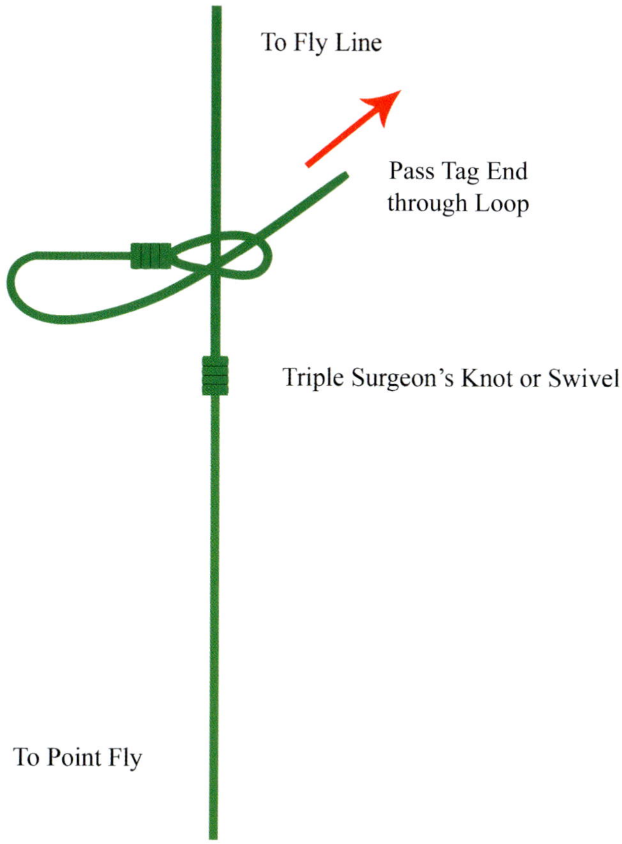

4. Pull the tag end tight, snugging the now-looped tippet section against the leader.

As with a tippet knot dropper, the sliding dropper also serves as a bite detector in the event of a missed strike. To set up a sliding dropper in bite detector mode, snug the sliding dropper tight approximately 2 inches above the tippet knot or barrel swivel stopper. If a fish takes the sliding dropper, the tension of the grab pulls it down the leader tight against the stopper.

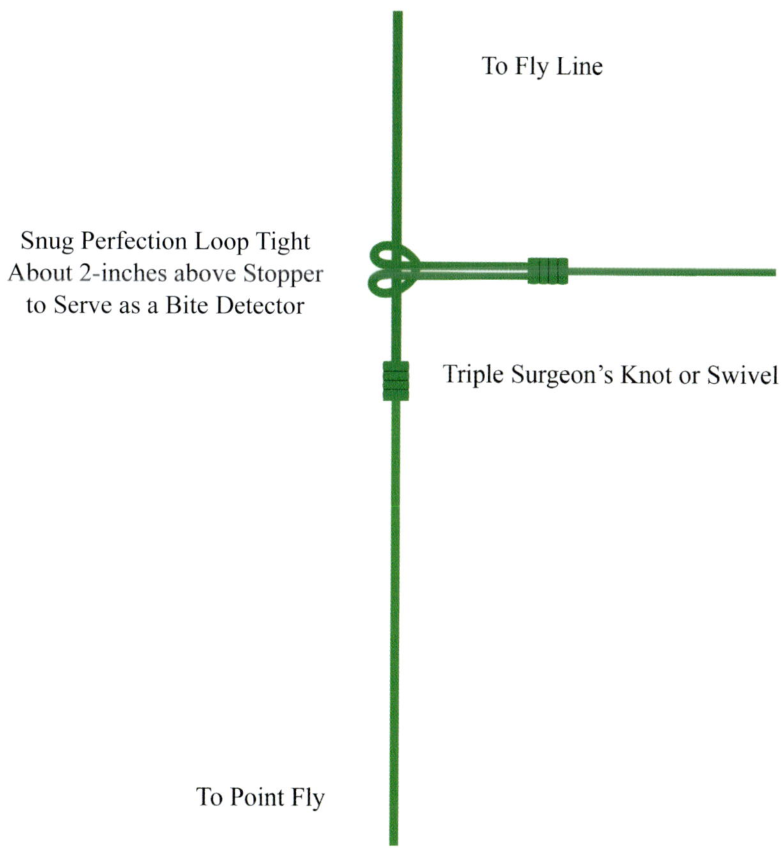

Reducing Dropper Tangles

Dropper systems are tangle-prone, but their presentation benefits more than outweigh any time lost managing tangles. By following the suggestions below, the intensity and frequency of tangles can be significantly reduced.

- Using stiffer tippet to form a dropper reduces tangles. If I am adding a sliding dropper to a 3X leader, I often use a 2X dropper.
- When casting, break the wrist slightly to facilitate wider, open loops. Wider, open loops are less tangle-prone.
- Use the properties of a weight-forward line to your advantage by shooting the line to the target. Keep false casts to a minimum. The more times the leader and flies are in the air, the higher the tangle risk.
- As with any casting stroke, always apply smooth power accelerating the stroke to a stop. Aggressive acceleration or punching the rod when applying power causes tailing loops and subsequent tangles.
- Allow the backcast to lay out completely before powering forward.

You can avoid most dropper tangles with a few simple tricks and good, practiced casting skills.

- Use your ears. Whistling flies are a sure sign of a tangle. As soon as you hear whistling, stop casting and check your flies. You may still be able to unravel a tangle.
- Use a high rod stop and allow the fly line to shoot tight to the reel or pinch the line as the cast unfurls. This tuck cast approach slingshots the flies and indicator, if present, allowing the leader to lay out entirely so the flies land separately, spread out, and in the case of a subsurface presentation, sink quickly.
- Watch for the flies to land separately. Depending on the presentation tactic, all of the leader components—flies, tippet rings, indicator, and swivel—should land independently. If they land in a collective heap, strip the flies in and investigate before they have a chance to form an unmanageable mess.

CHAPTER TAKEAWAYS

- Stillwater leaders, as with most leader systems, should assist and augment presentation and be practical to cast.
- Level or predominantly level leaders work best for sinking line presentations, as they keep the fly or flies in the same proximity as the fly line.
- The faster the sink rate of the line, the shorter the leader.
- Binder rings, available at most office supply stores, do a great job of storing and organizing tapered leaders.
- Use fluorocarbon tippet for all stillwater presentation techniques, both surface and subsurface.
- Use a simple suite of knots and become comfortable tying them. If you are a proficient knot tier, you are more likely to make the necessary leader and fly changes to be successful.
- Don't scrimp on leader and tippet material when tying knots. If you need glasses to see properly, use them.
- Use gradual tension and a strategic touch of saliva when drawing knots tight to avoid heat build-up due to friction and to ensure the knot forms correctly.
- Use a nonslip loop knot to attach flies to a leader, tippet, or dropper tag.
- Combining braided leader material and nylon or fluorocarbon to create low-stretch leaders requires a different connection than the knots used to join nylon and fluorocarbon.
- There are many benefits to using droppers in lakes. Droppers allow you to suggest a variety of prey items at once, they can be used to attract fish to a team of flies, they allow you to present flies at different depths, and a buoyant point fly can be used to suspend flies at a certain level or just above structure.
- The point fly is the fly at the end of the leader. Middle or top (bob) flies are between the point fly and the end of the fly line.

- To reduce tangles, keep your dropper tags short. Four to 6 inches is a good average length.
- Use shorter spacing when fishing multiple flies vertically versus more horizontal, cast and retrieve presentations. Eighteen to 24 inches is a good standard.
- When using non-indicator techniques, keep your flies 3 to 5 feet apart for subsurface presentations or approximately 3 feet apart for dry fly or emerger presentations.
- Tippet knot droppers and sliding droppers also serve as bite detectors in the event of a missed take.
- Use stiffer dropper tag material to reduce tangles.
- Use your ears: If your flies whistle on the cast, chances are you have a tangle. The quicker you identify a dropper tangle, the more likely it can be addressed.

CHAPTER 5

HOW LAKES WORK

Although not a biologist by profession, I have always been fascinated by the intricacies of nature, especially how and why things work. Inspired in part by this fascination, the biology of lakes and their inhabitants has a strong influence on my approach to stillwater fly fishing.

It is important to have a good working knowledge of various lake types, zones of a lake, and how lakes function throughout the seasons. Fish exist in an environment

As a stillwater fly fisher, it is critical to understand how lakes work and how they differ in order to predict fish location and behavior throughout the seasons. You soon learn all lakes are not created equal.

that is completely foreign to ours. It is critical to have at least a basic understanding of the properties of water along with the seasonal changes a lake undergoes to help us, as anglers, determine which lakes are the best to fish and to predict both fish location and their behavior.

When I began fly fishing lakes, I believed they were all the same. But after spending time on the water, most of it pretty frustrating in the beginning, my experience grew. As my knowledge and experience grew, I soon realized lakes are not created equal.

CLASSIFICATION OF LAKES

Lakes are classified by their productivity, or trophic state, based on their ability to support plant and animal life. Lakes are dynamic and complex. Factors such as depth, surface area, climate, and surrounding land use all affect a lake's trophic state.

Lakes can transition to a more productive state but not always for the right reasons. Cabins and houses featuring beautifully manicured lawns and sculptured shorelines are common to many lakes. However, the products and practices used

Potential hydrogen, or pH, is a measure of a lake's productivity, or trophic status. Most productive, eutrophic lakes have pH ranging from just over 7 to 8.5.

to maintain these properties exact a toll. Septic systems, fertilizers, and other contaminants leach into the lake, increasing its productivity but potentially causing substantial blue-green algal blooms. These seasonal blooms may temporarily render the water toxic, especially as the algae dies off. Algal blooms can induce summer fish kills.

Intensive forestry practices can also increase a lake's trophic status. Tree and plant roots within the watershed keep a lake's trophic status in check by filtering and retaining nutrients. Once trees and plants are removed, the increased nutrient load can have a devastating impact, particularly on smaller productive lakes noted for their trophy trout.

Water pH is an important consideration in regard to a lake's trophic status. pH, the power or potential of hydrogen, is a scale from 1 to 14 used to measure whether a solution is acidic or basic. Hydrochloric acid has a pH of 1. Drain cleaner has a pH of 14. Water is considered neutral with a pH of 7.

It is important to understand that an increase of one level on the pH scale is not a linear measure but rather a 10-factor increase. Multiple level increases are exponential. For example, water with a pH of 9 is 100 times more alkaline than water with a pH of 7.

Productive trout lakes range from a pH just greater than 7 to just over 8.5. The pH of every lake is different, even if they are in close proximity to each other. There can also be pH variances within a lake. As a lake's pH rises toward a level of 9 or above, it becomes increasingly toxic to trout, but there are exceptions, such as Nevada's famed Pyramid Lake. The leviathan-size cutthroat Pyramid is famous for have evolved to survive in water with a pH level of 9, an environment the vast majority of trout find lethal

There are three basic lake types, or trophic states, that all fly fishers should be aware of: oligotrophic, mesotrophic, and eutrophic. Having an understanding of the different lake types helps you anticipate the productivity of the lake you are on, what fishing you might expect, and, when faced with a choice, the option of choosing the best lake for success. As fly fishers, shallow, productive, slightly alkaline lakes always offer the best chance for success, not only for trout but for other species as well, such as bass.

Oligotrophic Lakes

Oligotrophic is the least productive class of lakes. *Oligo* means "little," and the productive state of these types of lakes reflects this name. Most oligotrophic lakes have a low pH, just under 7. Oligotrophic lakes are typically large, deep lakes with limited to minimal shoal or shallow areas.

Although often well oxygenated, due to their low productivity, oligotrophic lakes are typically clear, as there is little to no algae or zooplankton. In many instances, inflow and outflow streams are common, and any nutrients carried into the lake are soon flushed out. Bottom makeup is usually a blend of rock and sand as opposed to the rich, muddy bottoms common to productive trout lakes. Aquatic plants are practically nonexistent. Oligotrophic lakes provide tough environments for both fish and invertebrates to survive.

When I lived on the west coast of British Columbia, I spent much of my off-season practicing and honing my stillwater skills on the steep-sided, deep, unproductive lakes of the Coast Range. Most of these lakes featured little in the way of fishable shoals or weed beds common to productive lakes. It was not uncommon to be no more than a few rod lengths away from shore and be in over 30 feet of water. Trout in these lakes were small, emaciated, and spread out, having to roam considerable distances to support their meager existence. I found my best success near shore, working rock piles and sunken timber. Hatches were few and far between, and most invertebrates, if present, were small and tough to match. My best results were often on lakes containing crayfish or small baitfish populations.

Mesotrophic Lakes

Mesotrophic lakes feature a middle (meso) level of productivity. While they can be large in surface area, mesotrophic lakes typically have smaller rivers or streams entering and leaving them. Maximum depths are often less than a couple hundred feet, and there are often limited shoal or shallow water areas.

As with their less productive oligotrophic cousins, mesotrophic lakes are relatively clear bodies of water. As mesotrophic lakes are more productive, aquatic plants are often present on any existing shoal areas. Mesotrophic lakes are capable of producing quality fish, but as their food base isn't usually dense, it takes time for fish to grow. Many of the larger lakes in and around where I currently live in Alberta are mesotrophic in nature.

Eutrophic Lakes

For the stillwater trout angler, eutrophic lakes are the places dreams are made of. Eutrophic lakes are rich, productive bodies of water, often with a pH in excess of 7.5, capable of consistently producing trophy-size fish. It is safe to say that the world's best trout lakes are eutrophic. Think "euphoria" to associate which trophic class of lakes is best.

Eutrophic lakes are small and predominantly shallow, often less than 50 feet at their deepest point, landlocked bodies of water. If there is an outflow or inflow, it is seasonal. As a result, nutrients that wash into the lake, primarily through spring runoff, remain in the lake, creating a rich muddy bottom, ideal compost for lush aquatic weeds and vegetation. Aquatic weeds provide prime habitat for a stunning density and array of food items, enabling trout to feed and gain weight at a staggering pace.

Shallow, productive eutrophic lakes are home to both varied and dense populations of aquatic plants, which provide ideal habit for all manner of trout food, helping grow large, healthy fish.

Due to their high productivity levels, eutrophic lakes are predominantly murky due to suspended matter and summer algal blooms. There are exceptions, however. In the semiarid climate of western North America, eutrophic lakes abound, and there are also numerous eutrophic calcium-rich lakes featuring crystal-clear water, marl bottoms, and dense weeds. Marl is precipitated calcium carbonate that falls out of suspension, forming a thin, light-colored flock over the bottom. To the uninitiated, marl looks like sand, but if you try to wade across marl, you will soon find yourself entrenched in the rich soft mud that lies below.

ZONES OF A LAKE

Lakes are classified into zones, typically by water temperature. It is important to have at least a basic knowledge of lake zones, as fish move into or spend the majority of their time in or near certain zones throughout the season—critical knowledge that will help you, as an angler, target the most likely fish-holding areas. The old adage "90 percent of the fish are found in 10 percent of the water" bears fruit for the "zone aware" stillwater fly fisher.

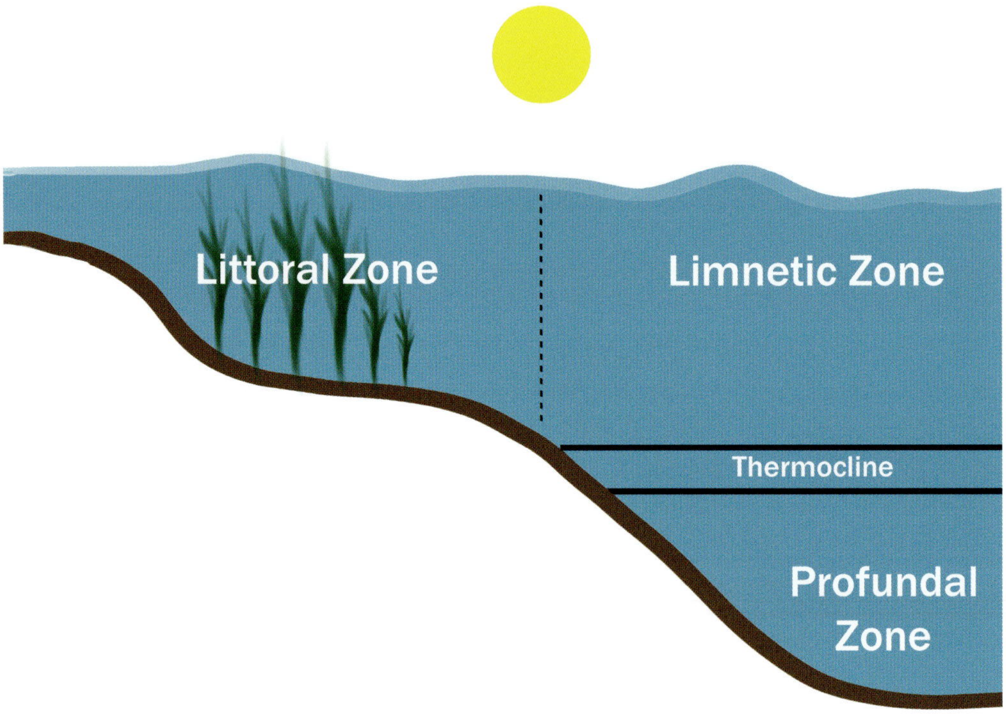

Lakes are broken down into zones, typically by water temperature. It is crucial to have a good working knowledge of all lake zones and how they are formed, as stillwater trout only spend time in a few of them throughout the season.

Littoral Zone

The littoral zone, or shoal, as it is often referred to, extends from the shoreline to open water. The depth of the littoral zone is governed by the physical structure of the lake and includes any region where the sun's energy reaches or touches the bottom. On clear lakes, the littoral zone may extend down 25 feet or greater. Sunken islands are also considered part of the littoral zone.

Due to the shallow nature of the littoral zone and the effect the sun has on it, water temperature varies throughout the year. During the late fall through winter and into early spring, the littoral zone is the coldest region of the lake. In the summer, shallow shoals become so warm that dissolved oxygen levels decrease, forcing trout to retreat to deeper, cooler areas of the lake. During the summer months, occasional nighttime forays onto the shoals are often the only time trout venture into shallows to feed.

The littoral zone is home to rooted aquatic plants and lush weed beds fueled through photosynthesis. Aquatic plants provide ideal habitat for almost all stillwater food sources. It is Mother Nature's supermarket and where you should spend the majority of your angling effort, due not only to the availability of trout food but also to the versatility shoals offer from a presentation perspective. Shallow shoal areas allow us to use a wide spectrum of presentation tactics including floating lines coupled with indicators, floating lines with long leaders and weighted flies, slow-sinking lines, fast-sinking lines, and buoyant patterns. Just about every presentation tactic discussed in this book can be used over shallow shoals.

Limnetic Zone (Epilimnion)

At first glance, the limnetic zone may appear similar, if not identical, to the littoral zone. The limnetic zone is also governed by the sun's energy and like the shallow shoal areas can be subject to water temperature variations throughout the year. The deciding factor is that the limnetic zone, or epilimnion, is away from the shore and defines the upper region of a lake. Sunlight does not reach the bottom in the limnetic zone.

As with the littoral zone, photosynthesis takes place, stimulating algae growth. In fact, it is this region of the lake where the greatest amount of photosynthesis takes place. There are, however, no rooted plants in the limnetic zone. The sun's rays govern the depth of this zone. As with the littoral zone, water clarity and suspended matter govern its depth: The clearer the water, the deeper the limnetic zone.

From a fly-fishing perspective, there are few food sources that live in the limnetic zone. Zooplankton including *Daphnia* and *Chaoborus*, a distant chironomid cousin, are two common inhabitants. Certain baitfish species may also school or stage in this region. Terrestrial and adult aquatic insects can be of localized importance should they land on or drift over the limnetic zone.

I have also found that environmental conditions such as weather change or elevated shoal temperatures can move trout into the limnetic zone. During the warm summer months, trout often spend time cruising this zone.

Presentation options are limited in the limnetic zone. Sinking line tactics are usually the best form of attack in this region, and deep-water indicator tactics can also pay dividends. Suspending small attractor patterns intended to suggest *Daphnia* clusters or chironomid patterns to represent ascending pupae transiting through the limnetic zone are two common indicator candidates.

Thermocline (Metalimnion)

The thermocline, or metalimnion, is a narrow distinct band of water that forms seasonally as a lake stratifies during the warm summer months. Forming at the extent of the sun's energy, the thermocline separates the warmer limnetic zone from the cold profundal zone below. Due to differing water temperatures and subsequent densities, the thermocline forms a physical barrier to mixing between the warm water above and cold water below. It is an important component of lake stratification and fall turnover.

By definition, the thermocline is a zone where water temperature reduces considerably over a short distance. Water clarity plays a key role in where the thermocline forms. In clearer water the thermocline forms at a greater depth, as the sun's energy penetrates farther into the water, warming it to a greater depth. On crystal-clear lakes the thermocline may be 50 feet deep. Conversely, turbid algae-stained water filters the warming effect of the sun. The thermocline will be shallower, perhaps as shallow as 20 feet. If you have ever dived into a lake, chances are you experienced the body-shuddering effects of a thermocline.

Wind also affects thermocline depth. Strong winds circulate the warmer, less dense water above the thermocline. As the warmer upper layer won't mix with the cooler deeper water, the thermocline tilts it down toward the windward end of the lake. As a result of the wind-induced swells, or seiche, thermocline depth can vary as the teeter-totter action of the water moves the thermocline deeper and shallower until the rocking motion subsides.

The thermocline can be seen on a sounder screen, as the transducer signal reflects or partially reflects off the cool dense water. Thermoclines often appear on-screen as a clear upper image with a blizzard-like lower image extending to the bottom. A well-established thermocline acts like plastic wrap, preventing tiny food sources such as zooplankton from penetrating the deeper water below. Stacked zooplankton can also appear on a sounder screen as a thin defined line.

Profundal Zone (Hypolimnion)

Beneath the limnetic zone and thermocline lies the profundal zone, or hypolimnion. It is a dark, cold region that I seldom, if ever, explore. Water temperature is consistent throughout the profundal zone as opposed to the limnetic zone, which is constantly in flux due to the effect of the sun's energy. In many instances, the profundal zone is an area of reduced oxygen content, making it inhospitable to most fish and aquatic invertebrates. Most trout species spend little to no time in the profundal zone. Char, such as lake trout and brook trout, have evolved to survive in the deep water of the profundal zone, especially during the warmer summer months.

As they are relatively buoyant, aquatic invertebrates also find tough slugging in the denser water of the profundal zone. The dense oxygen-reduced water of this zone makes it hard to move. Leeches, chironomid larvae, snails, and freshwater clams are typical profundal zone inhabitants.

I have on occasion targeted lake trout in deep water using fast-sinking lines, but you are definitely working the boundary of effective fly fishing. You stand a better chance of angling success targeting either the littoral or limnetic zone of a lake.

SEASONS OF A LAKE

Lakes, as with us on dry land, experience four seasons. Each season and the transition periods between have distinct characteristics that determine both fish location and their activity. It is important that we, as anglers, understand the seasons of a lake in order to provide ourselves with the greatest chance of success.

Water is unique, especially how its density varies in relationship to its temperature. Unlike other substances, water is not most dense in its solid form, ice. The density of ice is significantly less than liquid water, and as a result, it floats. Water is most dense at 39°F, or 4°C. It is this unique thermal property that allows lakes to stratify into layers of differing temperature on a seasonal basis, as it resists mixing. Lake stratification and the seasonal mixing process, or turnover, of these stratified layers is a critical process every lake and its inhabitants need to survive.

Winter

During the late fall, as the water temperature in the shoal areas of the lake cools into the mid to low thirties, trout retreat to deeper water. Here, they will spend the majority of the cold winter ahead. Trout are cold-blooded. Their metabolism is greatly affected by the surrounding water temperature. In cooler water, trout don't move with any urgency, so they need less food energy to fuel their metabolism. At times trout movement reduces to an almost hibernated state. Trout rely primarily on the body fat they generated by feeding during the open-water seasons of spring, summer, and fall to get them through the lean periods of winter.

Ice covers many productive lakes over the winter season. At this time, the lake begins to stratify. As snow covers the ice, light penetration reduces and plants start to die, generating heat and consuming oxygen. Toward the end of the season, trout begin moving into the shallows, where the most oxygenated water is.
BRIAN CHAN

When a lake freezes over, it stratifies into two distinct layers, cooler more oxygenated water sitting above warmer less oxygenated water below. Provided there is no snow, the sun's rays can still penetrate through the ice into the water to stimulate plant growth through photosynthesis. As snow covers the ice, light penetration steadily reduces. Aquatic plants begin to die and anaerobically decompose, generating heat and consuming oxygen. As fish are the largest oxygen consumers in a lake, they are pushed into the shallower, cooler, more oxygenated regions of the lake.

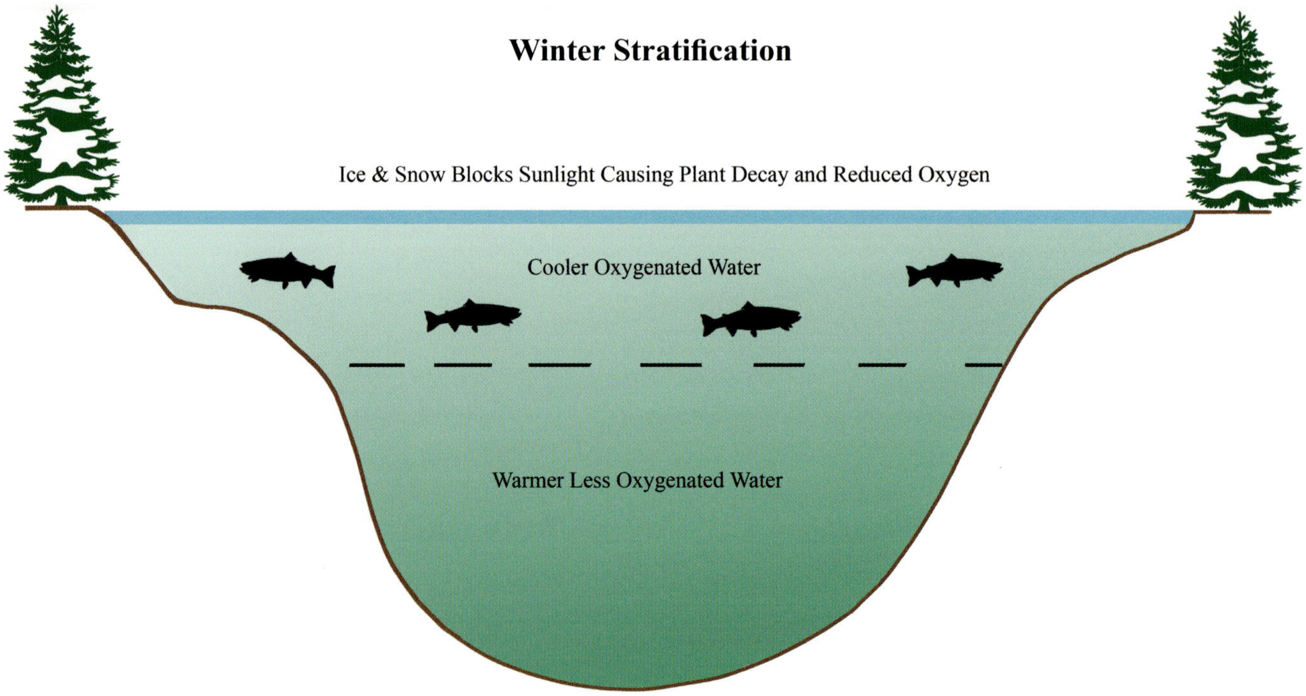

In the shallow, productive, often weed-choked, small eutrophic lakes famous for their trophy-size trout, harsh prolonged winters can have deadly results. In these circumstances the decomposition process consumes the majority of the available oxygen, suffocating the trout, a condition known as winterkill. The largest fish require the most oxygen. Unfortunately, they are always the first to die.

Winterkills can be complete or partial, as lake structure and the ratio of shallow to deep water has an effect. Trout inhabiting an oxygen-poor area of a lake such as a shallow bay become disorientated and trapped and die, resulting in a partial winterkill. In almost every productive lake, there is always some level of kill. Anglers visiting their favorite lake for the first time after ice-off always fear the worse should they see fish carcasses lying along the bottom in the shallow portions of the lake.

Many agencies install aeration systems in lakes to help prevent winterkill. The circulation current the aeration process creates keeps a portion of the lake ice-free, reoxygenating anoxic water as it diffuses with atmospheric air at the surface. Most aeration systems are turned on just prior to ice-on and shut down as soon

Immediately after ice-off, trout are in shallow water, often less than 10 feet deep, as that is where the oxygen is. In the Northern Hemisphere, target shallow northern muddy bays, as they are the first to warm, stimulating trout activity.

as the ice leaves the lake, allowing it to behave naturally throughout the balance of the year.

Lakes that don't ice over, such as those found in temperate coastal regions, still stratify, but as oxygen diffusion can still take place at the surface, winterkill is not an issue. Trout typically remain deep until spring temperatures warm the shallows to the point where they can reinhabit the shoal regions. On these lakes, exploring the deeper regions adjacent to structure such as drop-offs during the winter months works best.

Spring

Immediately after the ice leaves the lake, it is still in a stratified state. Trout are confined to the shallows, often in less than 10 feet of water, where the highest concentrations of oxygen can be found. Dark-bottomed bays in the east and north areas of a lake are the first to warm, stimulating fish activity. Make a point of targeting these areas, as the fishing can be outstanding for roughly seven to ten days after ice-off.

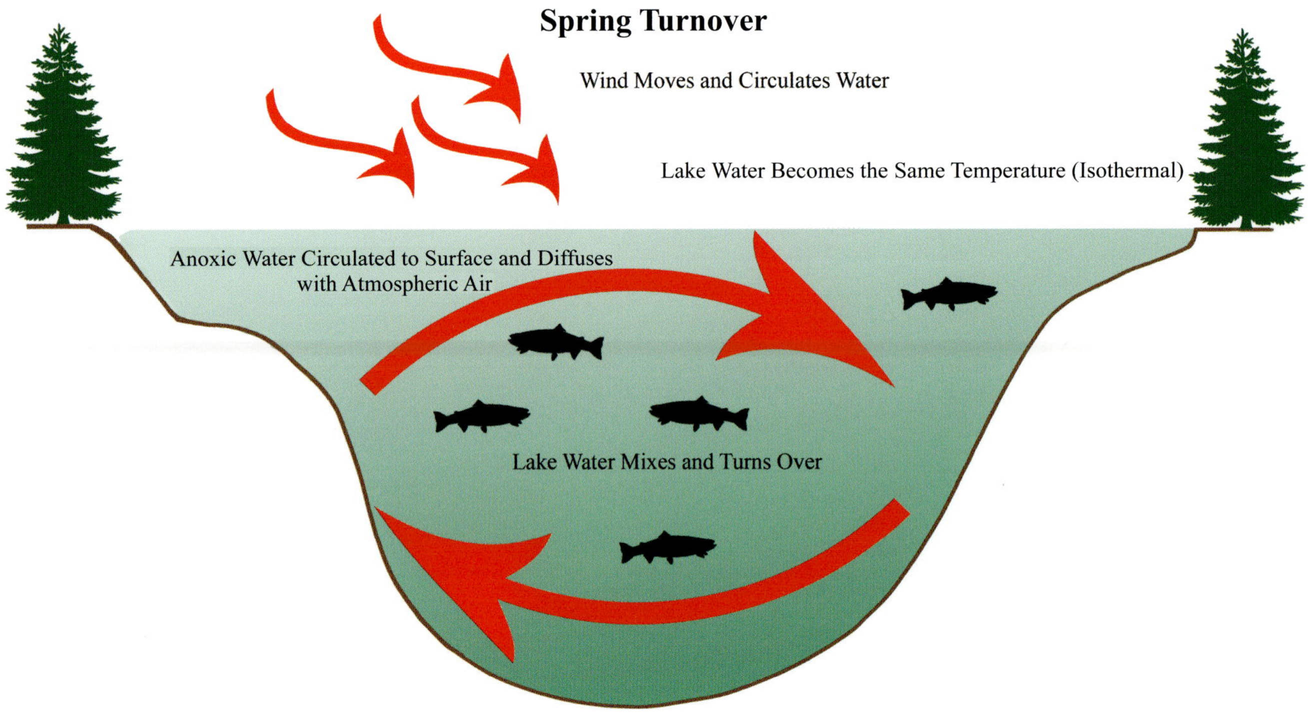

As the spring season progresses, water in both the littoral and limnetic zones continues to warm, to the point where these areas become the same temperature, or isothermal, as the lower regions of the lake. Stimulated by wind, the water begins to circulate, or turn over, anoxic water from the deep cycles to the surface, where it diffuses with atmospheric air.

This oxygen recharging process, known as turnover, is an essential ecological event. During turnover, oxygen levels are unsettled and water clarity is reduced. Methane and hydrogen sulphide gas, along with other chemicals, are released. Decaying weed matter from the bottom is dispersed throughout the water column. It is as though the lake has been given a solid shake. Turnover occurs within a few weeks of ice-off and typically lasts five to seven days. During turnover, fishing is usually poor. Your best bet is to choose a higher-elevation lake that has yet to turn or a lower-elevation lake that has already turned.

During turnover, the water remains murky and turbid. It is not unusual to see clumps of aquatic vegetation circulated up to the surface.

Rich, productive lakes that limp through winter teetering on the brink of winterkill are not out of the woods once the ice leaves. Strong winds may stimulate an aggressive turnover that mixes the water and quickly disperses what little oxygen remains over a wide area. Trout, now without enough dissolved oxygen to survive turnover, suffocate, a phenomenon known as spring kill. During a spring kill, trout appear to panic, often beaching themselves in a vain attempt to find sufficiently oxygenated water. As with winterkill, spring kills are a common occurrence on rich, productive eutrophic lakes.

Once the turnover process is complete, debris churned up through the mixing process settles, water clarity and chemistry improves, and much of the lake contains well-oxygenated water. Trout are free to roam throughout most of the lake. The sun continues to warm the littoral and limnetic zones, stimulating plant growth and increasing invertebrate activity and hatches. For many stillwater fly fishers, this is the best time to be on the water, until summer heat initiates additional changes.

Summer

As summer establishes, the littoral and limnetic zones warm. At the height of summer, the lake stratifies. Warm, less oxygenated water sits above the cooler profundal zone separated by a well-formed thermocline. As water temperature increases, the water's ability to hold oxygen decreases. Many cold-water species such as trout leave the shallows to seek deeper oxygenated water just above the thermocline. Only during

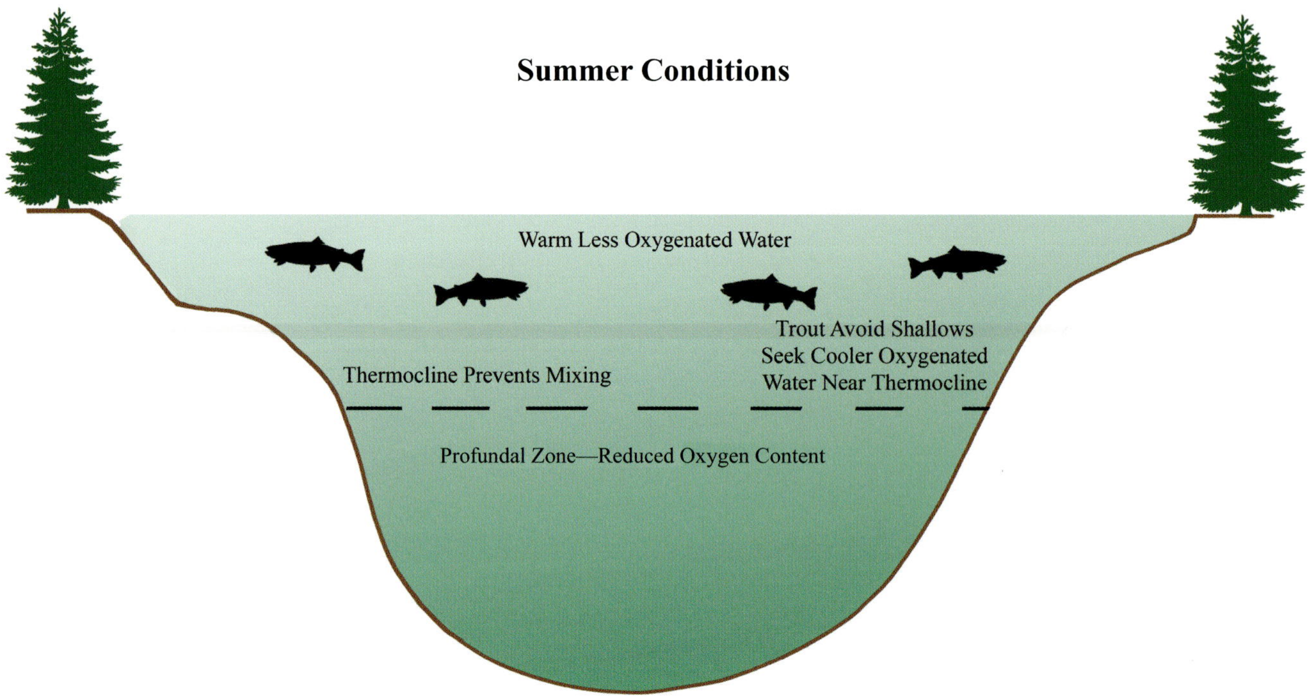

the night, until early morning, do trout venture into the shallows to feed. Many refer to this summer stratification period as the summer doldrums. At this time fishing is typically slow or spotty at best, but there are always exceptions.

On many productive lakes, algal blooms are a common summer occurrence. In many ways, algae aids fishing by keeping the water temperatures below the bloom cool. Most algae are plants and need sunlight to photosynthesize. Algal growth is always thickest at the surface and in the shallows, where sunlight penetration is greatest. Roughly 6 to 10 feet down, algae growth diminishes. Trout cruise beneath the algae cap in relatively cooler oxygenated water. Zooplankton, which feeds on smaller phytoplankton (plant matter), is a common summer food source. Attractor tactics are often employed at this time to cope with this tough-to-match stillwater food source.

In extreme conditions, heavy algal blooms coupled with warm water form a toxic partnership. During the day, blue-green algae respires, absorbing carbon dioxide and giving off oxygen. At night this process reverses. The algae now strips oxygen from the water, releasing carbon dioxide. At the peak of the bloom, blue-green algae begin to die. Through the decomposition process, dying algae robs the water of oxygen. Coupled with reduced oxygen due to high water temperatures, trout become stressed, feeding activity reduces, and in extreme circumstances, the combined lack of oxygen results in a summer kill. As with winterkill, summer kills range in intensity from partial to complete. Summer kills are most common in rich, productive lakes and those lakes prone to blue-green algal blooms.

By late summer most lakes are well stratified. It is not until the onset of fall that the lakes once again begin to change.

At the height of summer, the dreaded doldrums have kicked in on many lakes. Trout become lethargic, sliding into deep oxygenated water, where they often suspend just above the thermocline.

Fall

As summer wanes and transitions into fall, days become shorter and air temperatures begin to drop. At this time fish become increasingly active, venturing into the shallows to feed. Sensing the onset of winter, trout feed heavily as they put the finishing touches on the fat reserves that will, for the most part, carry them through winter. For many fly fishers, including myself, this is the best time to call in sick and get out on the water. Fish are aggressive and opportunistic, as the majority of stillwater hatches have long since ended. Some of the largest fish of the season are caught during the fall period.

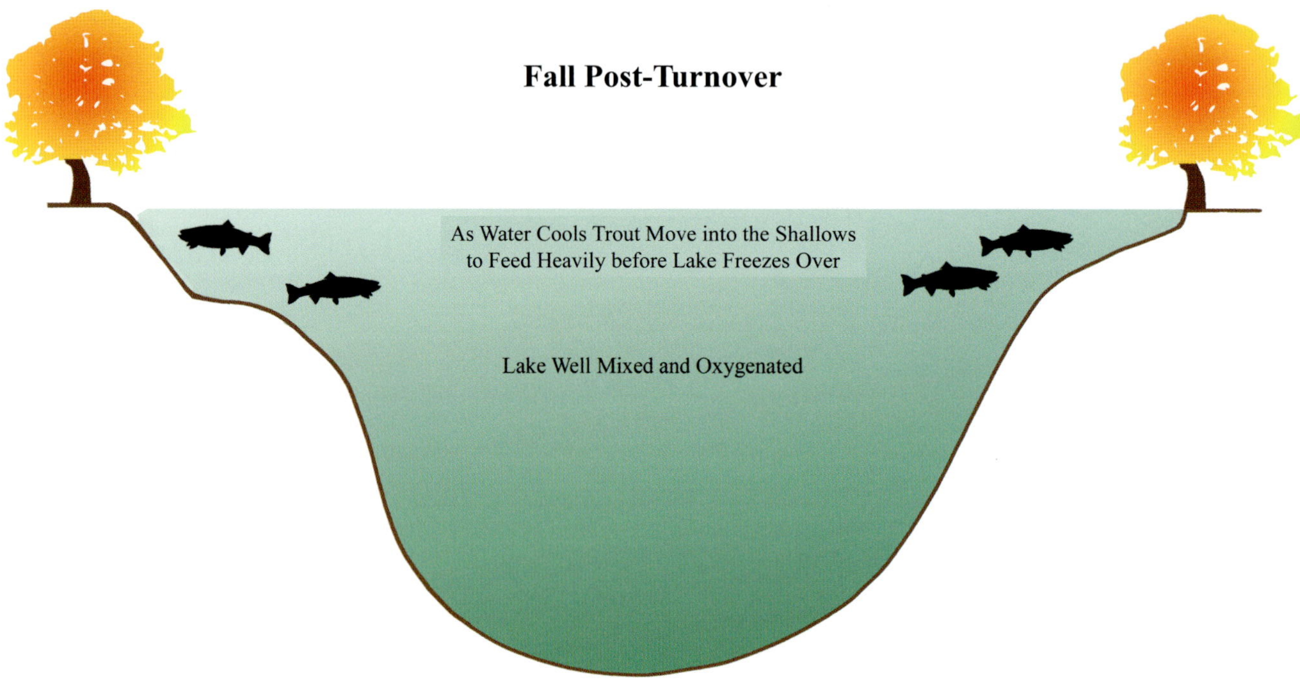

Along with the fish, the lake is also entering another period of change. Nights become cooler, and so do the upper regions of the lake. The upper layers continue to cool until they become of similar temperature to the cooler water at and just below the thermocline. When water reaches 39°F, or 4°C, it is most dense and begins to sink. Cool, dense water coupled with wind-induced wave action initiates turnover. As with spring, turnover recharges the lake's oxygen levels, allowing it to enter winter in the best possible condition.

Fishing is typically off for a few days until the water clears and oxygen levels stabilize. Fish continue to prowl the shallows until water temperatures cool to near freezing, forcing the fish to retreat to deeper water.

Not all lakes experience fall turnover. Many productive lakes are not deep enough to stratify, as the sun's energy penetrates throughout, maintaining uniform

Once fall turnover is complete, trout flood the shallows, feeding aggressively to build the fat reserves that will see them through winter. As with early spring, concentrate your efforts over the shallow shoal areas.
TODD OISHI

water temperature. These lakes rely on wind-induced current to circulate the water, reoxygenating it through surface diffusion.

Many lakes in temperate coastal regions or lower, warmer latitudes never ice over. These lakes only stratify during the summer period and, as a result, only experience one annual fall turnover event.

CHAPTER TAKEAWAYS

- All lakes behave differently.
- Lakes are broken down into three productivity types: low (oligotrophic), medium (mesotrophic), and high (eutrophic).
- If possible, target small, shallow, productive, slightly alkaline eutrophic lakes featuring muddy bottoms and dense weed beds, as these lakes are typically home to large trout.
- The shallow littoral zone is the best region to fish. Avoid spending much, if any, time prospecting the deeper areas of a lake.
- A thermocline forms as a result of summer stratification and separates the warm limnetic zone from the cool profundal zone.
- A thermocline can register on a sounder.
- Water is most dense at 39°F, or 4°C.
- Winterkills occur when the lake is still covered with ice.
- Spring kills occur during spring turnover.
- Some lakes turn over twice a year, other lakes only turn over once, while many shallow lakes never turn over.
- Early spring and late fall offer some of the best shallow-water fishing.
- Once a lake has completed spring turnover, trout spread out through most of the lake.
- As water temperature increases, the water's ability to hold oxygen decreases.
- Fishing typically slows during the warm summer months, known in some circles as the dreaded summer doldrums.
- Summer algal blooms are not always bad, as they absorb the sun's energy, keeping the water below oxygenated and cool.

CHAPTER 6

WHAT TROUT EAT: STILLWATER ENTOMOLOGY

In productive lakes, food concentrations can be overwhelming. I believe knowing and understanding what stillwater trout eat is an essential component of any fly fisher's toolbox. If you know and understand the life cycles and habits of what trout feed upon, you will make better presentation choices and present your flies properly.

I find trout food fascinating, from the smallest item on the menu to the largest. When I first began to fly fish, entomology and the study of trout food fascinated me, a fascination that continues today.

My fascination with bugs and other trout food starts along the shoreline. I always poke around the shallows, turning over rocks and logs or sifting through weed beds with an aquarium net to see what I can find. This practice continues on the water too. Correct and strategic use of a throat pump has also had a significant influence on my on-the-water observations. Throat pumps allow you to observe recently consumed, and often alive, prey. These samples allow you to see unique traits that only live food sources have, such as the shine of the trapped gas common to emerging chironomid pupae and mayfly nymphs.

In the beginning, I often gathered samples for future study, identification, or to have at my fly-tying bench to help guide future imitations. The challenge with sample collecting is that the small selection of little vials and alcohol I needed equated to more stuff in my kit bag and, as a self-professed klutz, an increased risk that I might spill the alcohol, break a vial, or both.

Alcohol preserved a sample, but after a short time, the natural colors of what I had collected disappeared. I had a great representation of the size and features but little else. The smartphone has refined my sampling process so that I don't sample

I break down both trout food and the patterns I use to suggest them into four key traits: shape, size, behavior, and color.
BRIAN CHAN

nearly as much as I used to. Smartphones allow you to create a reference library of quality hi-res macro images detailing key features, colors, and size when shot against a small ruler.

As my fascination grew, so did my desire to learn more. I took my fascination a step further and began setting up aquariums. My addiction culminated with a 30-gallon aquarium I used to study the inhabitants and take pictures, and now video. My knowledge and understanding of general entomology and stillwater entomology skyrocketed. I watched firsthand how the various food sources moved and behaved. My observations paid huge dividends, not only at my tying bench but on the water too. I soon learned that the underwater stillwater world was a tough neighborhood, as everything in the aquarium was always trying to eat each other.

My goal with this chapter is to break stillwater trout food into concise, manageable chunks and bullets to provide you with the primary essentials you need on the water, not only to identify what you see but also to learn how each prey item behaves so you can suggest it properly with your pattern selection. I use four common reference points many others use to help understand what trout eat in lakes: size, shape, color, and behavior, the same traits I use when designing stillwater trout flies. All four traits are important, and on any given day, this order can and often does change, so stay flexible. I have provided additional details below in the priority I find most important.

1. Shape: This is the overall profile or look of the prey item. Is it slender? Is it squat? The overall silhouette of a food source is a critical trigger trout use when feeding.
2. Size: What is the common size range of a particular food item?

3. Behavior: Behavior defines how each food source moves, which in turn guides your presentation, approach, and how you move the fly through the water. In the case of aquatic insects, how do they emerge and transform from their aquatic stage into a winged adult? What are the best depths to present the fly? Where will you position yourself for the best chance of success? What materials or construction techniques do you need to blend into the fly to make it come alive in the water?
4. Color: Trout food comes in myriad colors. Some insects, invertebrates, and baitfish have color schemes unique to themselves, while there are colors such as olive or brown that are common to many food sources. A number of factors influence color, including water clarity, lake location, season, and weed color. Each food source has evolved to blend into their surrounding habitat to avoid predators or, for those insects and invertebrates that hunt, provide camouflage.

DIGESTION RATES

People often ask about the digestion rates of the various insects, invertebrates, and baitfish trout prey upon in lakes. Trout digestion is not constant. Several factors influence digestion rates, including water temperature and its effect on the metabolic rate of the trout, how hard or soft the body of the food item is, and what percentage of the trout's stomach is full.

Many factors influence how fast trout digest food. Based on the number of dragonfly nymphs in this stomach sample, this trout wouldn't have been hungry for a while.
BRIAN CHAN

Soft-bodied prey such as chironomid larvae and pupae, caddis larvae, zooplankton, and smaller mayfly nymph species take approximately 12 to 24 hours to digest. Harder-bodied food such as dragonfly nymphs, water boatmen, and backswimmers take longer to digest, anywhere from 24 to 36 hours. Ants take a long time to process due to their hard exoskeletons and the formic acid within their bodies that they use to process and digest cellulose plant matter.

Having an appreciation for the digestion rates serves as a helpful guide to when fish might feed consistently and when you should be on the water. For example, when trout are feeding on soft-bodied prey such as chironomids, mayflies, and damselflies, you can expect them to feed daily, as these food sources don't take long to digest. Harder-to-digest food items may limit trout feeding, and attractor techniques intended to trigger a reaction may be required to catch fish.

STILLWATER FOOD AVAILABILITY, PHYSIOLOGY, AND LIFE CYCLES

No matter the season, there is always something for stillwater trout to eat. The underwater world is a blend of entirely aquatic organisms and others that spend a portion of their lives in the lake before transforming into winged adults.

Those organisms that spend their entire life in the lake I refer to as staples, bread-and-butter food sources that trout feed upon in the absence of a hatch. Staples include leeches, scuds, minnows, crayfish, and zooplankton. Some items on my staples list can be unique to certain lakes or regions, such as minnows and crayfish. For example, in the productive lakes of south-central British Columbia, baitfish such as redside shiners were eradicated many years ago to create monoculture fisheries containing only one type of fish, trout. In my home province, Alberta, our trout lakes are home to dense populations of fathead minnows and brook sticklebacks. These baitfish don't complete with trout but rather compete to get away from them, as trout love to eat them.

Although not intended to confuse you, there is a distinct asterisk to my staples listing. My staples list also includes any aquatic insect with a prolonged aquatic stage within their life cycle or hatch in such large numbers over the entire season that trout become conditioned to their presence, seldom refusing a well-presented pattern. Examples of these aquatic insects include dragonfly nymphs, damselfly nymphs, and chironomids, specifically the larval and pupal stages. Early and late in the season, at the start and end of the day, and when nothing seems to be hatching are great times to suggest a staple.

Physiology: Surviving Underwater

Entomology is complex. Each order, family, and sometimes species seems to have evolved its way of surviving and coping in the aquatic world. To better understand, we often try to interpret what we observe against how our own bodies function, especially when it comes to physiology, which rarely turns out to be correct. For example, for nearly all aquatic insects, the respiratory and circulatory systems function through completely separate processes.

An invertebrate's circulatory system performs three primary roles: It transfers metabolites to the body cells, carries waste, and serves as an essential part of the immune system. Invertebrates have a simple heart that runs through their body. The heart pumps hemolymph (blood) from the rear of the body to the front, where it runs back through the body cells before being pumped forward again.

Most crustaceans contain the respiratory protein hemocyanin, which is copper-based. When it binds with oxygen, it turns blue. Some invertebrates, such as scuds, use hemocyanin as a secondary oxygen supply when needed. Scuds may need to augment their oxygen levels when molting and often appear blue until their new exoskeleton hardens and matches their natural surroundings.

Iron-based hemoglobin, a protein common to human blood, is rare in aquatic invertebrates, but there are exceptions. The larvae of some chironomid species contain hemoglobin within their hemolymph, giving them a distinct scarlet red or maroon red coloration. Hemoglobin binds with oxygen, augmenting oxygen distribution to the cells and allowing some species to survive in oxygen-poor conditions.

The majority of aquatic insects extract oxygen from the surrounding water, which is called hydropneustic respiration. A few aquatic insects such as water boatmen and backswimmers use atmospheric air, trapping an air bubble along their bodies. The air bubble allows them to breathe surface air underwater, a process known as aeropneustic respiration.

In insects oxygen is transferred directly to the cells through a network of tubes called trachea.

Most aquatic insects possess external gills that are an extension of the tracheal system. Oxygen from the water diffuses across the gills' surface and is distributed throughout the body using a combination of differential gas pressure and capillary action. Gills can be feather-like, such as those on mayflies and damselflies, while other invertebrates have filamentous gills that resemble small hairs or tufts. Caddis larvae and pupae have hairlike filamentous gills. Some invertebrates have no external gills, and oxygen diffuses directly through their exoskeleton where it is thin and membranous, a process known as cutaneous respiration. A few invertebrates use both gills and cutaneous respiration.

Life Cycles of Aquatic Insects

Aquatic insects spend the majority of their lives in the water. When they reach maturity, they emerge, either at the water's surface or they crawl out of the lake, to complete their final adult stage. When aquatic insects emerge, they do so in large numbers to overwhelm any natural predators, ensuring the species continues. It is a hatch philosophy that insects have been using since prehistoric times with great effect.

The life cycle of any insect, including aquatics, can be broken down into two categories: complete and incomplete. An incomplete life cycle or metamorphosis is considered primitive on the evolutionary scale. It consists of three stages: egg, nymph, and adult. Once hatched, the nymph grows and matures by shedding its skin through a series of molts, or instars. The molting process is necessary, as the nymph's hard exoskeleton doesn't allow for expansion. With each molt, the nymph is a little larger, and toward the end of its nymphal cycle, certain features such as wing pads become more pronounced. After each molt, the nymph is vulnerable and is typically bright and visible, standing out in its environment until the new exoskeleton hardens and darkens to match its natural surroundings once again. Some aquatic insects molt ten times during their nymphal life, while others may molt more than twenty times.

At maturity, the nymph either swims to the surface or crawls from the water to complete its final adult transformation. Some insects like backswimmers, water boatmen, and aquatic beetles remain in the water even as adults. Mayflies have a slight twist to their adult life cycle. A short time after emerging, the sexually immature subadult, or dun, undergoes a second transformation into the sexually mature true-adult stage commonly referred to as a spinner. Aquatic insects featuring an incomplete life cycle include dragonflies, damselflies, mayflies, water boatmen, and backswimmers.

Advanced insect orders have a complete life cycle or metamorphosis consisting of egg, larva, pupa, and adult. Once hatched, the larva, equivalent to the nymphal stage of insects with an incomplete life cycle, begins to forage and grow, shedding its exoskeleton in the same manner as a nymph. Upon reaching maturity, the larva cocoons itself, where it transforms into the pupa. When the pupal transformation is complete, the pupa breaks free from the cocoon. Some insects may stage near the bottom for a few days in the pupal stage before ascending to the surface, while others swim to the surface immediately to hatch. Depending upon the specific insect, it may hatch at the surface or crawl from the water to emerge into the adult phase. Stillwater insects featuring a complete life cycle include chironomids and caddisflies.

STILLWATER FOOD SOURCES

I have prioritized the food sources stillwater trout feed upon in lakes from the most important to those of occasional importance. I base my priority sequence on over thirty years of notes, throat samples, stomach analyses, and on-the-water experience. Although my priority sequence is primarily western North America based, it has proven to be extremely reliable in other regions of the continent where I have strayed as well.

Chironomids

Class: Insecta
Order: Diptera
Families: Chironomidae, Chaoboridae

Chironomids are the most important food source of trout in productive stillwaters, outnumbering all other aquatic insects combined. River and stream anglers typically refer to chironomids as midges due to their tiny average size. English fly fishers call chironomids buzzers due to the high-pitched buzzing sound of the swarming adults.

Chironomid larvae. Due to the distinct red color of many species, fly fishers often refer to the larvae as bloodworms.
BRIAN CHAN

With over 2,500 species in western North America alone, chironomids hatch from ice-off to ice-on, and on lakes that don't freeze over, there is always some level of emergence. Stillwater fly fishers must come to terms with the value of these insects as a food source for trout and the presentation tactics associated with them.

The trapped gases chironomid pupae use to aid their ascent to the surface and final transformation to adult create a unique silver or gunmetal gray shine. This shine, along with the prominent white gills located at the head, are key pattern traits.

There are three stages upon which trout feed: the larva, often referred to as bloodworm due to the red coloration of its hemoglobin-based circulatory system, the pupa, and the adult. Chironomids, particularly the larvae and pupae, are easy to digest and rich in calories. Stillwater trout feed heavily on both the larvae and, to a lesser extent, the adults. They seldom refuse a well-presented pattern, regardless of the season.

Chironomid adults resemble their mosquito cousins. Thankfully they don't bite.

Of these three stages, I imitate the pupa approximately 80 percent of the time, the larva 15 percent, and the adult 5 percent. I often admonish myself that I should fish the larva stage more. If you bump into a fly fisher who states he was fishing chironomids, chances are he was using chironomid pupa patterns.

Chaoborus larvae and pupae are challenging to imitate due to their transparent bodies. The larvae are predaceous, feeding primarily on tiny zooplankton.
BRIAN CHAN

Most fly fishers have never seen or heard of *Chaoborus*, aka phantom midges or glass worms. *Chaoborus*, distant cousins to the more widespread chironomids, might be the toughest stillwater food source to imitate or suggest successfully. Why? Because the larvae and pupae are almost entirely transparent. When trout focus on *Chaoborus* larvae or pupae, it can be one of the most frustrating experiences, as few people, if any, are catching fish. After all, who, when going through their hatch or fly progressions in their attempts to figure out the mystery, decides on trying to imitate something transparent?

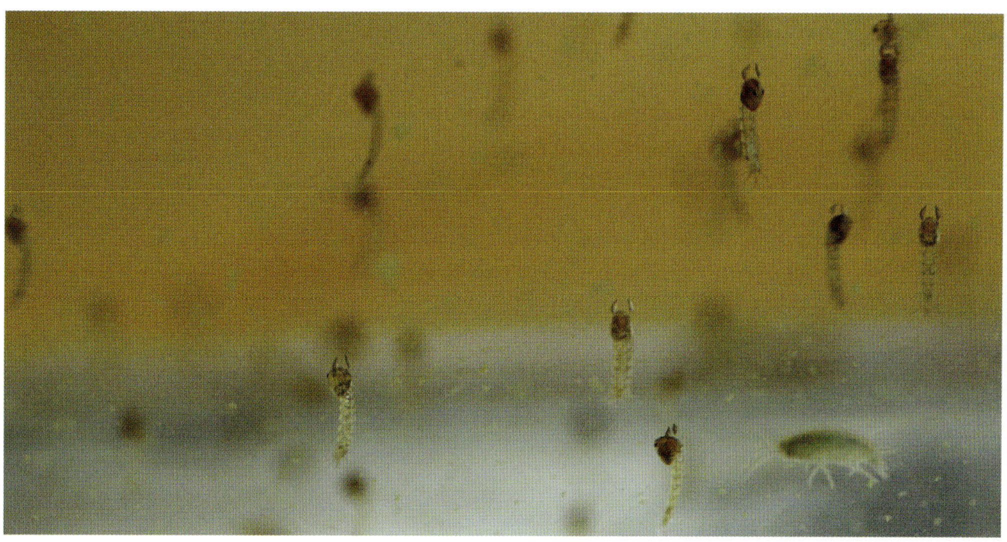

As with the larvae, *Chaoborus* pupae are often transparent. Often confused with their chironomid cousins, *Chaoborus* pupae are incredibly active. They also don't have prominent white gills but rather two hornlike appendages, which give them a unique satanic look.
BRIAN CHAN

Shape

- Chironomid larvae, or bloodworms, are slender, segmented, and wormlike—an uninspiring physique to many fly fishers. Trout consume large quantities of chironomid larvae throughout the season and, as with the pupal stage, seldom refuse a properly presented pattern.
- Chironomid larvae have a small head and two pairs of short prolegs, one pair located at the front of their body and a second, somewhat Y-shaped, pair at the rear.
- *Chaoborus* larvae are slender and tapered toward their head area. Located at their head is a short raptorial arm that the predaceous larvae use to grasp and hold zooplankton and other tiny organisms they feed upon.
- Chironomid pupae feature a slender, segmented, tapered abdomen and a short bulbous thorax that occupies roughly one-quarter of their overall length. The white, feather-like gills and wing pads are easy to see on larger species.
- *Chaoborus* pupae look similar to chironomid pupae, featuring slender, segmented, tapered abdomens and a bulbous head. If you look closely, you can also see hairlike fibers protruding from the tip of their abdomen.
- *Chaoborus* pupae have two hornlike appendages that give them a distinct satanic look. They do not have any white gills like chironomid pupae.
- Soon after transforming from the larval stage, chironomid pupae suspend with a predominately straight posture. In selective conditions, trout can key in to this body shape.
- As the pupae mature, they become more active, suspending in a curved, comma-like shape. They lever their abdomen back and forth, generating power as they wiggle to ascend to the surface. It is a good idea to have a cross section of straight and curved shank pupa patterns.
- After completing their ascent to the surface, the pupae often hang for a short period in a distinct comma-like shape. The pupae then lie horizontally with their body fully extended. A split then forms along the thorax, and the adult crawls out in front of its cast pupal shuck. Trout can focus on any one of these specific emergence profiles.
- Chironomid and *Chaoborus* adults resemble mosquitoes. Thankfully the females don't bite, as they do not require blood for egg development.
- At rest, adult chironomids and *Chaoborus* hold their pair of wings flat along their abdomen. The antennae of the females are slender and narrow, while the male's antennae are broad and feather-like.

Size

- Chironomid larvae range from too tiny to imitate to 1 inch in length, hook size 16 to 8. Patterns tied on size 12 or 14 2XL or curved scud hooks are a good starting point.

- *Chaoborus* larvae are small, approximately ⅜ inch in length, hook sizes 14 and 16 2XL.
- As with the larvae, chironomid pupae range from too tiny to imitate to close to 1 inch in length, hook size 18 to 8. A size 12 pattern tied on a curved scud hook is an excellent starting point.
- Clear alkaline lakes featuring light-colored marl shoals tend to be home to smaller chironomid species, from size 12 to 18.
- Adult chironomids range in size from tiny to ⅝ inch. Adult patterns size 10 through 18 cover most situations.
- Be observant. There are always exceptions. Above-average-size chironomid species may occur anywhere.
- The productive, muddy bottom lakes of the northwestern United States and Canada are home to some enormous chironomid species affectionately called bombers due to the abdomen-down-in-flight posture of the lumbering adults. Size 8 or larger patterns tied on 2XL nymph hooks are common when bombers are active.
- As with most insects, there is a downsizing between stages. At maturity, chironomid larvae are larger than the pupae, which are, in turn, bigger than the adults. Keep this trait in mind should you catch a recently emerged adult and are struggling to decide what size pupa pattern to try.
- I have found chironomid size, including larvae, pupae, and adults, diminish as latitude decreases. I believe this is due in part to a shorter winter season, which allows for an increased number of hatch cycles within a given species.

Behavior

- Although there are some free-living species, the majority of chironomid larvae construct tube homes along the bottom. It is not uncommon for trout to use their noses to root chironomid larvae out of their tube homes.
- Bloodworms feed on detritus, rotting plant matter, and algae, while other species are predaceous. They often leave the security of their tube homes during the low-light hours of morning and evening to forage, prime times to consider using a larval pattern.
- Chironomid larvae can establish colonies anywhere in a lake, but they prefer soft, muddy bottoms.
- Chironomids are capable of living in a wide range of water depths, from less than 10 feet to over 200 feet. Fishing chironomid larva and pupa patterns in water over 25 feet is not unusual during late spring into the summer. Whenever you are moving over deep water, always keep an eye out for emerging chironomids. Bird concentrations or groups of fish marking just above the bottom on your sounder are two signs to be aware of.
- As spring transitions into summer, trout migrate from warmer, less-oxygenated shallows to deeper water. Muddy deep-water flats are prime chironomid habit. This is an excellent time to fish a chironomid larva imitation.

- Chironomid larvae are feeble swimmers, moving through the water with a vigorous head-to-tail lashing motion coupled with periodic rests in an extended position. Wind-induced wave action and diving birds often disturb chironomid larvae.
- Once adrift, chironomid larvae are at the mercy of the elements, easy pickings for a cruising trout. Painstakingly slow retrieves with pauses or suspending larval patterns close to the bottom, static under an indicator, work best.
- Free-living *Chaoborus* larvae and pupae are incredibly active—seldom remaining stationary. The larvae move horizontally through the water by contracting and expanding their abdomen like a transparent spring. The pupae rise and fall, ascending when they move and descending slowly as they rest between body contractions. I believe their unique movement is a critical trout trigger.
- After transforming from the larval stage, chironomid and *Chaoborus* pupae stage a foot or so above the bottom. During this initial phase, staging pupae don't move very much. Accurate presentation depth is crucial for success.
- Pupae often stage above the bottom in staggering numbers for days before emerging.
- The staging chironomid pupae generate gas between the outer skin and the adult inside. This exchange increases the pupae's buoyancy. The buoyant pupae use a rhythmic wiggling motion to elevate slowly to the surface, where they will emerge.
- You can use the same dead, slow retrieves for both chironomid pupae and larvae.
- After hatching, the adults form mating swarms, usually not far from shore. On calm days the buzzing noise generated by the whirring wings of the swarming adults can be almost deafening.
- Females usually return to the water during the low-light hours of morning and evening, when the water is calm and there is a reduced risk of avian predation, to release their eggs.
- Females release their eggs by either dipping the tip of their abdomen into the water or using it to break the surface tension as they uses their wings to scurry across the water, creating a distinct V-like wake. The eggs sink to the bottom or begin hatching as they descend.
- When trout are feeding upon egg-laying females, pay attention to see if they prefer static or scurrying adults.
- The adult stage of the chironomid and *Chaoborus* is short-lived. Males die soon after mating, females shortly after laying their eggs.

Color

- Chironomid larvae come in an assortment of colors, including shades of red, maroon, olive, green, and tan.

- The larvae of some chironomid species have a hemoglobin-based circulatory system. The iron-based hemoglobin within the blood, or hemolymph, of these chironomid species' circulatory system turns them a distinct scarlet or blood-red color, leading to their popular nickname, bloodworm. Hemoglobin binds efficiently with oxygen, allowing chironomid larvae of these species to survive in oxygen-poor conditions such as deep water, high water temperature, and areas of high decomposition. Oxygen consumption is one of the byproducts of decomposition.
- Some chironomid species that are naturally not red may be able to adjust their hemoglobin levels to better bind with oxygen within their blood system to allow them to survive when dissolved oxygen levels are low. During the fall months, as the temperature of the water drops and its dissolved oxygen content increases, the larvae's reliance on hemoglobin reduces. It is not unusual to see some larvae a blend of red and their natural body color as the hemoglobin levels reduce.
- *Chaoborus* larvae are transparent or may have a subtle yellow tinge, hence their common name, glass worm. The larvae have two dark air sacs, located at the one-third and two-thirds point on their body, that they use to control their buoyancy.
- The digestive tract of the chironomid larvae often shows through their translucent body as a dark olive or black line running from one end of the body to the other.
- After feeding, the digestive tract of a *Chaoborus* larva can be a variety of colors depending on the color of its predominantly zooplankton diet, including bright orange, green, and reddish pink.
- Common chironomid pupae colors include black, maroon, brown, olive, and various shades of green and tan. Black is the most predominant chironomid color.
- Residual red hemoglobin from the larval stage often gathers at the tip of the abdomen and along the abdominal segments. A black pupal pattern featuring a short red butt and rib is standard for chironomid pupae across North America.
- It is not uncommon for pupae to change color as they mature prior to hatching. I have seen pupae that were a dark red to maroon color left over from the larval stage slowly change to a medium green a few minutes later. After this color change, they then begin to trap gas beneath their skin, becoming shinier and shinier.
- The gas the chironomid pupa generates beneath its pupal skin gives the abdomen of the pupa a distinct glow and a puffy, inflated look.
- At first, this shiny appearance is a subdued dark silver, pewter, or gunmetal gray. As the pupa generates more gas and surrounding water pressure reduces during its ascent, its outer skin expands. Its body coloration brightens, becoming a vibrant silver.

- *Chaoborus* pupae are predominately transparent or have the same yellowish tinge as the larvae. As the pupae mature, their body can turn greenish brown. The thorax region can be translucent, dark brown, or almost black.
- *Chaoborus* pupae have two dark, hornlike appendages protruding out of the top of their thorax. They have no white gills. Their active movement and lack of white gills are two primary keys you can use to separate *Chaoborus* pupae from chironomid pupae.
- Chironomid pupae have prominent white gills that are worth imitating. After hatching, the gills remain with the pupal shuck. Look for the white tufted shucks as a hatch indicator. You can also use the white gill tufts to separate chironomid shucks from any other shucks you find on the surface. Chironomid shucks can be easily confused with *Callibaetis* nymphal shucks.
- Immediately after hatching, the body of a chironomid adult is brighter than the pupa. Once their bodies harden, their body coloration also darkens. You can use this trait as a guide to figure out what color chironomid pupa to use should you capture a recently emerged adult.
- Chironomid adult coloration mirrors the pupa.
- *Chaoborus* adults are often a bright apple green.

Scuds (Shrimp)

Phylum: Arthropoda
Order: Amphipoda
Family: Gammaridae
Genera: *Gammarus*, *Hyallela*

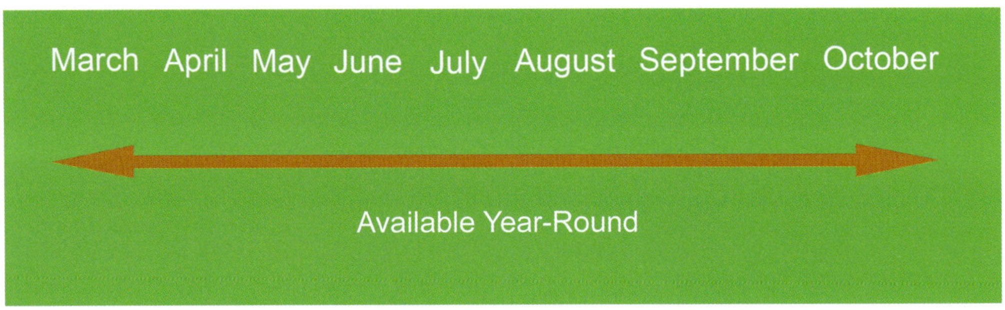

Scuds, or freshwater shrimp to many fly fishers, are one of the premier bread-and-butter food sources for trout in productive stillwaters, second only in importance to chironomids. With a fully aquatic life cycle, scuds are a readily available, year-round food source. There are approximately 150 species across North America contained within two primary scud genera: *Gammarus* and the smaller *Hyallela*. From a fly-fishing perspective, size is the only defining feature between the two genera. *Gammarus* require high concentrations of calcium to develop and maintain their chitinous exoskeleton. As there aren't as many calcium-rich lakes, *Gammarus* are less widespread than *Hyallela*. *Hyallela* are more tolerant of acidic water conditions.

Scuds are a critically important stillwater trout food source whenever present, second only in importance to chironomids.

Scuds are the carbohydrate of the stillwater world, as they help trout pack on pounds fast. Growth rates close to 2 pounds per season are not unusual. On Argentina's famed Lago Strobel, or Jurassic Lake, scuds are the trout's primary food source. They are the main reason Lago Strobel trout grow so large and maintain such an impressive 10-plus pounds average size. Early spring, midsummer, and late fall are the best times to fish scuds, as there are few hatches to preoccupy trout. In the fall months, trout are on a feeding rampage trying pack in as many calories as they can to provide the fat reserves needed to get through the long, cold winter ahead. Trout feed heavily on scuds at this time.

Shallow-water inhabitants, scud populations, in ideal conditions, can reach daunting proportions, roughly 10,000 per square meter. Population density is one of the reasons many stillwater fly fishers feel intimated when faced with trying to successfully imitate scuds. Many would rather fish anything else rather than face the prospect of having to work a scud pattern against such overwhelming odds. Rest assured, trout have no issues. Practice and perseverance pays off, and it is well worth the investment to become adept at fishing scuds throughout the season.

Scuds are omnivores, feeding primarily on detritus and algae. During my aquarium study, I have also seen groups of them tackle live prey such as damselfly nymphs and water boatmen. During the winter months, I would often drop brine shrimp into the aquarium to keep some of the predatory inmates distracted so they stopped eating the other inhabitants for a while. Scuds also enjoyed these brine shrimp treats.

Shape

- Scuds have a slender, tapered, segmented, armadillo-like body, flattened along each side; two pairs of prominent antennae; and seven pairs of underslung legs that always seem to be in a state of motion. The first and second pairs of legs feature hinged claws that the scuds use for holding food, mating, and crawling about the bottom debris and weeds within which they live.

- Scuds swim in an extended position; only the tip of their body, or telson, hangs down. The body posture of a swimming scud is an important pattern consideration. I prefer to tie my scuds on straight-shanked hooks and extend the body slightly into the bend to suggest the extended body and drooping telson of a swimming scud. I suggest swimming scuds most often using cast and retrieve techniques. A curved scud is either resting, feeding, or dead.

Size

- Scuds range in size from ⅜ inch (size 18) up to ⅝ inch (size 10). Although at maturity *Gammarus* are larger than *Hyallela*, there is no need to tie separate patterns for each genus.
- A size 12 or 14 scud pattern is a good basis point.

Behavior

- Scuds are most active in low-light conditions. As sunlight penetrates the water, scuds retreat within and under weeds, rocks, and other bottom debris.
- Mornings, evenings, and overcast days are prime times to fish a scud pattern. They are one of my preferred searching patterns before the hatches of the day begin.
- Scuds can become infected by a tiny parasitic worm called acanthocephala. Once infected, the parasite alters the scud's behavior. The scuds become attracted to light—not a recommended practice when foraging trout are around, as infected scuds are easy pickings. For the parasite to complete its life

The focused orange spot on the back of this scud confirms it is infected by a tiny parasitic worm called acanthocephalan. This parasite affects the scud's behavior, making it more available to foraging trout.

cycle, a duck or other waterfowl must eat the scud host. The parasite completes its life cycle within the small intestine of its new host. Once passed through the bird's digestive system, the parasite is deposited back into the water and the cycle begins again.

- Scuds are confident, capable swimmers, moving through the water in an erratic, almost intoxicated manner, swimming on their sides and upside down. A choppy hand twist and a brisk 3- to 4-inch strip retrieve punctuated with prolonged pauses to imitate the frequent rests they take when swimming are my two favorite scud retrieves. At times a long, slow, 6- to 12-inch retrieve also works to suggest a fleeing scud.
- Scuds typically mate once through their one-year life cycle, piggyback style, one on top of another. Some people tie mating scud patterns, though I haven't noticed if they work better than standard scud patterns.

Color

- Scuds are camouflage masters, blending in with their surroundings. When I watched scuds in my aquarium, their body colors faded to match the surroundings. Depending on their surroundings, common scud colors include shades of olive and green, gray-olive, light blue, gray, and tan. I even recall seeing an almost chartreuse scud.
- Olive or golden olive is probably the most common scud color.
- A scud's back is darker than its underbelly.
- The parasite acanthocephalan appears as a focused orange dot in the midsection of the scud's body.
- Pregnant scuds contain their eggs in an external pouch under their body called a marsupium. The developing eggs turn the underside of the scud orange.

Pregnant female scuds hold their orange-colored eggs in an underbody pouch called the marsupium. When the female sheds her exoskeleton, she releases her offspring to fend for themselves.

- No matter whether the scud is pregnant or infected, you should always have a selection of flies featuring a touch of orange. I tie scud patterns with orange heads, beads, or midsections, or, in the case of a pregnant scud, I mix a small percentage of orange dubbing with the base color to provide an overall orange hue.
- Orange scuds are dead. The orange color is a result of carotene within the scud's body. Carotene transfers to any trout feeding heavily on scuds, turning its flesh orange.
- Scuds must shed their exoskeleton to grow. When a pregnant scud molts, she releases her recently hatched offspring to fend for themselves.
- Immediately after molting, some scuds become blue to blue-gray due to their copper-based blood system becoming oxygen enriched. As a scud's new exoskeleton hardens, this blue coloration darkens and diminishes to match its surroundings.

Forage Fish

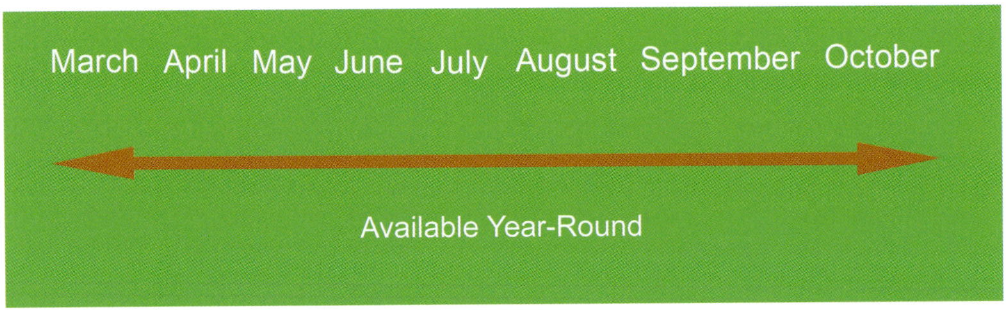

It's no secret: Big fish eat small fish. Although there are few exceptions, just about every stillwater trout species likes fresh fish in their diets—a diet that helps trout pack on weight fast. Many trout and char species, including rainbow, brown, brook, lake, and tiger trout, learn at an early age about the caloric value of fish. Trophy trout, in particular, are always searching for large quantities of protein, and forage fish quench this desire. The biggest fish on my local lakes have evolved into dedicated minnow hunters.

I spend the majority of my time using forage fish patterns in shallow water along the shoreline margins in water less than 10 feet deep. Most small baitfish need cover to protect themselves from marauding trout. Suspending in deeper water is usually a death sentence for an individual baitfish. Some of my favorite baitfish haunts include beaver lodges and along the edges of shoreline weeds and cattails. The majority of a beaver lodge lies beneath the surface. Baitfish love to school in and around the sunken branches and logs, safe in the relative protection they offer. Weeds and cattails provide similar protection.

There is a vast number of forage fish species throughout North America. Learn which species inhabit your local lakes and become familiar with their habits, preferred habitat, and coloration. In my local lakes, fathead minnows and brook sticklebacks

When present, stillwater trout, especially large ones, love to chase down and eat baitfish such as this fathead minnow. There is a wide range of baitfish spread across North America. If they are present in your local lakes, note their characteristics so you can have success suggesting them.

are common. My forage fish patterns, and presentation strategies, focus on these two primary species. In other regions, dace, shiners, or sculpins may predominate.

If you get a chance when a trout or a pod of trout attacks a school of forage fish, try to suppress your excitement and resist the urge to cast. Learn by watching what goes on. I recall watching a large brown trout targeting minnows in and around shoreline cattails on one of my favorite Manitoba lakes. Fathead minnows schooled loosely around the openings and channels within the cattails. A large brown effortlessly glided toward them. Upon sensing the brown, the fatheads clustered tightly together, creating a patch of nervous water, a result of too many minnows crammed into such a small space. The brown swam lazily through the school, parting them into

In my local waters, fathead minnows and brook sticklebacks are common inhabitants. Smaller forage fish such as these are common across North America.

two distinct groups. When the brown was in the middle of the path it had created, its attitude changed sharply. It started slashing left and right. Fathead minnows scattered everywhere. The brown snapped up any stunned or isolated minnows in the blink of an eye. Seconds after the frenzy, all went quiet as the brown slid off into the deep water adjacent to the shore.

I watched this pattern repeat for over half an hour. I learned that most of the attacks I saw weren't coming from multiple fish but rather a single fish working a section of the shoreline. This is valuable information I now use to work an area patiently should I see feeding action. Chasing a feeding fish up and down its hunting trail is tiresome and not all that effective.

Shape

- Depending on the species, forage fish come in a wide range of body styles from long and narrow to short and squat. Most of the minnows in my lakes are long and slender, under 3 inches in length.

Size

- Forage fish come in a wide range of sizes. Make a note of the average sizes in your waters and match them.
- Trout can become selective, choosing to feed on a specific size of baitfish. Choose patterns that match the size of the baitfish you observe.
- Forage fish size also varies seasonally. There will be times within a season when small, immature forage fish abound. These juveniles are favorite trout quarry, as they are still learning how to survive.
- Although trout are capable of consuming at least one-third of their body length, I tend to do best fishing smaller forage fish imitations, typically less than 3 inches. There are always exceptions, however. I have tossed flies the size of small birds in the hopes of coaxing huge lake trout from the depths. Smaller flies are much more enjoyable to cast for prolonged periods.

Behavior

- Forage fish often school in large numbers to protect themselves. The numbers within a concentrated school overwhelm potential predators, as they find it difficult to single out individual targets. Trout herd them into compact schools before slashing through them to break them into small manageable chunks.
- At times water temperature is vital. As the water temperature warms, many smaller baitfish species migrate into the shallows from deeper winter holding areas.
- Wind can also concentrate baitfish. The upwind edge of a weedy point or the downwind shorelines are excellent locations to find baitfish concentrations.

- Forage fish are vulnerable when light levels change during the early morning or evening, as their eyes don't transition as fast as a trout's.
- Baitfish rarely, if ever, suspend in a stationary manner. They are always in a state of nervous motion, moving in an erratic, stop-start manner.

Color

- Forage fish coloration usually matches their surroundings. Most shallow-water species I observe feature dark olive to brown backs, translucent sides, and pearlescent bellies.
- Open-water species, such as shiners, are often a bright silver or pearlescent color to reflect light, enabling them to blend in with their surroundings.
- The red gills of a frightened or injured baitfish can be a crucial trigger point. Many baitfish patterns incorporate a splash of red to represent the gills.
- The eyes of a forage fish are a prominent feature that is important to imitate. I believe trout use the eyes as a trigger point.
- During the spawning season, male forage fish often adopt bright color schemes to attract a mate. These often-vibrant color schemes make them easier to see, attracting the attention of foraging trout.

Leeches

Phylum: Annelida
Subclass: Hirudinea

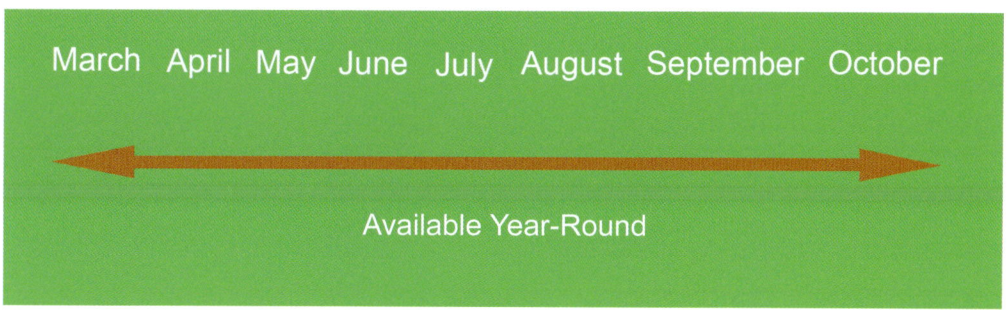

If there were ever a food source that needed a press agent, leeches would be it. Most people find leeches repulsive and are fearful about what they believe at leech will do to them. Hollywood hasn't helped either, with movies such as *The African Queen* and *Stand by Me* portraying leeches in a less-than-favorable light.

Leeches, close relatives of earthworms, are hermaphroditic, meaning they possess both male and female reproductive organs. Most leeches mate sexually, intertwining their bodies around each other, but they are also capable, if necessary, of reproducing on their own. After mating, most species deposit their eggs in a gelatinous cocoon, which they attach to weeds or other bottom debris. Other species carry their young along their bellies. The young leave their parent to fend for themselves after feeding

Most people loath leeches; stillwater trout, however, love them. Leech patterns are one of my preferred patterns, as they work all season long since trout seldom refuse them.

for the first time. Depending on the species, leeches can live several months or up to ten years. After reproducing one or two times, leeches die.

The majority of leeches feed on the blood of other animals, including humans, hence their lousy reputation. Capable of consuming a heavy meal, leeches can go months without feeding again. The leech stores the excess blood in a pouch called a crop and mixed with an anticoagulant to avoid clotting. Other species feed on carrion, decaying vegetation, and other invertebrates.

Leeches are a bread-and-butter food item that are available all year, and the trout love them. They are a must-have stillwater fly pattern for any stillwater fly fisher, regardless of skill level. Leech patterns can be suspended static under an indicator, retrieved slow or fast, and fished anywhere in the water, shallow, deep, or mid-water. It's practically impossible to present a leech pattern wrong. No matter the presentation

Some leech species' offspring remain with their parent until their first meal, when they venture out on their own.

style or line choice, keeping your leech patterns within a foot or two off the bottom works best.

Shape

- Leeches are slender, segmented, and ribbonlike. They are often referred to as dorsoventrally flattened, referring to how a leech's body is flat on both the top and bottom.
- The body of a leech resembles an elongated teardrop, wide and paddle-like at the back, narrow at the front.
- A threatened leech curls up in a defensive ball. I believe trout often bump a swimming leech, inducing it to curl up, making it easier to swallow—a behavior that we interpret as a short strike. If this happens, you can experiment with two options. First, stop your retrieve and let the fly fall for a second or so to see if the fish returns to take it. The long, flowing tails on most leech patterns rise, suggesting a curled-up leech. Second, keep retrieving. Often the trout returns and hammers the fly, almost as though it was frustrated that your fly didn't stop when it was bumped.

Size

- Although I have seen leeches over 6 inches long, the majority are under 3 inches.
- Trout seem to prefer smaller leeches, 3 inches or less. Leech patterns tied on hook sizes 6 4XL through 12 2XL work best.
- Leeches don't molt. They just get progressively larger.
- At times trout prefer small, approximately 1 inch long, baby or micro leeches. In the early spring and fall months up until ice-on, micro leech patterns tied on either size 10 curved scud or size 12 jig hooks are personal favorites.

Behavior

- Leeches prefer living in the shallow regions of a lake but can also live in deep water.
- Leeches can't see well. They would be considered, in human terms, legally blind.
- Early morning, evening, and into the night are excellent times to prospect with a leech, as this is when they are most active.
- When fishing leech patterns at night, use larger, bushy patterns such as a Woolly Bugger or Mohair-style leech. These patterns push water, creating an acoustic footprint trout track down using their lateral lines.
- Leeches are competent swimmers, moving through the water in a rhythmic, ribbonlike motion.
- Due to their confident swimming style, leech patterns are excellent searching patterns when fishing a new lake or when nothing seems to be hatching.

- Trout often favor leeches after a strong chironomid hatch, as though the leech was some sort of dessert or perhaps a plug to keep the mass of wriggling chironomid pupae down.
- Leeches use their anterior (front) and posterior (rear) suckers to latch on to and inchworm across rocks, logs, and other debris. They use their front sucker to attach themselves to hosts, including frogs, fish, and humans, to feed.

Color

- The majority of leeches are dark: black, brown, maroon, and olive. I have seen olive leeches with orange stripes down their sides.
- Mottled, variegated color schemes are typical, such as olive and brown, mottled tan and black, and tan and brown. As with all aquatic food sources, leeches tend to match their local surroundings.
- Dark colors such as black, blue, and purple and combinations of these colors are personal favorites in deep water and low-light conditions such as early evening.
- It is not uncommon to see leeches with dark backs and lighter-colored bellies.
- The best way to check leech colors is by turning over shoreline rocks and logs, as they often cling to the undersides of these items.

Damselflies

Class: Insecta
Order: Odonata
Suborder: Zygoptera
Families: Calopterygidae, Lestidae, Coenagrionidae, Protoneuridae

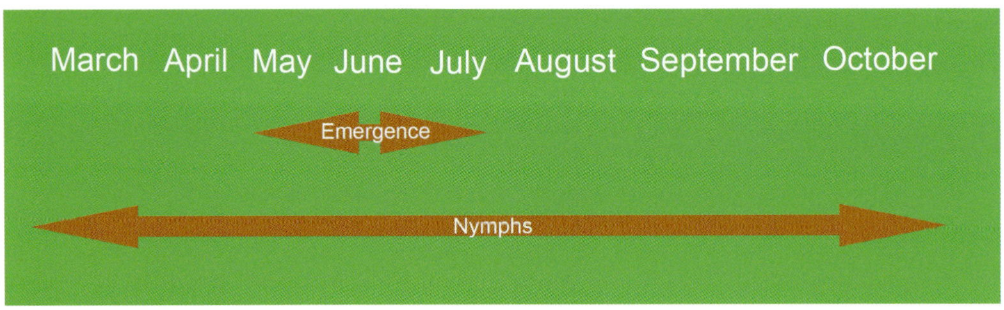

Although capable of living in slow-moving stretches of rivers and streams, damselflies inhabit lakes and ponds in large numbers. Damsels are a primitive insect with origins tracing back to prehistoric times. They have an incomplete, one-year life cycle. Trout feed predominately on the nymphs and occasionally on the adults.

After hatching, the nymphs begin foraging immediately. Damsel nymphs are capable predators. They use their hinged lower jaw to feed on almost anything they believe they can handle: mayfly nymphs, zooplankton, scuds, chironomid larvae, even each other. Damselfly nymphs reach maturity in mid- to late spring. The nymphs

Damselfly nymphs are active predators. Although capable swimmers, they love to ambush various prey, including scuds, chironomid larvae, mayfly nymphs, and even each other.

leave the security of the weed beds, swimming en masse just beneath the surface toward shore, where they crawl out of the water, usually onto emergent vegetation such as cattails, to emerge. Damsels will also creep up anchor ropes and onto a boat, float tube, or pontoon boat. If you have the time and patience, watch the entire emergence process. It is fascinating.

A damsel nymph's open-water trek silhouettes it against the bright sky, placing it in a high-risk position. Watch for aggressive slashing surface rises when trout are feeding on swimming damselfly nymphs. Fishing a damselfly nymph at this time can be spectacular.

Trout feed on damsel nymphs throughout the year. As predators, damsels are always on the move from one ambush position to another, exposing themselves to cruising trout in the process. This behavior is one of the reasons a damselfly nymph is a favorite searching pattern, especially around weed beds. Floating, clear-tip, hover, and clear intermediate lines are my preferred damsel nymph lines.

The damselfly emergence process takes time, depending on the species and air temperature. It can take up to an hour before the adult's wings and body has dried to the point it can fly.

At this time, the adults are vulnerable to other insects, birds, and foraging trout. Trout will also opportunistically

At rest, damsel adults fold their wings back over their body. Immediately after emerging, the immature tenerals are often olive, light olive, tan, or brown. As they age, they transform into their final adult coloration. Blue and black adults are common across western North America.

feed on any adults that end up blown onto the water or on egg-laying females. Female damsels lay their eggs in a variety of ways. Some species deposit their eggs by dipping the tip of their abdomen into the water, while other species encase themselves in a bubble of air, depositing their eggs directly onto subsurface aquatic vegetation. Still other species place their eggs just above the waterline. Immediately after hatching, the nymphs scramble into the water.

Capable pilots, adult damselflies maintain their predatory ways by taking prey on the fly. Adult mayflies, chironomids, mosquitoes, and other terrestrial insects are common menu items. Once captured in flight, the adult uses its legs as a basket to hold its victim steady as it consumes it. Damsel adults live through the season, until the first frosts of the fall kill them.

Shape

- Damselfly nymphs are long and slender. Successful damsel nymph patterns must match this thin, delicate profile. Located at the tip of their long, segmented abdomen are three paddle-shaped tails. Damsels have a short thorax and a distinct head and eyes. At maturity, the fingerlike wing pads are distinctive and worth imitating.
- The head and eyes are the widest part of a damselfly nymph. Keep the balance of the body proportions within the width of the head and eyes.
- The nymphs extract oxygen from the surrounding water by gently waving their tails and abdomen through the water. The distinct tails are a key identifying feature. Smaller immature damsel nymphs can be easily be confused with *Callibaetis* mayfly nymphs.
- As a damsel nymph swims from one location to another, it holds its six legs outstretched along its sides as stabilizers.
- During a damsel emergence, trout key on the nymph's snakelike swimming motion. Patterns tied on short-shank hooks featuring soft, flowing, mobile materials such as marabou, rabbit fur, or squirrel hair strips work best.
- It is not unusual for trout to fixate on resting nymphs. It pays to have a selection of realistic patterns tied on long-shank hooks for these occasions.
- Damsel adults are slender. When flying, their wings flutter like helicopter rotors.
- At rest, the damsel adult's wings lie parallel back along its abdomen. In addition to a difference in size, wing position is the easiest way to identify damselfly adults from their larger dragonfly cousins.
- Damsel adults that end up on the water adopt several different body positions. Straight and outstretched with their wings trailing behind in V-like fashion is one such position, or they can lie on the surface in a curled-up fetal position. Trout can become selective to either body position. It is a good idea to have adult patterns to match both body profiles.

Size

- Depending on species and location, most damsel nymphs range in size from ½ inch to 1½ inches long. Patterns tied on size 8 through 12 hooks work best.
- Damsel adults are larger than the nymphs, 2 inches or longer. Use short-shank size 10 or 12 extended body patterns.
- During fall, only the small, immature damsel nymphs remain. Simple, tiny patterns tied on size 12 and smaller scud hooks can work exceptionally well at this time.

Behavior

- Capable swimmers, damselfly nymphs move through the water using a unique plodding, side-to-side, sinusoidal, snakelike swimming motion coupled with prolonged pauses, as the nymphs take frequent rests. A five-turn hand twist with extended pauses is one of my favorite retrieves.
- On many western lakes, damselfly hatches often overlap *Callibaetis* mayfly emergences. At this time, both nymphs are active, and trout will eat them both. At times the *Callibaetis* emergence may be stronger, yet damselfly nymph imitations work best. The next day the opposite may be true. If multiple flies are legal, a damsel-mayfly nymph combination is one of my favorites when both insects are active.
- When fishing during a hatch, trout can become selective to the direction the natural nymphs are swimming. Make sure your positioning allows you to retrieve your imitations in the same direction as the migrating nymphs.
- As the nymphs swim just below the surface on their way toward shore to emerge, trout often become increasingly selective to presentation depth. At times trout may only take the nymphs if they are within a foot or less of the surface.
- Damselflies crawl out of the water to emerge. Look for the cast shucks stacked on the shoreline vegetation to determine if damsels are or have been hatching.
- During an emergence, recently hatched adults, or tenerals, waiting for their wings to dry and their bodies to harden, may be knocked or blown onto the water. Keep an eye out for this behavior should the trout choose the tenerals over the migrating nymphs.
- Adults knocked or blown onto the water struggle and twitch to get airborne. If enough adults are on the water, trout begin to take an interest. When fishing adult patterns, add the odd strip or twitch using a rod flick to suggest a struggling adult.
- If trout are taking damsels and other insects on the surface, use the severity of the rise to help determine which insect they might be taking. Trout typically take damsel adults in a splashy, aggressive rise.

Color

- Damsel nymphs, like most other aquatic invertebrates, match the color of their surroundings. Weed color is an excellent guide for choosing damsel nymph colors.
- Prominent damsel nymph colors include various shades of olive and green, brown, olive-brown, tan, and even maroon.
- In clear-water lakes, the nymphs are usually lighter, sometimes a tough-to-match pale, watery green. In darker, algae-stained lakes, darker olive, brown, or olive-brown nymphs predominate. Be observant, as there are always exceptions. Don't be surprised to sample a variety of different-colored damsel nymphs, all living in the same location.
- Damsel nymphs molt several times before reaching maturity. After each molt, the nymphs are pale in color. Light olive, tan, or ginger patterns work well to suggest a recently molted nymph.
- Right after emergence, damsel adults are often light olive to a mustard brown. Their bodies soon change to more vivid colors. In the West, blue-bodied damsels with black bands is a common color scheme.
- In some species, only the males adopt a vivid color scheme. The female adults may retain their somber, muted emergence colors.
- Other common adult colors include bright green, maroon, brown, red, and yellow.

Dragonflies

Order: Odonata
Suborder: Anisoptera
Families: Aeshnidae, Libellulidae, Gomphidae

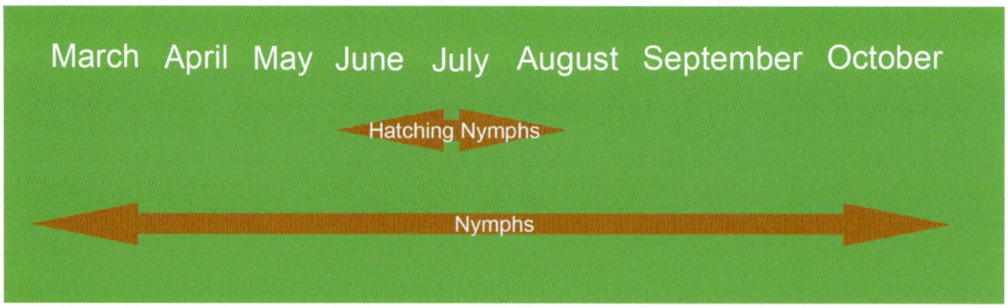

Dragonflies are the larger, more aggressive, predatory cousins of the damselfly. This is an insect that doesn't play well with others—something I have witnessed firsthand. During my aquarium studies, I decided to drop a small, roughly 1-inch Aeshnidae nymph, commonly referred to as a darner, into a thriving 30-gallon aquarium. Three months later, the darner was just over 2½ inches long and had eaten every other inhabitant except for two leeches, and it had tried to eat one of them. It decimated my aquarium. There is nothing a dragon nymph won't attempt to eat. I have seen them eat scuds, damsel nymphs, water boatmen, backswimmers, even each other. A single nymph can wreak havoc in a hatchery fry pond.

As with their smaller damselfly cousins, dragonflies trace their originals back to prehistoric times. They have an incomplete life cycle. From a fly-fishing perspective, spend your efforts on the nymphal stage. To date, I have never seen a trout eat an adult dragonfly or seen one in the stomach sample of a trout. I have a few friends who claim to have seen trout targeting low-flying adults, but I have yet to witness it myself.

There are three primary dragonfly families of concern to the fly fisher in North America: the slender Aeshnidae (darners), the squat Gomphidae, and Libellulidae (sprawlers). Of these three families, the darners garner all of the press and are probably the most well known due to their active habits and large size. In reality, the sprawlers are the most widespread, with over ninety species across North America. It is important to note that the family Gomphidae (clubtails) has a limited distribution in lakes. Gomphid nymphs are common inhabitants of slower-moving rivers and streams. *Gomphus*, a genus within the Gomphidae family, has become a common nickname many stillwater fly fishers use to describe any lake-dwelling sprawler nymph they see, despite the fact that sprawlers from the family Libelluidae are the most common stillwater dragonfly.

The nymphs of all dragonfly species are long-lived, up to four years among some species. Immature nymphs are a bread-and-butter stillwater food source, as they are always around. Dragon nymphs' large average size makes them popular with many fly fishers as both a searching and confidence pattern. The solid takes to a large dragon nymph pattern is a definite attraction too. Before I understood the importance of chironomids and developed my skills imitating them, casting and retrieving a large dragon nymph made more sense, as the bigger the bug, the more likely a trout might find it in the vast expanse of a lake. My tactics have changed considerably. Still, from time to time, retrieving a large dragon nymph pattern provides a pleasant break from the finesse tactics associated with imitating smaller prey items such as chironomids and scuds.

The large hourglass-shaped nymphs from the family Aeshnidae, often referred to as darners, are active, aggressive predators. They stalk the underwater jungle, hunting in catlike fashion and pouncing on anything they choose, from small fish to tiny scuds. BRIAN CHAN

Squat and spiderlike, sprawler dragon nymphs prefer to hide and ambush their prey. They like to bury and camouflage themselves among weeds and debris, where they lie in wait for dinner to come to them.

Upon reaching maturity, dragonfly nymphs, as with damselfly nymphs, crawl from the water to transform into adults. Unlike damsel nymphs, dragon nymphs don't swim just beneath the surface, preferring to crawl over the bottom and out of the water. Once out of the water, they are capable of trekking a considerable distance before transforming. I have found cast shucks 20 feet from shore, 6 feet up the trunk of a tree. Dragon husks are large and relatively easy to spot among shoreline vegetation, rocks, and other debris.

Of all the stillwater aquatic insects, dragonflies are the last to emerge. Depending on factors such as air and water temperature, elevation, latitude, and species, dragonflies can emerge well into July. If the air temperatures are warm enough, most dragonfly hatches take place at night.

Cooler air temperatures shift emergences to daylight hours. Dragonflies are most vulnerable during their transformation process, as it can take approximately two hours before the adult can fly. This vulnerability explains, in part, why they prefer nocturnal emergences.

Dragonflies mate similarly to damselflies. The male grasps the female behind her head using a pair of claspers mounted at the tip of his abdomen. If the female accepts his rough advances, she swings the tip of her abdomen up to the underside of the male's thorax to complete the fertilization process. The fertilized female dips and dances across the surface, dropping her eggs each time she touches the water. The eggs hatch soon after, and the dragonfly's cycle of carnage repeats once again.

When at rest, adult dragonflies hold their wings perpendicular to their body like helicopter rotors. Capable fliers, dragonflies continue their predatory ways, feeding on a variety of airborne prey. Adult dragons seldom, if ever, are fed on by trout.

Shape

- Dragonflies have two basic body shapes: slender hourglass and squat, almost spiderlike.
- Darner nymphs fall into the slender hourglass category. It is easy to overdress a darner pattern. Their head and middle of the abdomen are the widest. Even a fully grown nymph that may be more than 2½ inches will only be ⅜ to ½ inch wide.
- Sprawler nymphs are squat and spiderlike. Small hairs cover their bodies and trap sediment and other debris, masking their appearance and color.
- No matter the family, all dragon nymphs have six relatively long, stout legs; a prominent head; and a pair of eyes that are well worth imitating.
- Depending upon the family and species, dragon nymph legs extend back to just past the tip of the abdomen.
- Adults feature a long, slender abdomen; a compact, robust thorax; and a prominent head and eyes.
- At rest, dragonfly adults hold their wings outstretched like rotors on a helicopter.

Size

- Darners can attain sizes over 2½ inches. A range of patterns from size 10 3XL through size 4 4XL should cover the bases. A size 6 3XL or 4XL is a good average size. Adult darners can seem the size of small birds. Body lengths of 3 inches or longer are common.
- Smaller sprawler nymphs range in size from ⅝ inch to 1 inch; 2XL hooks in size 10 and 8 cover most situations. Adult sprawlers are about half the size of the darners; 2 inches would be average.
- Use larger dragon nymph patterns in the spring through early summer, as this is when the number of large nymphs is highest.
- In the fall months, use smaller patterns to match the remaining immature nymphs.

Behavior

- Darner nymphs are active predators, stalking among weeds, rocks, and other debris. They crawl to within striking distance of their prey before unleashing their lower hinged jaw to snatch their victim. Turning over shoreline logs and rocks is a great way to find resting darner nymphs.
- Sprawler nymphs are sedentary ambush feeders. They shuffle themselves into position among bottom sediment or weeds, waiting for their food to come to them. When an unsuspecting victim comes into range, their prey disappears in a puff of silt as their underslung jaw fires out and grabs it.
- Although more abundant than the larger darner nymphs, the camouflage and ambush tactics of sprawler nymphs make them challenging to find. Chara beds are often home to dense sprawler nymph populations.
- Located at the tip of the abdomen is the dragonfly nymph's gill chamber. The nymph extracts oxygen from the surrounding water by expanding and contracting its body, pumping water through its gill chamber. A sudden body contraction creates a focused burst, allowing the nymph to shoot forward in short, 3- to 4-inch spurts with its legs tucked along its sides. Dragon nymphs use this afterburner behavior to flee or to jet from one location to another. Darner nymphs also use these focused bursts to help capture prey. Adding quick strips to your retrieves imitates this behavior. Sprawler nymphs rarely use this tactic, preferring to crawl from spot to spot.
- Despite their aggressive disposition, dragon nymphs don't move very fast unless they are startled. I use buoyant materials in my dragon nymph patterns, such as spun and clipped deer hair or foam. A buoyant pattern tethered to a short leader and a fast-sinking line allows you to work your flies slowly around and above the weeds, rocks, and sunken debris dragonfly nymphs call home.
- A steady hand twist coupled with random 3- to 4-inch strips is a standard dragonfly nymph retrieve. When trout are prowling over shallow flats, retrieving a darner nymph using 4- to 6-inch strips can provide some heart-stopping takes. A steady hand twist works best when using sprawler imitations.

- Dragonfly adults are confident fliers. Some species reach airspeeds of over 30 miles per hour, roaming miles away from their home waters. Adult dragonflies are just as nasty as they were as nymphs. They feed on the fly, using their legs to snatch and hold all sorts of prey, including mosquitoes, mayflies, damselflies, and caddisflies. Their appetite has no boundaries.

Color

- As hunters, dragonfly nymphs need to match their surroundings. Darner nymphs are typically mottled blends of olive, green, dark olive, and brown. Sprawler nymphs are shades of brown, green, or olive. The debris the fine hairs catch on their bodies often masks their actual color.
- Although not necessary for success, as far as fly patterns go, dragon nymph bellies are lighter than their dorsal surfaces.
- Dragonfly nymphs molt numerous times. After each molt, the nymphs are pale and stick out against the surrounding background. Seemingly sensing their vulnerability, recently molted nymphs are shy and reclusive until their new exoskeleton hardens to match their habitat.
- Adult coloration varies greatly among families. Darner adults are usually bright combinations of blue and green. Sprawler adults can be a variety of colors depending on species, including red, green, blue, and black. Their wing bases are often a contrasting color, hence their "red-shouldered dragon" nickname.

Mayflies

Class: Insecta
Order: Ephemeroptera
Families: Baetidae, Caenidae, Ephemeridae
Genera: *Callibaetis, Caenis, Hexagenia*

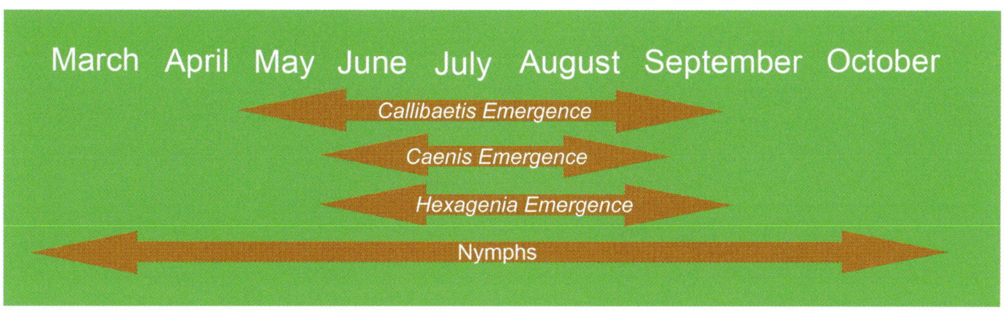

Mayflies are not as widespread in lakes as they are in rivers and streams. In lakes that they do occur, their population densities can be staggering. Belonging to the order Ephemeroptera (meaning "short-lived winged insect") mayflies have inhabited the planet for several hundred millions of years. Despite their long-term evolution, mayflies remain one of the more primitive insect orders, especially when compared to other aquatic insects such as caddisflies or chironomids.

Callibaetis nymphs are active swimmers, featuring a slender tapered body, fork-like tails, and prominent abdominal gills.
RICK HAFELE

The sexually immature *Callibaetis* dun, featuring speckled opaque wings, looks like a tiny sailboat as it sits on the water just before it takes flight.

After hatching, *Callibaetis* duns fly off to nearby vegetation, where they molt and transform into the sexually mature spinner. *Callibaetis* spinners feature predominantly transparent wings and two long tails.

Mayflies have an incomplete life cycle with a unique two-stage twist in the adult stage. The nymphs initially hatch into sexually immature duns. A short time after hatching, the duns molt into the sexually mature spinners and mate. After mating and egg-laying, both the males and females die soon after, as they can't eat or drink. A mayfly's entire adult stage exists for one purpose: reproduction. Mayflies are one of the few stillwater insects that offer reasonably reliable surface opportunities using adult and emerger imitations. Depending on the family, temperature, elevation, and latitude, stillwater mayflies emerge any time from late May through August.

Hexagenia nymphs are burrowers, requiring just the right substrate to build their U-shaped tunnel homes. When they find a suitable substrate, *Hexagenia* often occur in staggering numbers.
DAVE HUGHES

Hexagenia adults are massive. Emergence takes place at dusk and continues well into the evening. As Hexes hatch in typically large numbers, trout of all sizes throw caution to the wind to feed on these sizable protein-rich food sources.

As with all mayflies, *Hexagenia* spinners feature clear, transparent wings and large tails. Trout don't feed on them nearly as often as the emerging duns.

There are three lake-based mayfly genera I cross paths with most often: the mid-size *Callibaetis*, the massive *Hexagenia*, and the diminutive *Caenis*. Of these three genera, *Callibaetis* is the most widespread in western North America. *Hexagenia* is not as prevalent, but in soft, silty bottom lakes that are to their liking, their populations can be staggering.

Caenis nymphs are crawlers. They spend most of their lives smothered among the weeds and bottom debris, making it difficult for trout to find and feed on them consistently.
DAVE HUGHES

Due to their challenging-to-match minute size and emergence habits, fly fishers often refer to *Caenis* duns by their common name, "white-winged curse." Thankfully stillwater trout rarely feed on *Caenis* adults.
DAVE HUGHES

Caenis duns emerge at night in very shallow water adjacent to the shore. They transform into spinners within minutes of hatching.
DAVE HUGHES

Caenis are widespread, but you won't see them too often due to their minute size and emergence habits. They are frustrating to match, hence their nickname, "white-winged curse." Frankly, I have only seen sporadic feeding on *Caenis* nymphs. I don't even carry any specific *Caenis* patterns. However, I do receive a lot of questions about this hatch after people have seen large concentrations of spent spinners scattered across the water's surface. I thought it best to mention them so the next time you see a tiny, stout, three-tailed nymph or the pale adults, you are aware of them.

Other mayflies such as Tricos (*Tricorythodes*) and gray drakes (*Siphlonurus*) are also capable of living in lakes, though I have yet to run into any populations of note. If your lakes have any inflow streams or rivers, other species such as pale morning duns or green drakes may drift out onto the lake, where stillwater trout are only too happy to feed on them.

Shape

- There are four mayfly groups: clingers, crawlers, burrowers, and swimmers. The nymphs within each group have a unique body shape suited to their subsurface habits.
- *Callibaetis* nymphs are swimmers featuring a slender, torpedo-shaped body. At rest, *Callibaetis* nymphs arch their body and tails as they sit on weeds or fall through the water. The thorax is their widest feature. They have three forklike tails covered with tiny hairs.
- A set of heart-like gills runs externally along the sides of the nymphs' abdomen. Their gills are always in a constant state of motion, fluttering to extract oxygen from the surrounding water.
- *Hexagenia* (Hex) nymphs are burrowers. They have a large head complete with a set of tusks and short pair of stout forelegs they use to burrow into the bottom substrate.
- Located along each side of a Hex's abdomen is a set of external interlocking gills. Hex nymphs have three feather-like tails at the tip of their body.
- *Caenis* are crawlers. Their bodies are short and stout.
- The square-shaped gills of a *Caenis* nymph cover the top of their abdomen, adjacent to the wing case area of the thorax. They have three fine-diameter tails.
- Tiny hairs cover the body of a *Caenis* nymph, which help trap silt and debris for camouflage.
- Mayfly adults, both spinners and duns, have slender bodies. The tails of the duns are usually body length. Spinner tails are long, often one to two times longer than the mayfly's body.
- The upright wing position of a mayfly dun reminds you of a sailboat. A group of duns resembles a small sailing regatta.
- After mating, the spinners are exhausted and dehydrated. They are nearing the end of their lives. Upon returning to the water's surface to lay their eggs, the females don't hold their wings up for long, if at all. Most times, you will

see the spinners lying flush on the surface, wings outstretched in a crucifix-like posture.

- *Callibaetis* spinners sometimes hold their wings in an approximately 45-degree angle between vertical and spent. Trout at times can become selective to this posture.

Size

- At maturity, *Callibaetis* nymphs range from ⅜ to ⅝ inch long, excluding tails, hook sizes 12 through 16 2XL. A size 14 nymph is a good starting point.
- *Callibaetis* duns and spinners are slightly smaller than the nymphs, ½ to ¼ inch, sizes 14 and 16.
- *Callibaetis* are multibrooded, meaning they can have more than one emergence throughout a season. With each successive hatch, both the nymphs and adults become smaller due to the reduced time between broods.
- During the late fall, just before ice-on, trout often feed on tiny immature *Callibaetis* nymphs.
- Compared to other mayflies, *Hexagenia* nymphs are enormous. At maturity, the nymphs, including tails, reach close to 2 inches in size.
- *Hexagenia* duns are also large, averaging about 1½ inches long, excluding their tails. Size 4 extended-body adult patterns are common.
- *Caenis* nymphs and adults are tiny, seldom exceeding ¼ inch.

Behavior

- *Callibaetis* are excellent swimmers. They interlock their tails and rapidly undulate their abdomen to dart through the water in rapid 3- to 4-inch spurts. At first glance, their swimming motion might remind you of a small minnow. The nymphs tire quickly, falling as they rest, abdomen and tails arched. A slow five-turn hand twist punctuated with prolonged pauses is my favorite retrieve.
- Be prepared for takes as the fly falls or the moment you recommence your retrieve.
- Although widespread across many western lakes, I have found the best *Callibaetis* populations reside in productive, clear lakes featuring vast shallow marl and chara shoals. Floating, clear-tip, hover, and clear intermediate are my preferred *Callibaetis* nymph lines.
- Just before emergence, *Callibaetis* nymphs become active as they gather gas beneath their exoskeleton. The trapped gas adds buoyancy, causing the nymph to rise. The nymph instinctively fights this buoyancy, fluttering back down to the bottom to grab on to the aquatic vegetation. Many refer to this behavior as false hatching. Any shiny, gas-inflated nymph rising in front of a cruising trout is immediately snatched up. Just before any *Callibaetis* emerge, the nymph fishing can be spectacular.

- *Callibaetis* nymphs usually swim up to the surface on a shallow-angled trek. I have also witnessed some nymphs using a steep-angled, almost vertical, emergence swim.
- Once at the surface, the nymph's thorax splits and the dun crawls out. The dun rests on the surface for a short period before flying off to shoreline vegetation to transform into a spinner a few hours later.
- Spinners form large mating swarms that rise and fall along the shorelines. After mating midair, the females gestate their eggs for about five days before returning to the water to lay them. The eggs hatch within a few seconds of hitting the water. Egg-laying usually occurs in the early morning or evening, when the surface is calm and there is less risk of being eaten by birds, dragonflies, or damselflies. The males die soon after mating, and the females die once they have laid their eggs.
- Because of the prolonged time it takes for *Callibaetis* females to gestate, you can have some excellent surface action using spent spinners even though no duns are emerging.
- *Callibaetis* hatch in the late morning through the early afternoon. The strongest and most prolonged hatches take place on calm, dreary, overcast days.
- As *Hexagenia* nymphs are burrowers, trout seldom see them. They only venture out of their burrows at night to forage. That doesn't mean you shouldn't consider prospecting with a nymph pattern, however, as their large size makes them hard for a cruising trout to ignore.
- Hex nymphs have a bit of a Goldilocks complex when it comes to the makeup of the silty bottoms in which they construct their 4- to 12-inch-deep, U-shaped burrows. Too hard and they can't dig, too soft and their burrow collapses. When they find just the right bottom makeup, they establish themselves in huge numbers. Bottom makeup explains why one lake may have an incredible *Hexagenia* population while the surrounding lakes have none. The Great Lakes region has numerous lakes and rivers that are to a Hex's liking. Their population densities in this region are incredible.
- *Hexagenia* nymphs are competent swimmers. They move through the water by interlocking their gills and tails as they undulate their body. The best Hex nymph imitations utilize mobile materials that move and breathe.
- *Hexagenia* prefer to hatch in the early evening, using the security of low light to mask their large size as they rise toward the surface.
- Hex duns hatch quickly but often remain on the surface for a while, waiting for their body and wings to dry and harden so they can fly. Trout take full advantage of this delay. If legal and safe to do so, evening fishing offers the best chance of success.
- Hex duns rest among the shoreline vegetation for a few days before transforming into the spinner.
- Mating flights and subsequent *Hexagenia* spinner falls take place in the early evening as well. Trout view the spent spinners as a target of opportunity, and

your best chance for success remains with imitating the emerging duns. However, due to the Hex's large size, trout will opportunistically dine on any stage.

- *Caenis* nymphs live deep within the weeds and bottom debris. As a result, they are only an occasional food source.
- Prior to hatching, *Caenis* nymphs gather in extremely shallow water, often too shallow for trout to find or feed on them. The nymphs begin hatching in the early evening and into the night, crawling from the water to emerge.
- The adult stage of a *Caenis* is brief. Upon hatching, *Caenis* duns transform almost immediately into spinners. Mating and egg-laying take place soon after. Usually, the only clue you have that a hatch has taken place is the large numbers of tiny spent spinners clogging the water's surface.

Color

- *Callibaetis* nymphs match their surroundings. Common color schemes include mottled combinations of olive, light olive, and brown. Use a two-tone pattern featuring a dark back and lighter belly to match the natural nymphs.
- *Callibaetis* nymphs living in clear lakes tend to be darker than those inhabiting muddy bottomed algae-type lakes.
- At maturity, the wing pads of the *Callibaetis* nymph become dark and swollen.
- The trapped gases the *Callibaetis* nymph uses to aid its ascent and adult transformation gives it a reflective shine that is well worth matching using Mylar shellbacks, wing cases, and ribbing.
- *Callibaetis* duns have mottled opaque wings.
- Spinner wings are transparent. Female *Callibaetis* spinners retain a mottled leading edge from the dun stage.
- *Callibaetis* adult body coloration varies seasonally. Early in the season, their bodies are dark gray or olive so they can efficiently absorb the sun's rays to ensure they survive long enough to mate. Later in the season, light olive and tan predominate. The lighter colors reflect the sun's energy, reducing the risk of dehydration.
- *Hexagenia* nymphs are yellowish brown to dark brown.
- The body and wings of a Hex dun range from tan to yellowish brown, with distinct dark bands along the body. Spinner body coloration is similar to the dun except for their transparent wings.
- *Caenis* nymphs are mottled shades of brown. Duns and spinners are white to cream with a contrasting tan, brown, or black thorax.

Caddisflies/Sedges

Class: Insecta
Order: Trichoptera
Families: Leptoceridae, Limnephilidae, Phryganeidae

Caddisflies, or sedges, are complex. This complexity and diversity spread across the more than 10,000 caddis species worldwide enable them to survive in a wide variety of water temperatures and oxygen conditions. Caddisflies are a resilient insect. With so many different habits, adaptations, and behaviors scattered throughout their life stages, it seems that caddisflies were put on this planet to drive fly fishers crazy. Thankfully we only have to cope with three caddis families in lakes: Leptoceridae (long-horned case makers), Limnephilidae (northern case makers), and Phryganeidae (traveling sedge). In simple terms, small (Leptoceridae), medium (Limnephilidae), and large (Phryganeidae).

All stillwater caddis species in North America are case builders. Stillwater trout eat the larvae, case and all, along with any caseless larvae they find without their homes.

Compared to most river and stream caddisflies, stillwater caddis are large. All stillwater caddis are case makers, the most advanced division within the overall caddis family. With their complete life cycle, trout feed on the larvae and more frequently on the emerging pupae and adults, as they are the most exposed stages—ironic perhaps, as caddis spend the majority of their life cycle in the larval stage. At certain times, trout regularly consume caddis larvae. Early spring and late fall are two prime times trout feed on caddis larvae, as weed growth is low, leaving them exposed and easy to consume. Trout eat caddis larvae complete with case. Finding small sticks or sections of weeds within a stomach sample is a typical sign trout are targeting caddis larvae. The soft-bodied, grub-like larvae digest reasonably fast, while their cases take longer to process.

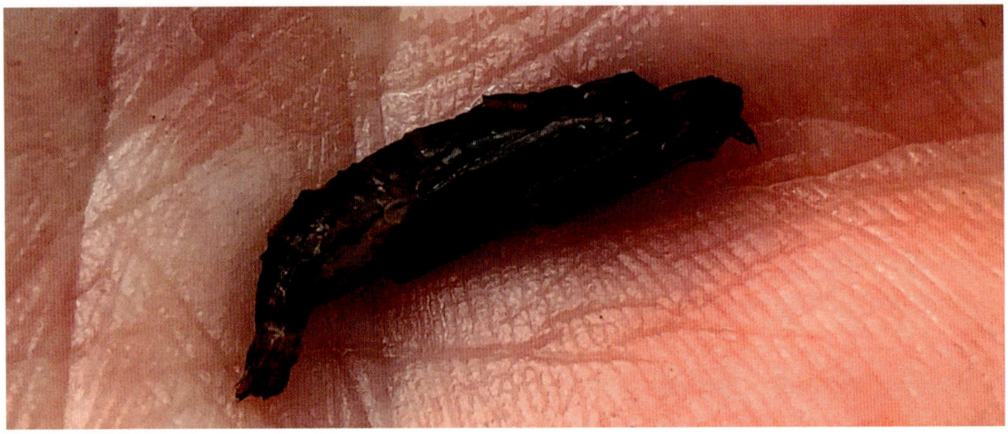

Seldom seen by fly fishers, caddis, or sedge, pupae use their elongated hind legs as oars to scull their way to the surface, the shallows, or the shore to emerge.

Each species within the three stillwater families uses different materials and construction techniques to build their unique cases. In addition to size, you can use case construction and shape to determine which caddis species are available in the lakes you fish. Once the larva seals itself within its case, pupation takes anywhere from two to eight weeks, depending on the species. The larger the caddis, the longer the pupation.

When adult caddis are scurrying across the surface, it is time to take a vacation or call in sick, as the explosive takes can be heart-stopping.
RICK HAEFELE

Most caddis hatch from late spring through early summer. Some emerge at the surface and others in the nearshore shallows, while still others crawl out of the water to complete their final transformation. When caddis are emerging, trout seem to lose their minds, chasing down the sculling pupae and scurrying adults with reckless abandon—time to consider calling in sick or taking an extended vacation.

Shape

- Caddis larvae are slender and grub-like. You rarely see an exposed caddis larva, as, for the most part, they remain within their self-made mobile homes.
- Smaller long-horned case maker cases are slender and made up of small sticks, pine needles, and, on occasion, small rocks and sand.
- Midsize northern case maker cases are more haphazard in their construction, resembling small sea urchins. Tiny pine needles are a common construction material.
- The large traveling sedge larvae build their neat, meticulous, longitudinally aligned cases out of various sections of cattails or tulles.
- Caddis pupa bodies feature a distinct abdomen, thorax, and head. Their cast pupal shucks are identical.
- The wing pads, antennae, and elongated hair-tipped hind legs of the medium to large caddis families are prominent and worthy of imitation.
- Caddis pupae hold their prominent wing pads along the sides of their thorax.
- Many refer to Leptoceridae as long-horned caddis due to the adults' long, twice-the-body-length antennae.
- The mothlike caddis adults hold their tentlike wings back over their bodies.
- Just after emerging, adult caddis raise their wings for a short while to dry them before folding them back over their body. At this moment, the pupal shuck sits directly behind the adult, with its wings held high. A Tom Thumb does an excellent job mimicking this profile.

Size

- Caddisflies vary in size, depending on the family. Within each family, the larva (less its case), pupa, and adult are all similarly sized.
- The smaller long-horned case makers range from ⅜ inch to ⅝ inch (size 14 and 12), the midsize northern case makers range from ⅝ inch to 1 inch (size 10 and 8), and the larger traveling sedges range from ¾ inch to 1½ inches (size 8 and 6).

Behavior

- Most long-horned case makers are carnivorous, crawling or using their elongated hind legs to scull through the maze of aquatic weeds, case in tow, in search of suitable prey.

- The smaller long-horned case makers are the most prolific, offering perhaps the best pupa and adult fishing. If larger caddis are hatching, smaller caddis species that may also be emerging alongside them often go unnoticed by fly fishers. Trout don't make the same mistake.
- Many long-horned case maker adults dive beneath the surface, enveloped in a shiny air bubble, to lay their eggs directly on the bottom vegetation. After laying their eggs, they bob back up to the surface and take flight once again.
- At first glance, egg-laying behavior can be confusing to figure out. Trout may take the adults anywhere along their egg-laying journey. If they begin targeting the adults as they return to the surface, we can mistakenly interpret this as hatch activity. If you are fortunate to catch a trout, carefully throat pump the fish. If the sample contains adults, look for the often bright green eggs on the tip of the abdomen to confirm whether subsurface egg-laying is taking place.
- As with chironomid pupae, the pupae of larger caddis species may take a few days staging and crawling along the bottom before emerging. Using a floating line and long leader to wind-drift a weighted pattern or suspending a pupal pattern just above the bottom are great tactics to suggest staging pupae.
- Once ready to emerge, caddis pupae use their elongated, feather-like hind legs to scull through the water in short bursts, punctuated with short rests, toward the surface or shoreline shallows. When the pupae are ascending, use a 3- to 4-inch strip-pause retrieve.
- Traveling sedge larvae use a bizarre defense technique. When threatened, they flee their homes using rapid undulations of their abdomen.
- After undergoing their last molt, traveling sedge larvae require increased protein before pupation. Their diets change, shifting from vegetarians to carnivores.
- After emerging, adult traveling sedges and northern case makers scurry and zigzag across the surface, leaving a distinct, trout-attracting wake. Due to both the large average size of these two caddis families and the speed at which they move, trout typically take these scampering adults in violent splashy rises. A choppy hand twist or 3- to 4-inch strip retrieve in conjunction with a waking-style pattern can produce some explosive takes.
- At times trout will tail slap and swamp the skittering adults in an attempt to slow them down. An aggressive missed take could be a trout trying to drown your fly. Be patient, and let your fly sit for a few seconds to see if the trout returns to take your fly in a relaxed, deliberate manner.
- The heaviest traveling sedge emergences take place in the early evening and into the night.
- The burnt orange shucks of the larger caddis species are visible to the trout as they float at the surface. It is not unusual for a throat sample to reveal opportunistic feeding on these cast shucks.
- As with most insect emergences, you usually have the best results imitating the pupa.

- After hatching, adult caddis live for a few weeks. During this time, adults return to the water to drink. This hatch-like behavior can be confusing. Always look for the pupal shucks to confirm if caddis are hatching.

Color

- Larval coloration varies depending on species and family. Common larva colors include olive, bright green, yellow, and tan. The head of the larva is often a darker color. The large traveling sedge larvae often have rust-brown vertical stripes running down their head.
- Northern case maker pupae are typically olive or ginger. I have also seen two-toned pupae consisting of a bright green body and rust-brown thorax and head.
- Bright lime green abdominal bands are characteristic of the larger caddis species. It is an excellent idea to incorporate this feature into your caddis pupa patterns.
- All stillwater caddis larvae and pupae have short, white or light tan, hairlike gill filaments running along their body.
- Adult coloration is similar to the pupa's, although their bellies are usually a lighter shade. I typically tie my adult caddis patterns with lighter-colored bodies to mimic this feature and to suggest recently hatched adults that have yet to darken as their exoskeleton hardens.

Water Boatmen

Class: Insecta
Order: Hemiptera
Family: Corixidae

On my local lakes and others across western North America, air-breathing water boatmen are a seasonally important food source. Especially during the spring immediately after ice-off and once again in the fall months when they have reached maturity, at the end of their one-year life cycle, boatmen can fly. On bright, calm, warm spring or fall days, mature boatmen take flight in large numbers to mate and populate other bodies of water. Once their journey is complete, they dive headlong into the water. The impact seems to stun them for a moment, as they dart around in tight circles before diving below. Trout soon become aware of these falls, taking the boatmen as they crash into the surface or as they swim through the water. Depending on elevation and air temperature, mid-April through early May and again from mid-September through mid-October are peak times to be on the water, as the fishing can be spectacular.

Smaller water boatmen are more widespread than their larger backswimmer cousins. Water boatmen feature a dark back and light belly.

With over a hundred species across North America, water boatmen are widespread, far more so than backswimmers, another air-breathing, beetle-like, seasonally available trout food source. During my travels, many fly fishers I speak to have never seen or heard of water boatmen in their local waters, let alone seen trout feeding upon them. The shallows immediately adjacent to the shoreline is the best place to see clouds of these aquatic insects scooting around.

Water boatmen are often confused with the larger backswimmers. From a fishing perspective, this is perhaps not important, as their life cycles, as well as the presentation techniques used to imitate them, are similar. Although some species are occasional predators, boatmen are primarily herbivores. Their beak-like mouth is best suited for chewing and grinding up aquatic vegetation. As a result, they don't bite. Backswimmers are a different story and are capable of inflicting a nasty bite if mishandled. That is the primary reason it is crucial to know the difference between the two insects.

Shape

- Water boatmen have a small head and oval-shaped, streamlined body.
- Mature boatmen fold their dark wings neatly along their back.
- As with all insects, water boatmen have six legs.
- Boatmen use their front legs for grasping and holding food, and the middle pair for holding on to weeds and other debris as they forage. Their signature oar-like hind legs are elongated and feathered.
- At rest, water boatmen hold their legs straight out, perpendicular to their sides. You can use this feature to help identify them from their larger, meaner back-swimmer cousins that hold their legs in a swept-forward position at rest.

Size

- Depending on the species, at maturity water boatmen reach up to ½ inch in length. I tie the majority of my boatman patterns on standard-shank size 12 and 14 hooks. A size 10 boatman would be a Goliath among its peers.
- Immature boatmen can be tiny, less than ¼ inch. They are tough to match.
- When trout focus on immature boatmen inhabiting the nearshore shallows, it can be a frustrating experience.

Behavior

- Water boatmen are an air-breathing insect. They have no gills.
- Using tiny body hairs, water boatmen trap an air bubble or physical gill along the underside of their body and wings, if present. The air bubble serves as a scuba tank that they use to extract air into their body through a series of tiny pores, a process known as aeropneustic respiration.
- Water boatmen can remain submerged for long periods. They can augment the air bubble, fanning their hind legs over it to diffuse additional oxygen into the bubble.
- Eventually boatmen exhaust their portable air supply, and they must return to the surface. This reliance on atmospheric air concentrates the majority of boatmen in the shallows in water less than 10 feet deep.
- The back-and-forth journey boatmen take from the bottom to the surface places them in constant risk of becoming trout food.
- Many water boatman species reach maturity in the early spring. They can live through the winter under the ice, using tiny air pockets to survive.
- Using short, choppy, erratic strokes, boatmen use their prominent rear legs to dart through the water. A brisk, choppy hand twist or 3- to 4-inch strip coupled with random pauses are my two favorite boatman retrieves.
- Water boatmen must always move or hang on to something if they rest. Otherwise, the buoyant air bubble bobs them back to the water's surface.

- Boatmen can't fly until they reach maturity, which occurs in early spring soon after ice-off or again in the fall.
- Trout often target boatmen immediately after ice-off, as they are one of only a few active and available food sources.
- Water boatman mating and migration flights, or more appropriately falls, cause the most concentrated trout feeding, at times driving them into a feeding frenzy. The best falls occur on warm, calm, sunny days.
- Returning boatmen crash headlong into the water, creating raindrop-like rings. Once they get their bearings, they scoot headfirst down to the bottom to feed. Pregnant females deposit their eggs on the vegetation below.
- Trout can feed upon water boatmen at any point in the water. At times the trout can become selective where they take them. Trout can target boatmen at the surface, mid-depth, or near the bottom.
- Your presentation choice depends on where trout are taking the boatmen. You can fish buoyant, foam-based boatman patterns at the surface or under the surface dragged down by a sinking line, or use beadhead boatman patterns in conjunction with a floating or clear-tip line.
- To simulate their air-replenishment trips, I often use buoyant patterns coupled with hover, clear intermediate, or type III full-sinking lines. A sweep line also makes an excellent choice. I let the line drag the fly down to simulate a brief surface rest followed by a dive to the bottom. Once the fly is near the bottom, a brisk retrieve moves it through the water. The final portion of the retrieve, followed by the hang, suggests the boatman's return trip to the surface.
- As trout try to crush and kill boatmen before swallowing, takes are typically aggressive, almost out of proportion to the size of the fly.

Color

- Mature water boatmen feature a dark brown to black back and light underbelly. Typical belly colors include light yellow, light olive, and tan, similar to masking tape.
- Water boatman eyes are distinct, often red to maroon in color. I always add a touch of red to my boatman patterns using red thread hot spots, beads, cones, or two red dots from a permanent marker.
- The shiny, reflective air bubble boatmen trap along their body and under their wings is a definite trout trigger. Make sure you use bright, reflective body materials, beads, and Mylar in your patterns to take advantage of this trigger point.
- Immature water boatmen haven't developed their dark wings. They have a light overall color scheme with mottled backs. Despite their small size, immature boatmen still have prominent eyes.

Backswimmers

Class: Insecta
Order: Hemiptera
Family: Notonectidae

Backswimmers are the bigger, nastier distant cousin of the water boatman. Completely predaceous, backswimmers move through the water using the same rowing motion as their smaller boatman relatives. They feed on anything they can, including other aquatic insects and even small fish.

The backswimmers in my aquarium seemed to have a particular taste for water boatmen. They grasped the boatmen using their two short, mantis-like legs, tucking them along their underbody, similar to how a mother holds an infant. The similarity ended there. The backswimmers would then stab their long, narrow proboscis into the boatmen, injecting an enzyme that turns their body tissue into a fluid. Once liquefied, the backswimmers drank the boatmen's insides like a Slurpee. So much for family loyalty. Be warned: If handled aggressively, backswimmers use this same process to inflict a painful bite, on the same level as a wasp or hornet sting. I am fortunate to have not yet been bitten, so I am relying on the experiences of those who have.

Predaceous backswimmers have a light back and a dark, usually olive belly. Handle backswimmers with care, as they are capable of inflicting a nasty bite.

Although widespread across North America, there are only approximately thirty species of backswimmers. They are not as commonly seen as their smaller water boatman cousins. Chances are you will see boatmen more than backswimmers when you are on the water.

For many years, I was led to believe that trout won't eat backswimmers. I have since found this to be false. On my local lakes, trout love backswimmers, particularly during the fall. As they are in the water bug family, backswimmers have a similar life cycle to water boatmen, so they are typically active at the same time. A boatman-backswimmer combination is one of my favorite early spring or fall fly combinations, especially on a washing line setup using a larger foam-based backswimmer pattern on the point.

Shape

- Backswimmers have the same oval-shaped body and head as a water boatman. The tip of their abdomen comes to more of a tapered point than the more-rounded end of a boatman.
- The raptorial front legs of a backswimmer resemble those of a praying mantis and are used to grasp and hold prey.
- At rest, backswimmers hold their long, hinged, feathered, oar-like legs at a 45-degree angle, swept-forward position so when they attack, their first stroke immediately pulls them forward. You can use this unique leg position to help separate backswimmers from water boatmen.
- Mature backswimmers fold their light-colored wings flat along their back.

Size

- Compared to water boatmen, backswimmers are large, reaching up to ¾ inch at maturity. As I fish mature backswimmers most often, I tie my patterns on size 8 and 10 standard-shank hooks.

Behavior

- Backswimmers, as their name implies, swim upside down. I factor this behavior into my patterns, tying the majority of them to ride upside down.
- At rest, backswimmers often hang, head down, at the surface. The tiny hairs at the tip of their abdomen pierce the water's surface so they can extract oxygen while they lie in wait for their next victim to pass below them.
- As backswimmers lack gills, they are reliant on atmospheric air. They use the same respiration process as water boatmen. As a result, backswimmers prefer shallow-water habitat.
- Backswimmers are completely predaceous, feeding on just about everything that comes within striking distance.
- Avoid handling a backswimmer if at all possible. Their bite packs a nasty wallop. Should a backswimmer land in your boat or on your pontoon boat or float tube, use a small aquarium net if you have to handle one.
- As with their smaller boatman cousins, backswimmers can only fly after their final molt. Like boatmen, they take flight to mate and migrate. Returning backswimmers plummet into the lake, leaving distinct raindrop-like rings in their wake. Sometimes they remain at the surface; other times they scull head-first to the bottom to hunt or deposit their eggs onto the vegetation.

- Backswimmers are capable swimmers and can move at a clip if they have to. I use the same fly line choices and retrieves for backswimmers as I do for water boatmen.

Color

- Backswimmer coloration is the opposite of water boatmen. Mature backswimmers have a predominantly white to cream back with black markings, a dark olive underbelly, a light olive head, and large dark red to maroon eyes. Their elongated hind legs typically match their body color. As with boatman patterns, I believe adding a splash of red to any backswimmer pattern is essential.
- The shoulder area of a mature backswimmer features a black wineglass-shaped marking. I use a black permanent marker on my backswimmer patterns to create these marbled dorsal markings.
- Backswimmers swim and suspend at the surface upside down. Their light back helps camouflage them against the surface reflection, while their dark olive body helps them blend into the dark water. It is a color scheme that serves them well when they hunt or need to avoid predators.
- The air bubble backswimmers trap along their body and under their wings gives them a shiny appearance. Use backswimmer patterns that incorporate reflective materials to suggest this effect.
- Immature backswimmers are predominantly white. Their red eyes are still a prominent feature.

Zooplankton

One of the reasons trout make such an excellent species to catch with a fly is their preference for small food. When trout eat little things, it takes a while to get full, so they have to feed often. Every time a trout opens its mouth to feed, we are provided with another opportunity to coax it into taking one of our flies. At times, however, when trout target minute zooplankton, they are taking this feeding behavior to the extreme. For many years when I found trout feeding on zooplankton, fishing was difficult, if not impossible. My best success came by stripping or hanging leeches. While I would prefer trout feed on slightly larger prey, I have since developed my presentation skills and tactics to better cope with this challenging-to-match food source.

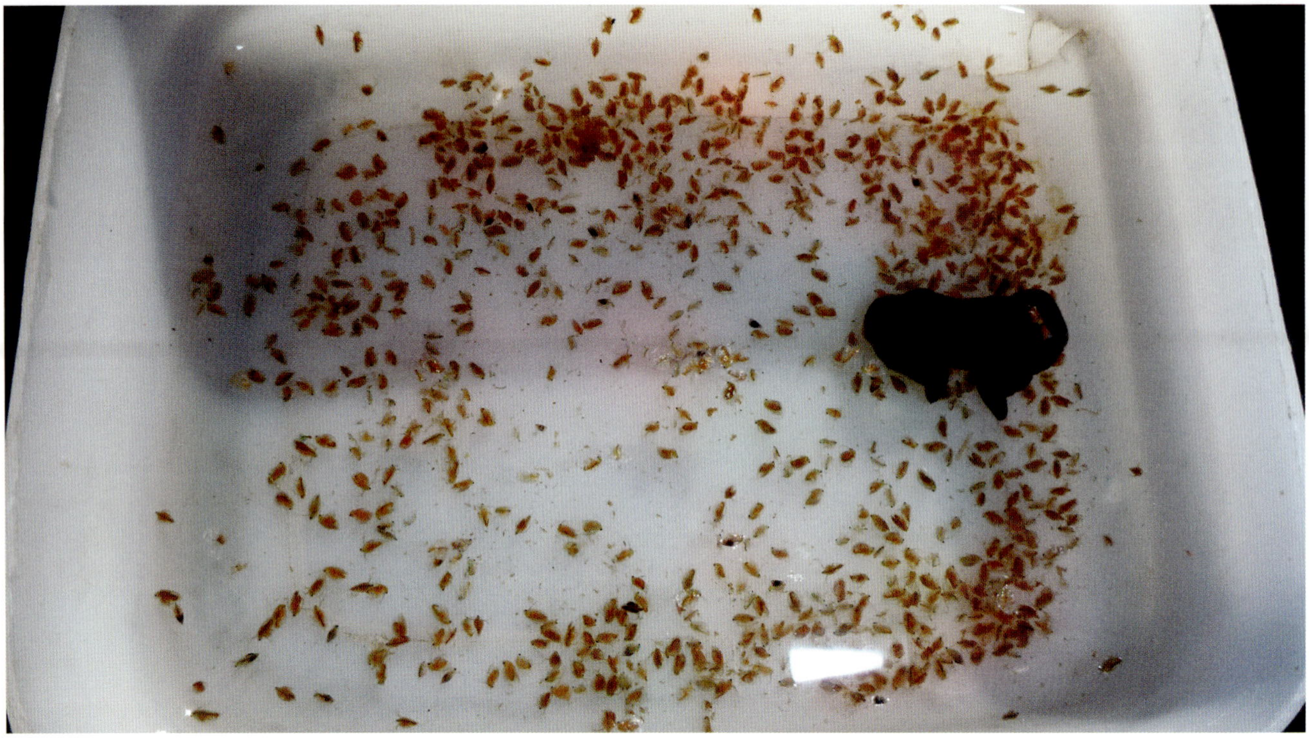

Despite their tiny size, zooplankton, such as *Daphnia* and *Bosmina*, are an essential food source for trout in stillwater, particularly during late summer and into early fall.

Zooplankton are at the base of the food chain. They inhabit oceans, lakes, rivers, and ponds. Despite their tiny size, they support animals many times their size: whales and sharks in the sea, trout in lakes. Zooplankton is an easy-to-eat, calorie-rich food source. Some zooplankton species scoot and dart, while others simply drift and go with the flow. It doesn't matter if they move or drift, zooplankton are no match for a trout. Trout simply glide through dense concentrations of zooplankton, straining them through their gill rakers.

A collage of organisms make up zooplankton, including juvenile scuds, the larval stages of insects, even fish. In stillwaters, there are four main groups: protozoa, rotifers, and two classes of crustaceans: cladocerans and copepods. Cladocerans, including *Cyclops*, *Bosmina*, and *Daphnia*, or water fleas, all fall within the class Crustacea, which also includes scuds and crayfish. In my local lakes, I see *Daphnia* and *Bosmina* most often.

Shape

- Zooplankton come in a variety of shapes, most of them alien-like. Thankfully trout don't seem to focus on any one particular shape.

Size

- Zooplankton are minute, usually ⅛ inch or smaller.
- I don't recommend tying any patterns tiny enough to match any specific zooplankton size.

Behavior

- Zooplankton are predators. They feed on phytoplankton, detritus, and each other.
- The largest concentrations of phytoplankton and zooplankton live in the limnetic zone. Trout spend time in this zone when unsettled and during the warm summer months into early fall, when water temperatures are high and oxygen levels are low. When trout are feeding heavily on zooplankton, it is usually a sign that they are spending the majority of their time in deeper water in the main lake basin or along the drop-off edges.
- Zooplankton and the phytoplankton they primarily feed upon are light sensitive. During the daylight hours, they descend into the depths, rising at night to feed in the dark.
- Trout are not the only zooplankton predator. *Chaoborus* larvae feed almost exclusively on zooplankton. It is common to find *Chaoborus* larvae and zooplankton mixed within a throat pump sample.
- Some zooplankton species don't move much, if at all. Other species such as *Daphnia*, or water fleas, are quite active, bouncing around like miniature pinballs.
- As with active *Chaoborus* larvae, movement may be a critical key trout use to help locate zooplankton.
- During the warmer summer months into early fall, clouds of zooplankton stack up along the thermocline. The difference in water temperature is a formidable barrier. In ideal conditions, stacked zooplankton help you to locate the thermocline, as they display as a band on a sounder.

Color

- Zooplankton come in a range of colors, including shades of orange, green, red, and pink.
- Trout can become selective to a particular zooplankton color. Matching the predominant zooplankton color is usually the best approach to catching trout.
- As fluorescent colors stand out in deep, dark water, I have had success stripping bright attractor patterns such as Blobs, Boobies, FABs, and Wotsits on fast-sinking lines.
- You can also try suspending size 10 and 12 beadhead Blobs that match the color of the predominant zooplankton below an indicator in deep water. I have used this technique in my local waters, even in Argentina, with excellent results.
- Hanging brightly colored Blobs under indicators is my most consistent zooplankton presentation technique but doesn't work all of the time.
- Natural patterns such as Pheasant Tails with hot spots, beads, and Mirage Opal Mylar shellbacks and wing cases also work well suspended beneath an indicator.

Crayfish

Phylum: Arthropoda
Subphylum: Crustacea
Order: Decapoda

Since I was young, whenever I see a crayfish, I can't resist picking it up. Stillwater trout seem to have the same reaction when they see one too. Crayfish are a large, calorie-rich food source trout seldom pass up. Unfortunately, from a stillwater trout food perspective, crayfish aren't all that widespread or they would be higher up on my priority list. I don't see a lot of crayfish in the lakes I frequent in western North America, although I am sure they are present, at least in some of them. The Midwest and Great Lakes region is North America's crayfish epicenter, home to the largest crayfish concentrations on the continent. Calcium-rich waters provide ideal crayfish habitat. Crayfish, as with all crustaceans, need high volumes of calcium for exoskeleton development.

Although primarily scavengers, crayfish have a diverse appetite. They are capable of eating most things they come across, including small fish, tadpoles, aquatic insects, and other invertebrates. I recall watching several crayfish in a small Manitoba trout lake eating dragonfly nymphs as they migrated over a rocky boat launch toward shore to emerge.

Although not present in every lake, crayfish, where present, are a welcome food source for stillwater trout, especially smaller juvenile crayfish.

Crayfish have a short, two- to three-year life cycle but in ideal conditions can live much longer. They mate in the spring, and the female carries the fertilized eggs inside her body at first before transferring them externally, storing them under her tail. The eggs look like dark split shot or berries. Some use the term "berried up" when referring to the gravid females. Depending on environmental factors such as water temperature, the eggs hatch within two to twenty weeks. Upon hatching, the juvenile crayfish cling to mom until they have completed their second molt. With their second molt complete, the young crayfish leave their mother to fend for themselves. Only a few survive the steep learning curve to adulthood.

Shape

- Crayfish resemble miniature lobsters, featuring a fused thorax, or cephalothorax, covered by a protective carapace.
- Crayfish have four pairs of legs and prominent eyes and antennae, along with a pair of pinchers that they use for foraging and as potent defensive weapons, as anyone who has mishandled a crayfish can attest. Crayfish are capable of regenerating any lost appendages.

Size

- Although capable of reaching large sizes, up to 5 inches or more, most adult crayfish average 3 to 4 inches in length
- Due to their inexperience and lifestyle, trout target young, immature crayfish. Young crayfish range in size from 1 inch to 2½ inches. Hook sizes 10 through 4 work best.

Behavior

- Crayfish live along the bottom. Snag-resistant patterns tied to ride upside down using jig hooks, dumbbell eyes, or balanced flies work best.
- Patterns tied to represent fleeing crayfish typically outperform realistic flies tied to suggest a crayfish in a "pinchers up" defensive pose.
- Mature adults are primarily nocturnal. During the day, they prefer to hide among rocks, weeds, and sunken logs.
- Young, immature crayfish tend to be more active during the day, as they have yet to learn the benefits of a nocturnal lifestyle. It is best to imitate smaller immature crayfish, as they are more visible and easier for trout to catch.
- It is not unusual to see a recently molted crayfish eating its cast, calcium-rich exoskeleton. Newly molted crayfish are shy and reclusive for approximately a week until their new exoskeleton hardens.
- As water temperature increases, so does crayfish activity. When water drops below 40°F (4°C), crayfish activity drops considerably. Late spring through early fall is the best time to use crayfish patterns and presentations.

- Crayfish appear to glide as they walk across the bottom on the tips of their four pairs of legs. If necessary, they can scurry at a high pace.
- When threatened, crayfish raise their claws and back away. Male crayfish are aggressive and often stand their ground. Less aggressive females and juveniles are more likely to flee.
- When they need to flee, adult crayfish use rapid undulations of the abdomen and fanlike telson to dart away from danger.
- It takes time for immature crayfish to learn how to use their tail-wagging propulsion system. Before developing this skill, juvenile crayfish use a combined pincher and leg paddling motion to flee
- The horizontal retrieve path of a sinking line makes it the best choice when imitating crayfish. Use a combination of hand twists mixed in with quick strips.
- Twitching or lifting the rod tip sharply jumps and accelerates the fly, suggesting a fleeing or swimming crayfish.
- Even if crayfish aren't present, you can catch trout using crayfish patterns retrieved at a pace to trigger a take.
- Flies utilizing soft mobile materials such as rabbit fur or squirrel hair do an excellent job suggesting a juvenile crayfish's swimming motion and profile. These materials are a common crayfish pattern component.

Color

- Common crayfish colors include olive, brown, and rusty brown.
- Some crayfish feature brightly colored pinchers or pincher tips, such as bright orange, blue, or red.
- Juvenile crayfish grow fast, molting anywhere from six to ten times in their first year. Recently molted crayfish are pale and easy to spot. Trout and other gamefish show a preference for recently molted, or "shredder," juvenile crayfish.

OTHER OCCASIONAL FOOD SOURCES

Snails (Order: Gastropoda)

Trout can and do eat snails. When trout fixate on snails, it can be frustrating. I have caught trout using snail patterns, but in my experience, it is a low-percentage game. You can tell if trout are eating snails because their bellies feel crunchy or their anal vent is red and swollen from passing the indigestible shell.

Snails prefer to live in alkaline lakes with high concentrations of calcium, which is an essential element for shell development. For the most part, they remain hidden and out of view. There are times when snails migrate, exposing themselves in large numbers, for seemingly unexplained reasons. They also cling to the underside of the

Snails can be seasonally important and a key food source in some lakes. Overall, however, they are an occasional food source for stillwater trout.
DAVE HUGHES

water's surface in warmer months. Wind-drifting a snail pattern on a floating line with or without an indicator can work well at these times. Suspending a snail pattern under an indicator with no movement has also worked for me.

As snails move so slowly, anytime they expose themselves, they are vulnerable. Although they can reach large sizes, trout can only eat small, ¼ inch or less, snails. Common snail colors include black, brown, olive, tan, and yellow. Mottled color schemes are typical. I have a few tapered peacock-based snail patterns in my fly box tied on standard-shank size 12 and 10 hooks. I rarely use them, but they are there if needed.

Terrestrials

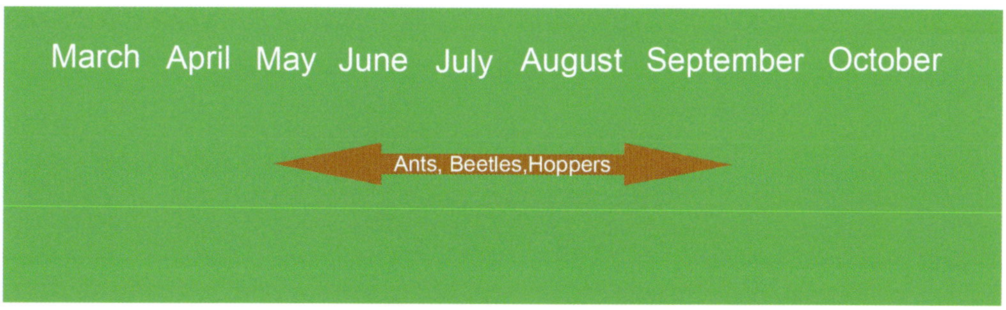

Terrestrial insects are not aquatic. They live around lakes, and their habits and activity unintentionally land them on the water. Once a terrestrial ends up on the water, it's usually a death sentence, either by drowning or digestion within a fish's stomach. Throughout the open-water season, a variety of land-borne insects wind up on the water. Trout, being opportunistic predators, willingly rise and take them. In most instances, this sporadic attention isn't worth worrying about. However, when large numbers end up on the surface, terrestrials can become an important localized food source. As there is always a chance of trout feeding on terrestrials, I always have a selection of patterns stashed in my fly box, just in case.

Ants, beetles, and grasshoppers are the most common stillwater terrestrials on the waters I fish.

I usually find ants and beetles the dominant terrestrials on lakes with high concentrations of trees and bushes. Grasshoppers prefer long grass, so you are more likely to use hopper patterns on lakes nestled among rolling meadows and fields. You may have other terrestrial insects of importance on your local waters, and it pays to do a bit of research to find out what terrestrials are unique to your favorite lakes. One of the best ways to figure out which terrestrials are important is to pay attention to local river and stream anglers. Terrestrials are a significant food source on rivers and streams, particularly late summer into early fall, when terrestrial growth and activity peaks.

Ants (Order: Hymenoptera; Family: Formicidae)

Ants are a busy insect that are always on the go doing something. Depending on the species, mature, winged males (drones) and females (new queens) leave the nest in large swarms, flying off to establish new colonies. Although most ants are small, less than ⅜ inch, I run across large, inch-long carpenter ants most often. Winged carpenter ants leave their downed rotting timber nests during the first hot stretch of the season; in western Canada, that's usually on, or just after, Mother's Day. The adults fall onto the water or attempt to fly over vast stretches of the lake and, becoming exhausted, drop to the lake below. This large food source soon causes a feeding frenzy.

After a few flying ant events, trout can become conditioned and will respond positively to an ant pattern. As with any food source trout have dined upon for a while,

Ants are often a focused, isolated food source on lakes. After feeding heavily on ants, trout often go off the bite, as the ant's hard body, combined with the formic acid within their body, takes a while to digest.

they can become selective. Only an ant that is the right size, shape, and color will work. The challenge with ants is that after prolonged feeding, trout often go off the bite. Ants are hard-bodied, and combined with the formic acid within their bodies, it takes a while for trout to digest them. Perhaps trout have a reaction similar to me after I have had a spicy meal. Although I enjoy a little spice in my food, I usually pay for it the next day.

Beetles (Order: Coleoptera)

Over 40 percent of the world's insects are beetles. That's a staggering percentage. In my experience, it takes a little longer to figure out if trout are taking beetles. Unlike swarming ants, beetles tend to trickle onto the water in small numbers that slowly add up to draw the trout's attention. You may start to see trout rise with increasing frequency, but there doesn't appear to be much, if anything, on the surface. Beetles ride low in the water and so aren't easy to spot, compounding the problem. Our first response is to suggest an aquatic insect by trying an emerger or adult pattern.

I recall one warm afternoon where enough fish were rising that I couldn't resist trying to coax a few to a dry fly. I began using patterns to match aquatic insects, followed by water boatman and backswimmer patterns, all with no success. After running out of ideas, I switched to a small soft-hackle coupled with a slow hand twist retrieve to keep it just below the surface. After about half an hour, I finally hooked a fish. After careful use of a throat pump, I found it had about a dozen size 14 black beetles in it. This discovery finally opened my eyes, and I began to notice a reasonable number of beetles on the water that had been blown downwind from a stand of trees.

If enough beetles end up on the water, stillwater trout will target them. Unlike other terrestrials, in my experience, beetles seem to trickle onto the water, so it is not as obvious to determine if they are present and if trout have discovered them.
RICK HAFELE

Grasshoppers (Order: Orthoptera)

I love it when fish eat grasshoppers. The takes are aggressive, and owing to the hopper's large average size, they can coax usually wary trout to the surface. Hoppers seem to have a leap-first, look-second mentality. This behavior mixed in with a breeze makes for some great late summer through early fall dry-fly fishing when hopper populations peak. Hoppers hit the water with a distinct splat that cruising trout sense using their lateral lines. Once a hopper hits the water, it is helpless. It struggles to hop out of trouble, but its rear jumping legs can't gain any purchase on the lake's surface to push off. It is doomed.

Grassy banks are excellent places to prospect when hoppers are active, especially those that slope off quickly into deep water. Trout cruise along the narrow, shallow water to deep water transition, pouncing on any hapless hopper that ends up on the water. In these instances, bouncing hopper patterns off the bank onto the water so they splat on the water like the naturals can pull trout from quite a distance.

Grasshoppers seem to have a leap-first, look-second philosophy that often gets them on the water. On lakes bordering grassy meadows, grasshoppers can be an important seasonal food source.

CHAPTER TAKEAWAYS

- Using your smartphone is a great way to catalog various stillwater food sources. Smartphones allow you to take both photos and videos for future reference and fly pattern design.
- Use four common reference points to help understand what trout eat in lakes: size, shape, behavior, and color. You can use the same traits when buying or tying stillwater trout flies.

- Those organisms that spend their entire life in the lake I refer to as staples, bread-and-butter food sources that trout feed upon in the absence of a hatch.
- Staples also include any aquatic insect with a prolonged aquatic stage within their life cycle or hatch in large numbers over the season, such as chironomids, dragonflies, and damselflies.
- Several factors influence digestion rates, including water temperature and its effect on the metabolic rate of the trout, how hard or soft the body of the food item is, and what percentage of the trout's stomach is full.
- An incomplete life cycle consists of three stages: egg, nymph, and adult. Aquatic insects with incomplete life cycles include mayflies, dragonflies, and damselflies.
- A complete life cycle, or metamorphosis, consists of egg, larva, pupa, and adult. There is no nymphal stage. Chironomids and caddisflies have complete life cycles.
- Many stillwater food invertebrates must molt by shedding their exoskeleton to grow. Recently molted invertebrates are soft and pale in color, making them easier for trout to spot.
- Chironomids are the most important food source of trout in productive lakes, outnumbering all other aquatic insects combined.
- Orange is an important scud color. Scuds infected with a parasite have a small, focused orange dot on their back. Pregnant scuds hold their orange-colored eggs in an underbelly pouch called the marsupium. Completely orange scuds are dead.
- Scuds swim with their body extended with only the tip of their telson hanging down. A curled-up scud is either dead, feeding, or resting.
- When touched, leeches curl up in a defensive ball. Trout often bump leeches to induce them to curl up so they are easier to consume. Many short strikes to our leech patterns are a result of trout trying to bump the pattern so it curls up like the naturals.
- *Chaoborus*, zooplankton, and snails are the most challenging stillwater food sources to imitate consistently.
- Dragonflies, damselflies, and some caddis species crawl from the water to emerge. All other aquatic insect species hatch at the surface.
- Avoid handling backswimmers if at all possible. Their bite packs a nasty wallop. Should a backswimmer land in your boat or on your pontoon boat or float tube, use a small aquarium net if you have to handle it.
- Terrestrial insects are not aquatic. They live around lakes, and their habits and activity unintentionally land them on the water. Ants, beetles, and grasshoppers are the most common stillwater terrestrials.

CHAPTER 7

HOW TO FIND TROUT IN LAKES

When I began spending more and more time targeting lakes, my initial trips were frustrating. The visible clues I used to guide me on rivers and streams were gone. The vast expanse of water was intimidating, and it offered few clues where the fish might be. Unlike a river or stream, I couldn't wade a lake very effectively, if at all. Some lakes were so big I couldn't even see all of the water. I was lost and didn't have any idea as to where I should go. Decisions were arbitrary. Should I try the right side of the lake? Perhaps I should try the left side this time? Or, as it seemed in the beginning, always go to the opposite end of the lake—the fishing has to be better there, right? I knew if I wanted to reduce my frustration and have consistent success fly fishing lakes, I

The vast expanse of a lake can be intimidating. At first glance, lakes seem to offer few clues as to where the fish might be.

Stillwater trout behave differently from river and stream trout, but they still have the same fundamental needs: comfort, protection, and food.

needed to figure out a better approach, some sort of system that I could apply to dissect not only my local lakes but other lakes and other fish besides trout.

One of the first things I realized was that stillwater trout behave differently than their moving water counterparts. Stillwater trout are cruisers, always on the move. Unlike river and stream trout, they don't hang out in holes or behind certain rocks, or hold tight against an undercut bank. Stillwater trout are constantly on the move, swimming, eating, and, on occasion, mating and reproducing.

As I continued developing my skills finding stillwater trout, it became apparent that they had the same basic needs as river and stream fish despite their behavioral differences. As with many successful river and stream anglers, I built the foundation of my process around searching for areas that offered one or all of the three fundamental needs common to all trout: comfort, protection, and food. Using this three-pronged approach, coupled with my powers of observation, I began to find trout consistently. It is an approach that continues to work to this day. Every time I am on the water, it is a system that I continue to refine, develop, and tweak.

COMFORT

To me, comfort is arguably the most critical factor when trying to locate stillwater trout. Comfort factors provide trout with the basics requirements they need to survive, so their metabolism functions at peak efficiency and their natural rhythms remain uninterrupted. If trout aren't comfortable, they become stressed. Environmental factors such as water temperature, weather, and how lakes function seasonally also influence trout behavior. If any of these influences aren't to a trout's liking, they are unlikely to feed and become pretty tough to catch.

Water Temperature

Water temperature is perhaps the essential comfort factor, and it has a significant influence on my fishing. Water temperature determines where I fish, my presentation depth, and my retrieve speed. The colder the water temperature, the slower my retrieve. When the water temperature is cold, static, or near static, indicator presentations are tough to beat, such as early spring, immediately after ice-off, and again in the fall, just before freeze-up. When I ask friends for a fishing report, one of my first questions is always, "What was the water temperature?" If they didn't make a note of or pay attention to the water temperature, I feel they missed a vital piece of the puzzle in trying to figure out trout location and activity.

So why is water temperature so important? It isn't about keeping trout warm or cold. Rather, the amount of dissolved oxygen water can hold is linked directly to temperature. The warmer the water temperature, the less dissolved oxygen it holds. Some fish are active over a wide temperature range. Their metabolism has evolved

Water temperature has a significant influence on trout activity and location within a lake.

and adapted to perform at both low and high temperatures. In comparison, trout have a relatively narrow temperature range. This narrow temperature window is one of the reasons they don't compete well with other fish, such as perch and suckers.

Every fish on the planet has a preferred temperature range. Within their preferred range, trout can comfortably extract the oxygen they need to survive, as their metabolism is functioning at peak efficiency. Trout are feeding, digesting, and feeding again. Although each specific trout and char species has a preferred range, I look for temperatures between 50°F and 65°F. Temperatures below 50°F usually require slower presentations. When water temperature begins to reach the high 60s, trout reduce or cease feeding, as the reduced oxygen content causes stress. You should avoid targeting stillwater trout and char in high water temperatures. In addition, 50°F is a critical temperature for insect emergences. In the spring, once the water temperature reaches 50°F, you can expect the first significant emergences of the season to begin.

Preferred stillwater trout and char temperature ranges are:

- Brook trout: 40°F (5°C) to 50°F (10°C)
- Brown trout: 55°F (13°C) to 70°F (21°C)
- Cutthroat trout: 50°F (10°C) to 60°F (16°C)
- Lake trout: 45°F (7°C) to 50°F (10°C)
- Rainbow trout: 50°F (10°C) to 55°F (13°C)

In the Northern Hemisphere, north bays with dark, muddy bottoms are the first to warm due to how the Earth sits on its axis. Right after ice-off, these are the prime places to explore, as the dark bottom absorbs the sun's energy, warming the surrounding water. It is amazing how a water temperature variation of only one or two degrees makes all the difference. Conversely, when water temperature increases, and dissolved oxygen decreases, trout struggle to extract the oxygen they need. They become stressed. If possible, the trout retreat to deeper, colder, oxygenated water. Should you catch a trout when water temperatures are high, acidosis often sets in. Trout become difficult to revive, as their white and red blood cells are out of balance. They slowly swim away, unable to recover, and die soon after. Increased mortality is why fishing trout lakes in the heat of summer is risky and, in most instances, should be avoided.

The moment I am on the water, I check my electronics to see what the surface temperature is. If you don't use or have a sounder, make sure you have a handheld thermometer. I carry a small traditional analog thermometer or Deptherm mounted to approximately 25 feet of cord, and lower it into the water to record temperatures at varying depths. In the early summer, water temperatures in the shallows begin to rise and trout begin sliding out into deeper water. Attached to a cord, I use either my thermometer or Deptherm to plumb the depths looking for temperatures between 50°F (10°C) and 65°F (18°C) along deep-water edges of drop-offs and points. Once I find a suitable temperature, I determine the best tactics, line choices, and retrieves to target the specific zone to catch fish.

Whenever you head out onto the water, using a thermometer, Deptherm, or sounder to determine the water temperature should be one of your initial priorities.

Springs provide cold oxygenated water and, as a result, concentrate trout, especially when water temperatures are high. On lakes such as Oregon's Upper Klamath, there are several shallow springs percolating air bubbles up to the surface. These types of springs are easy to find and target, but in my experience, most springs don't willingly reveal their location. You can use sudden drops in water temperature or a somewhat circular color change in an area as possible clues that there may be a spring below. If several boats are anchored around a specific, apparently isolated, area they might be sitting on a spring. Once located, target both the spring itself and the water immediately around it. Once you find a spring, mark its location via triangulating landmarks or drop a waypoint on your GPS so you can find it again. On many stillwaters, spring locations are a closely guarded secret. Locals rarely, if ever, surrender their location.

Underwater springs don't always bubble up to the surface like this one on Oregon's Klamath Lake. They are typically hard to locate. Springs provide consistent oxygenated water and usually hold trout, especially during the warm summer months.

Along with springs, not all lakes feature inflow or outflow rivers and streams. Most productive lakes are landlocked. This feature is what makes them so productive, as any of the nutrients that enter and remain in the lake create a rich compost-like base for aquatic plants to grow.

Where present, trout are attracted to inflow streams of all sizes for a variety of reasons, including current and cold oxygenated water. The current tongue masks the trout's presence while providing food and access to spawning habitat. Trout use inflow and outflow streams to spawn or follow other spawning fish up- or downriver to feed on their eggs and flesh. As the offspring hatch and migrate downstream, trout wait at the mouth to feed on them. I have had some great fishing concentrating on the inflow streams of large, typically unproductive lakes when salmon fry and smolt migrate into the lake as they begin their journey to the sea. One moment all is calm, and seconds later the water explodes as trout slash through schools of salmon smolt or fry, breaking them into smaller, easier to target groups.

Inflow and outflow streams offer several presentation options. When targeting an inflowing stream, I like to position myself on the deep-water edge of the alluvial fan or delta that forms from the debris and sediment brought into the lake. You can also fish inflow streams from the shore. Concentrate your efforts on the primary inflow current and the adjacent current seams. When fishing an outflow stream, you can walk and wade the nearby shallows as you search for cruising fish. It is common to

River and creek mouths provide all three fundamental stillwater trout needs: comfort, protection, and food.

Although not always present on all lakes, creek and river mouths are usually worth prospecting.

use flies intended to suggest river and stream invertebrates, as they are often carried out into the lake by the inflowing current.

One of the unique properties of water is that when it is of differing temperatures, it won't mix. You can use this property to locate old creek channels in reservoirs and impoundments. As dense, cold water enters a lake, it hugs the bottom, following the old creek channel for a distance until it becomes the same temperature as the surrounding water and mixes. A thermometer is useful to identify these oxygenated current tongues. In some lakes, the old winding creek bed may be less than 10 feet wide. Being able to find these narrow confines and place your flies there consistently can be the difference between the odd fish and a lot of fish. As with springs, once you locate an old creek channel, do your best to mark it so you can find it again.

Aquatic weeds are another oxygen source that attract trout. During the day, aquatic weeds photosynthesize by using the sun's energy to extract carbon dioxide from the water. This extraction process produces carbohydrates that the plant uses as food, generating oxygen in return. The photosynthesis process stops at night, but the respiration process continues generating oxygen.

Stillwater trout seldom stray far from weeds and weed beds. Weeds provide critical habitat for all sorts of trout food, protection, and, through photosynthesis, oxygen.
BRIAN CHAN

In addition to providing oxygen, aquatic weeds help protect trout and are home to a wide variety of trout food. Because of this, I consider weeds a stillwater prime lie, and barring extreme water temperatures, trout seldom stray from a healthy weed patch. In late fall or when the lake is iced over and covered with snow, sunlight penetration is reduced or eliminated and plants begin to die. Dying plants consume oxygen, and as a result, trout shy away from them. During the fall months, target green, healthy weed beds. Avoid brown, dying or decaying weeds.

Water temperature also influences trout food. Aquatic insect activity and emergence primarily center on water temperature. Some insects emerge when the water temperature reaches a certain point. Other insects curb their development at one temperature to allow others in their age class to catch up. When the water temperature increases to another trigger point, they then emerge all at once.

Water temperature has a significant influence on insect activity and hatch timings. Once a lake reaches 50°F, you can expect to see the season's first significant hatches.

I use 50°F (10°C) as a critical temperature trigger point, as this is when the significant emergences of the season kick off. Although tiny chironomids soon begin to hatch after ice-off, the first hatches of the season don't begin in earnest until water temperatures reach this 50°F threshold. Smaller insects such as chironomids, mayflies, and damselflies hatch first. Larger insects such as caddis and dragonflies are the last to hatch within a season.

Seasonal Changes

Water temperature plays a crucial role in how lakes function throughout the year. Seasonally, water temperature, and the changes it initiates, has a significant influence on trout location, behavior, and activity. As stillwater fly fishers, we need to be acutely aware of how lakes work throughout the year. You should develop a solid working knowledge and understanding of what happens to a lake throughout the year along with seasonal events, including turnover, summer stratification, winterkill, and spring kill. This critical knowledge helps you logically predict what lakes to fish, when to visit certain lakes, and where to concentrate your efforts throughout the season. I encourage you to invest the time to learn all you can about the dynamic world stillwater trout inhabit, starting with chapter 5, "How Lakes Work."

Weather Change

Trout, as with other fish, are sensitive to weather change, particularly cold fronts. When the weather changes, trout reduce or cease feeding altogether. Fly fishers and other anglers have long been curious as to what causes this behavioral change. I have always had an enormous interest in learning the reasons, and have devoted a considerable amount of time studying the writings of others, searching the internet, and discussing the issue with biologists. To date, my investigation has revealed a wide range of answers and theories, some plausible, others not so much.

A trout uses its swim bladder to regulate buoyancy, filling it by extracting oxygen from the water to increase buoyancy or reducing oxygen within the swim bladder to decrease buoyancy. This process helps trout swim efficiently by using less energy. The swim bladder can also detect, produce, and reflect sound waves. Sound wave reflection is what an electronic sounder picks up to mark fish. Some believe that changing barometric pressure has a strong influence on a trout's swim bladder and its ability to regulate its buoyancy and remain comfortable. A happy, comfortable fish is more likely to feed, providing us with a better chance of catching it.

Years ago, I used to scuba dive. One thing you learn when diving is the influence of pressure to avoid severe injury. When you descend from the surface, water pressure increases. At sea level, the pressure on us is one atmosphere, or 14.7 pounds. At 33 feet (10 meters), the pressure doubles to 29.4 pounds, a significant change. To remain comfortable and pain-free while diving, we must equalize the pressure on either side of our eardrums and mask. This knowledge also ensures we minimize our time in deep water to avoid increased nitrogen levels in our bloodstream.

Weather change and cold fronts, in particular, have a strong influence on a stillwater trout's feeding behavior and overall activity.

If a change in the weight of the Earth's atmosphere on water unsettles trout, then a sudden change from shallow to deep water should also have a negative impact, as often happens when you hook a fish along a shoal edge and it rockets into the depths. In this example the trout experiences a significant water pressure increase on its swim bladder, as opposed to a gradual reduction in barometric pressure due to approaching weather. I still believe changing atmospheric pressure plays a role, but it probably isn't the only reason for the downturn in fish activity.

Before a system moves in, fishing is typically steady. As the front approaches, trout feeding activity often increases, as though the fish sense the approaching change and begin stocking up to withstand a period of inactivity until conditions stabilize once again. Once the change occurs, fish activity ceases, as though someone threw a switch. At this time, fishing is tough. I believe trout retreat to deeper water until the change passes and their environment settles and stabilizes. When weather change negatively impacts trout activity and feeding, I fish deep, such as the deep-water transitions along drop-offs and points. I also slow down my presentations to compensate for the trout's reduced willingness to chase a fly.

As anglers, we are always looking for a single answer to the weather change riddle. I don't believe it is a single reason but a combination of several factors. Some possible reasons include changing atmospheric pressure, changing light levels, cold air reducing surface temperature and causing displacement, water current, and an increase in turbidity due to wind. There are probably other reasons only the trout are aware of. I look at weather change and its impact on fishing as though the trout's world was a snow globe. When conditions change, Mother Nature gives the snow globe a good shake. Until the transition period ends and the trout's environment stabilizes, fishing is challenging.

Lunar Phase

As with weather change, lunar phase is a complex riddle that can have a strong influence on trout behavior and location. I know of many anglers who use Solunar Tables. They adamantly believe in their ability to predict trout activity identified through minor and major periods, so much so that if a table lists no minor or major periods for a particular day, they won't go fishing.

I believe the lunar phase does influence trout behavior. When I look back at my records, my best fishing usually occurred during the period preceding a full moon. My toughest periods have been during a full moon and days immediately following. There are many theories and opinions as to why this is the case. Some believe that during a full moon, the bright light provided an opportunity for trout to feed all night. Consequently, when we hit the water in the morning, their bellies are full. The trout remain inactive until they finish digesting, refusing our best presentations and flies.

When the moon was full, I ventured out on many occasions, full of optimism of what the night ahead might bring. But my optimism was short-lived. On average, fishing was no better than it was during the day. As I thought about it, trout prey, such as scuds, are light-sensitive, preferring to hide among weeds and under bottom debris to avoid exposure and becoming trout food. Trout foraging under a bright full moon turned out to be not as profitable as I thought.

I believe the pineal gland, sometimes referred to as a trout's third eye, plays a crucial role during a full moon. The pineal gland is part of a trout's upper brain. It allows partial transmission of light, serving as a shadow detector, which helps the trout avoid predation, and establishing daily rhythms through the release of the hormone melatonin. My research suggested melatonin regulates resting periods where trout are less active, and the initiation of a trout's eyes transfer from cones to rods. Perhaps a bright, clear moonlit sky disrupts the distribution of melatonin, a disruption that negatively influences the feeding behavior and activity of the trout. Cloudy or overcast skies reduce moonlight levels and the subsequent impact on the trout. As a result, your odds of hooking a fish or two improve.

PROTECTION

I define protection as those factors that provide trout with a sense of confidence and security to feed. When a trout feels secure and protected, it is more likely to focus on feeding than predator avoidance. The critical protection factors I pay the most attention to include surface texture, light levels, and structure such as drop-offs, points of land, sunken islands or humps, and weed beds.

Surface Texture

A rippled water surface breaks up and defuses light. Under a rippled surface, trout venture into the shallows and feed. Think of a rippled surface as a riffle on a stream. Trout in riffles are typically easier to approach and catch.

Believe it or not, the wind is your friend when fly fishing stillwaters. Wind helps channel trout movement. Stillwater trout instinctively face into any current, including wind-induced current. As they were initially river and stream stock, it's in a stillwater trout's DNA. You can use this knowledge to predict where a fish might go when it rises or rolls at the surface. When there is no wind-induced current, trout cruise in a random manner, making it difficult to predict their direction of travel.

In the shallows, the wind not only provides surface cover for foraging trout but also churns up food. When the wind blows, I prefer, if safe to do so, to fish the downwind, windswept shore, especially rocky shorelines with adjacent weeds. The wave action dislodges all sorts of food that foraging trout are happy to take advantage of. A similar situation also occurs on the downwind side of a weed bed. The surface chop and subsurface swells knock unsuspecting invertebrates free, drifting them down to the waiting trout.

Believe it or not, wind, in moderation, is your friend when fishing lakes.

Wind often pushes and holds baitfish against the upwind side of a weed bed. Trout take full advantage of this situation, as they are much more agile than their smaller prey. They use the weed edge and the water's surface to concentrate and trap forage fish, slashing through them with reckless abandon. This scenario also happens on the upwind side of points. Targeting the downwind side of a windswept perpendicular point can also be important. The wind creates subtle back eddies on the downwind side. The circular currents within this subtle back eddy trap and concentrate food items while also offering a place to tuck in and escape the wind. During the 2007 Canadian Championships, I was able to set up several drifts through and along the outside edge of a large eddy behind a point. Once I completed the short drift, I gathered my drogue, taking a circular route back to the point to avoid rowing over any fish. I redeployed my drogue and repeated the drift. Targeting this back eddy yielded excellent results and was one of my best sessions of the tournament.

Wind also creates rotational currents at the surface, which trap food and concentrate fish. If you fish loch style, always take the time to explore wind lanes. Wind lanes always come in pairs: a flat caused by upwelling current and foam lines caused by downward currents. Trout can relate to both current types, or just one. Upwelling currents trap food at the surface and, in the case of an emergence, provide trout with a steady food source as they feed upwind. The downward current pushes down, suppressing ascending nymphs or pupae. Subsurface tactics work best in foam lines.

Although loch-style tactics provide the best opportunity to work the full length of a wind lane, you can also fish them from an anchored position. I recall fishing California's Lake Davis during a brisk wind. Chironomids were emerging, and fish concentrated in the foam lines to feed on them. Using subsurface, floating line techniques and a beadhead chironomid pupa, I concentrated my efforts in the foam line, enjoying a memorable day.

Light

Trout prefer to avoid situations that place them in direct light, preferring the protection and predatory advantage shadows and low light offer. Trout tend to feed shallow early in the day, before direct light bathes the shoals, and at the end of the day when the sun drops below the horizon. When direct sunlight strikes a shoal, trout are exposed. They often retreat to deeper water or patrol the edge of a drop-off or point where the security of deep water is a short distance away.

Water clarity and cloud cover also play a role: The clearer the water, the brighter the light, the warier the trout. Trout that inhabit crystal-clear lakes become reluctant to venture shallow, especially on calm, clear days. Unless cloud cover reduces direct light or an overwhelming concentration of food causes trout to throw caution to the wind, it is not unusual to see barren shoals. Generally, I tend to fish shallower early and late in the day. During the mid-portion of the day, I usually fish deeper.

You should also factor in the sun's travel throughout the day. In the morning, the sun's rays expose any east-facing drop-offs, shoals, or transitional edges of points, and trout may be reluctant to venture along the edges. At this time, concentrating your

Stillwater trout prefer to avoid direct light, choosing the protection and predatory advantage shadows and low light offer.

efforts along the west-facing drop-offs, shoals, and transitional edges that don't receive direct sunlight would be a wiser option. Later in the day, as the sun moves across the sky, concentrate your efforts along the western side of the lake that is now out of the direct light.

If there are no discernable steep or angled drop-offs, you can target the light lines created as the lake floor slopes gradually into deep water. As sunlight no longer reflects off the bottom, the water darkens. Trout love to cruise along the dark side of the light line, using the security of deep water to ambush prey and as an escape route.

If a lake doesn't have a defined drop-off, target the seam between light and dark water. Stillwater trout often cruise in the relative safety of the dark water immediately adjacent to the light seam.

Algae

Although an eyesore to some fly fishers, algae also offers trout an excellent source of protection. Algae is a plant. The vast majority of algae concentrates right at the surface, where it gathers to extract the sun's energy to photosynthesize. As a result, it only occupies the surface zone, typically extending down 10 feet or less. Algal concentrations also provide shade and reduce the influence of the sun's energy on the water temperature below the surface cap they create.

Although often shunned by fly fishers, surface algae provides excellent cover for foraging trout. Algal growth is most concentrated at the surface and seldom extends deeper than 10 feet.

During the summer months, when algal growth peaks, trout cruise comfortably in the relatively clear, dim water below. On some of my favorite western lakes, large chironomids begin hatching. Size 8 2XL pupa and larva patterns are standard. At this time, surface algae is thick and concentrated, but anywhere from 12 to 16 feet below trout are content feeding on staging and emerging chironomid pupae. The fishing can be outstanding. I have also had some memorable days fishing tight to the shore using small scuds, leeches, and immature water boatman patterns. Trout, content with the protection the surrounding algae provided, patrolled the shallows, pouncing on any food items they came across.

Structure

All fish relate to structure, including stillwater trout. My favorite lakes always have a mix of structure that separates and isolates shallow feeding areas from deeper main lake basins. If you target and explore structures such as drop-offs, points, sunken islands or humps, and weed beds, you should find fish.

Drop-Offs

Drop-offs are one of my favorite stillwater structures, as trout love to cruise along their edges. From here, they can make short, quick forays onto the adjacent shoal or seek the protection of the deep water adjacent to the drop-off should something startle them.

I break a drop-off into three regions: the shoal edge, the drop-off itself, and the deep water beside the drop-off. The shoal edge is worth exploring early and late in the day and during the spring and fall months. If fish aren't on the shoal adjacent to the drop-off or light or weather conditions appear to be keeping fish out of the shallows, I would then work the drop-off itself. As fish cruise the edge of the drop-off, try to position yourself so you can present your flies on an acute parallel angle to the drop-off without putting yourself directly where the fish are cruising. I target the deep side of a drop-off during the late summer when water temperatures in the shallows reduce dissolved oxygen content or if weather conditions have driven fish deep.

If you fish a lake consistently, you often learn that fish favor specific transit points on and off a shoal. Once discovered, use triangulation or the GPS function on your sounder to mark these locations so you can find them in the future.

Points

Points extend out into a lake, providing a shallow fingerlike shoal that extends out into the lake, surrounded along its sides by deep water. As with a drop-off, trout hang around points because of the deep-water cover they offer. Trout may patrol the transition along the deep-water edges or venture onto the shallow finger to feed. As discussed earlier, wind direction also plays a role in how and where I fish a point.

Sunken Islands and Humps

A sunken island or underwater hump can be a trout oasis. Trout frequently feed on and around sunken islands and humps of all sizes. They can venture onto the sunken island or hump to feed with the confidence that deep-water security surrounds them. I prefer to anchor upwind in the deep water adjacent to a sunken island or hump so I can target the edges and slopes along the sides as well as the shallow peak.

Weed Beds

Weed beds are trout magnets. They provide all three factors: comfort, protection, and food. From a protection perspective, trout use the dark background of the surrounding weeds to mask their presence. I love to fish the weed edges or over light marl patches, as this practice silhouettes and exposes my fly. If possible, I focus on any irregularities within a weed patch. Indentions, openings, weed points, and clumps of emergent or long-stemmed weeds often concentrate fish and are always worth exploring.

Hunting for Structure

Bathymetric maps, Google Maps, and Google Earth allow you to do a lot of structure hunting before you even leave the driveway. This pre-trip study pays huge dividends, allowing you to build an attack plan. When you arrive at the lake, you aren't wasting any time exploring, as you already have an idea where you want to go.

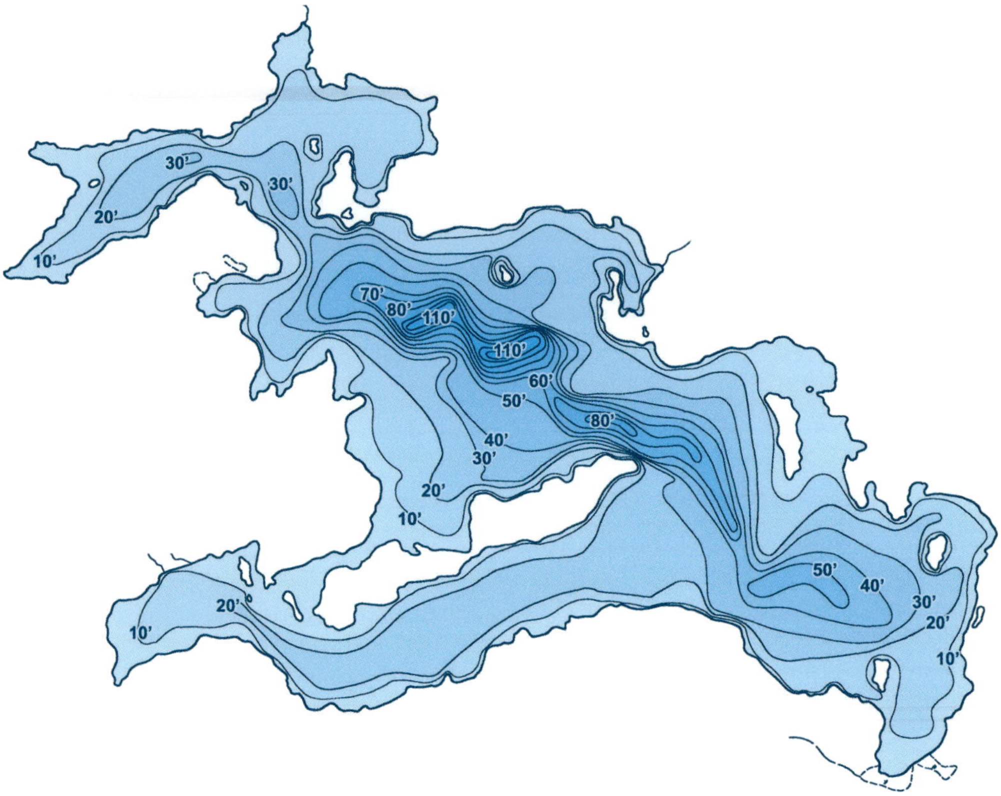

Bathymetric maps help you identify critical underwater structures such as drop-offs, shoals, sunken islands, and submerged points.
ANGLER'S ATLAS

Bathymetric Maps

I rely heavily on bathymetric, or underwater contour, maps. Bathymetric maps are available online, through mobile phone apps, via government agencies, and in regional map books. One of my favorite online sites allows you to save lake maps as PDF documents that can then be printed and taken on the water with you. You can place the printed map in a plastic sleeve available at any office supply store to protect it from the elements. The plastic sleeve also allows you to store maps of your favorite lakes in a three-ring binder.

Bathymetric maps help you identify essential structures such as shallow shoals, sunken islands, and drop-offs. Think of these areas as underwater game trails that concentrate trout. When used in conjunction with a sounder, bathymetric maps provide a high-level view of a particular lake's structure. A sounder helps identify smaller features within a specific piece of structure, often referred to as the spot within a spot. Many reasonably priced sounders feature built-in mapping software that allows you to produce bathymetric maps every time you are on the water.

The contour lines displayed on a bathymetric map join areas of equal depth. Spread-out contour lines indicate an acute transition to deep water. A steep drop-off appears as a series of compressed lines indicating a rapid depth change over a short distance. Sunken islands appear as small circular areas surrounded by deeper contour lines. Spread-out shallow contour lines indicate level shoal areas that are typically home to dense weed beds, one of my favorite structural elements.

Sounders are an integral part of my stillwater equipment and well worth the investment. I never venture on the water without one. I recommend purchasing the most comprehensive one you can and learn how to use all of its features. At first, some features may not appear useful, but if you invest the time to learn the benefits of a specific feature and how to use them, you wonder how you ever did without it. The manufacturer's website and YouTube are excellent resources, providing focused training on a variety of specific sounder features.

Google Maps and Google Earth

Google Maps and Google Earth are excellent tools to help identify promising areas to explore. I use Google Maps during my initial study phases at home to help identify likely-looking areas. When you first look at a lake on Google Maps, it doesn't identify much other than the roads leading into and surrounding it. However, changing to terrain view, by clicking the three horizontal bars in the search box located in the top left of the side panel drop-down menu if you are using a computer, provides some useful information. If you are using a smartphone, select the small diamond icon in the top right just below the search bar to reveal a drop-down menu and select "Terrain." You can get a measure of where the shallow and deep areas are in a lake by using the surrounding topography as a guide. Steep-sided shorelines indicate deeper areas with little to no shoal area. A low-gradient shoreline featuring a shallow trajectory would also extend out into the lake, creating shallow shoal areas and lush weed beds, prime trout and invertebrate habitat.

After studying a lake using Google Maps, on a computer you can swap to a satellite image in Google Earth by selecting the small satellite thumbnail. If you are using a smartphone, select the diamond icon in the top right once again and select "Satellite" from the drop-down menu choices. Google Earth allows you to zoom in on specific areas of interest and see features such as underwater points, drop-offs, and sunken islands. You can also inspect the shoreline surrounding the lake as part of your studying and planning process to identify boat launches, campgrounds, adjoining roads, and other important features.

FOOD

The third pillar in my "how I find trout, and other gamefish, strategy" in lakes involves understanding the habits and behaviors of the various food sources and where you are most likely to find them. Trout must eat, and the best place to find trout food is shallow weed-covered shoals, located in water 20 feet deep or less. Shoals are the supermarkets of the underwater world. In these shallow areas of a lake, weeds flourish, their growth stimulated through sun-enriched photosynthesis. Every potential prey item on the stillwater menu lives in water less than 20 feet deep.

Few food sources thrive in deep water, where oxygen levels are low. Chironomid larvae, snails, and leeches are among those capable of living deep. Cold, dense water is challenging for the majority of trout prey to move in. Life is more comfortable in the shallows. There are always a few exceptions, however. Sunlight penetrates farther in crystal-clear lakes. In these situations, it is possible to locate large weed beds in depths of over 25 feet. No matter the depth, you can almost always find trout patrolling weeds. When fishing is tough, I always spend the majority of my time prospecting where the food lives. At some point in the day, a trout or two should cruise by hoping to snack on an easy meal even if other factors such as weather or seasonal changes have them seemingly off the bite.

You should also have a solid working knowledge of the various trout food sources. A degree in aquatic entomology isn't necessary. Still, you should be able to identify them to avoid confusing two potential food sources, as is often the case with immature damselfly and mayfly nymphs such as *Callibaetis*. How does a particular food source move from one location to another? Do they crawl or swim? In the case of aquatic insects, how do they emerge? Do they emerge at the surface such as chironomids, mayflies, and most caddis species, or do they crawl from the water like dragonflies and damselflies to complete their adult transformation? This information helps you narrow down what insects might be hatching when you see shucks on the water or attached to shoreline vegetation, valuable knowledge that helps you confidently make the correct pattern and presentation choice. For more information on the myriad food items available to trout in lakes please refer to chapter 6, "What Trout Eat."

PUTTING IT ALL TOGETHER

The Power of Observation

I consider the power of observation as the skills and actions that bind how I use comfort, protection, and food to find stillwater trout consistently. Your eyes and ears are arguably your two best assets. The trouble with them is that they report to your brain. Many times, our brain makes assumptions and conclusions that are not based on actual observations, causing us to waste valuable on-the-water time. Don't be in a hurry to get on the water and fish. Instead, invest 10 or 20 minutes observing what is going on, both on the shore and on the water.

When I first arrive at a lake, I take the time to observe what is going on around me. I take a short walk along the shoreline. If there is a dock at the launch area, I walk along the dock too. During my walk, I am always looking for clues as to what might be on the menu. If you see any easy-to-reach rocks or logs, turn them over to see what is living under them. Shoreline rocks and logs are great places to find leeches, scuds, and dragonfly and damselfly nymphs. I have a small aquarium net on hand so I can swipe it through or against any aquatic or shoreline weeds to see what is living on or among them.

Look above the water. Check the shoreline vegetation such as bushes, trees, long-stem bulrush, or cattails. These are the places to find the cast shucks of recently emerged dragonfly or damselfly nymphs. Strong winds create a white foam that washes up onto the shoreline. This white foam traps all sorts of prey items, offering excellent contrast that enables you to spot them easily. If you see any spiderwebs, make a point of looking into them to see what they have trapped.

During your shoreline search, make a note of the most prevalent food sources. What size are they? What were the most predominant colors? Lastly, make a note of the surrounding terrain to link your pre-trip study using a bathymetric map or Google to confirm any potential structure that interested you.

Observation is not just a shoreline activity. When I am ready to head out, I move away from the shore slowly so I can continue to see what is going on. Move too fast, and you miss things. Look on the water's surface for any adult insects or cast shucks. Use your polarized sunglasses to penetrate surface glare and see into the water. Looking into the water allows you to see shallow shoals and weed beds as well as anything that swims by, including trout or trout food.

If present, always inspect any spiderwebs. They often provide a treasure trove of clues as to what insects may be hatching.

Before heading out on the water, always invest a few minutes to check shoreline vegetation for any signs of insect activity, such as this emerging damselfly.

Pay attention to birds. Birds such as swallows and terns feed on insects. If you see concentrations of birds working low to the water like helicopter gunships, this is an excellent clue that there is probably a hatch under way. Insect hatches aren't always long-lived or widespread. Birds help you find localized hatches. If I see intense bird activity, I usually forgo my orientation cruise and my initial plans and head over right away to see what all the fuss is about.

Watch the shorelines for bird activity as well. Emerging dragonfly or damselfly nymphs are easy pickings for any birds walking a shoreline. I recall watching an unusual number of robins bending over to pick up things from a small shoreline clearing. Curiosity eventually got the better of me, and I decided to investigate. Once on shore, it didn't take long to figure out what was attracting the robins. Legions of plump dragonfly nymphs were crawling out of the water to emerge. The plodding nymphs were an easy-to-eat, calorie-rich meal for the opportunistic robins.

You can also use diving birds such as grebes to locate baitfish. Grebes and other diving birds feed on small fish. If grebes are concentrated in an area, there is a good chance that other predators such as trout are nearby too. Find the prey, and you will usually find a predator such as a trout.

If the lake is relatively small, it is always a good idea to cruise its perimeter logically. If the lake is too big to do this, break it down into smaller chunks and investigate those areas thoroughly. Avoid spreading yourself too thin. You want to identify any structure that might be worth exploring. If you made up a plan as a result of your pre-trip research, stick to it. Be pragmatic and avoid a scattered, haphazard approach.

A sounder is a critical component of my initial exploration. I make a note of the surface temperature and any small pieces of structure, such as a small hump or trough,

Get in the habit of following the "Two Fish Rule." If a fish rolls twice in an area, move and investigate.

that may not appear on a larger-scale bathymetric map. My sounder has both GPS and side imaging, and I can use these features to mark areas on either side of my boat or pontoon boat. Once marked, I can drop a waypoint so I can explore them later.

When you are on the water, watch for moving fish that may indicate active feeding, aggressive fish chasing each other, or perhaps a fish that simply broke the surface as it was swimming. Among my closest angling friends, we follow the "Two Fish Rule." Should we see a fish roll at the surface more than once in an area, we move to investigate the rolling fish right away. If I am catching fish in my current location and opt not to move, I make a note of the location in preparation for a possible change of scenery later. Not only do rolling or leaping fish betray their location, but it is also a prime indication of active fish. Active fish usually take a properly presented fly.

On occasion, stillwater trout leap clear of the water. While there are isolated instances of trout leaping to take insects such as adult damsels, this is rarely a feeding rise. Trout leap for a variety of reasons: to rid themselves of skin parasites, or perhaps they are egg-bound. Stillwater trout in productive, landlocked lakes can't spawn, as they require moving water. Mature males and egg-bound females breach in an attempt to rid themselves of milt and eggs as they impact the water's surface.

You always want to strike a balance between moving occasionally and moving constantly. If I choose to anchor in a specific location, I typically stay between 15 and 30 minutes, depending on my presentation. If I am using a slow presentation, I move sooner based on the belief that at some point during my retrieve, any fish in the area would have seen the fly and reacted positively. If I am using a fast retrieve pace, I may extend my stay, as my fly might have moved through the area before a cruising fish had a chance to see it. If the fish aren't relating to any specific area or structure and seem spread out, a more dynamic approach such as fishing loch style from a drifting boat may be a better option.

Any time you are on the water, pay attention to other anglers, especially successful ones. While maintaining a respectable distance, use your binoculars to observe—you can learn a lot. Pay attention to what type of water they are working. Does it appear shallow? What type of structure are they concentrating on? Is it a point or a drop-off? A bathymetric map comes in handy for pinpointing their location.

Make a note of what color fly line they are using. Floating lines are bright, as are most indicators. Sinking lines are dark and difficult to see. If you suspect they are using a sinking line, how aggressive the rod tip bounces during a retrieve can provide clues to whether the line sinks fast or perhaps a bit slower. Due to its mass, a fast-sinking line bounces a rod tip more than a slower-sinking line.

If the successful anglers are using cast and retrieve tactics, are they getting fish on the hang? Does their hang involve a fast or slow rod raise? Are they hanging the fly for a short time or perhaps longer? Sometimes you can see if they are using any sort of unique retrieve. Be careful: I know of some anglers who pretend to be using a brisk strip retrieve when in reality they only actually pull the line once for every four or five strips. Other fly fishers tuck their hands down low so you can't see what they are doing. To gain a measure of the retrieve pace, I make a note of the time between casts. A long time between casts suggests a slow retrieve, while a short casting interval is indicative of a brisk retrieve. The retrieve speed coupled with the time of the year and your knowledge of insect activities and hatch cycles can help you eliminate or confirm what their fly choice might be.

Throat Pumps

Another critical tool to help determine how and what you should be fishing involves the careful use of a throat pump to sample what a trout was most recently feeding upon. You want to make sure you only sample the esophagus. Sampling further down into the stomach runs the risk of injuring the fish and can provide you with yesterday's news regarding food type and preference. You want to know what the trout ate moments before you caught it.

I am an advocate of using a throat pump with a subtle vacuum approach as described in the following instructions rather than the flush-and-pump process the instructions that come with the pump suggest. Using the vacuum approach, you don't have to touch the prey item to sample it. If you squirt water down the esophagus before pumping, as the directions suggest, you are compromising the sample by flushing what the trout recently ate down its throat.

Throat pumps are of critical importance during complex or overlapping hatches. For chironomid addicts such as myself, my throat pump is a critical accessory. I have successfully pumped a variety of prey items ranging in size from tiny zooplankton to leeches, even small baitfish.

A throat pump provides you with three key pieces of information to guide your presentation approach:

1. What have the trout been feeding on?
2. What depth were the trout feeding at?
3. Are the trout actively feeding?

Identifying what items are in any specific sample provides valuable information on what trout are feeding on by food type, size, and color. The ratio of one prey item to other prey items also provides clues to trout feeding preference and what aquatic insects are most available.

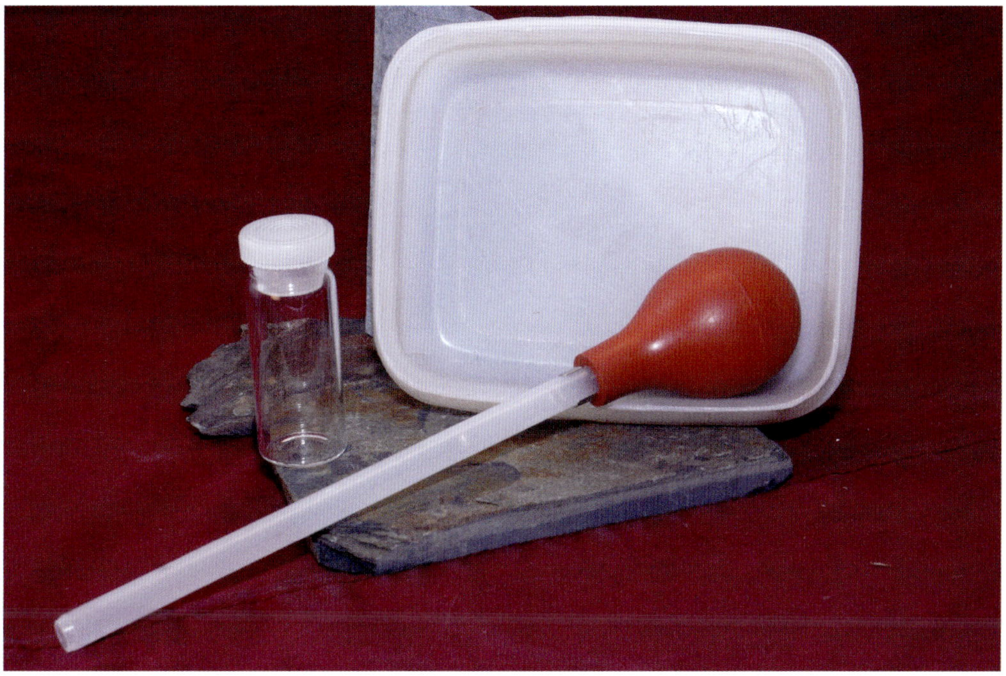

A throat pump not only identifies what a trout has been feeding upon but also provides clues to feeding activity and location within the water.

Linking the sample items with where they live or are most likely to be found provides critical clues as to where in the water the trout are feeding. A sample containing chironomid larvae (bloodworms) or scuds would signify feeding at or just above the bottom. Conversely, a sample containing mayfly duns or terrestrials is a clue trout are feeding at or near the surface. Zooplankton is usually an indicator of deep-water feeding.

If the sampled food items are still alive and moving, this is a clear indication that fish are actively feeding, dictating hatch-matching flies and presentation tactics. In these situations, if you match the fly to the food and present it properly, you should catch fish. If the sample reveals nothing or a limited amount of dead food items, this suggests that fish are not actively feeding, and perhaps attractor flies coupled with an aggressive presentation style to trigger a reactive bite might be in order.

How to Use a Throat Pump as a Vacuum

When using a throat pump, the welfare of the fish is paramount. I recommend only using a throat pump on fish 14 inches or longer. If you aren't comfortable using a throat pump, don't. Wait to be taught by someone proficient at using a pump.

You don't need to throat pump every fish. I always pump the first fish and, based on the sample provided, gauge how often I pump fish going forward. Changing location usually results in gathering another sample. When fish are fluctuating through a variety of particular prey items such as emerging chironomid pupae, increased pump frequency allows you to stay in touch with the various preferences which can, at times, change on an almost hourly basis. During the fall months, when trout focus on bread-and-butter food items such as scuds, leeches, immature dragonfly nymphs, and juvenile damselfly nymphs, I pump fish infrequently, some days perhaps only once.

With a bit of practice, throat pump usage is easy:

1. Place the pump into the water and squeeze the bulb a few times to fill and then empty the pump. This practice ensures that the pump tube is moist and lubricated inside and out. The bulb is empty.
2. Using your thumb and forefinger, depress the pump bulb.
3. Support the fish and gently slide the pump tube down its throat. As soon as you feel resistance, stop sliding the pump. The longitudinal muscles of the trout's esophagus instinctively grab the end of the tube, creating a vacuum. When you let go of the bulb, it should remain collapsed, confirming a vacuum has formed. If you feel strong resistance when sliding the tube down the throat, as though you were trying to push the tube through something hard, stop. Not being able to insert the tube is an indication of a constricted esophagus, a definite sign fish aren't feeding. A tight throat is a common occurrence during

BRIAN CHAN

BRIAN CHAN

late summer through early fall, when high water temperatures often cause trout to cease feeding.

4. Gently withdraw the pump from the fish. You should hear an audible sucking sound, and if you watch the opaque tube, you should see the dark sample shoot up into the bulb.
5. Set the pump aside. Take the time to revive the fish and release it.
6. Partially fill a small container with water. Ideal containers include sample vials, margarine containers, and small plastic trays. White containers or trays offer high contrast, allowing you to examine the sample. Place the tip of the tube into the water within the container. Draw water up into the bulb by pinching the bulb.
7. Squeeze the bulb to shoot the contents back into the container for examination. Avoid drawing water directly from the lake, as you run the risk of accidentally ejecting your sample into the water before you have a chance to examine it.

BRIAN CHAN

BRIAN CHAN

BRIAN CHAN

Taking Notes

Whenever you are on the water, get into the habit of taking notes that you can later transfer into a fishing diary. Over time your notes become a crucial part of your research for future trips, helping you accelerate your stillwater knowledge. Even though you may be fishing a different lake, the notes taken from previous trips begin to coalesce, forming patterns that help unlock other lakes too. You can purchase a specific fishing diary, jot your observations in a notebook, or record them electronically. In addition to the trip date and the location, here is a list of items I make a note of every time I am on the water:

- Weather conditions
- Wind direction
- Water temperature, both at the surface and near the bottom
- Insect activity and hatches
- Water clarity
- Throat pump analysis
- Equipment used, specifically line and leader choices
- Flies, both successful and unsuccessful patterns
- Presentation tactics, including water depth and where I caught fish

CHAPTER TAKEAWAYS

- Stillwater trout behave differently than their moving water counterparts. Stillwater trout are cruisers, always on the move.
- Stillwater fly fishers can use the same three factors moving water fly fishers use to find trout in rivers and streams: comfort, protection, and food.
- Comfort is arguably the most critical factor when trying to find stillwater trout. Comfort factors provide trout with the basic requirements they need to survive, so their metabolism functions at peak efficiency and their natural rhythms remain uninterrupted.
- Water temperature is perhaps the most essential comfort factor and has a significant influence on lakes. Water temperature determines where you fish, your presentation depth, and your retrieve speed.
- Springs, inflow streams, and weed beds are three primary oxygen-rich locations to find stillwater trout.
- A thermometer or Deptherm is a critical accessory to help you locate the preferred temperature range and subsequent oxygen levels for stillwater trout. If you find a temperature range of between 50°F (10°C) and 65°F (18°C), you should find stillwater trout.
- Water temperature also influences trout food. Aquatic insect activity and emergence primarily center around water temperature. Use 50°F (10°C) as a guide to when the first significant emergences of the season kick off.

- Environmental influences such as weather change and lunar phase also affect stillwater trout activity and subsequent feeding behavior.
- Protection factors provide a trout with a sense of confidence and security to feed. When trout feel secure and protected, they are more likely to focus on feeding than on predator avoidance.
- Critical protection factors include the surface texture, light levels, and structure such as drop-offs, points of land, sunken islands or humps, and weed beds.
- Bathymetric maps, Google Maps, and Google Earth are excellent tools to help you locate stillwater structure such as drop-offs, underwater points, sunken islands, and shoal areas.
- The best place to find trout food are shallow weed-covered shoals, located in water 20 feet deep or less.
- Your powers of observation are the skills and actions you use to bind comfort, protection, and food together so you can consistently find stillwater trout.
- Don't be in a hurry to get on the water and fish. Instead, invest 10 or 20 minutes observing what is going on, both on the shore and on the water.
- A throat pump is a valuable accessory. Appropriately used, a throat pump provides you with three key pieces of information to guide your presentation approach: what the trout have been feeding on, what depth the are trout feeding at, and whether trout are actively feeding.
- Whenever you are on the water, get into the habit of taking notes that you can later transfer into a fishing diary or journal.

CHAPTER 8

INDUCING A TAKE: STILLWATER PRESENTATION AND RETRIEVES

Lakes, unlike rivers, have little to no current to animate the fly. Other than suspending a fly static beneath an indicator, you must move the fly to induce a take. Our presentation skills, in particular the way we manipulate the fly by the manner in which we retrieve it, is the key to success, not usually the pattern choice.

Unlike rivers and streams, lakes have little current to help move and animate the fly. Retrieves are a critical factor for inducing a take.

How we manipulate the fly through our retrieves is the key to success, often more so than pattern choice.

ROD AND HAND POSITION

After making the cast, rod position is essential. Eliminating slack is critical when fishing subsurface. When using floating lines, I keep the rod tip no more than 3 inches from the water's surface. A low rod position maintains a tight connection between you and your fly. The moment a take is recognized, a positive rod raise immediately applies tension and sets the hook.

Correct rod position is essential for both recognizing and reacting to takes.

Strike indicator presentations require an immediate hook-set as soon as you recognize a take. As there is a 90-degree leader angle between you and the fly, brisk hook-sets are a must. Setting the hook from a low rod position to roughly 11 o'clock applies immediate tension to the fly through the line, leader, and tippet, transforming the 90-degree leader angle into a 180-degree straight line. A high rod tip creates slack, which muffles the strike, resulting in missed fish and frustration. When I am on the water, asking people to lower their rod tip within 2 to 3 inches off the surface is a standard correction.

Strike indicator presentations require an immediate hook-set as soon as you recognize a take.

I only recommend a slightly higher rod position when targeting surface-feeding fish using adult and emerger patterns. Often, an excited angler, upon seeing the trout rise to the fly, sets too early, pulling the fly away. To avoid missing a take, hold the rod tip a foot or so above the surface. The higher tip position creates just enough of a slack buffer to allow the fish to take the fly and turn down before setting the hook. If you are missing fish when fishing dry or emerger patterns, holding the rod higher off the water should fix the problem.

Sinking line presentations depend on feeling the take, as there are no visual clues, as is the case when using floating line tactics, either through line or indicator movement. With sinking lines, stabbing the rod tip into the water aids strike detection. Be sure to point the rod tip directly at the fly line and fly. Avoid having your rod tip to the side of the line and fly, as the flexible rod tip will absorb or potentially mute a strike. I stab my rod tip into the water to at least the first or second guide. Takes may occur on the drop as the fly falls through the water. I often blend in the slowest of hand twist or pinch strip retrieves as the fly descends. This practice eliminates any slack between myself and the fly so I don't miss any takes on the drop.

As with rod position, your hand position is essential. As soon as the fly line lands on the surface, transfer the fly line to the rod hand, either pinched against the cork by the forefinger or held between the tip of the thumb and forefinger. I prefer pinching the line between the tips of my thumb and forefinger, as I feel it provides increased sensitivity, especially with slow retrieves.

When fighting fish, particularly during the initial phases of the fight, pinching the fly line against the cork handle is your primary drag system, especially when fighting smaller fish. With large, aggressive fish, the forefinger remains your primary defense until the fish takes any loose line and the reel takes over.

During the fight, there is always a risk of stepping on the fly line or having it catch on something. It is always a good idea to get the fish onto the reel as soon as it is practically possible. I pinch the fly line against the rod handle to maintain pressure on the fish and use the pinkie finger of my rod hand to guide any loose fly line onto the reel. This practice allows for even line distribution across the spool, reducing the risk of a backlash or the line piling upon one side of the reel, where it may bind and cause a break-off. Avoid dropping your head when gathering fly line, as this lowers the rod tip, creating slack and subsequent fish loss.

When fishing subsurface using floating lines, the moment you recognize a take, use a swift rod raise to set the hook.

As with your rod position, hand position is essential for creating a proper retrieve to induce a take.

RETRIEVE ELEMENTS

No matter the retrieve, there are four common elements:

1. The length of the pull
2. The speed of the pull
3. The cadence, tempo, or rhythm of the retrieve
4. The pause between pulls

There are four elements common to all stillwater retrieves: the length of the pull, the speed of the pull, the tempo or cadence of the retrieve, and the pause between pulls.

Of these four elements, the pause is often the key. All trout prey move in an erratic manner punctuated with resting pauses. The pause portion of any retrieve mimics this behavior. As trout are primarily sight feeders, they are attracted to movement. Many times, trout follow the fly for a while before deciding to pounce. When the fly pauses, the trout has a predatory advantage and takes the fly. The majority of takes occur as the fly pauses and drops or the moment the retrieve resumes. Be sure to focus at this time to avoid missing a fish.

Figuring out the correct retrieve speed, governed by both the length and speed of the pull, is one of the variables we are continually experimenting with. Aquatic insects, baitfish, and other invertebrates are not Olympic athletes, nor do they have rocket packs to augment their movement. For the most part, trout food moves slowly, either to avoid becoming food for something else or, in the case of predators such as dragonfly or damselfly nymphs, to stalk as they hunt. Imitating how various trout prey move is a crucial factor that guides what retrieve you should use.

Environmental factors also impact retrieve pace. When water temperatures are cold, such as early spring or late fall, a trout's metabolism slows and they are less likely to chase fast-moving prey. In these circumstances, slow to almost static retrieves work best. Stillwater trout are also affected by weather changes such as frontal passages. At this time, the trout's world is in a state of flux. Barometric pressure, water temperature, and light levels all change. These changes unsettle trout, decreasing their activity and willingness to chase. During these periods of environmental change, slow, pedestrian retrieves work best.

As a general rule, stillwater retrieves are typically slow and erratic, as trout food doesn't move in a straight, steady, robotic manner. Brisk retrieves work best when fish are in an active, aggressive frame of mind or when using attractor patterns and techniques intended to trigger a non-feeding response. The best stillwater retrieves are usually a combination of different retrieve types. No matter the retrieve, I almost always begin with two brisk 3- to 4-inch strips. The strips ensure I have removed any slack so I am tight to my flies and don't miss any takes, and they may induce any nearby fish, attracted by the sudden movement, to take.

STILLWATER RETRIEVES

I use four types of retrieves: the hand twist, the strip, the pinch strip, and the rolly polly. Each retrieve has its window of use depending on the food source, environmental conditions, and presentation technique. The hand twist, strip, and pinch strip can also be combined to provide the trout with a variety of retrieve options. Varied, erratic retrieves work best. You can also use wind-induced current to move or drift the fly or to augment a retrieve.

I usually retrieve until roughly a rod length of fly line remains outside the guides. This enables proper rod loading for casting and allows you to execute the hang. The hang is a technique employed at the end of a retrieve to induce a following fish to take the fly.

Except for the rolly polly, all stillwater retrieves take place from behind the rod hand.

Hand Twist Retrieve

The hand twist, or figure eight or hand weave, retrieve is arguably the cornerstone stillwater retrieve. Depending on the pace, you can use the hand twist to match every prey item, from emerging chironomid pupae to fleeing baitfish. It is my preferred retrieve when I am imitating slow-moving food sources such as chironomid pupae, chironomid larvae, mayfly nymphs, and damselfly nymphs.

Depending on the number of fingers you use, the length of the pull can be easily changed. Using the pinkie finger to retrieve the line provides a long pull. The ring finger provides a moderate-length pull, and the middle finger provides the shortest pull. The hand twist is a busy retrieve that keeps the fly fisher's hands occupied while providing a jerky, natural, erratic pace. It is the perfect cure for the impatient angler.

Although arguably the most difficult retrieve to master, with a bit of practice, the hand twist is easy to learn.

1. Reach up behind the rod hand and pinch the fly line with the thumb and forefinger of your retrieve hand.

2. While still holding the line with your thumb and forefinger, open your hand and spread your fingers. Using your pinkie finger, pull a length of the fly line toward you by rolling or twisting your hand at the wrist. Depending on the retrieve, you can also use the middle or ring finger to retrieve the line.

3. Once the hand twist is complete, release the line. Re-grip the line with your thumb and forefinger and repeat the retrieve process.

4. The gathered line can be held in small figure eights in the palm of your hand or allowed to drop. A blend of these actions can also be used by gathering a few coils in the palm of your retrieve hand, releasing them if they become cumbersome to hold.

Strip Retrieve

As its name implies, the strip retrieve consists of pulling, or stripping, the line from behind the rod hand. It is a simple retrieve that you can use in a wide variety of scenarios, including moving water and the ocean.

You can use the strip retrieve to suggest a wide array of trout food. The length and speed of the pulls can be easily varied. A series of long pulls can suggest a leech, darting minnow, or gliding scud. Short, choppy, erratic pulls imitate water boatmen, backswimmers, scuds, or caddis pupae. A retrieve with quick strips suggests a fleeing dragonfly nymph or minnow and is the backbone retrieve for attractor patterns such as the Booby, Blob, or FAB.

The strip retrieve requires discipline when conditions dictate a slow retrieve. Impatient anglers usually retrieve the fly far too fast, making the strip retrieve a poor choice. When slow retrieves are required, self-governing retrieves such as the hand twist or pinch strip are a better choice.

1. Reach up behind the rod hand and pinch the fly line with the thumb and forefinger of your retrieve hand.

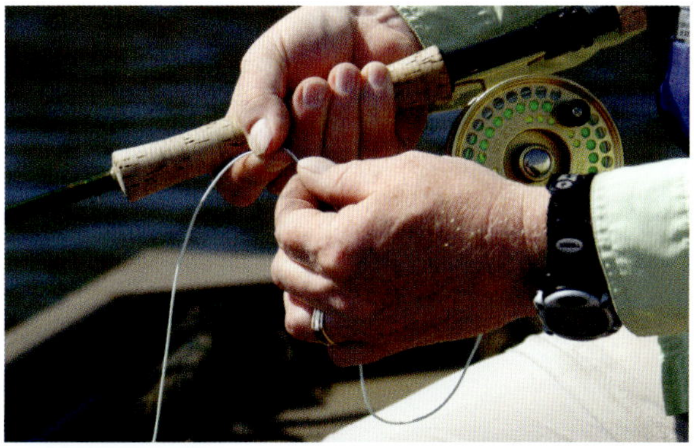

2. Pull a length of fly line from behind the rod hand. When using a strip retrieve, pulls can be long and slow, short and slow, long and fast, or quick and fast.

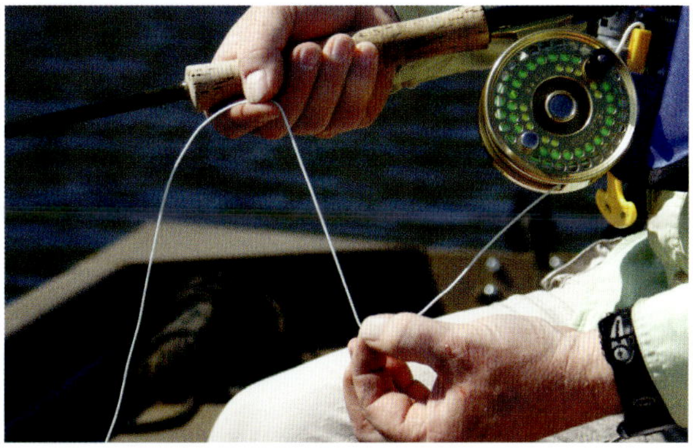

3. Remember that the pause is an essential component to any retrieve—wait before grabbing the line again. After grabbing the line again, repeat steps 1 and 2 until you hook a fish or there is no more line to retrieve.

Pinch Strip Retrieve

The pinch strip is an excellent alternative to the hand twist for those having difficulty learning or mastering the hand motions but need a slow retrieve. The key to the pinch strip is keeping the retrieve and rod hands together. With the hands touching, it is impossible to retrieve at any sort of pace. The pinch strip is ideal any time a snail-paced retrieve is required.

1. With your rod hand in the retrieve position, touch the fingertips of your retrieving hand to the palm area or heel of the rod hand.

2. Using the thumb and forefinger of your retrieve hand, pinch the fly line.

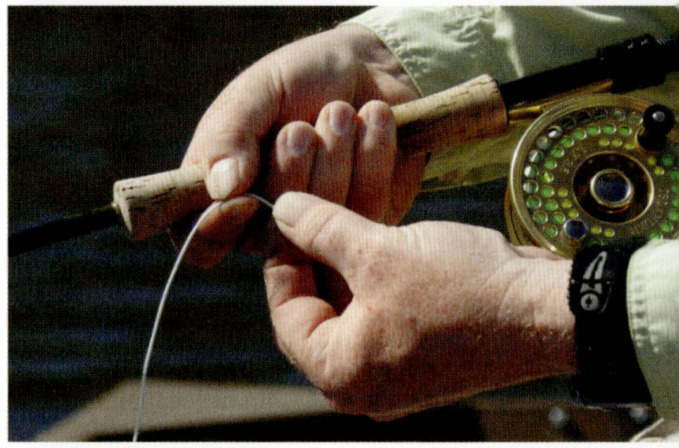

3. Without letting your rod hand and retrieve hand come apart, gather the fly line using the thumb and forefinger of your retrieve hand.

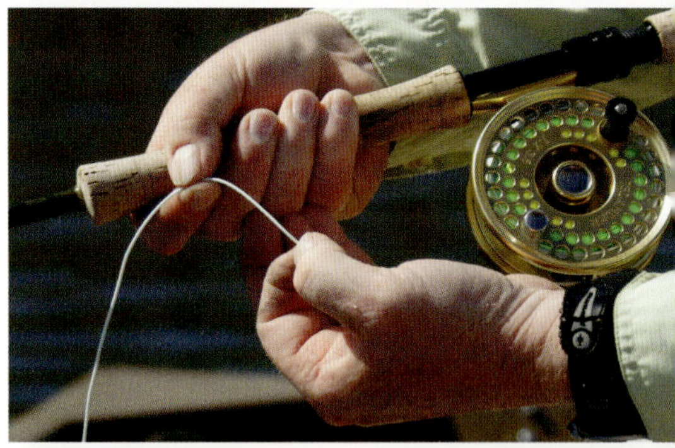

4. Release the pinch, re-grip, and repeat.

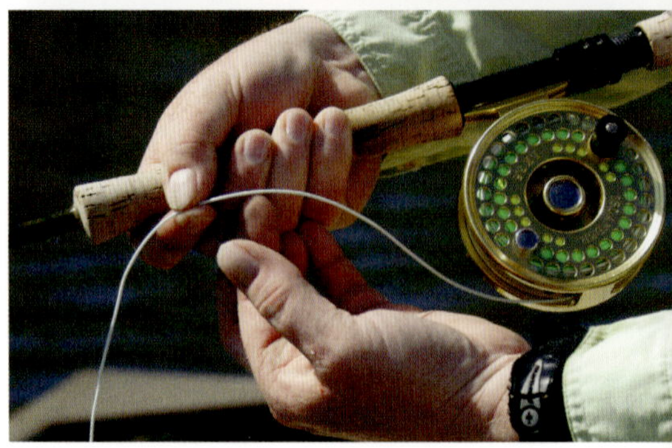

Rolly Polly Retrieve

The rolly polly is the retrieve of choice when a turbocharged retrieve is required. Attractor patterns such as Boobies, FABs, and Blobs are typical rolly polly candidates. You can also use the rolly polly for natural patterns, including leeches, minnows, and dragonfly nymphs. Although the pace of the rolly polly can be varied and slowed, I typically use it to trigger takes from aggressive trout. It is also an excellent retrieve for other stillwater inhabitants such as pike and muskie.

The retrieve position of the rolly polly differs from all other stillwater retrieves. Instead of holding the rod in one hand and using your other hand to retrieve line, place the butt section of the rod in the armpit of your casting arm. You retrieve line with both hands using alternating pulls from behind the stripping guide. I most often use the rolly polly for brisk retrieves using typically long, rapid pulls. The retrieve cadence can be varied simply by slowing and then speeding up the hand movements.

Setting the hook is usually never an issue with the rolly polly, as takes are aggressive. Continue stripping the line after the initial take to pull and set the hook into the trout's mouth. Once hooked, transfer the rod from the armpit to the rod hand to fight and land the fish.

1. Place the reel under the arm and into the armpit of your retrieve hand. Make sure the rod tip is either at or into the water.

2. Reach up with one hand and grab the fly line just behind the stripping guide.

3. Pull the line back toward you.

4. Release the line and grab it just behind the stripping guide with your other hand.

5. Pull the line back toward you as was done on the first portion of the retrieve. Repeat this retrieve process, alternating hands to retrieve the fly line.

INDICATOR RETRIEVES

Many people may think that when suspending flies under an indicator, a retrieve is not required. While letting the indicator sit static is one option, there are times when retrieving the line is necessary to induce a take. I use four different presentation options when using strike indicators: static, hand twist or pinch strip, strip retrieve, and upwind.

Static

No retrieve is involved with this approach. Once the cast is complete, let the indicator remain motionless. The wind-induced surface ripple provides the only movement to the fly suspended below. The static approach works best when water temperatures are cold such as early spring soon after ice-off and again in the late fall or when environmental conditions such as weather change reduce fish activity.

Hand Twist or Pinch Strip

A slow hand twist or pinch strip retrieve allows you to cover water and induce a take. It is my preferred presentation when prospecting structure such as a weed bed. Moving the fly is also a great way to break up the monotony that can set in when using a static approach. Many indicator critics contest that staring at an indicator is boring. I agree, staring at an indicator for prolonged periods can become tiresome. The cure for boredom with any stillwater presentation is to do something. By moving the fly, you are doing something.

Strip Retrieve

When fish are active and willing to chase a moving fly, a long, wake-inducing strip often triggers a response. The moment you stop the strip, watch for a take. Stripping raises the fly; stopping allows it to flutter and settle. This rise-fall motion often attracts the attention of nearby fish. Takes usually occur as soon as the strip stops or within a few seconds of the indicator settling—this is not time to be looking elsewhere. Pay close attention to the indicator.

At times a continuous sequence of short strips works. Short, choppy strips are always worth a try when trout are targeting fast-moving prey such as leeches and minnows. As with any retrieve, maintain a varied pace until you discover a consistent speed and cadence that fish respond to best. The strip retrieve can also be used with the hand twist or a pinch strip to ease periods of potential boredom between takes.

Upwind

An upwind presentation is the rough equivalent of upstream nymphing on rivers and streams. This presentation option works best with leech and minnow patterns, although it can certainly be used with other patterns too. An upwind presentation takes advantage of a trout's natural tendency to face and cruise into a wind-induced current. To avoid potential tangles from punching the cast upwind, you only want to present your flies using this presentation option when the winds are light.

From an anchored position, place an acutely angled cast upwind. Once you have completed the cast and the fly has had a chance to settle, begin gathering line as the indicator drifts back toward you and watch for the indicator to disappear. Always place your cast on the downwind side of your casting arm. In this position, you won't have the line crash into position should you lose control of the cast or succumb to an unexpected wind gust. If the downwind drift increases due to wind accelerating the surface current, it may pull on the indicator, lifting the fly out of the target zone. You may have to increase your leader length slightly to compensate.

Most of my indicator presentations are a combination of static, hand twist or pinch strip, and strip retrieve. After casting, I allow the indicator to settle so the fly can sink to the set depth. I let the indicator sit static until my attention begins to wane. I then start a short series of hand twists to move the fly and cover water. If there is no response, I stop the retrieve, allowing the indicator and fly to settle. As my attention wanes again, I strip the line, causing the indicator to wake. I stop the fly, letting the indicator and fly settle once more. At this point, I keep a sharp watch for any signs of a take the rising, and then falling, fly may induce. If there is no response, I repeat this entire pause and retrieve process until the cast is complete or I hook a fish. If I catch a fish, I do my best to remember what I was doing immediately before the take so I can duplicate it.

WIND DRIFTING (MOVING THE STRIKE ZONE)

Using wind-induced current, or wind drifting, is a personal favorite presentation option for floating line presentations, with or without indicators. Wind drifting allows you to cover water using a static or near-static presentation. It is an excellent presentation option for chironomid pupae and larvae, caddis pupae, and mayfly nymphs. When using non-indicator presentations, wind drifting resembles a traditional wet-fly swing on a river. Watch the line to stop, move upwind, or straighten suddenly to signal a take. At times takes are felt as a sharp pull, similar to that of a swung wet fly. Takes on the downwind swing are addictive—the kind of take you want to experience again and again.

From an anchored position with the wind blowing from behind, place a quartering cast on an acute angle downwind. An upwind reach cast is an excellent option to

Wind drifting, using any wind-induced surface current to move the strike zone, is an excellent floating line presentation technique, with or without indicators.

help establish the drift. Once the line, leader, and flies land, allow the wind-induced surface chop to drift and swing the flies downwind. As the fly line has a surface area along its length, the current pulls on the line, causing it to arc into a distinct C shape. This shape is a presentation detriment, as it accelerates and raises the fly. You must mend the fly line upwind to maintain a natural dead drift presentation and to stay in contact with the fly.

Mending is not an aggressive wrist flick but rather a slow, deliberate raise of the rod followed by a delicate repositioning of the fly line upwind. As soon as the line begins to get out of position, lift the rod vertically, high enough to eliminate the line arc that is starting to form. With the rod raised, reposition and lay the line on the water upwind. I am a firm believer in mend a little, mend often. Make frequent short, small mends rather than one large, difficult to control and execute mend. As with moving water, mending shouldn't move the indicator or the fly.

When using indicators, wind drifting allows for movement of the strike zone throughout the presentation. If you cast downwind and let the fly hang, a fish has to swim within sight of the fly to take it. It stands to reason that if you can move your fly over a greater area, you should catch more fish. Wind drifting an indicator presentation moves the radius of visibility around the fly downwind. Once the line and indicator have finished drifting and now hang straight downwind, let the fly sit still for a few minutes. If there are no takes, begin a slow upwind retrieve back to the boat. Using this approach moves the strike zone. The odds of catching a fish only increase as the fly or flies cover more water.

FAN CASTING

It is essential to cover as much water as possible both vertically and horizontally. Fan casting allows you to cover water horizontally, showcasing your fly or flies through a variety of angles. Looking from above, imagine a clock face around you. From an anchored position, with the wind placed at your back, the primary presentation area lies out in front from 9 o'clock off the left arm to 3 o'clock off the right arm. If wind conditions allow, place the occasional cast behind the boat. Rather than continuously casting in the same lane, use the hours or even half hours on the clock to fan casts from 9:30 through 2:30 on the imaginary clock face in front of you. I rarely place a cast along the axis of the boat to cover 9 o'clock or 3 o'clock, especially if there are two anglers in the boat. When two anglers are fishing together, the midsection of the boat divides the clock face. The stern angler works the area from 9:30 to noon, the bow angler noon to 2:30.

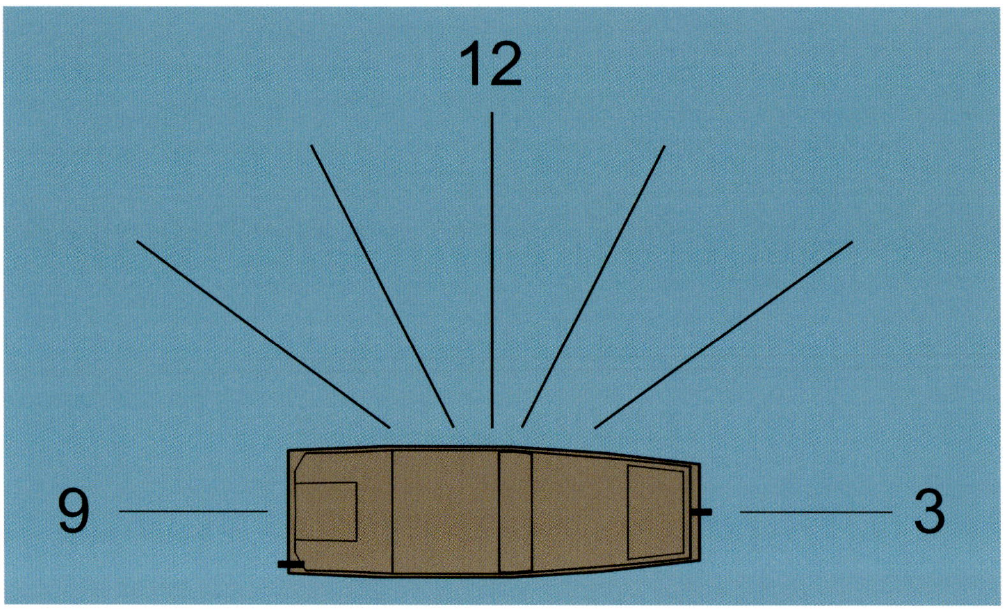

Fan casting allows you to present your fly at various angles while covering as much water as possible.

Fan casting works in a variety of situations, including fishing loch style from a drifting boat, cruising, paddling down a shoreline, even when fishing from shore. It just makes sense to present your fly or flies over a wide area.

THE HANG

If you have spent any time fly fishing lakes, you have probably experienced a sharp grab or seen a boil at your fly or perhaps a flash as you raise the rod to cast. Why does this always seem to happen at the end of the retrieve? Chances are the fish was following the fly for a while, interested in your fly but not committed. As you raised the rod, two things happened: The fly increased speed and changed direction. These two actions triggered a predatory or flee response from the trout, and it accelerated to take the fly. A technique called the hang gives you a solid chance of converting a following fish into a caught fish.

Incorporating the hang at the end of every stillwater retrieve is arguably the quickest way you can increase your catch rate when fly fishing lakes.
RYAN ERMET

Incorporating the hang at the end of every retrieve is arguably the single greatest technique to increase your catch rate on lakes. It is a technique that works with both floating lines without indicators and all sinking line presentations. The hang is easy to execute:

1. As you are nearing the end of the retrieve—one to two rod lengths of fly line outside of the rod tip is a good starting point—drop your retrieve hand away from your rod hand.
2. Raise the rod as though you were going to cast or position it for a roll cast. The retrieve hand continues to gather line during the rod raise. A hand twist works best.
3. With the rod at roughly the 11 o'clock position, pause, or hang, the fly for a while at or just below the surface to see if any fish have followed the fly and are poised to take it.
4. If there are no fish, cast and present the fly once again.

A low body profile from a seated position works best with the hang, as any fish looking up may be spooked seeing you in the background. Using a diagonal sweep of the rod from either side of center is also a good idea to keep you out of the trout's sightline. Long rods, 9½ feet or greater, provide a longer rod raise while keeping the flies away from you so you don't spook fish.

The speed of your rod raise and how long you hang the flies are important hang variables—variables you always experiment with until a consistent pattern emerges. Some days a fast rod raise works; other days trout prefer a slow rod raise. The length of hang can also vary from as short as a few seconds to over 10 seconds. I recall hanging a fly for almost 25 seconds on Idaho's Henry's Lake before a cutthroat rocketed from the depths to smash the fly.

When using multiple flies, hang each fly at or just below the surface. The upper fly serves as a strike indicator. If the fly darts suddenly, set the hook. The sudden fly movement is an indication that a fish has taken one of the flies below.

If a fish follows the fly but turns away or dives, lower the rod tip and allow the fly to fall through the water. The fish is often still in the neighborhood and can frequently be coaxed into taking the falling fly.

Hang markers help you recognize when your retrieve is coming to an end, signaling it is time to initiate the hang. I prefer my hang markers 20 feet from the end of the line. A 20-foot hang marker coupled with a long rod provides me with two hang points, depending on my leader length. The two hang points reduce the chance of spooking a following fish, as I can keep the flies a reasonable distance from my boat. When using a shorter leader, 12 feet or less, I initiate the hang with the marker at the rod tip. If I am using a long leader in excess of 12 feet, I have the option of hanging the flies when the line marker is at my reel.

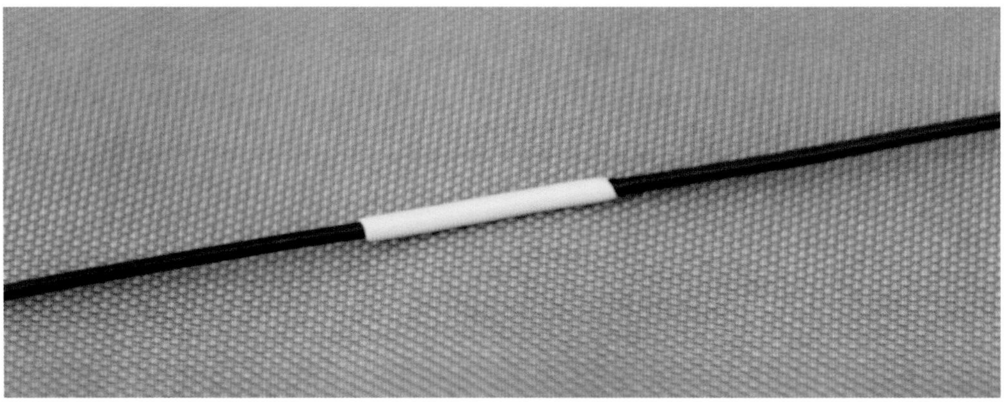

Hang markers help you recognize when your retrieve is coming to an end, signaling it is time to initiate the hang.

Many manufacturers incorporate hang markers into their fly lines. These marks may be short, while other line companies integrate an extended color change to identify the correct hang point. You can also add a hang marker to an existing line by wrapping bright-colored thread and whip-finishing it onto the fly line. A Dacron or braided bobber stop provides an even simpler option. You can also add a hang marker to the line using a uni or nail knot. Once you have added the hang marker to the fly line, a thin coat of brushable superglue binds the wraps. When the superglue is dry, coat the hang marker with Aquaseal or UV resin for further protection and to provide a smooth, guide-friendly coating.

You can also use a hang marker to identify the setup point when dangling flies vertically beneath the rod tip. Once you set the appropriate fly depth, make a note of which guide the hang marker is at or closest to. Should a fish take line during the fight, all you need to do is reset the line so it hangs at or near the same rod guide again. See chapter 11, "Going Deep," for a full explanation. The hang marker also marks the load point of the line. If you start a cast at the hang marker, there is sufficient line out to load the rod and cast.

CHAPTER TAKEAWAYS

- When using floating lines, keep the rod tip no more than 3 inches from the water's surface. A low rod position maintains a tight connection between you and your fly.
- Use a slightly higher rod position when targeting surface-feeding fish using adult and emerger patterns. If you are prone to strike too fast due to the excitement that is often associated with surface-feeding trout, the controlled slack helps avoid missed takes, as it creates a short hook-set delay when striking, allowing the fish to take the fly.
- With sinking lines, stabbing the rod tip into the water aids strike detection. Be sure to point the rod tip directly at the fly line and fly.
- Avoid having your rod tip to the side of the line and fly.
- There are four common elements to any retrieve: the length of the pull; the speed of the pull; the cadence, tempo, or rhythm of the retrieve; and the pause between pulls.
- Several factors govern retrieve speed: water temperature, fish activity, the way the food source you are suggesting moves, and environmental factors such as weather change. As a general rule, most stillwater retrieves are slow and erratic.
- Always begin any retrieve with two quick 3- to 4-inch strips to remove any slack or to induce any fish, attracted by the sudden fly movement, to take the fly.
- The hand twist, or figure eight or hand weave, retrieve is arguably the cornerstone stillwater retrieve. Depending on the pace, you can use the hand twist to match every prey item, from emerging chironomid pupae to fleeing baitfish.
- The pinch strip is an excellent alternative to the hand twist for those having difficulty learning or mastering the hand motions but need a slow retrieve.
- When you need to use a fast-paced turbocharged retrieve, as is often the case when fishing attractor patterns such as the Booby, use the hand-over-hand rolly polly.
- There are four retrieve options when using strike indicators: static, hand twist, strip, or upwind.
- Wind drifting, or the use of wind-induced current, is an excellent presentation option for floating lines, with or without indicators.
- Fan casting allows you to cover water horizontally, showcasing your fly or flies through a variety of angles.
- Incorporating the hang at the end of every retrieve is arguably the single greatest technique to increase your catch rate on lakes.

CHAPTER 9

FLOATING LINE TECHNIQUES: STRIKE INDICATORS AND LONG LEADER NYMPHING

If you asked me if you could fly fish lakes using only one line, my answer would be easy: "Yes, a floating line." To me, floating lines offer unparalleled versatility.

If fish are feeding at or just below the surface, a floating line with a dry fly, emerger, or unweighted nymph or pupa pattern should produce a few fish. If fish

Floating line presentations allow you to successfully fish subsurface to cover a wide range of water depths.

are in deep water, you can get down to them by suspending a weighted pattern at a set depth under a strike indicator. You could also fish a weighted pattern or a team of weighted flies using a floating line coupled with a long leader, a technique affectionately referred to as the "naked technique" because the leader does not have any indicator attached to it.

When I am fishing deep from an anchored position, I have successfully suspended flies beneath an indicator to over 22 feet. With the naked technique, you can easily explore water over 25 feet deep.

STRIKE INDICATOR TACTICS

Strike indicators allow stillwater fly fishers to control two of the most critical presentation elements:

1. Maintaining a constant presentation depth, governed by the distance between the strike indicator and fly.
2. Controlling your retrieve speed, dictated by how much or little you move the fly by retrieving the fly line. Strike indicators can be left to sit static. You can retrieve the line to attract fish to the fly, or you can use wind-induced current to drift the line, leader, and fly.

Strike indicators allow you to control your presentation depth and your retrieve speed, two critical presentation elements.

Whenever I fish with someone new to stillwater fly fishing, they typically haven't developed the patience to let their flies sink long enough or retrieve them slow enough. Strike indicators allow you to control these two crucial components easily. Plus, it is just plain fun to watch that indicator disappear below the surface, as typically only one thing can make that happen: a fish. It takes me back to my initial childhood fishing experiences using a bobber and bait.

In addition to the presentation benefits, it's just fun to watch an indicator disappear beneath the surface.
BARRY ACTON

Using strike indicators on lakes is not as simple as some might think. There is far more to using strike indicators than just placing an indicator on your leader, making a cast, and waiting for the indicator to disappear. Several complexities must be mastered for consistent success.

Why Indicators?

In addition to controlling presentation depth and retrieve speed, indicators offer many presentation benefits:

- As the depth of your presentation is set by how far you hang the fly or flies beneath the indicator, you can strategically keep your flies just above the bottom where trout most often hunt.

Indicators offer several presentation benefits, including working flies in and around weeds in shallow water.

- Indicators are ideal for probing weed pockets, allowing you to work these areas without the risk or worry of your fly hanging up on any bottom weeds or debris.
- A strike indicator provides the ultimate depth control. We first began using indicators to suggest suspended chironomid pupae. Controlling the depth at which you present a chironomid pupa or larva pattern is often the most critical aspect. It wasn't long after that we began suspending other pattern types under an indicator to suggest leeches, baitfish, scuds, and myriad other food sources, as once again presentation depth is vital with all food sources, not just chironomids.
- Using strike indicators to target trout in shallow water seems obvious, and it is. I use indicators most often in water 15 feet deep or less. Although you can certainly use indicators in deep water, for me, 15 feet or less is the indicator technique's sweet spot. When trout get into really skinny water, indicator presentations can be tough to beat, especially in weed-choked productive lakes. As the shallows of productive lakes are bathed in sunlight most of the year, they are typically home to dense concentrations of aquatic vegetation—prime habitat for trout food. As a result, trout spend much of their time hunting in these areas.

- A strike indicator allows you to explore weed pockets without worrying about hanging up or spooking fish. Weed pockets are gaps or openings in the weeds and are favored cruising spots for trout. Many resemble teacups, fringed by weeds along their sides and below to form the bottom of the cup. Repeatedly casting and retrieving in and around weed pockets risks spooking any nearby fish, especially if you accidentally drop a heavy, water-slapping cast. When using indicators, you can place a single cast into a likely-looking area with minimal disturbance. Once the indicator and fly settle, you can let the fly sit or creep it back at a snail's pace. Working flies in and around weed pockets during early spring or late fall is an ideal indicator scenario.
- Although indicator systems can be tangle-prone, they are the perfect presentation technique for neophyte stillwater fly fishers. As indicators work best when presented at short distances, long casts are not necessary or recommended. The roll cast is my preferred indicator cast. With some brief instruction, beginners can flop out a reasonable roll cast and be fishing and catching fish in short order. I want to ensure beginning stillwater fly fishers enjoy their initial on-the-water experiences through a gradual introduction to fly casting and catching a few fish. Asking them to execute more-complex cast and retrieve techniques can be both challenging and frustrating. With indicator presentations, all they have to do, for the most part, is watch the indicator and raise the rod when it shows signs of a take. Once they catch and release their first fish, there is a good chance they will carry on with this great sport for years to come. When I was first teaching my sons to fly fish lakes, we used indicators all the time. They could enjoy the splendors of nature, eat, and call Mom on the radio, all while they fished. As both father and guide, my day was far more relaxed, as I wasn't continually undoing casting-induced leader tangles or having to repeatedly cast.
- It might seem paradoxical, but indicators also work great in windy conditions. Continuous casting in the wind often causes tangles and unwelcome leader knots due to overpowering the rod or increasing the pace of the casting stroke. Using a roll cast or a single pick up and lay down, an indicator provides a prolonged presentation and reduced tangles due to the reduced casting. I have used this approach with excellent results using all sizes of flies from small chironomid larvae to larger balanced leeches and minnows in some incredibly windy conditions, including Lago Strobel (Jurassic Lake), one of the windiest places on the planet.
- As your presentation depth is set to avoid having your fly foul with any weeds or debris and your retrieves are typically slow, your fly remains in the water longer, increasing your odds of catching fish.
- Finally, indicators allow you to fish two rods at once if legal to do so. Depending on the provincial or state regulations, an angler may fish two rods if they are by themselves or have purchased an additional license. In these situations, indicators are an ideal choice. You can let the indicator rod sit, enabling fish

1. With the indicator in the assembled state, peg inserted into the indicator, slide the leader through the peg hole. Slide the indicator into position on the leader. I prefer the peg on the fly side of the indicator, as this reduces tangles since the leader is less likely to catch the peg. Also, when using a swivel below the indicator, the peg eliminates indicator loss in the event of a break-off, as the swivel acts a stopper, preventing the peg and indicator from sliding off the leader.

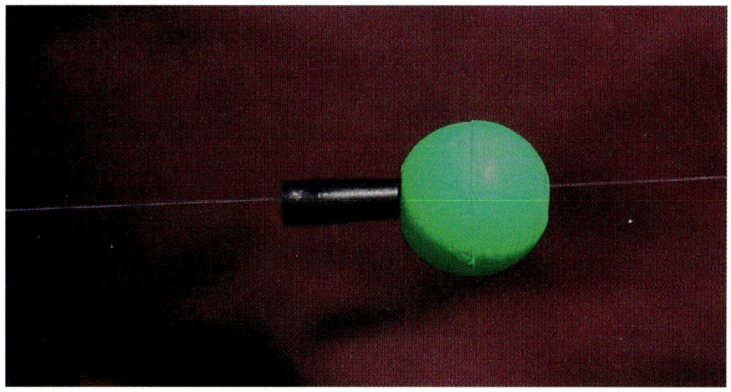

2. Withdraw the peg so it is about 2 inches away from the indicator. Using your fingers, pinch the leader on the opposite end of the indicator to the peg so it can't slip.

3. Push the peg back toward the indicator to form a large, approximately ¾-inch loop in the leader. I prefer larger loops, especially when using small-diameter leader or tippet material, as I feel the indicator releases better.

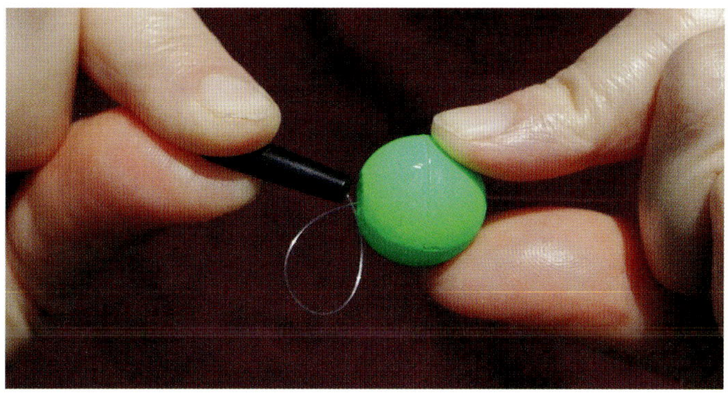

4. Pinch the loop between the plastic peg and the indicator hole to lock the Quick Release Indicator in place.

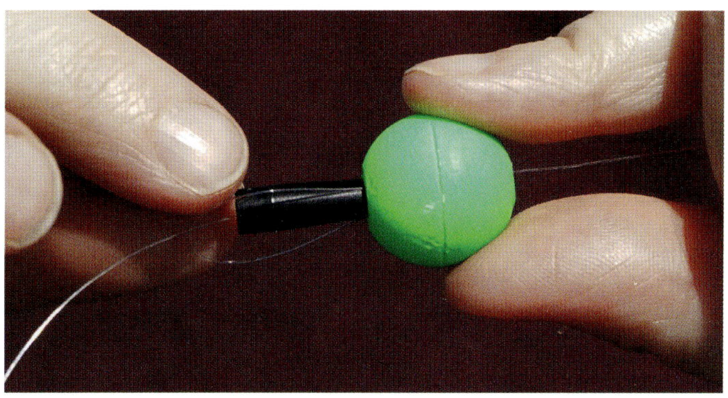

For me, the Quick Release Indicator was a game changer. It opened up my indicator presentations options, allowing me to suspend flies from shallow to deep. My personal best is currently over 22 feet between the indicator and fly.

Nothing is perfect, however, and there are a few drawbacks to the Quick Release Indicator. As with Corkies, Quick Release Indicators must precede the fly onto the leader. As a result, changing back and forth from indicator to non-indicator presentations takes a few steps. The hi-vis coating tends to chip over time, and the indicator hole becomes enlarged with repeated releases—a welcome problem in most instances, as this means you are catching lots of fish. A coating of clear nail polish adds a layer of protection to reduce chipping. A short length of black electrician's tape around the peg increases its diameter, allowing you to cope, for the short term, with a well-worn indicator.

Choosing the Right Indicator

Fly fishers are often looking for that one size fits all, silver bullet indicator solution. There isn't one. I carry a cross section of all indicator types in a variety of sizes and colors, as presentation conditions are always changing.

Light conditions vary, and people see colors differently. It pays to have a wide range of colors on hand. I find bright colors work best with the sun coming from above or behind. In low-light conditions, greens and yellows work best for me. When fishing into the sun or when surface glare makes bright-colored indicators tough to see, dark colors work best. For example, the bright green weeds in Nevada's Pyramid Lake make brightly colored indicators difficult to see. Many locals darken their indicators using black permanent markers to silhouette them against the bright green backdrop.

There is no one indicator type, style, or color for every situation. Having a range of indicators on hand allows you to meet any presentation challenge.

"What size indicator should I use?" is a common question. I prefer using the smallest indicator I can for the conditions, as I feel they offer the highest sensitivity, helping transmit subtle takes. Small indicators also keep you honest by making sure you keep the indicator close so you can see it. Long casts are a detriment when fishing indicators, as it is difficult to impossible to see subtle takes at a distance, and even if you can see the take, there is a delay before you can set the hook. When fish are taking soft, you miss fish. As a general rule, the deeper you are fishing, the closer the indicator should be to you. When I am fishing deep water, greater than 18 feet between the indicator and fly, I have roughly a rod length of the fly line extending from the tip.

Surface chop also has a bearing on indicator size. My general rule is the rougher the surface chop, the bigger the indicator. Small indicators in choppy water are tough to see. Pattern weight also has a bearing. Heavy patterns, such as balanced flies using tungsten beads, can drag smaller indicators flush or under the water, making strike defection difficult to impossible.

Takes are not always aggressive. They can be subtle. In these situations, indicator shape can provide salvation. Teardrop- or tapered-style indicators lie flat on the water. As the fish takes the fly, the indicator first stands and then pulls under the water. When fish are taking softly, a standing indicator might be your only sign of a take. Once a fish feels something isn't right, it spits out the fly without ever pulling it down, another argument for making short casts so you can see this indicator behavior and react.

Indicator Leaders

During one of my on-the-water stillwater schools, I had two anglers in my boat. Chironomids were hatching in 10 feet of water. Both anglers were using indicators to suspend their pupal patterns 1 foot off the bottom. It only took a few fly changes to figure out pattern size and color. The person at the bow began hooking fish at a steady pace, roughly one every 15 minutes. The person on the stern hadn't caught a fish, a pattern that continued for over an hour. As the instructor and guide, it was my job to figure things out. We went through all of the typical solutions: pattern size, pattern color, and depth. Nothing changed.

Eventually, the student who wasn't catching anything asked if we could confirm the correct depth by putting the two indicators together and stroking the leader and tippet down to the fly. The flies were within a millimeter of each other; the distance from fly to indicator seemed correct. During this process, I could feel that one leader was thin and level and the other had a definite taper to it between the indicator and fly. The tapered leader belonged to the person who wasn't catching fish. I suggested a change to the indicator-style leaders I prefer that feature a level tippet section. After making this change, my student caught a fish on his first cast. He then proceeded to catch fish on his next three casts.

For the balance of the day, both students enjoyed catching fish with similar frequency. Peace and harmony and a certain level of personal satisfaction ensued. So, the question remains: "Does the leader make that much of a difference when indicator fishing?" The answer, in short, is an emphatic "Yes!"

The example above illustrates why the correct leader setup when using strike indicators is a critical success factor. How you set up a strike indicator leader is the most crucial section of this chapter and perhaps this entire book. For your flies to hang at the desired depth, there must be level, thin-diameter leader and tippet material between your indicator and fly.

Most people think a standard tapered trout leader will work. Conventional tapered trout leaders feature a long, thick butt section—50 percent of the leader length in most instances—designed to facilitate the gentle transfer of casting energy so you can accurately present a dry fly to a feeding trout. If the leader didn't transfer energy efficiently, there is a risk the fly may land aggressively and spook the trout. When it comes to indicator systems, a thin level leader sinks vertically, whereas a tapered leader's sink rate varies along its length. The butt section of a tapered leader is typically 40 pounds or greater. Thick-diameter leader material sinks slower than thinner-diameter material. Although the indicator appears set to suspend the fly at the targeted depth, it won't, as the leader droops off the indicator in a subtle arc. A level indicator leader sinks straight down from the indicator to the set depth.

I strongly recommend the use of indicator-style leaders. These leaders feature a short butt section, typically 3 feet or less. The majority of the leader is thin, level leader material. The brand I prefer is 10 feet long regardless of the breaking strain. I simply add equal- or lesser-diameter tippet material to the leader to construct the overall leader length. I always use 2 to 3 feet of fluorocarbon tippet for my last leader section. Keeping in mind ethical catch-and-release practices and having the ability to manage large trout, I use 2X to 4X leader and tippet material most often.

As the indicator leaders I use are only 10 feet long, I only have 7 feet of level leader factoring in the short, 3-foot butt section. To fish deeper I must add equal- or lesser-diameter tippet material plus my final 2- to 3-foot tippet section. For example, if I need to suspend my flies at 15 feet, I would begin with the 10-foot indicator leader. I would then add 6 feet of tippet material followed by my 2- to 3-foot tippet section to have enough leader and tippet between my indicator to reach 15 feet. To minimize consuming the main indicator leader, I use the tippet section between it and the final tippet section as my adjustment zone. To fish deeper, I add tippet to this section. To fish shallower, I remove tippet.

Some ardent indicator fly fishers construct leaders made up entirely of tippet material. Level leaders are tangle-prone, especially for new fly fishers, when coupled with heavy flies such as balanced leeches. They require a bit of casting practice to get used to, and this is the primary reason I favor roll casts when fishing indicators on lakes. Thin-diameter tippet material can also bite into the welded loop at the end of the line, damaging it in the process. I prefer the short, thicker butt section of the indicator leader, as it aids casting and prevents fly line damage since it doesn't bite into the welded loop. Between the fly line and indicator, your leader has a bit of backbone to help cast and present the fly. The level leader and tippet between the indicator and flies ensure they sink to their set depth.

Standard Indicator Leader

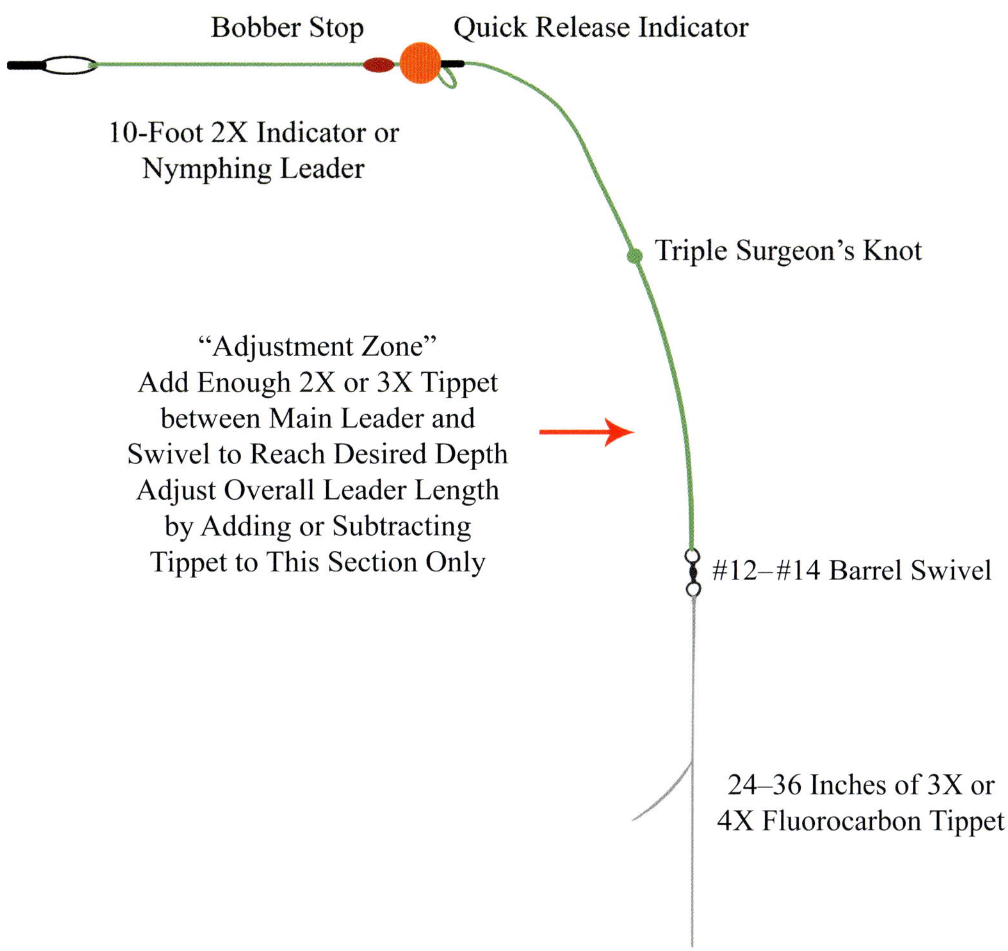

There are times when trout feed in extremely shallow water, a common occurrence when they are chasing and herding minnows tight against emergent shoreline vegetation. In these situations, you are fishing in water that is often less than 5 or 6 feet deep. This is the only time I stray from my usual indicator nymphing leader setup, as it is too long. In these situations, I build a short, stout, tapered leader using two different sections of tippet material. I begin with a short, approximately 3-foot, section of 15-pound nylon tippet. I then add enough 10- or 12-pound fluorocarbon tippet to ensure I can suspend a fly a minimum of 1 foot off the bottom. Most of the time, my overall leader length is roughly 7 feet. I don't use a swivel, as it would get in the way, prohibiting me from setting my indicator so I can work my flies 1 to 2 feet below the surface. The entire leader setup must be stout. When you hook a fish, you must fight it aggressively. You often have to horse the trout out of the shallows so it doesn't take you into the weeds lining the bottom or fringing the shoreline.

Deep-Water Indicator Leaders

When you begin suspending flies 15 feet or more below a releasing indicator, it soon becomes apparent that the indicator doesn't trip consistently. This trait is due to the inherent stretch in nylon leader and tippet. As you recognize a take and set the hook, the natural elasticity in the leader absorbs the majority of your set. You still hook the fish, but the indicator remains locked in place. You either have to trip the indicator at some point in the fight as you would with a fixed position Corky or set harder, which risks breaking the fish off. So, what's the solution?

I had the good fortune to fish California's Crowley Lake with local guide Ernie Gulley. Crowley is famous for its deep-water chironomid emergences. During my time there, I learned how Crowley's anglers and particularly guides such as Ernie developed a simple, no-stretch leader that consistently trips Quick Release Indicators.

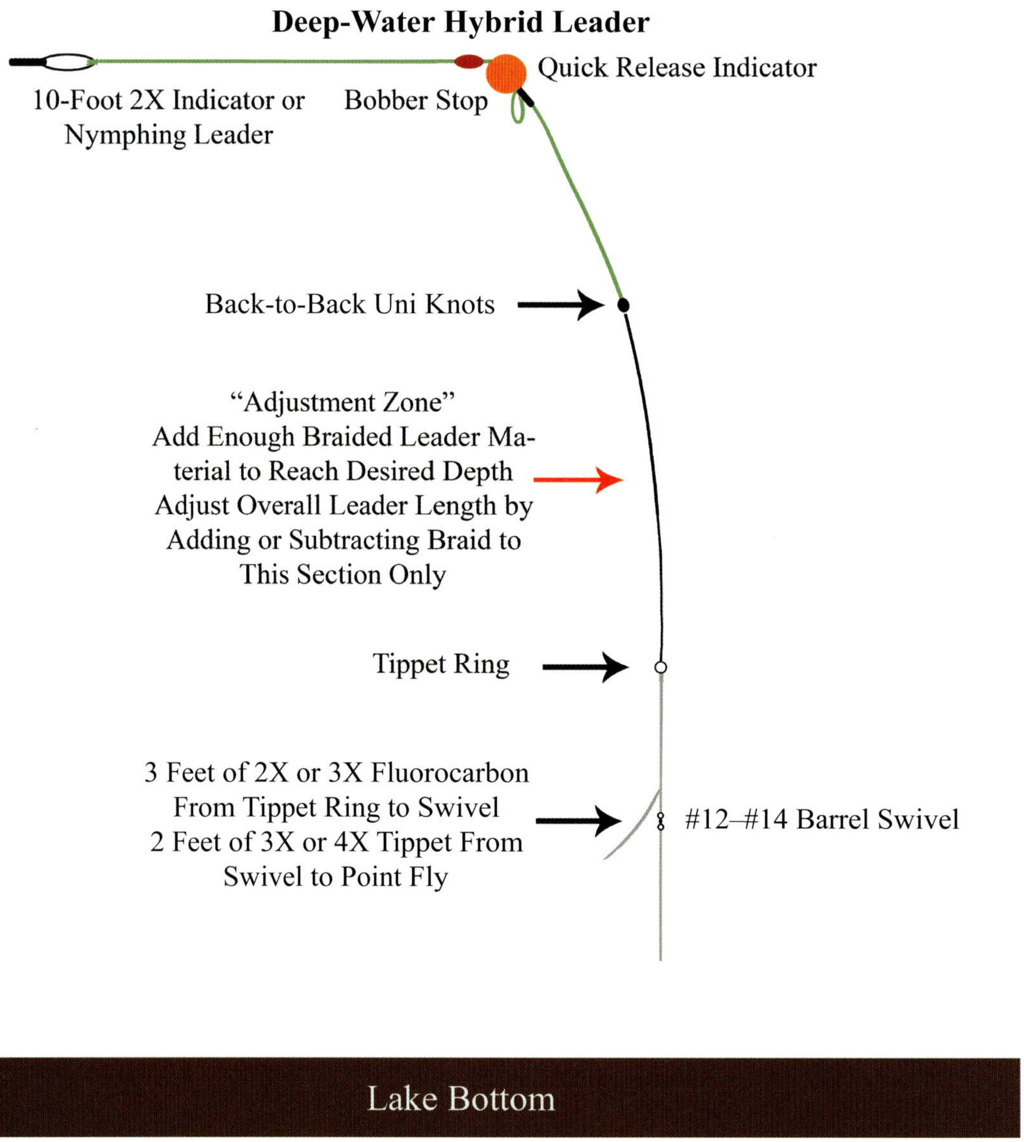

Rather than using a nylon-based leader, they use leaders built primarily out of low-stretch braided leader material, the same material used by many conventional anglers. I use 10 to 15 feet of 25- or 30-pound braid for my full-length low-stretch systems. A 4- to 5-foot section of fluorocarbon tippet, connected to the braid via a barrel swivel or tippet ring, completes my full-length low-stretch leader.

One of the hallmarks of braided leader material is its high strength versus low diameter. Breaking strain has nothing to do with why I prefer heavier braid, however. It is all about reducing tangles. High-strength braid is thicker and less tangle-prone. Once a braided leader tangles and knots, it is almost impossible to undo. You have to rebuild the leader. As this system is an "end justifies the means" solution, I strongly recommend using short roll casts to present this rig. As a general rule, the deeper you are fishing, the shorter the cast. Provided you aren't making a lot of surface noise, fish will cruise comfortably below. Also, due to the increased distance between the indicator and fly, you need to keep things close so you can react to any signs of a take.

I now use a hybrid low-stretch leader the majority of the time when using indicators in deep water. The hybrid uses a 10-foot indicator leader as the primary foundation connected by back-to-back uni knots to a short, 5- to 10-foot section of thinner, 8- or 10-pound braid. I attach the final fluorocarbon tippet to the braided section using a tippet ring. The final tippet section is usually 4 to 5 feet long, broken into two sections separated by a small barrel swivel. As with the nylon-based indicator leader, increase or decrease the braided section to shorten or lengthen the overall leader.

I try to keep the final tippet section, from swivel to fly, to approximately 2 feet. If you want to add a second fly, simply add a sliding dropper just above the swivel. When using smaller flies, consider adding one or two small split shot to overpower the floating tendencies of braided leader so you can get your flies down to the desired depth in an expedited manner.

The hybrid leader offers a couple of advantages. You can quickly transform a nylon-based indicator leader into a low-stretch leader without having to replace the leader with a full braided leader, and there is no risk of the braid biting into the fly line loop and damaging the line.

Setting Indicator Depth

When indicator fishing, it is critical to know the depth of water you are exploring. An electronic sounder or, as described in chapter 3, "Getting Around," a marked anchor rope makes determining your depth easy.

If the bottom is flat and featureless, begin by hanging your flies a foot above the bottom. If the bottom is irregular—dotted by weed clumps, sunken logs, rocks, and other debris—begin 2 feet above the bottom to compensate for working your flies over these obstacles. When fishing over submerged weeds, start by hanging the flies 1 foot above the weed tops.

As fish in lakes prefer to feed just above the bottom, always start working your flies in that area. If you have no takes, begin shortening the distance between your indicator and flies in 1-foot increments to work through the water column. Flies intended to represent smaller prey usually dictate small incremental changes, as fish are less likely to alter their feeding depth for an apparent minor caloric reward. There simply isn't enough food energy to warrant moving any significant distance to feed. Larger flies designed to imitate minnows and leeches offer higher value, and trout are more likely to move a greater distance.

I believe that it is better to err on the side of presenting your flies slightly higher than the trout's feeding level rather than below. Trout are more likely to rise to take a prey item than tip down. Once a trout takes the fly, it usually descends to its original cruise depth. This trick results in a positive pull-down, giving you a better chance of a positive reaction.

Many times, approximately setting depth works well, but some situations dictate a more precise approach. Using a ruler mounted on your boat or one that is part of the markings on a float tube or pontoon boat is an excellent way to accurately measure and set indicator depth.

How to Set Indicator Depth

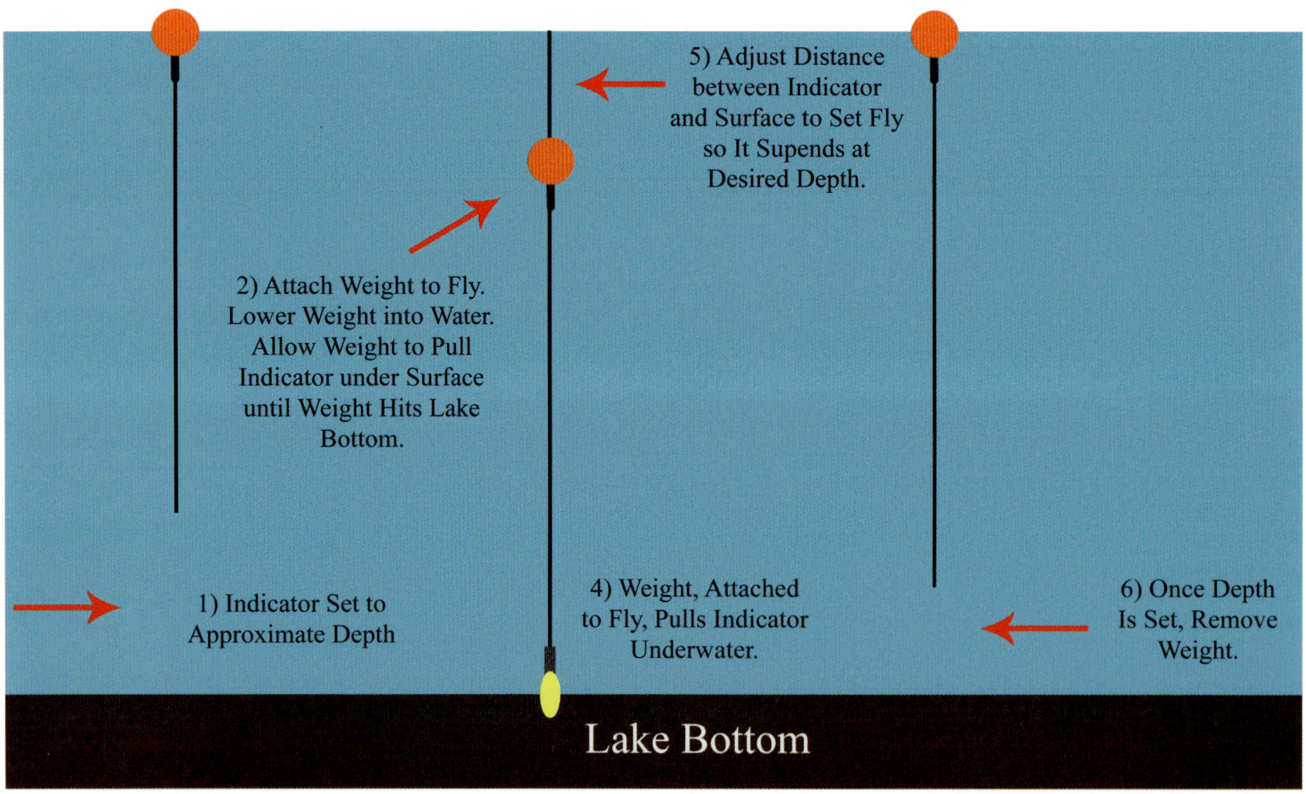

When trout are being fussy due to cold water temperatures or weather change or are rigidly feeding at a specific level on tiny prey such as zooplankton or chironomid pupae, a depth locator is invaluable. A depth locator is nothing more than a weight used to set indicator depth surgically. Depth locators are also used to set fly depth when dangling or when fishing vertically using fast-sinking lines. For a detailed explanation, refer to chapter 11, "Going Deep." The weight source can be a pair of forceps, a bell sinker, a steelhead slinky, or an actual depth locator designed for ice fishing.

Using a depth locator is easy:

1. Set your indicator for the approximate depth you wish to target.
2. Carefully attach the weight to the fly, being careful not to damage it.
3. Lower the weight into the water, allowing it to hit bottom gently. Don't let the weight plunge into the bottom, as this leads to inaccurate readings.
4. The weight pulls the buoyant indicator underneath the surface. The distance between the indicator and the surface tells you how far your fly will suspend above the bottom once you remove the weight.
5. Generally, you want to begin suspending your flies a foot off the bottom. With this in mind, adjust your indicator so it sits a foot below the surface.
6. With the indicator now set, remove the weight, slide the bobber stop down to the indicator to mark your depth, and cast.

THE NAKED TECHNIQUE

Before the introduction and subsequent popularity of strike indicators, we used floating lines in conjunction with long, 15-foot-plus leaders to fish small weighted flies—a method christened the "naked technique" due to the absence of a strike indicator to control depth. Although not as widely used today as strike indicators, the naked technique is an essential option in the stillwater fly fisher's presentation arsenal.

Although tricky to learn at first, the naked technique teaches two key elements that transfer to other presentation techniques: patience and touch. Patience as a result of taking the time to allow the fly or flies to sink to the proper depth and retrieving them at a snail's pace, touch by learning to recognize the subtle takes associated with this method. Using floating and later midge-tip lines coupled with long leaders, this was how I first learned to fish chironomid pupa patterns. In addition to chironomid pupa and larva patterns, the naked technique works when using a variety of other pattern types, including scuds, damselfly nymphs, caddis pupae, mayfly nymphs, and even leeches. If I had only one way to fish lakes, it would be the naked technique.

Mastering the naked technique involves balancing four variables: leader construction, sink time, weight, and retrieve speed.

Naked Technique Elements

At first glance, the naked technique seems simple. Cast as far as you comfortably can. Let the flies sink. Retrieve the flies and catch fish. Nothing different from any other presentation technique. But there are four crucial elements to this technique that must be mastered and balanced for consistent success:

1. Leader construction: Allows the flies to reach the targeted depth.
2. Sink time: Allows the patterns to sink and reach the targeted depth.
3. Weight: The naked technique works best with weighted patterns. Additional weight, including barrel swivels integrated into the leader, multiple flies (if legal), and split shot or putty, may be required to get the flies deep.
4. Retrieve speed: Painstakingly slow retrieves are needed to keep the flies tracking at a consistent depth.

Leader Construction

Although you can use the naked technique at almost any depth, it is a method I prefer to use in water between 16 and 25 feet deep. To reach the required depth and to allow your flies to track correctly through the water, long leaders are required. Long leaders are intimidating to most fly fishers. Visions of frustrating tangles and an inability to effectively cast run rampant. If you can cast a 9-foot leader, you can cast a 20-foot leader. My elder son learned to fish long leaders when he was nine. He didn't realize or worry about the leader. Catching fish was his goal, and if that dictated long leaders, so be it.

I am not aware of any company that produces leaders longer than 15 feet. You have to build your own. Many anglers, particularly competition anglers, use long, thin, level leaders. Casting level leaders takes a bit of practice and can be challenging. I use a formula that provides enough leader length to reach the targeted depth but also aids casting. Begin with either a 12-foot or preferably a 15-foot tapered leader and add equal or lesser diameters of fluorocarbon tippet to complete the overall leader. To build a 20-foot leader, begin with a 3X 15-foot tapered leader and add 5 feet of 4X fluorocarbon tippet. For a 25-foot leader, I would start with the same 15-foot tapered leader and add 5 feet of 3X fluorocarbon followed by another 5 feet of 4X fluorocarbon.

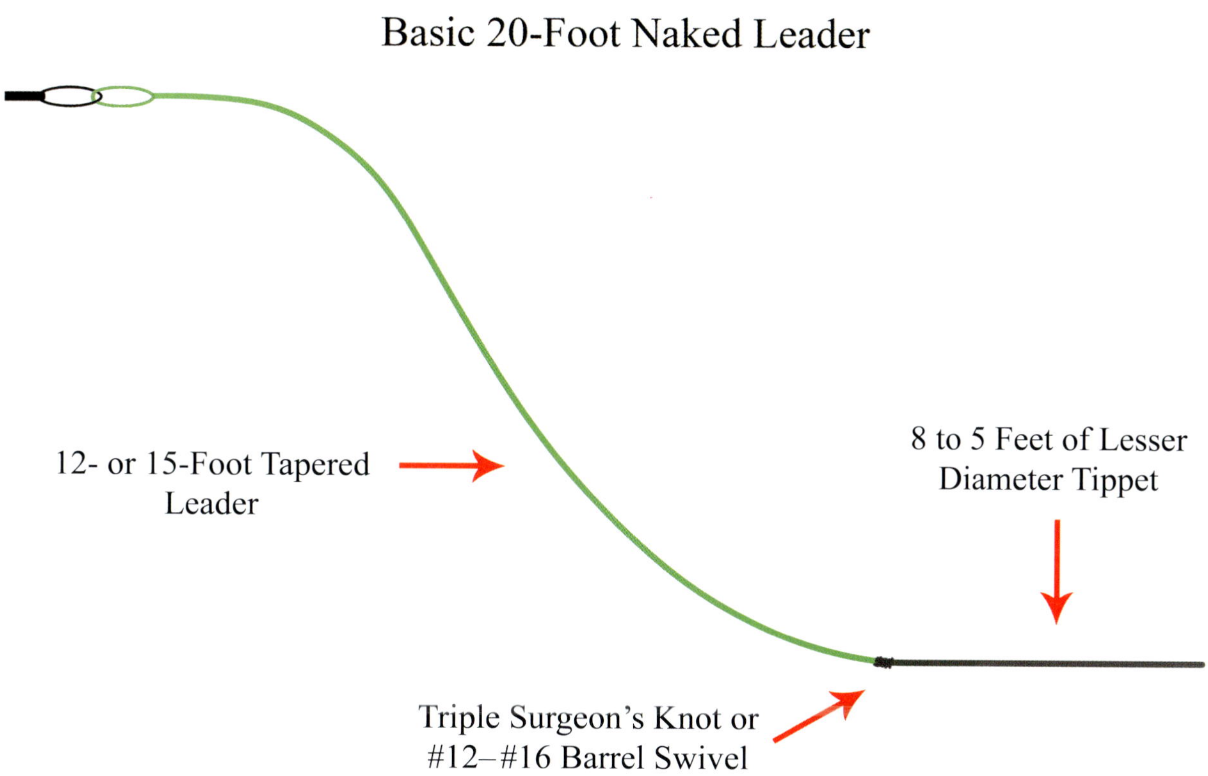

A tapered leader's diameter varies from the thick butt section down to the thin tippet section. Unlike dedicated indicator leaders, we are using this feature to our advantage for both presentation and casting. The thick butt section provides the leader with some backbone, helping it turn over while reducing the risk of tangles and subsequent frustration. The differing diameter also causes the leader to sink at different rates along its length, allowing a slow, controlled sink rate that allows for slow, natural, pedestrian retrieves.

There is a method to the madness when it comes to determining the correct leader length. Factoring in the varying sink rate along its length, I want a leader that is 25 percent longer than the water I am targeting. The additional length compensates for the arched profile of the leader as it sinks and tracks back during the retrieve. To reach 16 feet, I need a 19-foot leader (16 × 1¼). The table below provides a complete leader length listing for water depths from 12 to 25 feet.

Naked Technique Leader Length vs. Depth

Depth Target	Required Leader Length (Depth Target x 1.25)
10 Feet	12.5 Feet
12 Feet	15.0 Feet
14 Feet	17.5 Feet
16 Feet	20 Feet
18 Feet	22.5 Feet
20 Feet	25 Feet
25 Feet	31.25 Feet

Sink Time

Once the cast is complete, the fly or flies must be allowed to sink. Water depth plays a role in determining sink time, with shallow water requiring less sink time than deep water. As I prefer to use this method when prospecting water 16 to 25 feet deep, my minimum sink time is 30 seconds in most instances. I use the sweep hand of my watch to ensure consistent, accurate sink times. There is always an element of experimentation. Just be sure to note your sink time if you hook a fish so you can duplicate it again on future presentations.

Weight

The naked technique is essentially long-leader nymphing. As the wind is almost always a constant stillwater companion, patterns should be weighted to cope with the wind-induced current. As the wind increases, lake current behaves similarly to river current, inhibiting the sink rate of your fly or flies. Additional weight may be required to ensure your patterns sink to the targeted depth and don't get swept downwind.

I often incorporate small (size 12 to 16) barrel swivels into my leader between the last tippet section and the remainder of the leader to compensate for wind-induced current. In extreme circumstances, weighted putty massaged around the swivel or split shot may be needed. When the wind is brisk, I often switch to a midge-tip line. The clear tip bites through the surface chop, reducing any adverse action imparted to the floating line while allowing you to maintain contact with your flies.

Retrieve Speed

Retrieves with the naked technique must be painstakingly slow to keep the flies tracking through the water at a consistent level. A brisk retrieve causes your flies to climb out of the zone you are trying to target, typically within a foot or two of the bottom.

I use a snail-paced two-finger hand twist or pinch strip retrieve. If there is any line memory, your retrieve pace should not straighten it. After making the cast and allowing the leader and flies to sink, begin with two brisk 3- to 4-inch strips. I always start my retrieves in this manner. The two quick strips remove any slack that may have formed while the leader and flies were sinking. Plus, the sudden movement of the flies may trigger any fish in the vicinity to investigate and hopefully take. Always be prepared for a strike within a few seconds after the two brisk strips.

If you aren't having success with the naked technique, moving the fly or flies too fast and not letting them sink long enough are the two most likely causes.

Recognizing Takes

As the retrieve is slow with the naked technique, trout rarely take the fly aggressively. If the line is under tension, as can happen in windy conditions, you feel most takes. The take is addictive—a sharp stab, similar to the grab associated with swinging wet flies on moving water. At times takes can also feel as though someone has closed a book onto the leader, creating a sensation of weight. If you feel any resistance to the retrieve, set the hook. Hook-sets are always free.

When a trout grabs the fly, this action transmits through the tippet and leader, down the fly line, and is eventually sensed by the rod hand. The touch with this method comes from recognizing takes before you feel them. You should see the majority of naked takes before you feel them.

The fly line is essentially a long hi-vis indicator. With practice, takes can be detected by merely watching the line. Takes manifest themselves in several ways: The

The naked technique teaches you two essential presentation elements: patience and touch. These two skills, once mastered, will help you across a variety of presentation techniques.

DOUG PULLAN

curve of a gently sweeping line straightens, the tip section pulls down or veers left or right, or, my favorite, subtle line curves straightening.

When a floating line sits on a relatively calm surface, there are often small line curves, or "squiggles." Watch one of the subtle line curves as closely as possible to the tip. If the curve begins to straighten, signifying a take, pinch the line against the rod handle and raise the rod swiftly to set the hook. Tension, on the other end, is the reason the line straightened. If you are using the correct retrieve speed, the line will be moving so slowly that any subtle curve will not straighten, as you aren't applying tension to your end of the line. If the line straightens, a fish at the other end of the line is applying tension

On flat, calm, windless days, pay particular attention to where the tip section of the line enters the water. The tip section sliding just subsurface is ideal, as it ensures direct contact with your leader and fly. If a fish takes the fly, the tension often creates a small circular ripple at the junction, as though someone had used an eyedropper. As with a line take, it takes a leap of faith to set the hook without feeling anything.

With practice, recognizing takes provides you with almost a sixth sense. It is this touch that is such an essential element to the naked technique, a skill that transfers to other presentation disciplines. Your catch rate should increase while improving your overall stillwater experience.

WHEN TO FISH INDICATORS OR FISH NAKED

"When should I fish indicators and when should I use the naked technique?" is a common question. Here are a few guidelines:

- Although you can fish indicators in deep water, I use indicators most often in water 15 feet or less.
- If, when fishing in deeper water with indicators, you are having trouble picking up subtle takes, try the naked technique for more direct contact with the fly. With the 90-degree connection between you and the fly when using an indicator, a fish can swim a short distance then sense the tension of the leader and spit the hook, causing the missed take.
- If fish want a moving fly, use the naked technique.
- If fish prefer a static or near-static presentation due to cold water temperatures or weather change, use an indicator.
- When trout seem fixated on a particular depth, use an indicator.
- Use a strike indicator when prospecting in an around shallow weed pockets.
- If you are allowed to fish more than one rod at a time, use a strike indicator setup and allow a fly to suspend while you explore other options using cast and retrieve presentations.

- If you have someone new to fly fishing or is an inexperienced caster, set them up with a strike indicator. Although you may have to cast for them at first, the indicator eliminates hang-ups and, perhaps most importantly, gets them catching fish and enjoying their time on the water.
- If fish seem to be spread out vertically over a wide area, try the naked technique.

CASTING INDICATORS AND LONG-LEADER SYSTEMS

Due to the long skinny leaders, swivels, and multiple flies, strike indicator systems are tangle-prone. Conversely, many people unfamiliar with the naked technique are intimidated when it comes to casting long leaders. With a bit of discipline and by following some fundamental principles, casting indicator rigs and long leaders can be relatively problem-free. Here are some tips to keep tangles and subsequent frustration to a minimum:

- Long rods, 9½ feet or longer, help form wider casting loops. An open casting loop is less likely to foul.
- You can also open your casting loop by breaking your wrist slightly.
- Always place the wind at your back whenever possible.
- Use only enough leader and tippet as necessary. If the situation requires a 15-foot leader, don't use 20 feet. If conditions change, you can always extend the leader. Conversely, if you move from deep to shallow water, shorten the leader.
- As with any cast, a smooth application of power to a crisp stop on both the forward cast and backcast is critical. Aggressive use of power causes the rod tip to travel in a curved path. As the fly line follows the rod tip, this helps cause the casting loop to tail and tangle.
- Allow the backcast to lay out entirely before coming forward. Coming forward too soon, without allowing the backcast to lay out, introduces slack, which causes the loop to tail and tangle.
- Keep false casts to a minimum. The more time your line and leader remain airborne, the higher the chance of a tangle. I follow a "twice and gone" philosophy, meaning no more than two false casts before letting the line shoot. If any amount of wind is present, often a single false cast suffices.
- Shoot the line. I use weight-forward lines, which concentrate their weight, or mass, in the head section. The remainder of the line is level, shooting line designed to follow the head section on the cast. Once the head section is outside the rod tip, complete the cast. Don't continue to false cast once the head section is past the rod tip or the cast will collapse. Tangles and frustration soon follow.

- When casting indicators, use a roll cast whenever possible. With the roll cast, the leader, indicator, and flies only leave the water as you apply power on the forward stroke. Roll casts virtually eliminate leader tangles.
- Make sure you have enough line out of the rod tip, typically a rod length minimum, to flex or load the rod properly. Casting a short line promotes excessive power and rod speed, causing nasty tangles.
- Don't be in a rush to lower the rod when casting. Allow the line and leader to completely unfurl and land on the water before dropping the rod.
- Allow the line to come tight to the reel on the final cast or pinch the line as the line shoots to the target to slingshot the leader and flies to turn over completely.
- Using a tuck cast featuring a high rod stop on the final forward cast allows the flies to land first and sink.
- Look for distinct, separate splashes of each fly, swivel, and strike indicator as they hit the water. If everything lands within a short radius, chances are the leader is fouled. Strip in the line—you might be able to sort out the tangle. Repeated false casts will only exacerbate the problem.
- Keep the strike indicator within 3 feet of the end of the fly line. If the indicator is too far from the line, the leader becomes unbalanced and difficult to cast. This situation often occurs when moving from deep to shallow water without shortening the leader.

CHAPTER TAKEAWAYS

- A floating line offers incredible versatility. From an anchored position, you can fish from the surface to over 25 feet deep.
- Strike indicators help you control two of the most critical presentation elements: depth and retrieve speed.
- Indicators offer several presentation benefits including precise depth control, prospecting shallow weed beds and pockets, targeting fish that will only accept a static presentation, managing windy conditions, and when fishing two rods at once.
- There are a variety of indicator types available. No indicator ticks all of the boxes, and each type has its pros and cons. You should have a cross section of different indicator types, colors, and sizes on hand.
- Leader construction is crucial to a successful indicator presentation. The leader and tippet between the indicator and fly must be level and of similar or equal diameter along its length to ensure your flies sink to the set depth. Avoid using a standard tapered leader due to the differing diameter along their length. Tapered leaders don't allow your flies to sink to the required depth.
- Integrating a no-stretch component to a strike indicator leader when fishing water 15 feet or greater removes any elasticity in a nylon-based leader so a Quick Release Indicator trips consistently.

- Rubberized bobber stops and swivels are critical indicator accessories to have on hand.
- You can use a variety of weight sources including hemostats or a depth locator to set indicator depth surgically.
- There are four crucial elements to the "naked technique" that must be mastered and balanced for consistent success: leader construction, sink time, weight, and retrieve speed.
- Use a snail-paced two-finger hand twist or pinch strip retrieve with the naked technique.
- The floating line often serves as a strike indicator when using the naked technique.
- There are situations where indicators are the best presentation over the naked technique, and vice versa.
- Fly fishers can be intimidated when faced with the prospect of casting long leaders or complex indicator rigs. If you follow basic casting guidelines, you can cast these leader systems with ease.
- Avoid long-distance casts with indicators. The deeper the presentation, the closer you keep the indicator, so you don't miss subtle takes and you provide yourself with ample reaction time.
- When using tangle-prone indicator rigs, use the roll cast as often as you can.

CHAPTER 10

FLOATING LINE TECHNIQUES: DRIES, EMERGERS, AND TARGETING SIGHTED FISH

The majority of stillwater trout in North America feed near the bottom. That is where most food lives, and the risk of becoming lunch for an osprey or other avian predator is reduced. Your best chance of catching trout on lakes lies prospecting beneath the surface. However, if trout are feeding at or just beneath the surface, you should be prepared for this presentation challenge.

Let's be honest: Lakes are not widely known for their surface action. Lakes are deeper than rivers or streams, so it is safer and more efficient for trout to feed near the bottom, as that is where the majority of stillwater food lives. There is also a reduced risk of falling victim to an eagle, osprey, loon, or other predator if a trout remains deep, hidden from view. If you want to place odds in your favor, subsurface tactics are the way to go. For example, I only have the opportunity or choose to fish adult chironomids roughly 5 percent of the time. Imitating the pupae and larvae offers a higher probability of success.

Yes, there are always exceptions, such as Montana's Hebgen Lake. Some stillwaters such as Hebgen have become famous for often-consistent surface action, so much so that you can plan a visit to take advantage of the dry and emerger opportunities Hebgen's gulping trout have become famous for.

Nonetheless, if trout are feeding at or just beneath the surface, it is tough to resist the urge to cast to rising fish. It is also important to remain adaptable to whatever is going on any given day. Although fishing dries and emergers isn't as productive as prospecting the depths, I believe all stillwater fly fishers should be prepared to take advantage of any surface-feeding fish. Targeting surface-feeding trout is an addictive experience, fly fisher versus fish. It requires patience. Your powers of observation are crucial. Trout also provide you with instant feedback on both your pattern choice and presentation techniques.

Targeting surface-feeding trout is an addictive, fly fisher versus fish, experience.

In western North America, there are numerous lakes with healthy populations of caddisflies, chironomids, and mayflies. Trout in these lakes are aware of the adult and emerger opportunities these insects offer. They have become conditioned surface feeders, so much so that it is possible, at times, to prospect and explore using dry and emerger patterns in the same manner as you would with nymphs and streamers.

Stillwater trout have a wide range of potential surface prey, such as this adult damselfly.

Due to the generally low percentage of dry and emerger opportunities across North American lakes, however, I have a broad definition of what trout prey might provide me with the chance to take a surface-feeding fish. River and stream anglers are familiar with mayflies, caddisflies, and chironomids (midges), but surface-feeding opportunities for these insects also exist in lakes. Terrestrials, including grasshoppers, beetles, and ants—food sources most moving water fly fishers are very familiar imitating—can also have localized importance.

When targeting surface-feeding trout on a lake, any potential food source can provide surface action, including baitfish, water boatmen, and backswimmers.

Stillwater trout also feed on water boatmen and backswimmers during their mating and migration flights, damselfly adults, and baitfish that have been corralled just below the surface or crippled survivors struggling to swim after a trout attempted to break up a school. I have even taken large rainbows, browns, and brook trout on mouse patterns, an addictive experience all fly fishers should try if they haven't already.

The explosive, aggressive rise to larger flies such as mouse patterns is easy to become addicted to.
BARRY ACTON

EQUIPMENT REQUIREMENTS

As with moving waters, controlled, relatively short, accurate casts work best, whether targeting rising trout or prospecting an area where surface-feeding trout have been active. I prefer floating lines designed with surface-feeding trout in mind. Lines featuring long front tapers dissipate casting energy, allowing delicate presentations. Your flies land softly and you are less likely to spook trout.

Some of the best surface opportunities take place when there is little to no wind. Sunny, calm conditions are some of the most challenging. Trout are wary. There is no wind to channel their movement, and cruise paths are random and, at times, difficult to predict. Dry fly–specific lines, featuring long head sections, allow for quick, quiet pickups and lay-downs to cope with moving, unpredictable fish. Clean your floating line frequently to remove dirt and other contaminants. A high-riding floating line is less likely to grip the surface during the pickup portion of the cast.

Water conditions often have an impact on your choice of dry and emerger patterns. In flat, calm conditions, smaller flies usually work best. A rippled surface allows you to increase your fly size.

There are instances where aggressive floating lines featuring short front tapers and large head sections are a wise choice. Large, wind-resistant flies such as adult caddis, grasshopper, baitfish, and rodent patterns are prime candidates for floating lines that might seem better suited for casting large streamers and indicator rigs.

When fishing dries and emergers, the goal is to target specific trout whenever possible. There are times when trout are rising in a random, difficult-to-predict fashion or the surface conditions mask subtle surface rises to adults or emergers. In these circumstances, shotgunning casts over likely areas, where fish have been rising, is a standard approach. When using a shotgun approach, let the flies sit on the water for a short period, perhaps 5 or 10 seconds, before casting to a new area. In these situations midge-tip, or clear-tip, lines featuring short, 3-foot, slow-sinking intermediate tips are also an excellent presentation option when coupled with one or more damp patterns that are nothing more than a wet fly with a stiff hackle.

After making a cast, let the flies sit at or in the surface film. After a short time, the clear-tip drags the flies beneath the surface. As soon as the flies disappear, begin a slow, erratic hand twist retrieve. Be prepared for a take. Many times, fish take flies on the retrieve more than when they sit on the surface. This approach takes advantage of both surface-feeding fish and those cruising just beneath the surface feeding on emerging nymphs, pupae, or sunken adults.

Although targeting surface-feeding trout using floating lines is the standard approach, a midge-tip line is another great option.

Midge-tip, or clear-tip, lines also work well with buoyant mouse, baitfish, and large attractor patterns such as Boobies or Chernobyl Ants and their many variations. Use a hard strip to drag or pop the fly beneath the surface and then let it sit. This approach often draws aggressive trout from a distance. Be prepared for a vicious, heart-stopping strike, often when the fly is sitting still and all seems quiet.

Compared to subsurface floating line presentations, dry and emerger leaders are shorter. I use 9- to 12-foot leaders for the majority of my surface feeding. The extended butt section of a tapered leader muffles surface disturbance by further dissipating casting energy while helping to facilitate short, accurate casts when targeting surface-orientated trout.

To build a 12-foot leader, I begin with a 9-foot leader and add 3 feet of fluorocarbon tippet. I form a tippet knot dropper so I can fish adults and emergers on the same cast until the fish tell me which stage they prefer. On calm, bright, clear days, I may extend my leader to 14 feet. Leaders over 14 feet are less accurate and require practice to master. Most times, leaders 12 feet or longer aren't necessary.

I use fluorocarbon tippet almost exclusively with dries and emergers. In calm, clear conditions, fluorocarbon cuts through the surface film, reducing the risk of creating a tippet shadow, which often alerts fish that something isn't quite right with the fly. Some fly fishers use nylon tippet, believing it helps better float the fly. As we seldom, if ever, leave a fly sitting for prolonged periods, any issues of fluorocarbon dragging a fly beneath the surface are eliminated. In calm conditions, proponents of nylon tippet degrease their leaders with special leader mud. In Europe, fly fishers use Fuller's earth, a difficult-to-obtain fine clay powder, mixed with liquid dish soap to create a degreasing mud.

Although it may seem contradictory, I often switch to lighter tippets to avoid straightening smaller, light-wire dry-fly hooks. I prefer using heavy tippets for subsurface work so I can strike and fight fish aggressively. When larger fish are on the prowl, heavy tippets coupled with low-stretch lines and moderate to fast rods make small, light-wire dry-fly hooks the weakest link. With larger flies, this isn't an issue, as I use standard or heavy-wire hooks. Larger dry flies contain a higher volume of buoyant materials, and, in many instances, a stout hook helps ensure the fly lands properly, hook point down.

Where legal, I almost always use multiple flies when targeting rising trout. Multiple flies allow me to cover more water, and I can imitate both adults and emergers at the same time. Washing line tactics also work well with surface-feeding fish. The buoyant point fly can be used to suspend nymph or pupa patterns. Waking flies such as a Booby can also attract fish to more-imitative flies as well. Due to the trout's reduced window of vision at the surface, I keep my flies 2 to 3 feet apart—the clearer the water, the greater the spacing. Other than when regulations dictate, I might only fish a single fly in sunny, calm conditions, as multiple flies landing near a fish or group of fish may startle them.

FLOATANT AND DESICCANTS

Fly floatant and desiccant are two kit bag essentials for surface-feeding trout. As both of these accessories have different purposes, they work best when used together. Floatant works best when applied to flies that are dry, yet to be soaked, or smothered in fish slime. I apply desiccant or powder to saturated or slimy flies to dry them out and recharge them for reuse. Once recharged, floatant may be applied once again.

Applying floatant is easy. The key is moderation. Avoid applying floatant like a toddler squeezing toothpaste onto a toothbrush. There should be no floatant slicks emanating from your fly. To apply floatant:

1. Squeeze a conservative amount of floatant onto the tip of your forefinger.
2. Rub the floatant between the tips of your forefinger and thumb to allow your body heat to liquefy the floatant.
3. Pat and squeeze the liquefied floatant on and into the various components of the fly you wish to float.

Try to avoid squirting floatant directly on the fly. Liquefy the floatant on the tips of your thumb and forefinger and pat it onto the fly or portions of the fly you want to float.

Larger patterns and foam-based patterns may require multiple applications to ensure the fly is saturated and ready to float. You may only wish to apply floatant to specific parts of a fly, such as a wing post or the thorax area of an emerger, so the fly floats partially on the surface. Floatant can also be used to grease the tip section of a floating line. A high-riding tip section lifts off the water easier with a minimum of surface disturbance.

Where you place floatant depends on the fly's design and purpose. My Para Pupa represents a chironomid pupa hanging just below the surface. I only apply floatant to the hi-vis wing post.

Desiccant, by design, is intended to remove moisture from a sunken or slimy fly. Begin by first patting the fly dry on a shirt sleeve, chamois cloth, towel, or amadou patch. Amadou is a natural fungus that absorbs water unbelievably well. Once the fly is dry, applying desiccant powder is easy:

1. Remove the lid of the desiccant powder bottle.
2. Drop the fly in the bottle, still attached to the tippet.
3. Place the lid back on the bottle, being careful not to pinch or nick the tippet.
4. Shake the bottle aggressively a few times to coat the fly with desiccant.
5. Remove the fly from the bottle and blow off the excess desiccant.

Use desiccant powder to recharge saturated flies.

Your fly is recharged and ready for action. Don't forget to tighten the lid on the desiccant bottle. From personal experience, spilled desiccant gets everywhere in a kit bag. Some desiccants come with an applicator brush, allowing you to rub the powder into the fly. There is no need to drop the fly into the bottle with applicator brush desiccants.

READING AND REACTING TO THE RISE

One of the most challenging things to do when surrounded by rising fish is to suppress your excitement to begin casting to the rises and expecting an immediate take. Too often, we assume all rising fish are taking adult or terrestrial insects sitting on the surface. Many times, however, trout are feeding on emerging pupae, transitioning nymphs, or spent spinners sitting in or just under the surface. The rise to an insect sitting on the surface is different from the rise to an emerging insect in or just below the surface. Reading the rise is critical to success so you choose the right pattern and style to match what the fish are feeding on. Having the opportunity to find and target surface-feeding fish is already rare enough. Don't compound things by choosing the wrong fly.

When you find fish feeding at the surface, learning to read the rise becomes a critical skill for success.

Reading the Rise

Surface-feeding fish often poke their noses out of the water. You often see their dorsal fins followed by a deliberate tail sweep. As a trout rises, its head creates a bow wave at one end of the rise. The bow wave, coupled with the tail sweep, provides both the speed and the direction of travel, valuable information that helps determine where to place your fly and how far you should lead the fish in the hope of hooking it.

A bubble in the middle of the rise is a definite tell that the fish is taking something off the surface. When the fish pokes its nose out of the water to grab the insect, it takes not only the insect but a mouthful of air too. As the fish descends, it swallows the bug and exhales the air through its gill plates, leaving a telltale bubble in the process.

Reading the Surface Rise

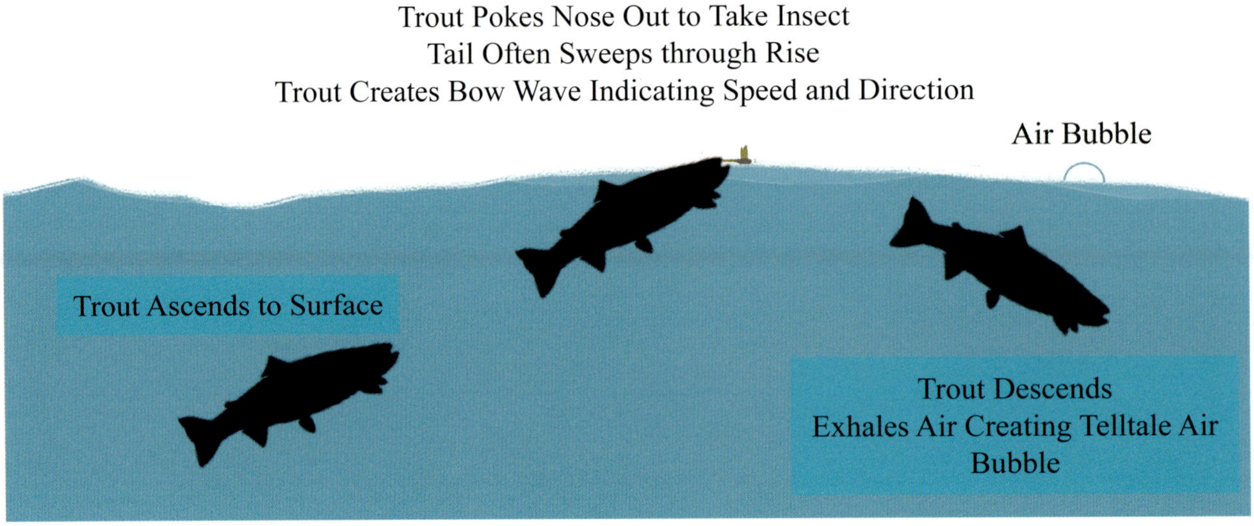

Trout feeding on food just below the surface, such as emerging nymphs and pupae, only show their back, from the rear of their head to the dorsal fin, a riseform behavior often referred to as porpoising. Rarely do you see a tail sweep as the fish arcs through the surface to take the suspended nymph or pupa.

Emerger rises can be challenging to see at times. In extreme circumstances, you might only see a bulge or subtle swirl, as the feeding trout doesn't break the surface. Emerger rises tend to be slow and deliberate, as the suspending pupae or nymphs aren't going anywhere as they hang helplessly during their transition process. More often than not, surface rises are to food suspending just below the surface rather than on it. When in doubt, it is always best to start with an emerger, wet fly, or unweighted nymph with a porpoising rise.

Reading the Emerger Rise

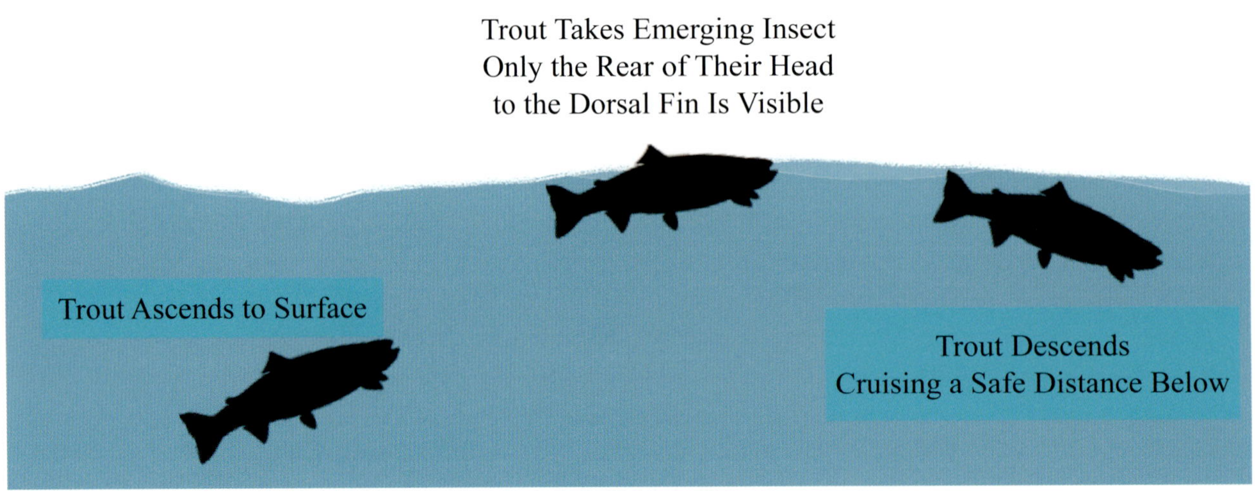

Rises can be slow and deliberate or violent—clues we can also use to determine what they might be feeding upon. A trout only expends just enough energy to feed. Slow, deliberate rises are usually to something small or something that can't escape, such as an emerging pupa, nymph, or mayfly spinner. Trout typically reserve violent, aggressive rises for larger terrestrials or nimble prey such as water boatmen, backswimmers, caddisflies, and damselfly adults.

Surface rises to forage fish are typically explosive. Fleeing baitfish are quick and agile, and trout need to move fast to feed. Targeting trout chasing baitfish at the surface is both intense and chaotic. One moment all is calm and the next, it is as though a detonation occurred. Baitfish fly everywhere as trout slash wildly at them.

Trout size also has a bearing on the intensity of the rise. Juvenile trout rise aggressively as they compete for food with their rivals. Large, lazy fish tend to rise less aggressively for the same food item.

Surface-feeding trout can also be tricksters, appearing to rise when they initially aren't. When targeting more-substantial surface fare, trout may swamp or tail-slap their victim to immobilize it. With their quarry damp and subdued, the trout leisurely returns to take it. This behavior is a common occurrence when trout are taking large adult caddis. The challenge is being observant to recognize this behavior and to let your fly sit at what initially appears to be a botched rise. When trout are swamping adults, it is a nerve-wracking experience. More often than not, we strike, pulling the fly away. It takes practice and discipline to leave the fly until the fish returns to take it.

Reacting to the Rise

After a fish has risen, the question "Where to cast next?" is often asked, as the rise tells you where the fish was, not where it is. Again, reading the rise is essential. Try to suppress your excitement and gain a measure of the trout's direction of travel and speed. If I am unable to see or determine the direction, I have a specific casting sequence.

If there is any wind-induced ripple on the surface, my first cast is always upwind of the rise. Due to the stillwater trout's river and stream roots, they instinctively cruise upwind into any wind-induced current. If there is little to no wind, things can become tricky, as the trout tend to cruise randomly. Determining their direction of travel becomes difficult to predict. In these circumstances, you have to make an educated guess. I always start by casting to the near side of the rise. If that doesn't work, I pick up quickly and target either left or right of the rise. Avoid casting across to the far side of the rise, as you may spook the trout or, if it is cruising with other trout, the entire group.

Slack-line casts are also crucial stillwater presentation elements. Once the fly lands, there must be enough slack in the line and leader to allow the fly to drift with any wind-induced current. A fly presented on a tight line creates drag, which alerts fish that something isn't right. At times, slack-line presentations such as parachute, serpentine, or puddle casts may be necessary.

Stillwater trout love to lurk in the depths adjacent to a drop-off or sunken island. As the naturals drift over the deep dark water, trout rocket up to take them.

You can take advantage of a trout's lateral line to call the fish to your fly as it lands.

In these circumstances, slack-line presentations allowing for a natural drift from the shallows to deep water may be essential for success. At times popping the rod tip vertically to feed slack line into the drift may also be necessary. When feeding line, do so in a controlled manner so you can react to a take. Dumping in too much line creates excessive slack that won't be absorbed by the strike, resulting in missed takes.

At times trout can be called back by the delicate splat of your fly. Trout use their lateral line, a group of sensory organs located along either side of their body, to detect movement or vibration in the water. The cells within the lateral line process the signals into electrical impulses. The impulses are then sent to the brain, which determines if the trout has sensed food or a potential predator. If your fly lands correctly, it should send out a signal that the trout interprets as food. If so, there is a good chance it might return to investigate and take your fly.

A strategic rod twitch, slow strip, or hand twist retrieve to move the fly after it has landed often induces a take, even if the food source you are imitating sits still or drifts downwind, such as a mayfly dun. This tactic works well when there are lots of naturals on the surface. Movement makes your fly stand out in the crowd, triggering a reaction. Prey such as baitfish, adult chironomids, caddis, terrestrials, water boatmen, and backswimmers all move. Many times, moving the fly is the only action that might induce a take. Be prepared for aggressive takes to a moving fly.

At times the number of fish rising is overwhelming. Choosing a target is difficult, and you risk spooking the pod should your line land among them. I have often had success in these circumstances by retrieving hackled nymphs or wet flies just beneath the surface. The trick is placing your fly in the zone the fish are feeding.

After rising, surface-feeding fish descend a few feet below the surface to avoid predators and to provide a better window of vision so they can spot and target prey. Using a floating line or midge tip with unweighted wet flies or hackled nymphs such as a Cruncher keeps your offering in the zone the trout are moving in. A Cruncher is a variation of the Pheasant Tail Nymph. It has no wing case and a sparse Indian cock hackle. The hackle slows the fly's descent, so it rides just below the surface. Using wet flies and hackled nymphs is one of my preferred tactics for surface-feeding trout. Fly size often doesn't matter when trout are in the mood to feed, intercepting anything that crosses their path. When trout are feeding on tiny emerging chironomids, I have used wet flies and nymphs as large as size 12 with excellent results using this approach.

The Cruncher is an excellent stillwater pattern. It is a personal favorite when targeting surface-feeding trout.

Setting too early is a common mistake when fishing dry flies, a mistake created by the excitement of the moment or our inability to adapt from the quick reactions required when using subsurface tactics. As soon as we see the rise, we often set immediately, pulling the fly away from the feeding fish. When a trout rises to the fly, we must give it time to take the fly and delay our set until the fish turns down, pulling the fly into the corner of the trout's mouth. Many fly fishers count to two to ensure this happens.

Holding the rod tip just above the surface induces controlled slack that helps you avoid missing fish due to too fast a hook-set.

Maintaining a slightly higher rod tip when fishing dries and emergers also helps reduce missed strikes. Holding the rod tip 6 to 12 inches off the water introduces controlled slack. When a fish rises, the controlled slack causes a slight delay during the hook-set, allowing the fish to take the fly before the line tightens.

SIGHT FISHING

One of the greatest rewards when using dry flies is drawing sighted fish to the surface to take your fly. Whether you are using surface or subsurface techniques and patterns, there are some crucial considerations when targeting sighted fish in lakes.

Refraction and the Trout's Window of Vision

Understanding the effects of refraction is an essential sight-fishing factor. Refraction is the bending of light when it travels from one medium, air, to another, water. Stabbing your fly rod into the water is one of the best ways to understand this phenomenon and how it relates to sight fishing. Once submerged, the rod tip appears to bend up toward the surface. We know this isn't the case, however, as the submerged tip section continues on a straight path beneath the surface.

The illusion this exercise illustrates relates to where a fish is in the water when you see it. A sighted fish always appears farther away and closer to the surface than it is. In reality, the fish is closer to you and lying deeper due to refraction. The farther we are away from the fish, the higher the distortion. From a presentation perspective, we need to keep our casts shorter to account for the actual proximity of the fish. If you are attempting to get the fish to take a sunken fly, you also need to let it sink deeper than where the fish appears to be to compensate for the effects of refraction.

Stabbing your rod tip into the water helps you understand how light bends, or refracts, when it travels from air into water.

Refraction also affects apparent fish proportions, providing clues we can use to gauge a fish's depth. The closer a fish is to the surface, the skinnier it appears. Deeper-lying fish appear large and more robust.

Refraction also affects how much a fish sees through the surface out into our world, creating a 97-degree circular window, or cone, of vision. Any light outside of this cone reflects off the underside of the surface. Due to how the light bends, a small

Understanding the impact of refraction on ourselves and stillwater trout is essential to sight-fishing success.

acute-angled blind spot forms, roughly 10 percent, from the surface to the point where the fish can see us. At the junction of the blind spot and where the fish can see us, objects, such as a casting angler, appear distorted and are challenging to make out.

The actual window the fish sees out of depends on how deep it is. The closer the fish is to the surface, the smaller the window, and consequently the closer we can get to the fish. Multiplying the trout's estimated depth by a factor of 2.26 determines the size of the trout's window. For example, a trout 2 feet down has approximately a 4½-foot window of vision. A trout 5 feet down has a window of vision just over 11 feet in diameter. I believe that many times when we cast toward a sighted fish, refusals stem from the fact that the fish didn't see our fly.

We can use the small size of the window to our advantage to allow us to get closer when targeting trout feeding at or just below the surface. A closer position allows for a more controlled, accurate cast as well as the best chance for the fish to see our dry or emerger pattern. Despite the narrow window of a trout cruising just below the surface, exercise caution when making a presentation. Excessive or aggressive casts above the trout's 10 percent blind spot alert it to our presence. It is best to anticipate the trout's direction and place your cast ahead so your fly naturally appears in its window.

A little strategic fly movement isn't a bad idea either to draw a trout's attention. Adding movement often works well when your fly is sitting among a sea of naturals or a rippled surface. A rippled surface disrupts the trout's window of vision, making it difficult for the fish to see both the naturals and your fly. Many times, once the wind has rippled the water, all surface feeding stops.

Spotting Fish

When targeting surface- or subsurface-feeding trout, your odds of success dramatically improve if you can see the fish. On bright, calm days this can work against you, as the fish also have a better chance of seeing you. The sooner you see a fish, the better your odds of success. Polarized sunglasses are an essential piece of sight-fishing equipment, as they eliminate surface glare. If you can't see through the surface glare, you won't be able to spot trout.

The majority of my sight fishing involves more time watching than casting. It is important to remember that in lakes trout move and the water doesn't. We can use movement to help identify fish and then determine the best presentation option and angle. A high vantage point such as that from a pontoon boat or boat helps. Remember the trout's window of vision. Keep your movement to a minimum so you don't inadvertently spook the fish. If you have to move, do it slowly. Avoid sudden movement.

I used to be a pilot. Watching out for other traffic is critical. You can use the same techniques to spot fish that I used to use to watch for other aircraft. Hold your head

Use distinguishing features such as the white leading edges of the fins on brook trout to help spot fish.
BARRY STOKES

steady and focus on a specific area, and watch for movement. If your head is moving and your quarry is moving, chances are you won't see the fish. Another trick came to me from a friend and former soldier. When looking for bad guys, he was trained to scan from right to left, opposite to the way we read. Scanning in this direction makes picking out targets, such as a moving fish, easier.

You can also use species-specific traits to identify fish. All char, such as brook trout, have distinct white leading edges on their fins. On dark, overcast days, when spotting fish can be challenging, their white leading edges stand out, making them easier to spot. Conversely, silver-sided rainbows can be very difficult to spot at times.

Once you spot a fish, know your casting limits. Avoid risky long-distance casts. If possible, wait for the fish to come closer, where you can make an accurate, higher percentage cast. Employ a high rod stop so the line and leader have a chance to lay out, dissipate casting energy, and land delicately. The last thing you want is to spook a fish by driving a cast into the water. At times we can get almost paralyzed with fear, afraid that any presentation we make to a cruising fish might spook it. I find this especially true on bright, clear days. Don't be afraid to cast. Be prepared to accept that you might only get one shot at a cruising trout.

Learning to interpret the mood of a sighted cruising trout helps you determine your odds of success.

Interpreting the Mood of the Fish

As with humans, I firmly believe that trout have individual personalities and moods. Being observant is key. Learning to interpret the moods or actions of a trout helps you determine which fish offers the best chance of success or is best left alone. I break fish into four categories when sight fishing: static, slow cruiser, sprinter, and pods. Based on my experiences, here are my thoughts on each of these four categories:

1. Static: Fish that move very little. A typical brook trout behavior. Although it may take some work to wake them from their apparent slumber, static fish can be coaxed to take.
2. Slow cruiser: Trout that are cruising at a relaxed, comfortable pace. Slow cruisers, as their attitude might suggest, are usually cooperative and should take a properly presented fly.
3. Sprinter: Fish that dart and move at a quick pace, as though they were late and on their way somewhere. They appear skittish and spooked. I find sprinters difficult, if not impossible, to catch.
4. Pods: Trout cruising in groups. They are usually catchable due to their naturally competitive nature. Exercise caution: If you are careless with your presentation and spook or startle one member of the pod, the entire pod scatters too.

Stealth is critical when targeting sighted fish and when stillwater fishing in general. Noise discipline is crucial. Whenever possible, always approach the shallow shoal from deep water. When I am using an outboard motor, I turn off the motor well out over deep water. The wake of a boat approaching at speed and then shutting down at the last minute alerts fish, causing them to evacuate the shoal and head for deep water. I always make my final approach using my electric motor or oars.

Flat, calm conditions are one of the most challenging situations you can face on a lake. You see the fish, and the fish see you. Stealth and good noise discipline are crucial.

If I am going to anchor, I prefer to do so in deep water and cast onto the shoals. On some clear lakes, if you spook fish by setting up on the shallow shoals, they scatter. In extreme cases, they won't return, spoiling not only your fishing but that of anyone else who was working the shoal. Anchor quietly by lowering the anchors gently into the water. Never toss your anchors into the lake "cowboy style." Sound travels much farther in water than in the air. The loud splash of rough anchor deployment alerts, or more often spooks, fish. Make sure you anchor away from the trout's travel path, wind permitting, on the deep-water side of the drop-off if possible.

CHAPTER TAKEAWAYS

- Avoid long, potentially inaccurate casts. Choose a closer target or be patient and wait for the trout to come closer to you.
- Dry fly–specific floating lines are a worthwhile investment when chasing surface-feeding stillwater trout.
- Use fluorocarbon tippet with dries and emergers. Fluorocarbon cuts through the surface film, reducing the risk of creating a tippet shadow.
- Don't be afraid to try using waking attractor flies such as a Booby to draw fish to more-imitative flies.

- Avoid liberal floatant application. There should be no floatant slicks emanating from your fly.
- Reading the rise is critical to success so you choose the right pattern and style to match what the fish are feeding on.
- More often than not, surface rises are to food suspending just below the surface rather than on it.
- Slow, deliberate rises are to something small or something that can't escape. Larger caddis, terrestrials, or nimble prey usually disappear in violent, aggressive rises.
- When targeting more-substantial surface fare, trout may swamp or tail-slap their victim to immobilize it.
- A bubble in the middle of the rise is a definite tell that fish are taking something off the surface.
- When figuring out where to cast after seeing a fish rise, if there is any wind-induced surface ripple, make your first cast upwind.
- Don't be afraid to move a dry fly or emerger. A strategic rod twitch, slow strip, or hand twist retrieve often induces a take.
- Maintaining a slightly higher rod tip when fishing dries and emergers reduces missed strikes. Hold the rod tip 6 to 12 inches off the water to introduce controlled slack.
- When faced with an overwhelming number of rising fish, try retrieving hackled nymphs or wet flies just beneath the surface.
- Understanding the effects of refraction is an essential sight-fishing factor.
- A sighted fish always appears farther away and closer to the surface than it is. In reality, the fish is closer to you and lying deeper.
- The closer a fish is to the surface, the skinnier it appears. Deeper-lying fish appear large and more robust.
- Refraction affects how fish see out of the water, creating a circular window, or cone, of vision.
- The actual window the fish sees out of depends on how deep it is. The closer the fish is to the surface, the smaller the window.
- Polarized sunglasses are an essential piece of sight-fishing equipment.
- The majority of sight fishing involves more time watching than casting.
- There are four fish behavior categories when sight fishing: static, slow cruiser, sprinter, and pods.

CHAPTER 11

GOING DEEP: SINKING LINE TECHNIQUES

As the majority of stillwater trout feed subsurface, using sinking lines makes sense. The predominantly horizontal retrieve path a sinking line provides also mimics the direction most trout food moves.

Sinking, or wet, lines allow you to prospect deeper regions of the lake, keeping your fly in those regions consistently. As there is a wide range of sink rates, sinking lines provide you with the versatility to cover a variety of water, from shallow shoals to deep main lake basins. Depending on the sinking line type, you can work and cover water both horizontally and vertically.

Sinking lines shine in windy conditions. The wind-induced surface chop often negatively affects floating line indicator and long-leader presentations, causing the fly to move unnaturally and a loss of connection that can result in a missed take. Sinking lines slice through the surface chop, allowing for varied natural retrieves and no loss of connection between you and the fly. Long, thin-diameter leaders are common to subsurface floating line presentations. To compensate for variable wind speed and gusts, we tend to apply inconsistent, abrupt power, which leads to wind knots, tangles, and frustration. Leaders for sinking lines are shorter and far less affected by wind. The thin diameter and density of a sinking line also slices through the wind, providing superior casting control.

Staunch sinking line advocates argue that a sinking line is a better presentation tool. They feel floating lines create wake and surface disturbance that may spook fish and the fly or flies won't remain at a consistent depth. This is true when using a brisk retrieve or trolling. However, as discussed in chapter 9, "Floating Line Techniques: Strike Indicators and Long Leader Nymphing," a floating line coupled with a long

Sinking lines are a great option in windy conditions, as the line isn't affected by the surface chop and the leaders are shorter than those used with subsurface floating line presentations.

leader or strike indicator remains an excellent subsurface presentation tool when used in conjunction with snail-paced retrieves.

UNDERSTANDING SINK RATES AND USING THEM TO YOUR ADVANTAGE

Sinking lines are available in a variety of sink rates. You may wonder if they are necessary, and the short answer is "yes." Sinking lines are referred to by type: type I, type III, type V, etc. The type designation corresponds to the sink rate of the line in inches per second, or ips. For example, a type V line would sink at approximately 5 ips. This type rating is an approximation, as each manufacturer's lines can sink at different rates depending on the line's design and function.

When purchasing any fly line, it is crucial to learn the specific line characteristics and sink rates for each line. Some lines also sink at different rates within their given line type depending on fly line weight. For example, a type V 5-weight sinking line may sink slower than a type V 7-weight line. It always pays to learn the traits and behaviors of any fly line so you can use it for the correct situation and get the value out of your investment.

Placing the flies in a specific zone and keeping them there for as long as possible is the goal of any subsurface presentation, no matter the tactic or line choice. Knowing and understanding how to take advantage of the sink rate of your sinking line is critical for consistent success. The countdown method and the Rule of 12s allow you to use a sinking line's sink rate to your advantage.

Know and use the sink rate of your sinking lines so you can consistently target specific depths and catch more fish.

Although somewhat similar to the Rule of 12s, the countdown is a systematic approach best used when the water depth isn't known or when targeting suspended fish in deep water. I count increments of 5 seconds before starting the retrieve after making an initial cast. Make two or three casts using the five count. If you don't catch the bottom or a fish, increase the count by five for the next sequence of casts. Continue adding five counts until you either catch a fish or begin snagging bottom. Back off by two or three counts if you touch bottom, and continue this count until you hook a fish or it is time to move to a new location. Should you catch a fish, remember the count and repeat it for the balance of your presentation. Keeping your flies at a consistent depth is vital, as stillwater trout tend to be selective where they feed and, for the most part, opportunistic on what they feed upon.

The Rule of 12s is a surgical option based on knowing the sink rate of your line and the depth of water you wish to target. The number 12 corresponds to 12 inches in 1 foot. Begin by dividing the sink rate of your line into 12 to determine how long it will take the line to sink 1 foot. Multiply this number by the depth you wish to target to determine the correct sink time.

For example:

Target depth: 10 feet

Sinking line: type III

Divide the sink rate of the line into 12: $12 \div 3 = 4$. It will take the fly line 4 seconds to sink 1 foot.

Targeted depth is 10 feet. 10×4 seconds to travel 1 foot = 40 seconds. It will take approximately 40 seconds for the line to reach 10 feet.

The countdown method and the Rule of 12s help you to consistently target specific depths by training yourself to pay attention as the line sinks. While the line sinks, our minds often wander as other distractions take hold, clouding our ability to recall how long the line and flies sank if we caught a fish.

Fly Line Sink Rate Chart

Note:

Sink times are approximate.

Due to factors such as water density in relationship to water temperature, fly lines sink slightly slower in cool dense water.

Use of weighted flies will accelerate sink times.

Line Type	Sink Rate	5 Feet	10 Feet	15 Feet	20 Feet	25 Feet	30 Feet	35 Feet	40 Feet
Hover	1"/sec	60 sec	120 sec	180 sec	240 sec	300 sec	360 sec	420 sec	480 sec
Slow Sink Clear Intermediate	1.5"/sec	40 sec	80 sec	120 sec	160 sec	200 sec	240 sec	280 sec	320 sec
Fast Sink Clear Intermediate	2"/sec	30 sec	60 sec	90 sec	120 sec	150 sec	180 sec	210 sec	240 sec
Type III Full Sink	3"/sec	20 sec	40 sec	60 sec	80 sec	100 sec	120 sec	140 sec	160 sec
Type V Full Sink	5"/sec	12 sec	24 sec	36 sec	48 sec	60 sec	72 sec	84 sec	96 sec
Type VI Full Sink	6"/sec	10 sec	20 sec	30 sec	40 sec	50 sec	60 sec	70 sec	80 sec
Type VII Full Sink	7"/sec	8.6 sec	17.2 sec	25.8 sec	34.4 sec	43 sec	51.60	60.2 sec	68.8 sec

These methods are approximate. Water density varies with water temperature. The colder the water, the greater the density, the slower the sink rate. Pattern weight and leader length also play a role. Heavily weighted patterns accelerate the sink rate of the line, causing inaccurate sink counts. The risk of an erroneous sinking count is why I primarily use unweighted or even buoyant foam or deer hair–based flies for my sinking line presentations. This approach means I only have to tie one version of a particular pattern, which conserves fly box space, plus I don't have an inexpensive, heavily weighted fly negatively influencing the much more expensive fly line.

CHOOSING THE RIGHT SINKING LINE

When deciding which sinking line to use, it is easy to base your decision on water depth. Avoid basing your line choice on winning a race to the bottom. If you are fishing from an anchored position, all sinking lines will reach the bottom. It is just a question of time and patience.

Choosing the right sinking line is based on a variety of factors. It is not always about getting deep fast.

The retrieve speed in relation to the food source I am imitating and the water temperature always factor into my decision. If you are fishing from an anchored position and suggesting a slow-moving food source, a slow-sinking line would be the best choice. It is crucial to select a line with a sink rate that will not overpower the retrieve, dragging the fly below the fish or fouling along the bottom. Proper presentation is one of the reasons I prefer to fish slow-sinking lines such as a hover or clear intermediate from an anchored position. If the fish are active and willing to chase a fast-moving fly, a faster sink rate line would be the best choice. A fast-sinking line gets the fly down quickly, and the brisk retrieve keeps the line's sink rate in check.

Pattern weight also has an impact. A heavy fly accelerates the sink rate of the line by at least another inch per second. Sink rate acceleration due to pattern weight is the reason I prefer unweighted flies when using sinking lines, particularly fast-sinking lines.

Boat, pontoon boat, or float tube movement also affects line choice. If you are trolling or fishing loch style, you need a faster sink rate line than you would when anchored. Fast troll speeds create an acute line angle, dictating a fast-sinking line. If you

If you are trolling or fishing loch style, you usually need a faster sink rate line than you would if you are fishing from an anchored position, as you have to factor in the movement of your boat, float tube, or pontoon boat.
NICK SLIWKANICH

are slowly paddling in a pontoon boat or float tube, a clear intermediate or type III line is a good starting point.

When fishing loch style, you are casting and drifting downwind. The wind speed and a drogue or drift sock govern your drift speed. As soon as the fly line lands, you are creeping forward, requiring a faster sink rate so the line can sink and provide you with an effective retrieve. If fish are feeding deep, a slow-sinking line won't drop fast enough. You end up drifting over the line before it ever has a chance to get to depth. The quicker the drift speed, the faster the sink rate line.

No matter the sink rate, the goal is to choose a line that complements your retrieve pace to keep your flies tracking at the depth fish are holding or feeding at for as long as possible.

Leader length also impacts where the fly or flies are in the water in relation to the fly line. A nylon leader sinks at a slower rate than a sinking line. The countdown or Rule of 12s allows you to have a good idea where your fly line is in the water, but your leader and fly could be elsewhere. When using sinking lines, leader length decreases as the sink rate increases. In other words, the faster the sink rate, the shorter the leader. Keep in mind that multiple fly rigs increase leader length to allow flies sufficient space to work.

The goal of any sinking line system is to allow sufficient working distance between the flies and the line, ensuring the leader is sinking at the same rate and presents on the same plane as the line to add accuracy to the countdown and be functional to cast.

Listed below are the leader lengths I prefer for a single-fly setup from a slow-sinking hover line through a type VII density-compensated full sink. For a dropper setup, add 3 to 5 feet of length for each fly. I space my flies about 5 feet apart when fishing clear water, 3 feet for murky water. When using forage fish patterns, I often compress my spacing to as little as 2 feet to simulate fish trying to reform after a trout has fractured and scattered their school.

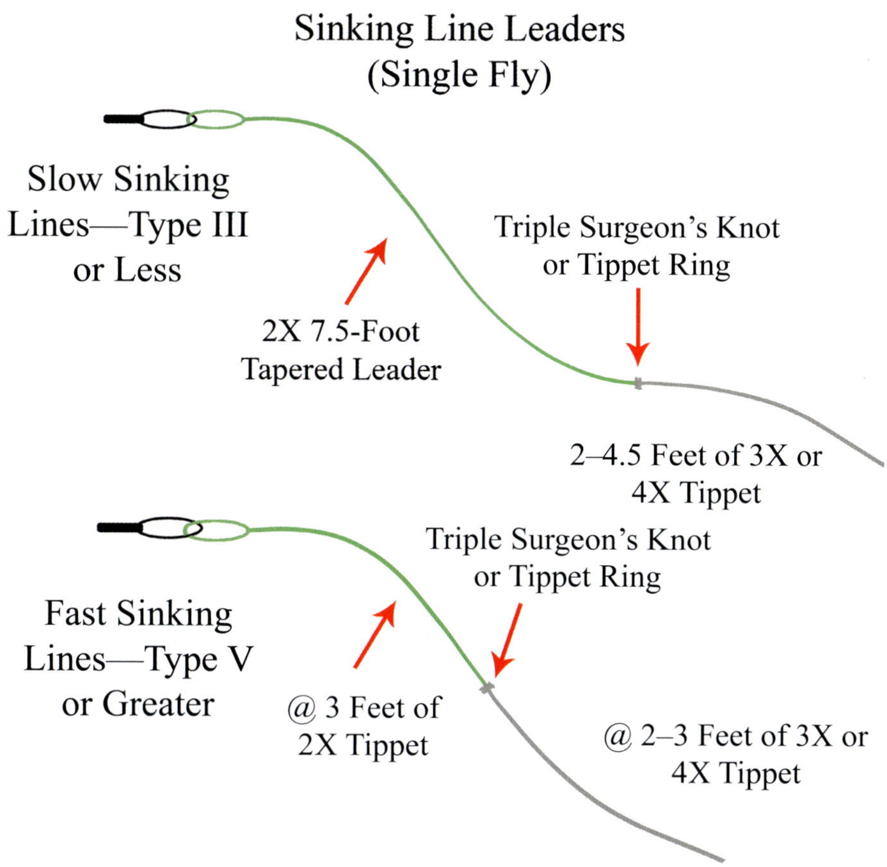

For sink rate lines type III or faster, I place my first fly roughly 6 feet from the end of the fly line. It is crucial to keep the distance between the upper fly and the other flies in the fly setup less than a rod length apart so you can land a fish. If the fly spacing exceeds the rod length and a fish takes the point fly, the upper or bob fly could catch the rod tip, causing a break-off or, worse, a broken tip section.

- Hover (1 ips sink rate) and clear intermediate (1½ to 2 ips sink rate): 9 to 12 feet depending on water clarity. Clear water usually dictates longer leaders. I use a 7½-foot leader as a foundation and add tippet, typically equal or lesser diameter fluorocarbon, to complete the overall leader. Depending on the brand, a 7½-foot tapered leader features a short, approximately 3- to 4-foot butt section. This butt section aids the turnover of longer leaders and doesn't bite into the welded loop of a fly line.
- Type III (3 ips sink rate) to type V (5 ips sink rate): 9 to 10 feet depending on water clarity. Depending on the overall leader length I am trying to achieve, I begin with either a 5- or 6-foot section of 2X nylon tippet followed by a 3- to 5-foot section of equal or lesser diameter fluorocarbon tippet. You can use either a triple surgeon's knot or a small tippet ring to connect the two sections.
- Type VI (6 ips sink rate) and type VII (7 ips sink rate): 5 to 7 feet depending on water clarity. Start with a short, 3-foot section of 1X or 2X nylon tippet followed by a 2- to 4-foot section of equal or lesser diameter fluorocarbon tippet.

CASTING SINKING LINES

Due to line density, fast-action rods are the best option for casting sinking lines. Fast-action rods have enough backbone to carry the weight of a heavy sinking line, helping you cast farther with less effort. Using a double haul to increase line speed is also recommended when casting sinking lines. As with floating lines, keep false casts to a minimum to avoid tangles, especially with multiple-fly rigs.

Once the head section is outside of the rod tip, let the line shoot to the target. Make sure to have a reserve of running line stripped from the reel to ensure the line casts as far as possible. Long casts work best with sinking lines, allowing you to cover water to induce fish to follow and hopefully take your flies.

Always hold the rod tip high on the final cast so the line and leader shoot tight to the reel. The fly line lays out entirely and the leader and flies sink on a tight line, so you rarely miss takes on the drop. Lowering the rod too soon causes the line to puddle and crash, creating slack and connection loss between you and your flies. Slack-line management is essential when fishing loch style from a drifting boat. As soon as your fly lands, gather any slack using a slow hand twist retrieve to stay in contact with your flies. Losing touch as your flies sink leads to missed or deeply hooked fish should a trout intercept your flies on the descent. Once the flies have sunk to depth, as with all retrieves, use two quick 3- to 4-inch strips to confirm contact with the flies. The sudden jump of the flies may also trigger a response from any nearby trout.

As a sinking line doesn't lie on the surface like a floating line, trying to pick up and cast an extended length is challenging. You have to use a roll cast pickup to bring the line up to the surface. Once the line is at the surface, lift it from the water to recast. To be honest, I don't use the roll cast pickup much, as I always retrieve the line to within approximately 10 feet of the rod tip to initiate the hang. The hang brings the line up to the surface, eliminating or significantly reducing the need for the roll pickup.

REDUCING TANGLES

Sinking lines have a deserved reputation for tangling. The thinner the fly line, the more it wants to tangle. Thankfully there are a few strategies to reduce or even eliminate tangles.

Before your first cast, always restack the line after stripping it off the reel. When you initially strip line from the reel and pile it at your feet, or on a stripping apron, the front of the line is at the bottom of the pile. When you try to shoot the line on the initial cast, the front section of the line has to fight through the pile, causing tangles. After peeling enough line from the reel, strip it back through the forefinger of the rod hand and cork as though retrieving and re-pile the line. This practice places the tip section on top of the line pile, eliminating tangles while providing a chance to stretch the line and remove any memory.

To avoid tangles when casting, pile your line so the front of the line is at the top, not underneath the rest of the line.

Sinking lines can also tangle during the retrieve. A lubricated, wet line tangles less than dry line. If you are fishing from a boat, fill a collapsible gardening bucket or cheap, plastic dollar store basket with a skim of water. Use enough water to keep the line wet. Drop the retrieved line into the bucket or basket to keep it wet and tangle-free on the recast. If a bucket or basket isn't available or practical, such as when fishing from a pontoon boat or float tube, place the line on a wet hand towel. The damp cloth keeps the line moist and reduces tangles.

Sinking lines love to tangle as you drop the line at your feet during the retrieve. Place a skim of water in a small basket or collapsible gardening bucket. Drop your line as you retrieve it into the basket or bucket to keep it wet and reduce tangles.

SLOW-SINKING LINES

Slow-sinking hover and clear intermediate lines are arguably my two favorite sinking lines. The slow sink rate of these lines makes them ideal for prospecting shallow shoals and weed beds. These lines slice through the surface chop, and their sink rate doesn't overpower the retrieve, making them excellent line options for imitating slow-moving food sources such as scuds, mayfly nymphs, and damselfly nymphs. You can also use a brisk retrieve pace to suggest a fleeing baitfish, darting scud, or jetting dragonfly nymph.

Floating lines, coupled with long leaders or indicators, are the standard for chironomid pupa presentations, but they can be challenging to use and control in windy conditions. The wind-induced surface chop often plays havoc with floating line techniques, transmitting down to the flies via the bouncing indicator or causing a loss of connection when using long leaders without indicators. There is also a risk of creating tailing loop tangles and frustration if we accidentally overpower the cast to compensate for the wind. In these conditions, a slow-sinking line such as a hover or clear intermediate is an excellent option. The slow-sinking line slices through the surface chop, allowing you to stay in contact with your flies, and the short, 9- to 12-foot leaders are more comfortable to cast and manage.

Whether it is windy or not, slow-sinking lines are a favorite choice when trout are feeding on staging and emerging chironomid pupae, in water 15 feet or more, but aren't targeting a specific depth. This feeding practice often happens early in an emergence or as the hatch begins to wane. Fish have to spread out vertically to find food. The more intense the emergence, typically the more focused the feeding depth.

From an anchored position, cast as far as you comfortably can. Allow the line, leader, and flies ample time to sink. The reduced sink rate of the line results in increased sink times compared to using floating lines coupled with a long leader and weighted patterns. Sink times of two minutes or more are standard. As with floating line presentations, retrieves are painstakingly slow. The hand twist or pinch strip are your best retrieve options. Takes with this method are typically solid and hard to miss due to the short leader.

Slow-sinking lines are typically not density compensated. As a result, these lines sink in a somewhat U-shaped path due to the dense midsection of the head. Powered by a slow hand twist or pinch strip, the flies are retrieved sweeping through an arc. Knowing this trait helps determine where the fish are in the water based on where, in the retrieve, takes occur. Early in the retrieve, the natural sweep of the line has the flies higher in the water. A take at this time signifies fish are up in the water, as that is where the flies are. Conversely, takes occurring from the midpoint to the end of the retrieve, when the flies are at their deepest, means fish are holding deep. Most of the takes when using this method occur late in the retrieve, as trout typically hang out near the bottom where their food lives.

FISHING BUOYANT FLIES

As with nymph fishing on rivers, you have to place your flies in harm's way near the bottom for consistent success. Drifting flies near rocks and sunken debris often results in snags and subsequent fly loss. The same presentation logic is also true in lakes, as trout love to forage in and around weeds and bottom debris.

Presenting and keeping the fly just above these obstructions is usually very productive. Suspending flies under an indicator just above the bottom is one option. Sinking lines, particularly type V sink rate or higher, can also be used to drag buoyant flies down and hold them just above the bottom. It may be necessary to give the fly a sharp strip to pop it and break the surface tension to get it to sink. Pay attention right after the pop, as any surface-orientated fish could be attracted to the pop and take the fly as it begins to descend.

Tethered to a short level leader, twice the anticipated length or height of any bottom debris is a good reference point: The fly line lies along the bottom as the buoyant foam-based or spun and clipped deer hair body fly skips above the weed tops. This presentation tactic works well for a variety of pattern styles, including dragon nymphs, scuds, water boatmen, backswimmers, and minnows. It is also an excellent presentation tactic for foam-based attractor patterns such as a Booby or FAB.

The Washing Line

You can also use buoyant flies in a washing line arrangement. Originating in Great Britain, the washing line is a reverse-order dry-dropper using a buoyant point fly, in conjunction with an appropriate sink rate line for the conditions, to suspend one or more conventional flies on separate, short, 4- to 8-inch droppers—like clothes on a washing line.

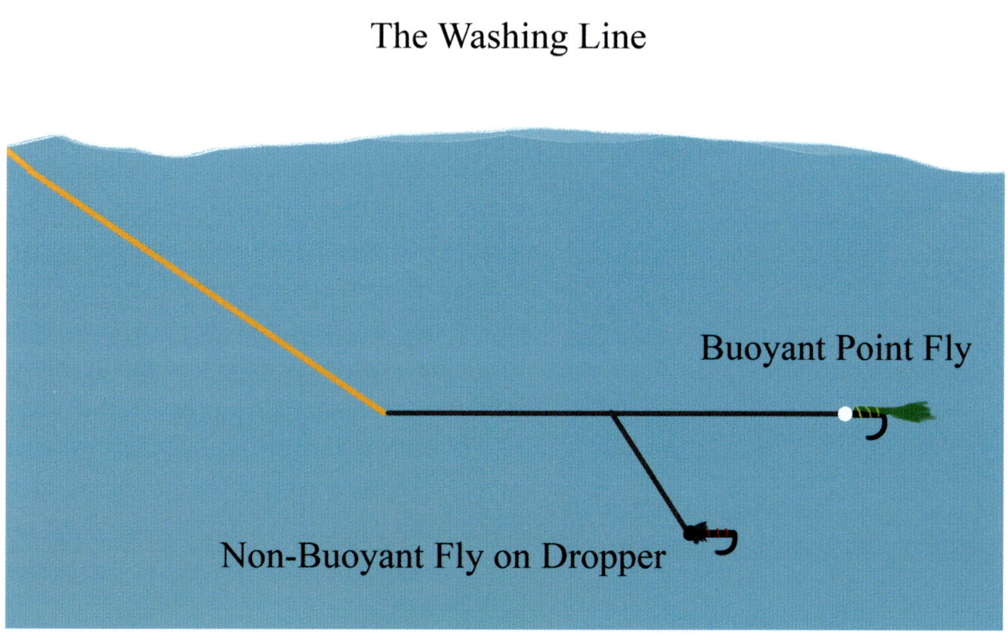

The washing line is a dropper technique that features a buoyant fly on the point and standard, non-buoyant patterns on separate droppers. You can use a washing line setup from the surface to just above the bottom.

You can use a washing line from the surface to just above the bottom. During the fall months, it is an excellent shallow-water presentation tactic in areas where weeds have grown up, creating a thin band of workable water between the water's surface and the weed tops. The washing line allows you to target this narrow section with minimal hang-ups. It is an excellent presentation option for damselfly nymphs, dragonfly nymphs, baitfish, scuds, water boatmen, and backswimmers. A bright, buoyant pattern such as a Booby can also be used as a point fly to attract fish to one or more natural patterns suspended from the droppers.

The washing line also works well during an emergence. Trout could be feeding at the surface on both the adults and emergers. A washing line setup on a floating, clear-tip, hover, or clear intermediate line keeps your flies at or near the surface where the fish are feeding.

As with faster sink rate lines, you can use a buoyant attractor pattern in a washing line arrangement as a waking fly with surface presentations. The waking fly draws trout to the surface. If they don't take the waking fly, they may move up the leader and choose a natural pattern hanging off a nearby dropper.

DANGLING

Fishing fast-sinking lines vertically, so the fly suspends just above the bottom, is a deadly technique.

From an anchored position, presenting fast-sinking lines vertically, or dangling, is an excellent way to suspend chironomid larva, pupa, leech, and minnow patterns just above the bottom. Dangling works best in deep water, 20 feet or greater, though I have used this method in water as shallow as 14 feet. As the fish are taking the fly below the rod tip, water clarity is critical. The murkier the water, the shallower you can dangle.

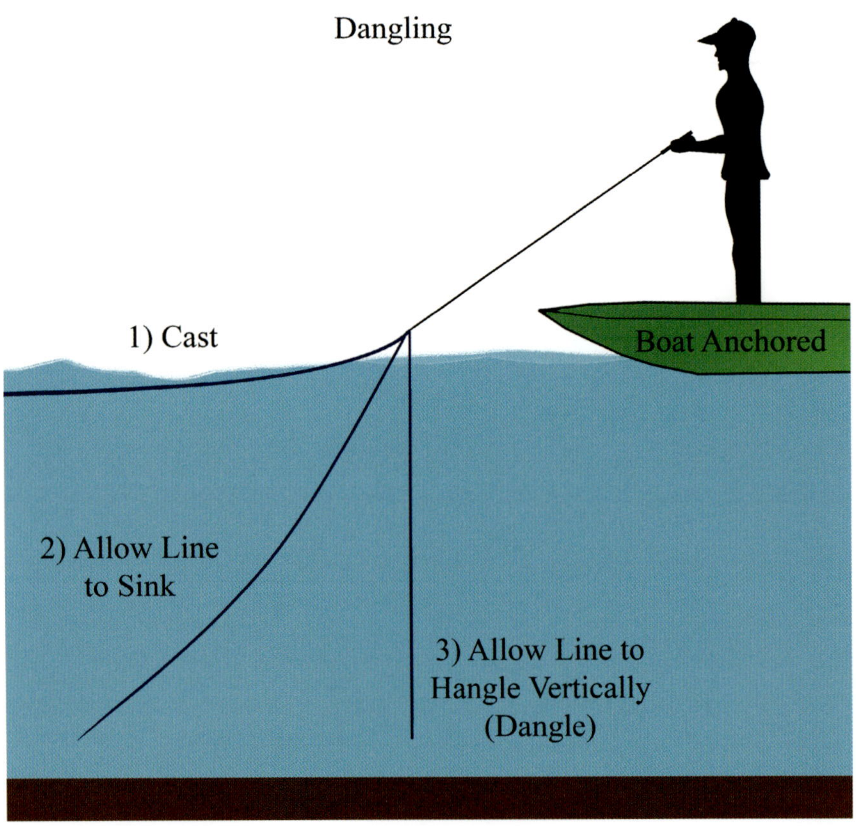

The most consistent dangling opportunities on productive lakes occur after spring turnover. Once turnover has occurred, the water chemistry and dissolved oxygen levels allow trout to inhabit the deeper regions of a lake.

Dangling is also an excellent presentation option when bright, clear conditions persist. On clear lakes, trout may feel exposed and are hesitant to prowl the shallows. If this is the case, dangling is a presentation option worth trying.

Brisk wind makes casting long leaders challenging. The wind-induced surface chop also makes it challenging to maintain presentation control. Dangling is an excellent option in this situation. Casts and leaders are short, and a fast-sinking line slices through a brisk wind easier than the thicker, more wind-resistant floating line. If necessary, it is possible to dangle into the teeth of the most aggressive wind.

Dangling is not about hanging your feet over the side of the boat to catch fish. There is no fly line or indicator to watch when dangling. Just never let go of the rod, as the takes are typically savage.

The primary dangling draw is the aggressive, typically savage, takes. One of my students said it best: "It's like a train taking a mailbag." Floating line presentations demand complete focus on the line or indicator to react to a take. Dangling requires no such attention. There is only one requirement: Do not, under any circumstances, let the rod out of your hand. Never lay your rod down for a second to grab a fly box, sandwich, or anything else. Should a take occur while your rod is unattended, you are most likely to experience a costly life lesson. If you have to put the rod down, place it in a rod holder.

Dangling Leaders

Dangling leaders are short: 5 feet is ample, 4 feet is typical. Begin with a 3-foot section of 1X or 2X fluorocarbon tippet. From there, add 2 feet of 3X (8-pound) tippet via a triple surgeon's knot or barrel swivel to complete the leader. The leader junction between the two sections acts as a fusible link in the event of an aggressive smash take. In the event of a break-off, it is better to have the leader break midway than at the welded loop of the fly line.

In strong winds, the weight of a barrel swivel helps mitigate wind-induced current by keeping the leader and flies hanging vertically below the fast-sinking type VI or VII density-compensated lines associated with this technique. It is possible to dangle with slower-sinking lines, but it takes longer for the flies to sink to depth, and when the wind-induced currents are present, it can be challenging to keep the line hanging vertically.

Dangling Setup

The key to dangling is ensuring your fly suspends a foot above the bottom to start in the same manner as hanging flies beneath an indicator. Setting fly depth is similar to setting indicator depth:

1. Attach a weight to the fly, such as a depth locator, forceps, or a bell sinker.
2. Lower the weight and fly into the water and let it hit bottom. Try not to let the weight plunge into the bottom, as this may lead to an inaccurate setting.
3. Lower the rod tip to what I refer to as the "fishing position," a few inches above the surface.
4. Reel the line in until the rod tip bends downward, signifying that the weight is just touching the bottom.
5. Grab the fly line 1 foot up from the fly reel and pull it back. Reel in this extra foot of slack. You have now set your fly to hang 1 foot above the bottom.
6. Strip in the line and remove the weight from the fly.
7. Make a cast and let the line sink until vertical.

Once the fly is suspending 1 foot above the bottom, let it hang, or dangle, for as long as you can stand it. As soon as boredom begins to set in, start a slow, steady hand twist or pinch strip retrieve. Retrieve the line until the connection between the fly line and leader is between the rod tip and the water's surface. Let the fly hang for a second; if there are no takers, cast and repeat.

Takes can happen at any point. The majority of takes occur when the fly is hanging a foot off the bottom or at the end of the retrieve. Fish often follow the fly up to the surface and have to decide to take the fly or not. If the fish takes the fly, it comes down over it, resulting in a savage, heart-stopping take.

One of the first times I used this method, I was in my float tube. The savagery of the take startled me. In the blink of an eye, my rod tip went from just above the surface to between my legs and behind my back. When I got the fish in, it was barely 16 inches long. Larger fish can be tough to handle at first. The first part of the fight resembles a bronco ride where you are just hanging on until the fish tires.

When fishing from a boat, be careful that the rod butt doesn't bend over the gunnel at an awkward angle. It might not seem possible at first, but do your best to try to keep the rod away from the boat.

I only dangle from an anchored boat. It is critical to keep the line vertical so the fly suspends at the set depth. Anchor ropes are a liability with this method, as fish can and do get into them. If a fish gets wrapped around an anchor rope, stay calm. Resist the urge to pull the fish in. This response pulls the leader around the anchor rope, and the trout usually ends up spiraling around the rope like a tetherball. Fine-diameter

Any time a fish wraps around an anchor rope it's exciting, especially when dangling. Remain calm, and let line play against the anchor rope as you either raise the anchor or work your rod around the rope.

leader bites into the rope, and if you are fishing multiple flies, the second fly will likely embed into rope. Either scenario results in a lost fish.

Although it might seem counterintuitive, let the fish run so the fly line is around the anchor rope. The thicker fly line won't bite into the rope. The rope acts as shock absorber, playing the fish as you manage the situation. With the fish playing against the rope, slowly raise the anchor and slide the fly line free, or, in extreme circumstances, carefully pass the fly rod under the anchor rope.

Anchor locks are a definite asset when raising an anchor one-handed. Should the anchor slip, the anchor lock cam grabs the rope, preventing it from plunging to the bottom. I have experienced many anchor rope adventures with students and clients. My personal best involved a fish that wrapped itself around the bow anchor, stern anchor, electric motor, transducer, and outboard motor. My student and I remained calm, managed the situation, enjoyed the humor of the moment, and successfully landed the fish.

Finding Fish when Dangling

When dangling, fish have to come to you. As a result, choosing high-percentage spots is critical. Over a deep flat basin, there is little structure to attract and hold fish. A concentration of food is arguably the only thing that will concentrate fish over a deep flat.

Chironomids are a prime food source in these areas, as larvae, or bloodworms, inhabit mudflats in large numbers. Trout root the larvae out of their homes, so larval patterns are always worth dangling. Eventually, the larvae transform into pupae, so mudflats are always prime places to watch for a chironomid emergence. Watch for the cast shucks drifting on the surface or birds such as swallows working low to the water, feeding on the emerging adults. I have stumbled onto some outstanding deep-water emergences and great dangling as I was moving from one shoal area to another. At some point on my journey, avoiding low-flying birds or trying not to swallow an adult chironomid was a definite clue to tie on a chironomid pupa pattern, drop anchor, and dangle.

If nothing seems to be hatching to focus a trout's attention in the main basin, fish the deep edges adjacent to a shoal such as the base of a drop-off or along the edges of a point. Sounders are an asset when dangling. They mark deep-water structures such as rock piles, subtle trenches, or sunken humps. They, of course, can also mark fish. Sounders are a crucial piece of equipment all stillwater fly fishers should have and use. Take the time to learn the various features and use them. The internet and YouTube are excellent resources.

Don't stick around too long in one spot, either. Make short moves until you find fish. With each location change comes a renewed sense of optimism and concentration that often makes a difference between success and failure.

A sounder is a definite asset when dangling to locate structure and determine bottom depth as well as mark fish.

CHAPTER TAKEAWAYS

- The predominantly horizontal retrieve path a sinking line provides mimics the direction most trout food moves.
- Sinking lines are a great option in windy conditions, as leader lengths are shorter, making them less likely to tangle while slicing through the surface chop, helping you maintain contact with your flies.
- Knowing and understanding how to take advantage of a sinking line's sink rate is critical for consistent success.
- The countdown method, along with the Rule of 12s, allows you to use a sinking line's sink rate to your advantage.
- The Rule of 12s is a relatively simple method based on knowing the sink rate of your line and the depth of water you wish to target.
- No matter the sink rate of your line, the goal is to choose a sinking line that complements your retrieve pace to keep your flies tracking at the depth fish are holding or feeding at for as long as possible.
- As a line's sink rate increases, leader length decreases; in other words, the faster the sink rate, the shorter the leader.
- Due to line density, fast-action rods are the best option for casting sinking lines.
- Slack-line management is essential when fishing loch style. As soon as your flies land, gather any slack using a slow hand twist retrieve to stay in contact with the flies.
- Sinking lines can tangle during the retrieve. Keeping the line wet by retrieving it into a bucket or basket or onto a damp hand towel helps reduce potential line tangles.
- You can use a washing line setup, featuring a buoyant fly on the point to suspend other flies off separate droppers from the surface to just above the bottom.
- Using fast-sinking lines fished vertically, or dangling, is an excellent way to suspend flies such as chironomid pupa, larva, leech, or baitfish patterns just above the bottom in deep water.

CHAPTER 12

THE POWER OF ATTRACTION: ATTRACTOR TECHNIQUES

Matching the hatch is one of the cornerstones of fly fishing: observing, studying, and imitating the various food items fish eat with our flies and presentation tactics. Often it is a combination of both fly choice and presentation that provides the answer.

Fish, particularly trout, don't always take our flies out of a feeding response. Often the flies, coupled with the correct presentation, trigger a reaction. The trigger can be deliberate or accidental.

Trout don't always take our flies out of a feeding response. You can use attractor techniques to trigger a response out of curiosity, territoriality, or aggression.

An example of an accidental trigger can occur when using an imitative presentation. After several unsuccessful casts, you decide it's time to switch locations. In preparation for your move, you reel the fly in as fast as you can. Halfway through the retrieve, as your fly is moving at high speed, a trout crushes your imitative pattern. The trout was instinctively drawn to the pace of your high-speed fly, triggering the aggressive response—a clue, perhaps, that a deliberate, energetic presentation to trigger a take might be in order. Triggering a strike is a core principle of attractor techniques and flies.

Aggressive fishing techniques are common to many fishing disciplines. Tournament bass anglers use reaction baits and tactics to cover water rapidly and target aggressive fish. With a limited amount of time at their disposal, an aggressive approach catches a lot of fish and has made more than a few millionaires along the way.

Attractor techniques and flies are also common in fly fishing. Renowned fly fisher, guide, and author Kelly Galloup has been using aggressive attractor techniques to trigger a reaction on rivers and streams for years. His book *Modern Streamers* changed how we view, present, and tie streamer patterns. Kelly realized the importance of a reaction bite, incorporating his observations into the flies and techniques necessary to trigger a reaction from non-feeding trout.

The techniques and patterns Kelly Galloup uses to trigger a response from non-feeding trout have had a considerable influence on many fly fishers.

Attractor flies, both dry and wet, are commonplace on rivers and streams. Patterns such as the Royal Wulff, Royal Coachman, and foam-based patterns like the Fat Albert possess more elements of attraction than imitation. Many salmon and steelhead patterns feature bright, gaudy color schemes. Large pike and muskie streamers also have design elements to trigger a take. Competition-based river and stream nymphs frequently incorporate an element of attraction using a variety of methods including thread hot spots, bright tags, or flashy beads—features that are also worth blending into stillwater patterns. Competitive fly fishing, in which competitors face time demands and a need to catch as many fish as possible within a limited window, has had a distinct effect on stillwater attractor presentations and patterns.

Patterns featuring trigger-point hot spots are excellent choices when presenting flies in deep or murky water and to have your fly stand out among a crowd of natural food sources, as evidenced by the hot orange bead peeking out of this trout's mouth.

In North America, stillwater attractor techniques and patterns are becoming more widespread, due in part to the growing influence of competitions, the internet, and social media. Attractor flies and techniques are commonplace on European stillwaters, so much so that some European fisheries ban or frown upon attractor techniques. These bans are intended to reduce a one-dimensional reliance on attractor techniques in the hopes of encouraging fly fishers to reconsider more imitative patterns and presentations. It seems the presentation pendulum is always in motion.

WHY ATTRACTORS?

There are several reasons you should consider using attractor patterns and techniques in lakes:

- Environmental changes: Stillwater trout are sensitive to environmental changes including weather systems, sudden storms, and frontal passages. During these periods of change, trout often become unsettled and cease feeding. At these times, triggering a reaction using attractor patterns and techniques is often the only approach that works.
- Prospecting deep water: Although trout can and do feed in deep water, the majority feed in the shallow shoal areas where food is most plentiful. At times trout slide out into deep water when conditions aren't to their liking. I often refer to these fish as "just not happy." As fish aren't feeding consistently in these situations, they stage and suspend in deep water. Attractor patterns and techniques can save the day.

Environmental changes, drawing fish to a team of flies, triggering a reaction, and vicious takes are a few reasons you should consider using attractor patterns and techniques.

- Matching tiny prey: One of the primary reasons fly fishers chase trout is their preference for feeding on small prey items. This habit gives us lots of chances to trick them into striking, as they have to feed frequently for prolonged periods. Stillwater trout can and often do take this to an extreme when they target small, tough-to-match prey such as zooplankton and transparent *Chaoborus* larvae (glassworms) and pupae. Zooplankton color varies; shades of orange, reddish pink, and bright to chartreuse green are common. Attractor flies are often tied to match these colors and suggest zooplankton clusters. When it comes to dealing with transparent *Chaoborus*, aggressive attractor presentations are needed to draw the trout's attention. Matching transparent food sources is a tough proposition.

- Targeting aggressive fish: Attractor techniques and patterns are an excellent approach for targeting aggressive fish, especially at the start of the day. Although not all fish may be in an aggressive frame of mind, you can use attractor tactics to catch that initial fish. Once caught, careful use of a throat pump may reveal focused feeding and a subsequent change in tactics—feeding that might not have been readily apparent.
- Attracting fish to a team of flies: Where permitted, using an attractor fly in conjunction with natural flies works well. A large, gaudy attractor placed above or below a natural fly or flies draws curious fish to investigate. Trout may or may not take the attractor pattern, but they often turn away from the attractor and happily take one of the natural patterns. At times a washing line setup, with a buoyant attractor on the point, also works. The buoyant attractor works in conjunction with the fly line to suspend one or more natural patterns off separate droppers between the point fly and the fly line, like clothes off a washing line. It is crucial to avoid the temptation to remove the attractor from the team of flies if you are consistently taking fish on the natural patterns. In many instances, it is the attractor pattern that is drawing the fish in. Removing it could negatively impact your catch rate. Even though the attractor may not be hooking fish, it is still doing its job.
- Triggering non-feeding fish: If careful use of a throat pump reveals no samples or it contains dead and partially digested food, imitative flies and techniques may not be the best approach. Triggering a take using attractors might be your only option.
- Targeting recently stocked fish: Many fisheries stock trout at a catchable size. These fish have lived, up until their release, in a controlled environment where food rained from above. Dropped into a new, natural environment, stocked trout must learn how to feed so they continually sample. As a result, they are susceptible to attractor patterns and techniques. Stocked fish also cluster together in the same age class. Fish, as predators, compete with each other, making them ideal candidates for attractors. Using attractor techniques to target stocked trout in England is commonly referred to as "stocky bashing."
- Aggressive takes: Due to the pattern style and how you fish attractor patterns, takes are seldom delicate. At times, it is nice to take a break from watching an indicator for subtle takes or a floating line for signs of a take, or recognizing the soft take to a nymph or pupa. Everybody needs a heart-stopping take now and again. Attractor techniques provide that.

TRIGGERING A GRAB

For me, attractor techniques and patterns are all about provoking a reaction. I factor three primary triggers into my attractor philosophies: curiosity, territoriality, and aggression.

Curiosity

Of my three primary trout triggers, curiosity is probably the one I feel offers the most trout appeal. Trout are tactile feeders—their mouths are their hands. Trout touch and sample all the time. A friend of mine says, "Trout are like a two-year-old. Everything seems to end up in their mouths." The internet is full of videos showing river and stream trout mouthing everything that drifts by to see what it is. Leaves, twigs, and other drifting debris all receive a quick exploratory chew. Most attractor patterns don't resemble any natural food sources, but trout, as with other fish, can't help themselves and sample the fly. From our perspective it doesn't matter why a trout puts a fly in its mouth so long as it does.

Just like us, trout are curious creatures. When unsure of something, trout use their mouth to sample a potential offering, such as an attractor pattern.

Territoriality

Trout, as predators, are aggressive and defend their area. Should something come through their living room, there is a good chance they will lash out with their mouth to protect their space. One might argue that a territorial attack is almost defensive. Attractor patterns and the presentation techniques used with them help trigger a territorial response.

Aggression

As with a territorial trigger, aggression is all about making the trout the predator it was born to be. Attractor techniques also trigger an aggressive response. Many attractor flies feature built-in action coupled with loud, obnoxious colors. Powered by a fast-paced retrieve, the pitching, wobbling, and undulating movement of these flies drive trout mad. These actions, either individually or as a team, trigger an aggressive response—no different than sprinting from a bear as opposed to backing away slowly in a non-aggressive manner. Sprint from a bear, and you will most likely trigger an instinctive predatory response that will in all probability have serious consequences.

THE ART OF EXAGGERATION

In addition to the three primary triggers, the art of exaggeration also comes into play. Attractor techniques employ exaggerated sizes, colors, and presentation techniques.

The art of exaggeration is a key pattern component to attractor flies, including chironomid pupa and larva patterns.

Size

Unlike natural presentations, size doesn't usually govern attractor patterns. Attractor patterns tend to be larger to stand out in a crowd. Coupled with a brisk retrieve, trout find large patterns easy to find and target.

At times during a hatch, particularly with chironomids, I have used oversize patterns with great success, even though throat samples revealed focused feeding on smaller chironomid pupae. Despite my best attempts to match the hatch, success was sporadic at best. Not until I decided to fish a gaudy pupa pattern, two sizes larger, did I begin to experience consistent success. I have also had success using much larger natural-looking chironomid pupa patterns. Playing the size card appeals to a trout's naturally greedy nature.

Color

Attractor patterns are typically bright, loud, and obnoxious. Color is often a critical pattern consideration. At depth, light is always in a state of flux. The deeper the presentation, the more light diminishes. Long-wavelength colors such as red and orange are the first to attenuate or fade as light levels reduce. At a distance, either vertically, diagonally, or horizontally, faded long-wavelength colors appear gray. Short-wavelength colors such as blue, indigo, and violet are the last to fade. If you remember the simple acronym Roy G. Biv (red, orange, yellow, green, blue, indigo, violet), determining the effect of light on color is easy. It is important to remember that water clarity affects color too. Turbid water clouded by algal blooms and other suspended solids muffles light and increases the rate of attenuation.

Stillwater attractor patterns are typically bright, loud, and obnoxious. Their primary purpose is to trigger a response from inactive trout.

In recent years, much has been discussed surrounding ultraviolet light (UV) and its effect on fly patterns and how trout see. It seems science is always changing. For many years it was believed that trout could see into the UV range. Now it is widely believed that only juvenile trout utilize UV vision to separate the microscopic food items they feed upon from inert floating debris. As the trout mature and begin feeding on larger prey items, the UV cones are no longer needed and transform into the blue range. A trout's eye, like the human eye, possesses both cones and rods: cones for color vision, rods for contrast. Cones are used during daylight hours, while rods rise to the forefront during low-light conditions such as morning, evening, and night.

Bright fluorescent materials are important attractor pattern components. In his book, *What Fish See*, author Colin J. Kageyama defines fluorescence as "the ability of an object to reflect light of a longer wavelength than it receives." Fluorescent patterns reflect light, both visible and invisible, appearing brighter, especially in low light. As a result, fluorescence is important in low-light conditions such as overcast days and deep water. I believe fluorescent attractor patterns stand out in comparison to surrounding natural tones and colors and consequently trigger a response.

Almost all attractor patterns feature some level of fluorescence. Some patterns utilize fluorescent hot spots, beads, thread collars, or eyes, while other attractor flies are completely fluorescent. When tying chironomid pupa patterns featuring yarn or floss gills, I prefer gill materials that fluoresce. Testing if a product fluoresces is simple. Shine a UV resin curing lamp on the material. If the material is fluorescent, it lights up and glows.

One of my favorite attractor chironomid larva patterns is Jerry McBride's Bionic Worm. In deep water, typically over 15 feet, the fluorescent pink tail and orange bead stand out. Rainbow trout, in particular, seem to love this fly. Many fly fishers, including myself, also use fluorescent patterns to match various zooplankton colors, including shades of orange, hot pink, red, and chartreuse. Contrasting color combinations are also deadly at times.

Jerry McBride's Bionic Worm is a vibrant chironomid larva, or bloodworm, pattern that performs exceptionally well in deep, dark water.

Presentation

Stillwater attractor presentations are typically aggressive. Fast, strip-pause retrieves are designed to induce a fish to follow and crush the fly. As the fly is moving at pace, savage takes are common—one of the key attractions to this method. Fish often follow a stripped attractor. As with many cast and retrieve presentations, takes often occur at the end of the retrieve. Don't be in a hurry to cast again. Always remember to hang the fly at the end of each retrieve to avoid missing takes.

When fishing chironomid pupa patterns under an indicator, you can also employ a nontypical up-tempo retrieve. Chironomid presentations are typically associated with static or painstakingly slow hand twist or pinch strip retrieves. When this natural approach isn't working, try a 12-inch strip with enough pace to cause the indicator to wake, followed by a prolonged pause. The strip raises the fly; the pause allows it to settle. Trout, attracted by the movement, often grab the fly almost immediately after the strip. Always pay close attention to the indicator immediately after the strip, as the indicator often dives, signaling the confident take of a trout below. This approach works well when coupled with large, overt chironomid pupa patterns, especially when you know, or suspect, trout are feeding on chironomid pupae and regular match-the-hatch–style presentations and patterns aren't working.

Fast-sinking lines are needed to drag buoyant foam-based attractors such as a Booby or FAB deep. Although you can trigger a trout to take a buoyant fly waking across the surface, your best chance for success involves using a fast-sinking type III or higher sink rate line.

Buoyant attractors attached to a fast-sinking line by a short, less than 5 feet, leader works well when targeting cruising fish in shallow clear water, a typical occurrence in early spring and late fall. If you spot a fish, cast ahead of its anticipated cruise path

As you are trying to trigger a reaction from a fish, attractor retrieves are typically brisk. Fast, aggressive retrieves also minimize the risk of hooking fish deep when using buoyant flies.

and allow the sinking line to drag the buoyant pattern down. As the fish comes into range of the fly, begin an aggressive 4- to 6-inch strip-pause retrieve. Upon seeing the fly, the cruising trout switches gears, accelerating after the fly and crushing it, often right at the end of your retrieve.

When fish are excited and willing to chase, a rolly polly retrieve is also a good option. Triggered by the movement, trout latch onto the fly, following almost to your feet before smashing it. If more than one fish follows the fly, a take is virtually guaranteed, as the fish compete with each other to take the fly. The visual aspect of this presentation technique provides some incredibly exciting opportunities.

PERILS OF BUOYANT FLIES

Buoyant foam-based attractors such as the Booby and FAB have become worldwide favorites. Powered by an aggressive strip-pause retrieve, these patterns shimmy, pitch, and dance—a seductive action few trout can resist. You must stay in contact with foam-based flies to avoid trout taking them deep. A buoyant fly, whether built of foam or spun and clipped deer hair, fished slowly or paused for a prolonged period, suspends or rises slightly, creating slack in the leader and a loss of connection between you and your fly. As the fish feels no resistance, it instinctively inhales and swallows the fly. If you are using a regular or weighted pattern, a sinking fly sinks on a tight leader. You feel these "on the drop" takes right away, as there is no loss of connection.

If you lose connection with a regular fly, trout can also take the fly deep. I had a fish inhale a fly once fishing loch style from a drifting boat. My fly line had tangled. As I worked out the tangle, my retrieve stopped. The fly line, leader, and fly sank

Whenever you are using buoyant flies such as the Booby, you must maintain contact with your flies to avoid hooking fish deep. If a fish feels no resistance when taking the fly, there is a chance it could swallow it.

without tension as the boat continued to drift. As soon as I sorted out the tangle, I stripped in the slack. The moment I came tight to the fly, I was surprised to hook a fish immediately. Once landed, the regular, non-buoyant nymph pattern was lodged deep in the trout's throat. Upon taking the descending fly, the fish felt no tension and swallowed it. I couldn't remove the fly without injuring the fish. My only alternative was to cut the tippet and leave the fly lodged in the fish in the hope it would later work its way free.

To avoid deep-hooking fish, the connection to buoyant flies must be constant. A brisk, choppy, 4- to 6-inch strip featuring minimal pauses maintains contact with your flies throughout the retrieve. If a fish does take the fly deep, don't attempt to remove it. No matter how cautious, your best attempts to retrieve the fly could nick or sever a gill raker, causing the fish to bleed uncontrollably. Although unfortunate, the best option is to cut the tippet and leave the fly in the trout on the assumption it will dislodge later.

USING ATTRACTORS TO MATCH THE HATCH

Not all attractor presentations feature fast, aggressive retrieves. Attractor patterns are often tied in colors that mirror zooplankton: shades of orange, chartreuse, red, and hot pink. When trout fixate on zooplankton, fishing can be tough, as it is impossible to match the size of the naturals. Zooplankton color, however, can be matched.

Although unorthodox, suspending small, size 8, 10, or 12, beadhead Blob patterns under an indicator, as you would to suggest chironomid larvae or pupae, works surprisingly well for zooplankton. You must use beadhead patterns to ensure the fly hangs on a tight tippet to avoid trout taking the fly deep. As trout cruise slowly, they inhale or filter feed on zooplankton. The best indicator Blob presentations involve predominantly static presentations or wind drifting to complement this feeding behavior. You can add the odd strip to coax a take. Often, the surface chop is the only action needed. Suspending beadhead Blobs under indicators during the late summer and through fall has saved the day for me on more than a few instances to be coincidental.

Attractor patterns such as beadhead Blobs suspended under an indicator can be used to suggest zooplankton. Choose a color that best matches that of the natural zooplankton.

CHAPTER TAKEAWAYS

- Fish, particularly trout, don't always take our flies out of a feeding response. Often the flies, coupled with the correct presentation, trigger a reaction.
- There are several reasons you should consider using attractor patterns and techniques in lakes, including targeting non-feeding trout or trout focusing on tiny, almost impossible to imitate food items, and to attract trout to a team of flies.
- Attractor techniques and patterns are all about provoking a reaction by appealing to a trout's curiosity, territoriality, or naturally aggressive nature.
- In addition to the three primary triggers, the art of exaggeration also comes into play.
- Although often presented in an imitative manner, you can also present chironomid pupa and larva patterns as attractors using the art of exaggeration.
- You must stay in contact with foam-based flies to avoid trout taking them deep. A buoyant fly, whether built of foam or spun and clipped deer hair, fished slowly or paused for a prolonged period, suspends or rises slightly, creating slack in the leader and a loss of connection between you and your fly.
- You can also use attractor patterns in an imitative role to suggest zooplankton. Beadhead Blobs that match the color of the zooplankton suspended under an indicator work exceptionally well at times.

CHAPTER 13

INTRODUCTION TO LOCH STYLE

I prefer to fish from an anchored position. It is the way I first learned to fly fish lakes. I believe for many of the presentation techniques and tactics covered in this book, an anchored boat offers superior presentation control. This is especially true with sub-surface floating line methods such as strike indicators and long-leader nymphing, aka the naked technique. However, there are situations where fishing from a drifting boat, loch style, offers superior benefits as opposed to fishing from an anchored position.

Loch style is commonplace in Europe, particularly in the United Kingdom. Steeped in tradition, loch style has been a standard for so many years that many lakes in Great Britain feature historical drifts, named in the same manner as specific runs and sections on North American rivers and streams.

Fly fishing from a drifting boat, loch style, is popular in Europe, particularly England and other Commonwealth countries such as Australia.
TODD OISHI

In North America, loch-style techniques are growing, primarily due to the increasing popularity and awareness of fly-fishing competitions in which fishing from an anchored boat is not allowed. The no-anchoring rule ensures an even playing field so no one can camp out on one spot. Stillwater competition anglers are only allowed to fish loch style. In North America, many competition fly fishers choose to regularly fish from a drifting boat to maintain and hone their loch-style skills. Loch-style competition circuits have been established and are growing in popularity, which only helps increase loch-style awareness and further fuel its growth.

So, besides competition and European influences, what are the practical benefits to fly fishing lakes from a drifting boat? Here are a few:

- As your boat or pontoon boat is drifting downwind, you are continually covering water. Loch style allows you the benefit of working large areas of a lake—areas that would be challenging to explore from an anchored position in more of a stepping-stone approach. Loch style is one of my favorite ways to fish dry flies and emergers over large shoal areas as pods of trout cruise and hunt terrestrials, adults, transitioning nymphs, and emerging pupae.
- With each cast, you are always presenting your fly or flies to fresh fish. Although trolling is a productive method for some, it is not a method I use, primarily because you first move over the fish and your flies follow. With loch style the flies precede the angler, eliminating the risk of the boat alerting or spooking fish.
- Trout in lakes retain their river and stream DNA, instinctively moving and feeding upwind in wind-induced current. As you are drifting downwind, you are presenting your flies into their path in a nonthreatening manner. Trout, as with many fish, are easily spooked by flies approaching from the side or from behind.
- Loch style and fishing from an anchored position can work together. You can drift over vast expanses of water to isolate specific areas that you might wish to anchor on and explore. If, on successive drifts, you hook fish over a sunken hump or adjacent to a point, you may want to anchor and further explore these structural elements.
- As with anchored techniques, you are always fishing with the wind at your back. Having the wind at your back eases casting, reduces tangles, and adds casting distance.
- When it is windy, surface conditions make fishing from an anchored position challenging. Drifting downwind using a drogue to slow and control your drift is an excellent presentation option. In these conditions a drogue or sea anchor is a necessary piece of loch-style equipment. Once deployed upwind, the drogue inflates with water, slowing and controlling the boat so it drifts broadside downwind, allowing you to cover water methodically.
- Loch style offers a dynamic approach to stillwater fly fishing. Some fly fishers shy away from stillwater fishing, as they perceive it is dull, slow, and tedious. As you are always on the move with loch style—casting, retrieving, and casting again—there is lots of activity to keep you busy. If slow or static stillwater presentations aren't your thing, give loch style a try.

There are numerous presentation benefits when fishing from a drifting boat. You are always presenting your flies to fresh fish, and you cover water so that your flies precede the boat, unlike trolling.

From a personal perspective, I simply enjoy fishing loch style. If anchored techniques aren't working or it makes more sense to drift, I won't hesitate to fish loch style.

EQUIPMENT REQUIREMENTS

There are a few specific equipment requirements and considerations unique to fly fishing lakes from a drifting boat.

Boats

You can fish loch style from a wide range of watercraft. As with most types of watercraft, there are pros and cons for each option. The main goal is that the boat or pontoon boat you choose to drift from is stable and wide—stability for angler comfort and safety, with width also providing stability while slowing the drift. An unstable watercraft that drifts too fast makes proper presentation difficult, frustrating, and potentially dangerous.

In Europe and in the UK in particular, clinker-style boats are commonplace. I have yet to see a clinker-style boat on any of the lakes I have fished across North America, though there are a few devoted "loch stylers" who I understand have built their own.

Clinker-style boats are commonly used loch-style boats in the United Kingdom and elsewhere. They are long, stable, wide, and heavy.
DEVIN OLSON

Original, wooden clinker boats are long, predominantly wide, and heavy. Today most of are made of fiberglass. Both wood and fiberglass are heavy, which helps provide a stable wind-resistant boat that drifts at a slow pace. Heavy boats are less prone to rocking, which creates waves. Fish can sense the wake through their lateral lines, which makes them wary or, in shallow conditions, causes them to spook. Most clinker boats feature a short keel, which also helps reduce drift speed. Clinkers are long, some over 17 feet, allowing three or more anglers space to cast, usually relay style to avoid everyone casting at once.

Large, heavy clinker boats require trailers to move them around. With many of the informal launches common to North American stillwaters, heavy boats can be challenging to launch, especially for a single angler.

In North America, aluminum jon boats are commonplace in many regions. Many anglers use them for loch style too. Aluminum jon boats are light, making them easy to handle and maneuver at the launch. They are my preferred loch-style boat. In my experience, they provide the best alternative to a clinker-style boat while providing the flexibility to fish from an anchored position too.

As with clinker boats, wide-bottomed jon boats drift extraordinarily well. A wide-bottomed jon boat is stable and provides a wide contact area, which aids the drifting process. I have a 14-foot flat-bottomed jon boat that is over 55 inches wide. In a light breeze, it drifts beautifully, perpendicular to the wind. V-hull aluminum boats also work, but due to their tapered bow, they don't always drift consistently.

Loch style is growing in popularity across North America due in part to competitions. You can only fish from a drifting boat in most fly-fishing competitions.

Fiberglass drift boats are also a common loch-style platform. Many anglers use these boats, as their versatility works for those who like to fish both lakes and rivers. As with a clinker boat, they are heavy and wide. The drawbacks to a drift boat are its rockered bottom and how little water they draw—maneuverability traits that serve them well on moving water but work against them as a loch-style platform. A drift boat's bottom design reduces its surface contact with the water and can lead to drift challenges, as the boat may spin in certain conditions.

Single anglers can also put pontoon boats and float tubes to good use for loch-style techniques. Many of these boats offer an excellent wide profile for drifting, even though they drift along their length nose down, feet first, as opposed to the broadside posture of a boat. In light winds, the odd left or right fin kick provides enough corrective action to maintain a controlled downwind drift. The portability of inflatable watercraft makes them ideal for smaller, less vehicle-accessible lakes. Their drawbacks become apparent on larger stillwaters. If a strong wind rises, it can become potentially dangerous or at least one long, hard kick and paddle upwind. Many pontoon boat anglers add an electric motor, which increases both safety and maneuverability.

Seats and Thwart Boards

In most situations, fishing in a boat from a seated position is best, from both a presentation and safety perspective. When fishing loch style, from a drifting boat, this is especially true, particularly from a safety perspective in windy conditions. If you decide to participate in a fly-fishing completion, fishing from a seated position is mandatory.

Fishing from a slightly elevated, seated position creates reduced boat wake from casting. Less wake helps you catch more fish, especially at the end of your retrieve, because you are less visible to following fish. If you stand up, you are more visible to fish, especially when you move your arms to cast. It is the movement that spooks fish.

Thwart boards lie across the boat's gunwale, allowing you to sit in an elevated position with your legs straddling each side of the board. In North America, most loch-style fly fishers make their own thwart boards. Commercially made aluminum thwart boards / boat seats are available in Europe.
TODD OISHI

When it comes to boat seating, you have a couple of options: seats or thwart board. Thwart boards lie across the gunwale of the boat, allowing you to sit above the boat floor with your legs straddling each side of the board. Thwart boards are easy to make using a 2-by-12-inch or 2-by-10-inch plank cut to length so approximately 4 inches hang over each side of the boat. Two-by-3-inch or 2-by-2-inch spacer blocks are then attached to the underside of the thwart board to prevent it from sliding off the gunwale. I wouldn't recommend building a thwart board without the spacer blocks. If the thwart board slips or slides as you cast, it could become potentially dangerous. Keep your feet firmly planted on the floor of the boat too. Any side motion might tip the thwart board, creating another possibly hazardous situation.

Thwart boards are easily removed and don't require permanent or semipermanent attachment as with a boat seat. They are commonplace in Europe, as the vast majority of European anglers don't own boats. Many European loch-style anglers purchase their own, commercially made thwart boards complete with a padded seat and carrying case. Some models even have roller wheels so you don't have to carry them from your vehicle to the boat. These portable thwart boards are made of lightweight aluminum and collapse to half their size for easy storage. In North America, commercially made thwart boards are difficult to obtain. If you are serious about getting a commercially made thwart board, you will probably have to order it from overseas.

Homemade wooden thwart boards, at least in my experience, are uncomfortable to sit on for prolonged periods. In practical terms, they are a pain in the butt. You can sit on a padded cushion, or rig a padded seat on your board for much-appreciated comfort. I participated in the 2007 Canadian Fly-Fishing Championships. Each competitor was provided with access to boats and simple wooden planks, or thwart boards. I was thankful that our team captain recommended bringing a cushion of some sort, as after one day of competition, my butt was killing me. It is tough to fish when you are in pain.

I prefer to fish from the comfort of a mounted padded seat secured by a bracket to the built-in seat of the boat or, depending on the boat layout, a pedestal seat. Mounted seats still allow you to fish from a low but slightly elevated position and, since they can spin, offer a safe, stable platform.

Drogues

In calm, light winds, most boats drift broadside downwind without incident. On occasion, a corrective oar stroke, fin kick, or stab of power from an electric motor may be required to keep the drift square. As wind and subsequent drift speed increases, maintaining a broadside drift becomes increasingly challenging. The bow is narrower and lighter than the stern, and left uncorrected the boat soon swings, bow pointing downwind. This position makes casting and proper presentation challenging and is further magnified when there are two people in a boat. These situations require a drogue or sea anchor.

A drogue is essentially an underwater parachute. It is deployed by tossing it over the side of the boat, upwind. Once submerged the drogue inflates with water, reducing drift speed while providing boat control, a combination that creates an excellent, slow-moving presentation platform.

There are two basic drogue shapes: conical and rectangular. In North America, the conical drift sock, or sea anchor, is more readily available. Rectangular para drogues are more common in Europe. As with a portable thwart board, you will most likely have to order a para drogue from overseas. I got mine from Great Britain.

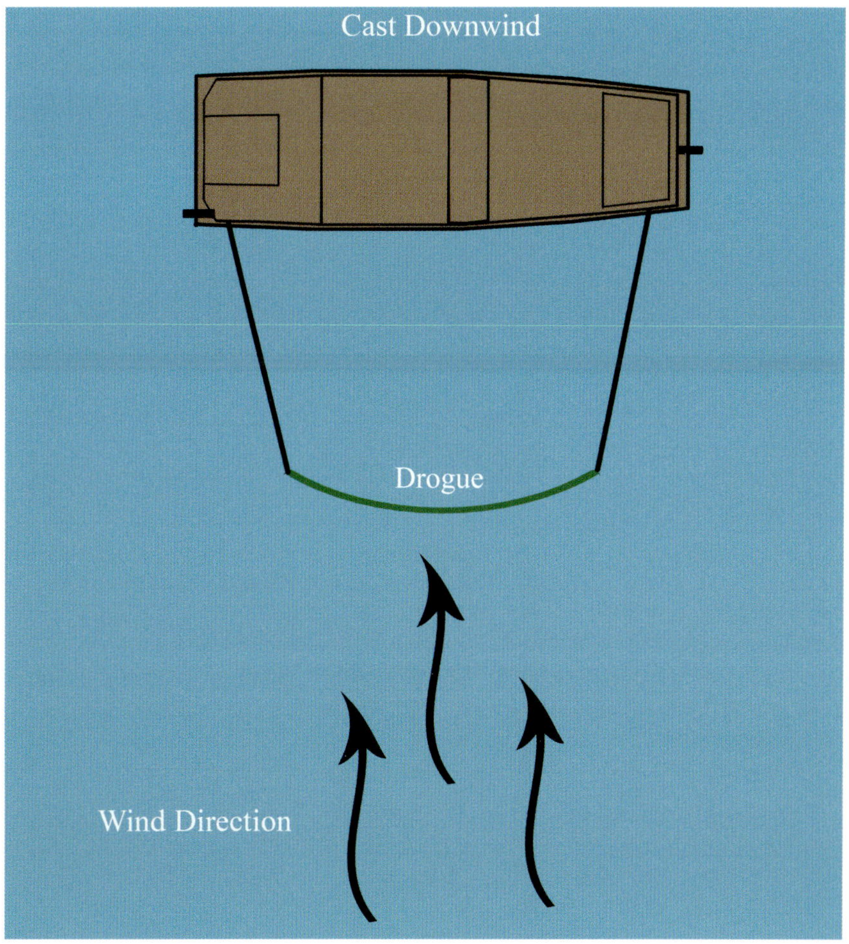

To fish loch style, position the boat perpendicular to the wind. Deploy the drogue on the upwind side of the boat and allow it to inflate with water to slow and control the drift of the boat.

Conical drogues, or sea anchors, are readily available across North America. If possible, purchase the largest one you can.

Conical drift socks are available in several sizes. Use the largest you can find. Large drogues offer the most drag, providing slow drift speeds. Some brands feature draw-string closures at the narrow end of the drogue to allow additional drift speed adjustments. The smaller the opening, the slower the drift speed. Conical drogues tend to have higher drift speeds than their para drogue counterparts.

Conical drogues have to be mounted centrally to the gunwale so the boat balances and drifts perpendicular. The weight distribution of the anglers, gear, motor, and other equipment affects the balance point on any boat.
TODD OISHI

It is possible to fish loch style from a float tube or pontoon boat using a conical drogue.

Most conical drogues feature a single anchor point, requiring a bit of experimentation to locate the balance point so the boat drifts perpendicular downwind. Weight distribution affects the anchor point: Angler, gear, boat motor, battery, and fuel tank location all play a role. Drift socks are the best choice for float tubes and pontoon boats due to this single anchor point.

Once the boat is in position, perpendicular to the wind, toss the drogue upwind to deploy. As the boat drifts downwind, the drogue inflates with water, slowing and controlling the boat.
TODD OISHI

A rectangular para drogue features two attachment points. It can be mounted centrally on the gunwale or at the bow and stern of the boat. If you attach the drogue straps at the bow and stern, the para drogue self-centers, balancing the boat for a perfect drift. Para drogues aren't easy to find in North America and are only available from a few select dealers.
BRETT COLPITTS

The straps or ropes of a rectangular para drogue attach to the bow and stern sides of the boat. Due to this double attachment, a para drogue self-centers once inflated, allowing for a quick, efficient setup. Of the two types, I prefer the rectangular para drogue due to its easy deployment and how it self-centers once inflated. Conical drogues have to be recovered and brought back into the boat at the end of a drift. Para drogues can be left outside the boat, as they trail along the sides of the boat as you work your way back upwind to set up for another drift. Make sure to make wide-open turns as you head upwind. A tight turn could result in the drogue becoming fouled in a motor prop.

The straps or ropes of a drogue attach by a clamp or clamps to the upwind gunwale of the boat. You can use a variety of clamps, including C-clamps, lock clamps, and spring clamps, all of which can be found at your local home improvement store. I am currently using spring clamps. Clamp choice is up to you so long as they hold the drogue ropes or straps without slipping. I half hitch the drogue straps around the clamps a couple of times for added security. If possible, look for drogues with bright,

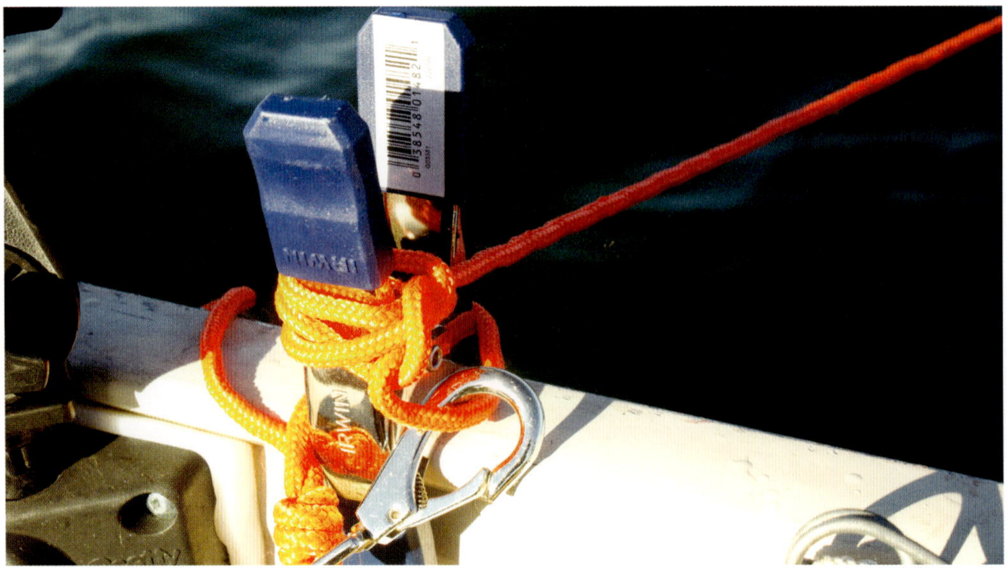

A C-clamp, lock clamp, or spring clamp, available at any home improvement or hardware store, attached to the upwind gunwale of the boat holds the drogue cords in place. A para drogue requires two clamps if you wish to secure the cords at the bow and stern.

visible straps. Should a fish get around the back of the boat during the fight, the visible ropes make steering the fish around the drogue easier. The last thing you want is a fish becoming entangled in the drogue ropes. Adding floats or hot water tank foam tubes to the straps is also a good idea. In the unlikely event your drogue should break free, you stand a better chance of recovering it.

Perpendicular drifts aren't always necessary, and there are situations where it is best to crab downwind on a diagonal track deliberately. Crabbing is an ideal tactic to allow the boat to drift diagonally parallel to a shoal, allowing both anglers to cast onto and retrieve back across the shoal. Of the two drogue styles, para drogues are easier to set up for crabbing. Shorten the rope in the direction you wish to angle the boat. If you wanted to crab to the left of a shoal, shorten up the right drogue strap or rope.

Take care when using a drogue in strong winds. In extreme circumstances a deployed drogue may dig down, pulling the upwind gunwale down and potentially swamping the boat. With the possible exception of bank angling, it is best to stay onshore in strong winds whether you fish loch style from an anchored position or otherwise. Care must also be taken when drifting in shallow water or over sunken logs and branches so that the drogue doesn't become entangled. These hazards may cause drogue loss or, worse, a capsized boat.

To crab a boat diagonally, shorten the rope in the direction you wish to angle the boat. If you wanted to crab to the left of a shoal, shorten up the right drogue strap or rope.

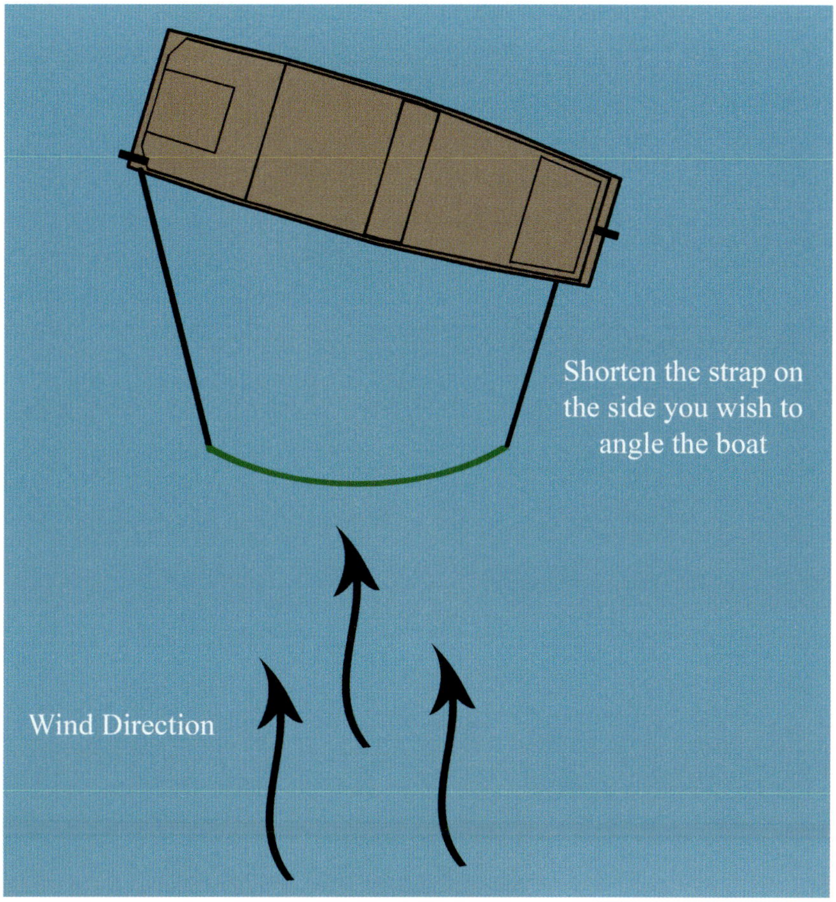

Shortening the length of one the straps or ropes of a para drogue allows the boat to crab diagonally, allowing both anglers to drift parallel to a structure such as a shoal.
TODD OISHI

Caution must be exercised when fishing loch style in windy conditions or over shallow water containing sunken logs or debris.
DEVIN OLSON

Rods and Lines

I still favor long rods, minimum of 9½ feet and preferably 10 feet, for loch style. One primary advantage of long rods is an extended, higher hang. As you are pulling or retrieving flies the majority of the time on the drift, many fish come at the end of the presentation as you hang the fly or flies before recasting. Sweep lines, featuring different densities along their length, are excellent loch-style lines. The less dense tip and rear sections of these lines help set up a sweep profile, allowing you to cover water vertically as you cover water horizontally downwind. Many ardent loch-style fly fishers believe this provides a superior hang, as the dense midsection tends to hang the line more vertically at the end of the presentation. This profile allows you to raise the fly or flies vertically through the water to hopefully intercept a fish.

Fly rods 9½ feet or longer work best when fishing loch style, as they provide a superior hang.
TODD OISHI

When fishing loch style, you cast more than from an anchored position, as the boat is always in motion. As soon as the line lands, you are advancing on to your cast. As a result, I use higher line weight rods so the rod does the work, not I. A 6-weight would be the minimum for trout. I know of other anglers who prefer 7- or even 8-weight rods. The heavier the line you are casting, the higher the weight rod. Wind speed also affects rod selection. Higher wind speeds result in faster drifts, which usually dictate faster-sinking lines to get down and more casts, as you are covering more water.

Loch-style line choices are the same as those for fishing from an anchored position or the bank. If the fish are up near the surface and the wind speed is light, floating, midge-tip, and slow-sinking lines would be preferred options. If the trout are deep and wind speeds are high, fast-sinking lines will be the best choice so your line, leader, and flies have a chance to get down to the fish. As a general rule, the faster the drift, the faster the sink rate. Varying wind and subsequent drift speed is one of the reasons competition fly fishers carry so many different lines. Each line has a presentation range that makes it the best choice for various wind and drift speeds.

PRESENTATION TECHNIQUES

The basic stillwater presentation techniques such as rod position and retrieves still hold for loch style, but there are a few adjustments unique to this method.

The first time you watch someone fishing loch style, you may think that brisk, fast-paced retrieves are standard. This is an optical illusion of sorts, as you must gather line in order to stay in contact with your flies as the boat drifts downwind. The faster

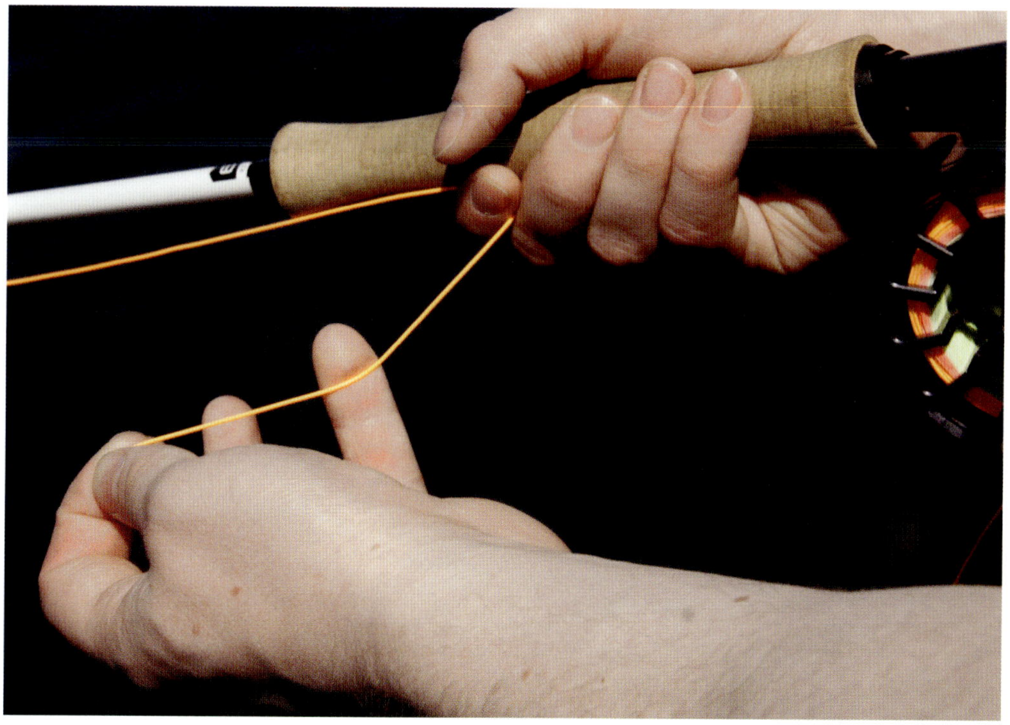

As the boat is always moving forward, retrieve your line just enough to stay in contact with your flies as they sink to avoid missing takes as they descend.

the drift, the faster the apparent retrieve. Use the line sag at the rod tip as a guide. The line should not hang vertically or move back under the rod, indicating that you aren't in direct contact with your flies. Losing contact results in missed takes and in extreme circumstances may result in fish swallowing your fly, as they feel no resistance when they mouth the fly.

Whenever possible, present your flies on an angle across the drift. Stillwater trout are hardwired to face into any current, and this trait is one of the primary benefits of loch style. As you always cast with the wind at your back, downwind, your flies are in front of or crossing the paths of cruising trout as they move upwind into the wind-induced current. An angled presentation also allows slower retrieves, as you aren't drifting straight down on your line, requiring a brisk retrieve to stay in contact with your flies. This presentation angle exposes the flies in profile view, across the path of any nearby fish. A straight, downwind cast provides a narrow view of the fly and doesn't cover nearly as much water.

Long casts aren't always necessary or advantageous when using loch-style tactics. When fishing shallow water or if conditions require or allow slow retrieves, a long

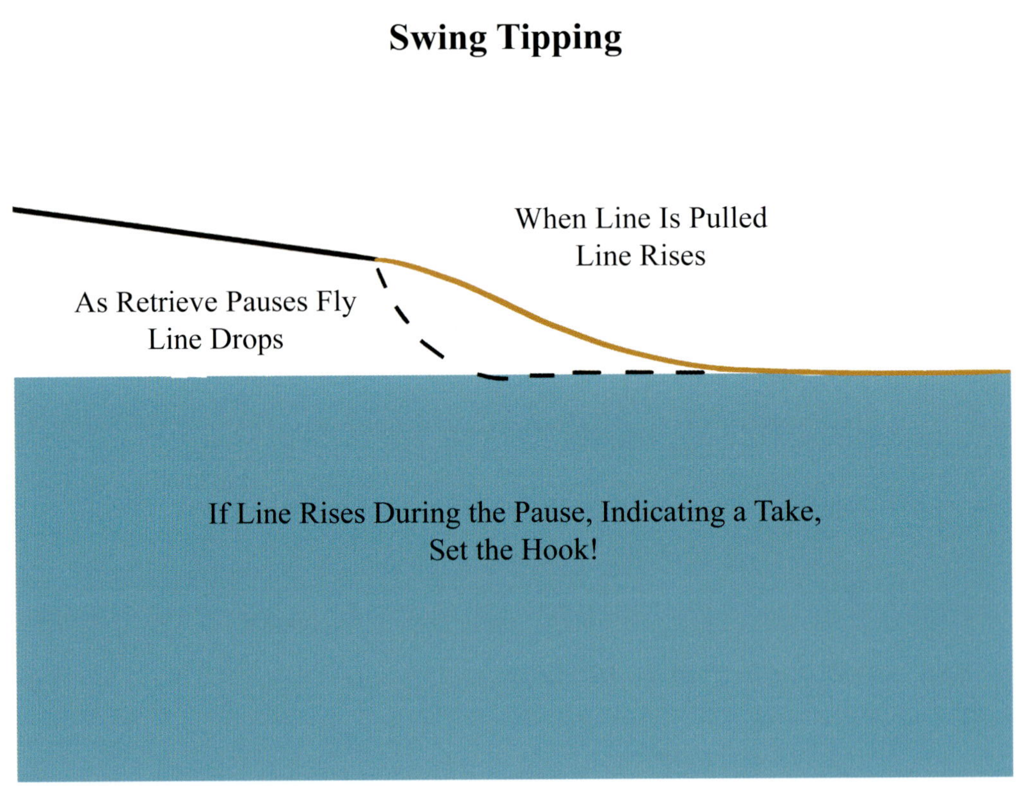

Watching the rod tip during the retrieve, or swing tipping, allows you to see signs of a take before it is felt.

cast results in the flies hanging up on the bottom before the presentation can be completed. As the boat is always moving forward, flies sink quickly, especially if you lose contact with the flies. Even if you are counting flies down before commencing the retrieve, use a slow hand twist to stay in contact with your flies to avoid any missed takes should a fish intercept them on the drop. Short, accurate casts also work best when fishing dry flies when drifting, as they help prevent drag due to the flies landing tight on a long line. When fishing dries, slack-line presentations such as a puddle cast also help the flies drift naturally.

When using floating and clear-tip lines, the tip sag can be used to recognize subtle takes—a European technique called "swing tipping." The movement of the fly during the retrieve mimics that of swing-tip rods that are popular with European coarse fish anglers. It is a technique well suited to loch style to help recognize takes before they are felt. If you watch the section of fly line from the rod tip to the surface during the retrieve, you will notice how the line rises on the pull and falls on the pause. I call this the rhythm of the retrieve. Tension on either end of the line causes the line to rise. If, during the pause portion of your retrieve, your fly line starts to rise, tension is being applied at the other end in the form of a fish. As soon as you recognize the line rising, signifying a take, raise the rod to set the hook. When fishing from an anchored position, I always watch for takes near the tip of the line. When you are fishing loch style, it isn't always easy to see the end of the line. Swing tipping is the next best thing.

Setting up a drift is straightforward, but there are a few tactic considerations. If possible, drift over water that is the same average depth so you don't have to make any mid-drift line changes. Drifting adjacent to structure or transition changes such as the edge of a shoal is also preferred, as trout frequent these places to hunt. Longer drifts are also preferred so I spend more time fishing and less time repositioning and deploying my drogue. I also make a point of drifting through unfished water, as targeting fresh, unfished water is best.

After deciding on a suitable drift, turn the boat broadside and square to the wind. If there is enough wind, set up and deploy the drogue. Once the drogue has been deployed and it has inflated, make any necessary adjustments to maintain a consistent broadside, downwind drift. Complete the drift. When the drift is completed, recover the drogue, if needed or desired, and make a wide return back upwind for another drift. To avoid spooking fish, never motor through the water you plan to, or others may decide to, drift through.

To reduce tangles, frustration, and, in extreme competitive circumstances, conflict, a few adjustments need to be made when there are two people in the boat. As when fishing from an anchored position, divide the boat in half. With the wind at the anglers' backs, drifting downwind, the bow angler works a quadrant from noon, a vertical line drawn from the center of the boat, to 3 o'clock, directly off his right shoulder. The stern angler works the other side, noon to 9 o'clock.

CHAPTER TAKEAWAYS

- As you are always on the move, one of the primary benefits of loch style is that you are always presenting your fly to fresh fish as you drift downwind.
- Wide, heavy boats work best for loch style.
- Fishing from a slightly elevated, seated position creates reduced boat wake from casting, helping you catch more fish, especially at the end of your retrieve.
- Thwart boards are easy to make. They lie across the gunwale of the boat, allowing you to sit above the boat floor with your legs straddling each side of the board.
- If you use a homemade wooden thwart board, use a cushion or consider adding a seat so you can fish comfortably throughout the day.
- There are two types of drogues in use today: conical sea anchors, or drift socks, and rectangular para drogues.
- Para drogues are easier to deploy, as they self-center.
- Conical drogues require you to locate the balance point of the boat. Balance points constantly change due to the weight distribution of anglers, gear, and boat equipment such as motors and batteries.
- Drogues can be set up to allow the boat to deliberately crab on an acute angle downwind. Crabbing allows two anglers to drift downwind while covering structure to one side of the boat or another.
- Para drogues are the easiest to set up for crabbing downwind on an angle. Shorten the rope in the direction you wish to angle the boat.
- Avoid using a drogue in strong winds, as it can pull the upwind gunwale down, potentially swamping the boat.
- As you cast more when fishing loch style, use a heavier rod than you would use when fishing from an anchored position.
- As with anchored presentations, fan cast to cover water and provide fish with a broadside profile of your flies.
- The faster the drift, the faster the sink rate of the fly line. As the flies are sinking, maintain contact with them by using a slow hand twist to avoid missing takes on the drop or potentially deep-hooking fish.
- Use shorter casts coupled with slow retrieves when fishing shallow water. Shorter casts also work best with dry flies to reduce line drag on the flies.
- When using floating or clear-tip lines, watch the line between the rod tip and the water for signs of subtle takes.
- To avoid spooking fish, never motor through the water you plan to, or others may decide to, drift through.
- When two anglers are fishing in a boat, divide the boat in half. The bow angler works a downwind quadrant from noon, a vertical line drawn from the center of the boat, to 3 o'clock, directly off his right shoulder. The stern angler works a downwind quadrant from noon to 9 o'clock.

CHAPTER 14

WHAT'S IN YOUR FLY BOX? STILLWATER FLIES

When I first started fly fishing lakes, stillwater-specific patterns weren't readily available. There were only a few books that even referenced stillwater patterns. This lack of stillwater-specific flies was a primary reason behind my first fly-tying book. I wanted to provide stillwater fly fishers with a reference they could use to help them stock their fly boxes and, more importantly, inspire them to create and develop their own stillwater flies.

Since that time, much has changed. Interest in stillwater fly fishing continues to rise, and the growth of social media, particularly YouTube and Instagram, further cultivates this interest. Now there is a steadily increasing number of unique and innovative lake flies available.

Whether you are an ardent tier or purchase your flies, it is essential to have a solid understanding of what constitutes a good

Whether you buy or tie your flies, it is essential to understand the traits that go into a solid stillwater fly pattern.

stillwater pattern—vital knowledge that helps you tie better flies or know what to look for when purchasing suitable lake patterns. As with almost every fly pattern, less is more when it comes to stillwater flies. I prefer slender, sparse, lightly dressed flies.

KEY PATTERN ELEMENTS

There are four pattern elements I incorporate into any fly: size, shape, color, and behavior. Trout can focus on one, two, three, or all four of these elements. These are the same elements I use to prioritize the key traits in the naturals too. Early in the hatch, fish seem to accept a range of pattern sizes and colors, provided the presentation depth is correct. As the hatch progresses, fish refine their selection process, and their feeding zone also narrows. Our flies must now match the body profile, size, and color of the naturals for consistent success. Chironomid pupae are probably the best example of this focused feeding behavior. Thankfully trout are most often in an opportunistic frame of mind, feeding on whatever crosses their path, providing a level of forgiveness and reason with our pattern shortfalls.

I believe that all four of these elements are essential pattern considerations. These priorities often fluctuate, so be prepared to adapt. One day a fly must have a particular shape, the next day the fly may need to be a specific size, and on another day, matching the color suffices. These fluctuations are part of the enjoyment and frustrations of fly fishing lakes. Based on my experience, I most often prioritize these considerations in the order of shape, size, behavior, and color.

Shape

When trout are feeding selectively, shape, or profile, is arguably the most critical pattern consideration. As trout concentrate on a specific food source, they become attuned to its particular form, a common predator trait referred to as search image formation. In his book *Trout Sense*, author Jason Randall defined search image formation as "the template that trout establish for feeding and a measure against which they measure future prey encounters." As humans, we use search image formation too. If you are in a busy mall looking for a friend or spouse, you know their build and what they are wearing—information you use to focus your search.

Ensuring your pattern shape, or profile, matches the naturals is arguably the most important of the four traits of every fly pattern.

Many anglers, frustrated by the trout's inclination to only accept flies that match a particular prey item's shape, attribute this behavior to a supreme intelligence. Thankfully trout aren't that smart. Choosing to only accept flies that match the specific food item is nothing more than an instinctive trait intended to promote efficient feeding. This is why I firmly believe that stillwater patterns, as with the majority of trout patterns, must be slender. Even large dragonfly nymphs aren't as robust as many would think. The large, aggressive nymphs from the Aeshnidae clan, commonly referred to as darners, are long and slender. The head and midsection of their body are their widest features. Many dragon nymph patterns are too fat. In selective feeding conditions, obese patterns don't work as well as those that complement the body profile of the natural nymphs. When trout focus on a particular food source, make sure your pattern matches the shape of the naturals.

Size

The overall size is important, as you want to do your best to choose patterns that match the overall dimensions of the targeted food. However, there are times where exaggeration works in our favor. Using a pattern that is one size larger than the naturals is one of my favorite tactics. I believe that if your fly stands out in the crowd of naturals, it appeals to a trout's greedy, predatory nature. Size exaggeration is one of the primary components of attractor flies. I have also found that when imitating chironomid pupae and larvae in deeper water, trout often accept larger flies despite their usual preference for flies that match the size of the naturals. Perhaps the security of deep water makes them less cautious?

There is also a seasonal component to size. In the spring through early summer, most insects are at the peak of their aquatic development. Once hatched, subsequent generations are smaller. Insects capable of multiple broods during a season, such as *Callibaetis* mayflies, are smaller with each successive generation due to their reduced growth time between cycles. As a general guideline, use larger flies in the spring, smaller flies in the fall.

As simple as they appear, chironomid pupae are among the most demanding food sources to match during selective feeding conditions.
BRIAN CHAN

Behavior

Behavior is a twofold process: the presentation techniques we use to bring the fly to life, and the choice of materials blended into the fly. Successful stillwater patterns must be mobile and translucent. As there is little current to animate a fly, I incorporate soft mobile materials such as marabou, aftershaft feathers, fur, and soft hackles into my flies. These materials move and breathe almost on their own, suggesting life and convincing fish to take.

Translucence is a key pattern trait. Dubbing blends, particularly long-strand mohair and synthetic-based blends, do a fantastic job of suggesting translucence when incorporated into leech, scud, dragonfly nymph, or caddis pupa patterns. Although difficult or illegal to obtain in some countries, seal's fur remains one of my favorite dubbing materials.

Material choice affects how a fly functions. Buoyant patterns such as a spun and clipped deer hair Gomphus allow you to work around weeds and other debris relatively snag-free.

Material choice also affects how a fly moves or functions. Blended into a fly, buoyant materials such as foam or spun and clipped deer hair help the finished pattern remain snag-free as it skips above the weeds and bottom debris. In the case of foam-based attractors such as a Booby or FAB, foam also adds a unique action to the fly.

Color

For many anglers, color is the most important pattern consideration. While color is important, it is not the most important pattern consideration. Why? Because there are so many variables that influence how colors appear underwater. Presentation depth, water clarity, and available light such as a bright sun versus overcast influence how trout see different colors. I believe patterns containing contrasting colors perform best.

As depth increases, the amount of available light decreases. Depth has a definite impact on color. Long-wavelength colors such as red and yellow are the first to fade. Blue and violet are the last to fade. These are two of my favorite deep-water pattern colors. Patterns containing some level of fluorescence are also among my favorites for deep water or low-light conditions such as overcast days or evenings. Fluorescence may dominate the fly's overall color or provide an accent in the form of a hot spot or bead. I also use fluorescent thread thoraxes and floss gills on many of my chironomid pupa patterns.

Aquatic invertebrates are camouflage masters. This damselfly nymph illustrates that when unsure of what pattern color to choose, you can't go wrong selecting a fly that matches the surrounding vegetation.

Water clarity also influences pattern color. In clear water, my patterns tend to be somber natural colors with perhaps a touch of flash. When fishing darker algae-type lakes featuring lots of suspended matter, my flies feature more flash in the form of Flashabou accents and flashy reflective body materials. If you are in doubt as to what pattern color to use, choosing flies that match the vegetation color is always a good starting point. In murky, turbid conditions, dark patterns tend to silhouette and stand out the best.

Water clarity impacts fly color. My clear-water patterns tend to be somber natural tones with perhaps a splash of flash. When prospecting turbid water, my flies feature a bit more flash, sparkle, and fluorescence to stand out better.

FLY CATEGORIES

I break my stillwater flies into three specific categories: suggestive, imitative, and attractor. Although you can use patterns from any category at any time, there are certain instances where I favor one category over another.

Suggestive Flies

As their category title would suggest, suggestive flies are patterns that possess features and characteristics common to many different food items. Denny Rickard's Stillwater Nymph is an excellent example, blending the traits of a scud and damsel into one. Suggestive patterns utilize translucence, mobility, flash, and contrasting color combinations. These traits appeal to a trout's naturally opportunistic nature. Suggestive flies look buggy and trigger trout to eat.

As illustrated by the peacock herl thorax of my Herl May, color contrast is always a good stillwater pattern trait.

For many stillwater fly fishers, suggestive flies are their preferred pattern choice. They subscribe to a belief that presentation trumps pattern every time, a concept I firmly believe in. The most realistic pattern on the planet will not work if it isn't presented at the right depth and moved in such a way as to convince a trout that it is food.

The Woolly Bugger is perhaps the best example of a suggestive fly. Depending on its size, color, hackle density, and tail length, a Woolly Bugger may suggest a variety of prey items including dragonfly nymphs, damselfly nymphs, leeches, and baitfish. It is a pattern, as with many suggestive flies, that looks like everything and nothing.

I carry a range of suggestive patterns in my fly boxes. They are patterns I use at the beginning of a day, or when fishing a new lake for the first time. My goal is to catch the first fish as quickly as I can. Through careful use of a throat pump, I can adjust my presentation strategy from there. Many times, a throat pump reveals sporadic, varied feeding with a range of prey items. In these instances, suggestive patterns are ideal choices. This is a typical early spring or late fall scenario, as the significant insect hatches have yet to start or have finished for the season.

The Woolly Bugger, and all of its variations, is perhaps the most recognized suggestive pattern in rivers and lakes.

Suggestive flies also work when trout appear focused on a specific food item, such as during the fall months when trout tune in to tiny scuds. In this situation, small suggestive micro leeches often outperform more realistic scud patterns.

Buoyed by the fact that trout are feeding, I believe that if I get my fly in front of a fish using the right presentation, it should eat it.

You can also use a larger suggestive pattern in a two- or three-fly system. The suggestive pattern draws fish from a distance to the smaller imitative flies that better match the food source the trout are focused upon. At times trout may only take the imitative fly, while on other occasions they target both flies. If fish appear to be preferring the imitative pattern, avoid the temptation to remove the suggestive fly. Chances are it is attracting fish to the imitative fly. Removing it may reduce your catch rate.

Too often, we become focused on specific, match-the-hatch–style patterns. Many times, a suggestive, cover-the-bases pattern is the best choice.

Imitative Flies

Imitative flies are designed and intended to represent a specific food item or stage within an aquatic insect's life cycle. Chironomids—larvae, pupae, and adults—are the pinnacle of imitative stillwater flies, particularly the pupal stage. The sheer volume of patterns to imitate this stage is overwhelming. Fly tiers are always attempting to create the ultimate chironomid imposter.

I enjoy trying to solve the match-the-hatch puzzle. If fish are feeding on damselfly nymphs, chances are I will tie on a pattern that matches the natural nymphs and present it as a natural nymph. I sort the majority of my flies by food source type—a definite clue that I enjoy trying to convince trout my flies are the real thing.

Imitative flies are usually the best option during a hatch when trout fixate on a specific prey item or stage. When the hatch is strong, trout become acutely aware of the size, shape, color, and behavior of a particular food source. This is a frustrating

For many stillwater fly fishers, chironomid pupa patterns represent the pinnacle of imitative stillwater flies.

situation, as the trout usually reject all of our offerings—a trait that many attribute to acute intelligence rather than instinct. I have had instances where trout were targeting ascending chironomid pupae and changing to a fly with a different rib made all the difference.

Attractor Flies

Attractor flies are the obnoxious party guest of the fly box. These are flies that are typically large and flashy, and look like nothing any self-respecting stillwater trout would eat. Attractors trigger a predominantly non-feeding response through curiosity, territoriality, or aggression.

Stillwater attractor flies are nothing new, but in recent years their use and application have increased. I first heard of attractor patterns as a serious pattern consideration at the 1993 World Fly Fishing Championship in Kamloops, BC. The English, Scottish, and Welsh teams were well aware of the charm their attractor patterns had on stillwater trout.

I always have a healthy supply of gaudy attractors such as Boobies, Blobs, and FABs on hand for those times when fish refuse to take suggestive or imitative patterns. Attractors can also be used to fool fish focused on minute zooplankton. In these instances, match attractor colors to those of the natural zooplankton.

An attractor pattern's primary intention is to trigger a non-feeding response through curiosity, territoriality, or aggression.

As with suggestive flies, attractor patterns are an excellent choice in multiple-fly rigs to draw trout to a team of flies. Trout may not take the attractor, but after venturing in to investigate, they readily take a nearby natural-looking pattern. I most often place my attractor patterns on the top dropper. I believe fish tend to peel off and back after seeing but not taking the attractor. Having the attractor as the top dropper places the other fly or flies into the path of the turning trout. As with suggestive patterns, avoid the temptation to remove the attractor from the team if the other fly or flies are getting attention. The attractor still plays a role in your success by drawing fish to your flies. Removing the attractor could negatively affect your success.

Attractors and the presentation techniques associated with them have become an essential component of my stillwater repertoire, so much so that I dedicated a chapter in this book to their use.

WEIGHTED FLIES

I tend to use weighted flies for specific presentation techniques: under indicators, floating lines coupled with long leaders (naked technique), leech and baitfish patterns on slow-sinking lines, and balanced flies. I prefer unweighted flies when using faster-sinking lines, type III or greater.

Sinking lines are categorized by sink rate, so you can choose the correct sink rate for the conditions. As discussed in chapter 11, "Going Deep," knowing the sink rate allows you to count your line and flies down to consistently prospect a specific depth. Tying on a heavily weighted fly unbalances the presentation, accelerates the sink rate, and lessens presentation control. I prefer to let the fly line drag the fly down so I have accurate control of my presentation. Quality sinking lines, as with all quality fly lines, are expensive. It doesn't make sense to allow an inexpensive weighted fly negatively impact the performance of the expensive fly line.

Hook style also impacts weighted flies. I prefer tying many of my patterns on curved shank hooks. Weighting a curved shank hook such as a scud hook with lead wire or a lead wire substitute concentrates the mass of the fly at the apex of the curve, causing the fly to roll over. Unweighted, curved shank patterns track and swim correctly.

I use brass beads 90 percent of the time, as I don't always use indicator presentations. Brass-bead flies work across a range of presentation methods. I find that other than with indicator presentations, tungsten-bead flies sink too fast. If I need more pattern weight to combat wind-induced current or to explore deeper water, I integrate a swivel into my leader or, if legal to do so, add flies on separate droppers. I only use tungsten beads on balanced flies and jig flies and when using small, size 18 or less, chironomid pupa patterns. I find the added mass of a tungsten bead pays dividends on smaller flies, as there isn't much material remaining on a small bead after the hook hole is bored. On the practical side, I have a hard time keeping my tungsten flies separated from my brass-bead flies. On a busy day featuring lots of fly changes, my fly boxes soon become messy and in need of reorganization.

As with moving-water flies, brass, tungsten, and glass beads have had a prominent influence on stillwater fly patterns.

Almost all of my chironomid pupa patterns and most of my larval patterns are weighted. Beads provide compact weight, add an element of flash and attraction, and contribute to the overall shape of my chironomid patterns. As pattern profile is critical, beads have become an integral chironomid pattern component. I am a firm believer in skinny chironomid pupa and larva patterns. Slender patterns sink fast, and when fish focus on a particular profile, size, and color, they perform well. This is especially true in pressured conditions, when there are numerous fly fishers on the water. I use a bead one size smaller than most bead-to-hook-size charts recommend for all of my chironomid larva and pupa patterns. Listed below are my preferred brass bead to hook sizes for these patterns:

Size 8: ⅛ inch (3.5 mm)
Size 10: 7/64 inch (3.0 mm)
Size 12 and 14: 3/32 inch (2.7 mm)
Size 16 and 18: 5/64 inch (2.0 mm)

Balanced Flies

There are several different approaches to weighting flies, but one style in particular has had an enormous influence on my pattern design: balanced flies. It is a weighting option worthy of more than a passing mention.

Spokane, Washington, fly fisher Jerry McBride originated the balanced fly concept. Jerry realized that a standard beadhead pattern suspended below an indicator hung vertically. However, except for emerging chironomids, caddis pupae, and mayfly nymphs, all other stillwater food sources move horizontally. Challenged by this shortcoming, Jerry experimented with several options before settling on a tungsten bead slid onto a sewing pin extension. The pinhead prevented the bead from sliding off. The pin extension, tied onto the shank out in front of the hook eye, balanced the fly so it suspended horizontally under an indicator, like most trout food.

When I first began using balanced flies, I wondered if they made a difference. Then one fall a friend and I were fishing identical leech patterns, one balanced and the other a standard beadhead. Both leeches were suspended beneath an indicator at the same depth a mere 5 feet apart. Would the trout care? It didn't take long to find out. The trout did notice, preferring the balanced leech ten to one. I was convinced. Since that initial experiment, a balanced fly such as a leech is perhaps my top choice when I am prospecting any lake.

Originally, balanced flies were mostly tied on standard shank down-eye hooks. Down-eye hooks allowed you to tie the finished fly onto your tippet, as a balanced fly rides upside down. The challenge with a down-eye hook is that if you aren't careful, you can accidentally obscure the hook eye through the tying process—a common occurrence when tying mohair-based leech patterns. You would then end up with a perfectly balanced fly that was impossible to tie on. I joke that these versions were what you gave to friends who lament that you never tie any flies for them!

My contribution to the balanced fly was based on the introduction of the 60- or 90-degree jig hook. Small jig hooks ensure the hook eye remains clear, regardless

Thanks to the variety of jig hook sizes and styles now available, we can tie balanced flies to suggest a variety of stillwater trout food, from larger leeches and minnows to smaller nymphs, scuds, and chironomid larvae.

of the materials used. Originally, small jig hooks that could stand up to the rigors of a trout were hard to find. Most of the small jig hooks I experimented with were designed for soft-mouthed panfish. These panfish-style, light-wire jig hooks straightened when subjected to a larger, aggressive, hard-mouthed trout. With the explosion in the popularity of European nymphing and jig nymphs, we now have a wide range of stout jig hooks available in a variety of sizes. I tie large balanced leeches and baitfish for walleye and bass and small balanced scuds and nymphs for trout. Balanced flies also make excellent river and stream patterns. Try suspending a balanced fly below a dry fly, dry-dropper style, or as part of a Euro nymphing rig.

Twice as dense as brass beads, tungsten beads are a must for balanced flies. Lighter brass beads require a considerable extension to balance a fly. I match hooks to specific bead sizes to ensure my flies balance consistently, and use the smallest tungsten beads possible to ease casting. Heavy balanced flies are not easy to cast on a thin, level indicator leader, especially the long leaders that are necessary for prospecting deeper water.

These are my recommended hook and bead sizes for the size range of the Daiichi jig hooks I prefer to use:

Daiichi 4640-4647: size 6, 5⁄32 inch (3.8 mm)
Daiichi 4640-4647: size 8 and 10, 1⁄8 inch (3.5 mm)
Daiichi 4640-4647: size 12 and 14, 7⁄64 inch (3.0 mm)

The hook, pin extension, and tungsten bead chassis are key to a balanced fly. I first began using sewing pins that I cut to length using a pair of side cutters, typically the distance from the hook eye to a vertical line up from the hook point. The risk with this method is that the ragged, cut end of the sewing pin may sever the tying thread. I have since switched to sequin pins. Sequin pins are shorter than sewing pins, coming out of the box just the right length. The machined tapered tip of the pin minimizes the risk of thread breakage as you secure it to the hook shank. You can find sequin

The chassis—consisting of a 60- or 90-degree jig hook, tungsten bead, and an extension such as a sewing pin, sequin pin, or escutcheon pin—forms the backbone of any balanced fly.

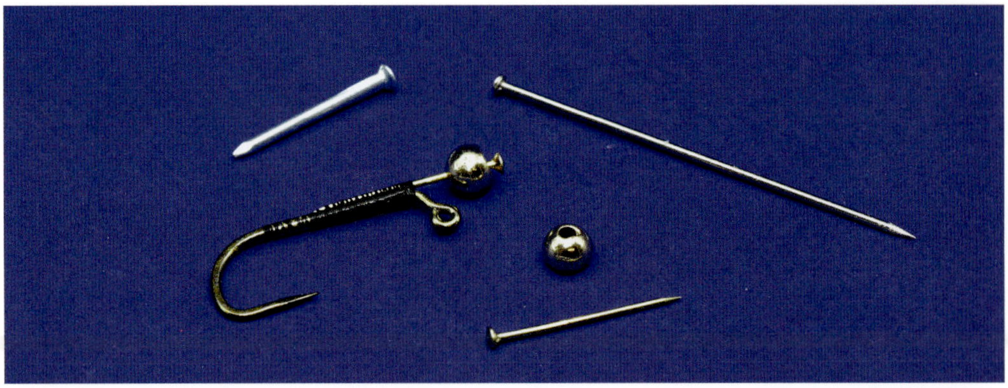

pins at craft stores, hobby shops, and online. Larger beads, over ⅛ inch (3.5 mm) diameter, slide over and off the head of a sewing or sequin pin. In these instances, use small brads or escutcheon pins. These can be found at most home improvement stores.

Begin by sliding the tapered bead onto the pin. I prefer to position my beads so the wide tapered end envelops the pinhead. Place the bead and pin assembly onto the shank. Secure it in place at a point where you can envision getting another two beads onto the pin extension between the rear of the bead and the hook eye. This proportional standard works no matter the hook or bead size.

When you first begin tying balanced flies, it is a good idea to remove the hook, extension, and bead chassis from the vise and do a test balance. When you "air balance" the hook, a slight tail-down profile is best. At first, this may seem wrong. Most balanced flies feature a tail of some sort. In the water, the tail supports the fly, tipping it horizontally. Don't be too concerned if your finished fly doesn't balance perfectly level. Under an indicator, bounced around by the surface chop, balanced flies dance seductively.

When tying a series of balanced flies, I find it best to tie in steps, production style:

1. Begin by loading beads onto all of the pins.
2. Bind the loaded pins to the hook.
3. Whip-finish and remove the tying thread.
4. Add a coat of brushable superglue to the thread wraps for added durability.

When suspended under an indicator, balanced flies hang horizontally, mimicking the natural direction most stillwater food sources travel. Balanced flies also make excellent cast and retrieve patterns due to their jigging action.

The pin and bead play no role when fighting a fish, as the tippet attaches to the hook eye as with an unbalanced fly. If you grab the bead and pin extension while removing the fly, you may knock it out of position or, worse, pull it right out of the fly. When using balanced flies without an indicator, the bead and pin can pinch and jam on rocks and other bottom debris during the retrieve. The superglue coating alleviates these risks.

Balanced flies are not just indicator flies. A balanced fly pitches the fly nose down as it falls, just like a conventional jig. Flies such as balanced leeches and minnows perform exceptionally well when presented using cast and retrieve tactics. A 4- to 6-inch strip retrieve with a prolonged pause is deadly. Presented in this fashion, trout and other game fish find the jigging action of a balanced fly tough to resist. Over a lightly weeded or rocky bottom, a balanced fly lands bead down, hook point up.You can walk it over the bottom with little risk of a hang-up. Bass, walleye, and panfish love balanced leeches and minnows using this presentation technique, similar to how traditional bass anglers crawl jigs over the bottom to induce dour bass to strike.

FACTORS GOVERNING FLY CHANGE

To me, the fly pattern is the ultimate scapegoat. If you aren't catching fish, it always seems to be the fly's fault. If someone is having a great day on the water, everyone else wants to know what fly they are using. Cagey fly fishers guard their pattern identity as though it were a government secret.

If you ask someone what fly they are using, there are several potential answers. Some may be truthful. Others may lie or provide a pattern name that means nothing. There are so many unique pattern names today, and many of them have no relation to what the fly is or what it is designed to suggest.

When it comes to figuring out if a fly change is in order, think DRP: depth, retrieve, pattern. First, are you presenting your pattern at the correct feeding depth? Most times your fly needs to be within 1 or 2 feet of the bottom, as this is where the majority of stillwater trout food lives. Next, are you moving the fly at the correct pace? What retrieves are you using? Depending on the situation, long pulls, a slow hand twist, a strip-pause retrieve, or quick strips may be in order. Did you try a static presentation beneath an indicator? Finally, consider your fly pattern.

If you aren't catching fish, before changing flies, think DRP. Make sure you are fishing your flies at the right depth and pace before changing patterns.

If you ask a successful fly fisher what is working, even the most secretive person will likely let you know what depth they are fishing and how little or much they are moving the fly. As I stated previously, the best pattern in the world won't catch anything unless it is presented at the right depth and retrieved at the correct pace. Presentation always trumps pattern. In my experience, most people new to stillwater fly fishing don't let their flies sink long enough to reach feeding trout and then retrieve them too fast. Low and slow works best. If I am using a pattern that I have confidence in for the conditions, and I believe I am presenting my fly at the correct depth and retrieve speed, chances are I will change location before changing flies.

FLY STORAGE

Fly storage varies from fly fisher to fly fisher based on their personal preferences, logic, and the number of flies they carry. I admit, I prefer to carry a lot of flies with me in the most compact fashion that I can. My system is relatively simple and has evolved over many years on the water. It is not, however, a system cast in stone. I always keep my storage options open.

I currently use a Montana Fly Company (MFC) 12-by-11-by-4-inch slit-foam boat box with a leaf insert as my primary fly storage. Within my main box, I sort my flies by food source: leeches, damselflies, dragonflies, scuds, caddis pupae, mayfly nymphs, generic nymphs, baitfish, water boatmen, and backswimmers.

There are lots of fly box options. I use a large, slit-foam boat box to carry the majority of my flies. I also have a selection of smaller slit-foam boxes within my kit bag to hold my chironomids, balanced flies, and attractors.

I also carry several smaller, 7-by-3½-by-¾-inch Tacky-style slit-foam fly boxes in my kit bag. I use these to hold my chironomid larva and pupa patterns, balanced flies, dry flies, and attractor patterns. These slender boxes fit neatly into my boat bag. When I fly to various stillwater destinations, I can't bring my main fly box. The smaller slit-foam boxes pack well, and I can stock them with a cross section of patterns that I anticipate using on my trip.

I prefer the slit-silicone-mat fly boxes as, in my experience, they hold flies the best. There is nothing more irritating than opening your fly box to find the majority of its inhabitants rattling around, free from their moorings.

FAVORITE CROSSOVER PATTERNS

If you are a river and stream fly fisher, there is no need to build a stillwater fly collection from scratch. Many patterns designed and developed for rivers and streams also work in lakes. Here are some popular river and stream patterns that I feel should be in every stillwater box.

Beadhead Prince Nymph

Hook: #10-14 Daiichi 1760 or 1710
Thread: Black 8/0 or 70-denier
Tail: Brown goose biots
Rib: Gold Ultra Wire or oval tinsel
Body: Peacock herl
Hackle: Brown hen saddle
Wing: White goose biots
Bead: Gold, brass

Flashback Gold Bead Pheasant Tail Nymph

Hook: #10-14 Daiichi 1120 or 1710
Thread: Hot Orange or black 8/0 or 70-denier
Tail: Pheasant tail
Rib: Gold Ultra Wire
Shellback: Mirage Opal Mylar
Body: Pheasant tail
Wing case: Pheasant tail topped with Mirage Opal Mylar
Thorax: Peacock herl
Legs: Pheasant tail
Bead: Gold, brass

Soft-Hackle Hare's Ear Jig

Hook: #12-16 Daiichi 4640 or 4647
Thread: 8/0 or 70-denier, color to complement body
Tail: Partridge or Brahma hen fibers, color to complement body
Shellback: Mirage Opal Mylar
Rib: Gold or copper Ultra Wire
Body: Hare's ear dubbing
Hackle: Partridge or Brahma hen saddle fibers, color to complement body
Bead: Gold or copper slotted tungsten

Parachute Adams

Hook: #12-16 Daiichi 1170 or 1110
Thread: Black or gray 8/0 or 70-denier
Tail: Moose body hair, mixed brown and grizzly hackle fibers, or Coq de Leon fibers
Body: Adams gray dry fly dubbing or natural muskrat fur
Wing post: White calf body hair, Widow's Web, poly yarn or EP Trigger Point Fibers
Hackle: Mixed grizzly and brown

Elk Hair Caddis

Hook: #12-16 Daiichi 1170 or 1110
Thread: 8/0 or 70-denier, color to complement body
Rib: Extra small gold, copper, or silver Ultra Wire
Body: Fine & Dry Dubbing, color to match naturals
Wing: Natural elk hair
Hackle: Brown

Zebra Midge

Hook: #16-18 Daiichi 1120
Thread: 8/0 or 70-denier, color to match naturals
Rib: Extra small gold, silver, copper, or red Ultra Wire
Bead: Silver, copper, gold, white, brass, or tungsten

Woolly Bugger

Hook: #6-12 Daiichi 1720
Thread: 8/0 or 70-denier, color to complement body
Tail: Marabou, mixed with two strands of pearl (6905) or ice blue pearl (6904) Flashabou tied along each side
Rib: Extra small gold, silver, or copper Ultra Wire
Body: Chenille, crystal chenille, dubbing, color of choice, or peacock herl
Hackle: Grizzly saddle, color to complement or contrast body

FAVORITE STILLWATER PATTERNS

I enjoy designing and tying flies. Although I firmly believe in presentation over pattern, I still carry a lot of flies, not because I necessarily need to, but because I want too. Each season I experiment with new patterns. Some excel, others fall short. Designing a fly to match a specific food source or situation and having it work consistently is one of my favorite aspects of fly fishing. During the winter months, time at the vise is well spent and keeps me fishing, at least from a mental perspective.

Despite the volume of flies I carry with me on the water, I have several confidence patterns that always seem to perform. Here are some of my favorite patterns sorted by category.

Suggestive Flies

Carey Special

Hook: #6-10 Daiichi 1710 or 1720
Thread: 8/0 or 70-denier, color to complement body
Tail: Pheasant tail or guinea fibers
Body: Chenille, dubbing, color to suit, or peacock herl
Hackle: Pheasant rump or dyed guinea, color to complement body

Stillwater Nymph

Designed by Denny Rickards
Hook: #8-10 Daiichi 1710
Thread: Olive, 8/0 or 70-denier
Tail: Olive, marabou
Rib: Extra small gold, copper, or silver Ultra Wire
Shellback: Olive, marabou, or Mottled Thin Skin, color to complement body and tail
Body: Olive Ice Dub, hare's ear, or seal's fur
Hackle: Grizzly, dyed burnt orange

Fly Craft Fullback (Flashback)

Hook: #8-12 Daiichi 1710 or 1760
Thread: 8/0 or 70-denier, color to complement body
Tail: Pheasant tail
Rib: Copper, gold, or silver Ultra Wire
Body: Peacock herl or Ice Dub
Shellback: Pheasant tail
Wing case: Pheasant tail topped with Mirage Opal Mylar
Hackle: Natural or dyed partridge or Whiting Brahma hen saddle

Halfback

Hook: #6-12 Daiichi 1710
Thread: Black, olive, fluorescent orange, or fluorescent chartreuse 8/0 or 70-denier
Tail: Pheasant tail
Body: Peacock herl
Wing case: Pheasant tail
Thorax: Peacock herl
Legs: Pheasant tail

Diawl Bach

Hook: #10-14 Daiichi 1550 or 1530
Thread: Black, olive, fluorescent orange, or fluorescent chartreuse 8/0 or 70-denier
Tail: Reddish-brown hackle fibers
Rib: Copper or gold Ultra Wire
Shellback: Mirage Opal Mylar
Body: Peacock herl
Beard: Reddish-brown hackle fibers

M & M (Mirage Micro) Leech

Hook: #10-12 Daiichi 1120
Thread: 8/0 or 70-denier, color to complement body
Tail: Black, olive, or maroon Saddle or schlappen marabou from the base of the feather, mixed with two strands of red or pearl Krystal Flash
Rib: Red, copper, or silver Ultra Wire
Body: Mirage Opal Mylar
Hackle: Black, olive, or maroon ostrich herl
Bead: Gold, copper, or silver tungsten

Imitative Flies

Chironomids

Frostbite Bloodworm

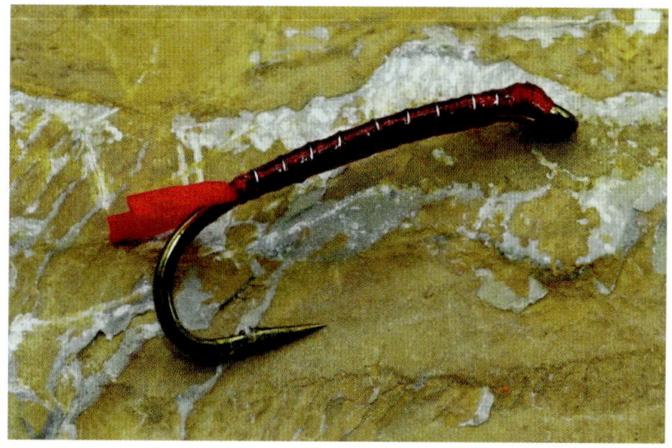

Hook: #10-14 Daiichi 1760
Thread: Red 8/0 or UTC 70
Tail: Red stretch floss
Rib: Silver Ultra Wire
Body: Bibio red Buzzer Wrap

Bionic Worm

Designed by Jerry McBride
Hook: #10-14 Daiichi 1120
Thread: Red 8/0 or UTC 70
Tail: Hot pink marabou
Rib: Gold Ultra Wire
Underbody: Gold holographic Mylar
Body: Bibio red Buzzer Wrap
Bead: Fluorescent orange

Chromie

Hook: #10-14 Daiichi 1120
Thread: Black 8/0 or UTC 70
Butt: Red holographic Mylar
Rib: Red holographic Mylar
Body: Silver Flashabou
Bead: Black nickel
Gills: White UNI Floss or UNI Stretch

PBR (Phil's Black & Red)

Hook: #10-14 Daiichi 1120
Thread: Black 8/0 or UTC 70
Rib: Red Ultra Wire
Underbody: Red holographic Mylar
Body: Dark reddish-brown Stretch Flex
Thorax: Black 8/0 or UTC 70
Bead: White, brass

Black Sally

Hook: #10-14 Daiichi 1120
Thread: Black 8/0 or UTC 70
Butt: Red holographic Mylar
Rib: Red holographic Mylar
Body: Black Flashabou
Bead: Black nickel
Gills: White UNI Floss or UNI Stretch

Collaborator

Hook: #10-14 Daiichi 1120
Thread: Burnt orange UTC 70
Butt: Red holographic Mylar
Rib: Gold Ultra Wire
Body: Root beer Buzzer Wrap
Bead: Gold, brass
Gills: White UNI Floss or UNI Stretch

Raccoon

Designed by Paul Lasha
Hook: #12-16 Daiichi 1170 or 1110
Thread: 8/0 or 70-denier, color to complement body
Tail: Natural Grizzly hackle tip, mallard flank or teal fibers, white Z-Lon or Antron
Butt: White ostrich herl
Shellback: Elk hair or tan 2 mm sheet foam
Body: Fine & Dry Dubbing, color to match naturals

Leeches

Balanced Leech (Bruised)

Hook: #10 Daiichi 4640
Thread: Black 8/0 or UTC 70
Tail: Black marabou, mixed with four strands of ice blue (6904) Pearl Flashabou, two strands tied along each side of tail
Body: Black/blue Arizona Simi Seal
Bead: Gold tungsten, mounted on a gold sequin pin and secured to the hook shank

Baby Leech (Bruised)

Hook: #12 Daiichi 4640
Thread: 8/0 or UTC 70, black
Tail: Saddle Schlappen marabou from the base of the hackle stem, black, mixed with two strands of pearl Krystal Flash
Body: Arizona Simi Seal, black/blue, spun in a dubbing loop of small blue Ultra Wire
Bead: Flourescent orange, $\frac{7}{64}$-inch slotted tungsten

Glenn's Leech

Designed by Glen Gerbrandt
Hook: #10 Daiichi 1120
Thread: 8/0 or UTC 70, color to match body
Tail: Micro mink or squirrel Zonker, color to match naturals
Rib: Small gold or red Ultra Wire
Body: Marabou, color to match naturals
Cone: Red $\frac{3}{32}$-inch micro cone

Damselfly Nymphs

Grizzly Damsel

Hook: #10-12 Daiichi 1760
Thread: Olive 8/0 UTC 70
Tail: Grizzly marabou, color to match naturals
Rib: Small copper Ultra Wire
Shellback: Mirage Opal Mylar
Wing case: Olive Scud Back
Thorax: Grizzly marabou aftershaft feathers, color to match naturals
Hackle: Olive partridge or Brahma hen
Bead: Copper, brass

Pearly Damsel

Hook: #10-14 Daiichi 1530
Thread: Olive 8/0 or UTC 70
Tail: Marabou, color to match naturals
Rib: Small copper Ultra Wire
Shellback: Mirage Opal Mylar
Body: Marabou, color to match naturals
Legs: Marabou (tips from strung marabou plume), color to match naturals
Eyes: Black extra small mono
Head: Marabou, dubbed, color to match naturals

Strip Tease Damsel (Olive)

Hook: #10-12 Daiichi 1120
Thread: Olive 8/0 or UTC 70
Tail: Olive micro mink Zonker
Rib: Fine chartreuse Ultra Wire
Body: Light olive dubbing
Legs: Olive partridge or Brahma hen
Head: Light olive dubbing
Eyes: Chartreuse knotted vernille (plush chenille)

Dragonfly Nymphs

Draggin

Hook: #4-8 Daiichi 1730 or 1720
Thread: Olive UTC 140
Underbody: Black 2 mm sheet foam
Body: Peacock Arizona Simi Seal and olive Brill UV, spun together in a dubbing loop
Wing case: Dark brown raffia
Thorax: Olive deer hair, spun and clipped
Legs: Barred Sexi-Floss or Sili Legs
Eyes: Black 5 mm Booby foam
Head: Peacock Arizona Synthetic Dubbing

Grizzly Dragon

Hook: #6-8 Daiichi 1720 or 1730
Thread: Olive UTC 140
Tail: Olive and light olive grizzly marabou
Underbody: Black 2 mm sheet foam
Body: Grizzly marabou, olive and light olive, folded in a Magic Tool and spun in a dubbing loop
Wing case: Olive Thin Skin
Legs: Barred Sexi-Floss, olive
Eyes: Black 5 mm Booby foam
Head: Arizona Synthetic Dubbing, peacock
Tying note: Trim finished body and tail to resemble the shape of a natural dragonfly nymph. Be careful not to overtrim.

Gomphus

Designed by Jim Crawford
Hook: #8-10 Daiichi 1710
Thread: UTC 140 or GSP 100, color to complement body
Body: Natural or olive deer hair, spun and clipped to shape
Legs: Natural hen or cock pheasant tail fibers
Head: Natural or olive deer hair, spun and clipped to shape

Scuds

Pearl Shrimp

Hook: #10-16 Daiichi 1120
Thread: 8/0 or UTC 70, color to complement body
Rib: Gold, copper, or red Ultra Wire
Shellback: Pearl braid or Mirage Opal Mylar
Body: Ice Dub, color to match naturals

Mayfly Nymphs

Herl May (Flashback)

Hook: #12-16 Daiichi 1760
Thread: Tan or olive UTC 70
Tail: Tan mottled turkey flat, three fibers
Rib: Fine silver Ultra Wire
Shellback: Tan mottled turkey quill
Body: Two strands of tan ostrich, one strand of light olive ostrich
Wing case: Tan mottled turkey quill, covered with Mirage Opal Mylar
Thorax: Peacock herl
Legs: Tan mottled turkey flat
Tying note: Cover wing case with UV resin

Caddis

Crystal Sedge Pupa (Dark Olive)

Hook: #8-10 Daiichi 1760
Thread: Olive 8/0 or 70-denier
Body: Peacock Arizona Simi Seal, combined in a dubbing loop with olive Brill UV or Micro Polar Chenille
Wing case: Olive Thin Skin
Thorax: Peacock Arizona Simi Seal
Wing pads: Olive raffia or Swiss straw
Hackle: Olive Whiting Brahma hen
Swimmerets: Olive Barred Sexi-Floss
Antennae (optional): Two strands of natural pheasant tail
Head: Peacock herl

Mikulak Sedge

Designed by Art Mikulak
Hook: #6-10 Daiichi 1760
Thread: Olive UTC 140
Tail: Natural elk hair
Wings: Natural elk hair, tied in three clumps along shank
Body: Hare's Ice Dub, caddis green (#49) or olive (#263)
Thorax: Hare's Ice Dub, caddis green (#49) or olive (#263)
Hackle: Brown

Tom Thumb

Hook: #8-14 Daiichi 1170
Thread: Black or olive UTC 140
Tail: Deer hair
Shellback: Deer hair
Wing: Deer hair

Baitfish

Balanced Minnow (White Satin)

Hook: #10 Daiichi 4640
Thread: White 8/0 or UTC 70
Tail: White marabou
Body: Crystal Arizona Simi Seal
Hackle: White/black barred schlappen
Eyes: 4 mm molded eyes
Lateral line: Pearl Krinkle Mirror Flash, two strands tied along each side of body
Bead: Silver ⅛-inch tungsten, mounted on a silver sequin pin and secured to the hook shank

Baby Fat Minnow

Designed by Clarke Pierce
Hook: #8 Fulling Mill Bonio Carp Hook
Thread: White 8/0 or 70-denier
Tail: White marabou
Collar: Callibaetis (#50) or pearl (#284) Ice Dub
Bead: Silver 7/64-inch (3 mm) tungsten
Head: Fly Fish Food's Jr. Bruiser Blend, darker color on top, cream dubbing on bottom
Eyes: ⅛-inch 3D holographic eyes

Balanced Ice Minnow

(Variation of Bob Morenski's Ice Minnow)
Hook: #10-12 Daiichi 4640
Thread: Red 8/0 or UTC 70
Tail: Black marabou, mixed with four strands of ice blue (6904) Pearl Flashabou; two strands tied along each side of tail
Body: Silver Brill UV
Bead: Silver tungsten, mounted on a silver sequin pin and secured to the hook shank

Water Boatmen / Backswimmers

Greater Water Floatman

Hook: #8-10 Daiichi 1550 or 1530
Thread: Olive 8/0 or UTC 70
Shellback/head: White Booby body foam
Body: Peacock green Straggle String
Legs: Olive stretch floss
Tying note: Use permanent markers to provide shellback and head markings. Coat finished markings with Softex.

Water Floatman

Hook: #12-14 Daiichi 1550 or 1530
Thread: Black 8/0 or UTC 70
Shellback: Black Booby foam
Body: White Straggle String, white UV Brill, or clear or UV clear Micro Polar Chenille
Legs: Burnt orange Sexi-Floss

Attractor Flies

Booby (Tequila)

Hook: #8 Daiichi 1120
Thread: Fluorescent orange UTC 140
Tail: Fluorescent yellow marabou, mixed with four strands of pearl Krinkle Mirror Flash; Pearlescent, two strands tied along each side of tail
Butt: Atomic yellow Jelly Fritz
Body: Safety orange Jelly Fritz
Eyes: White 5 mm Booby cord

FAB (Sunburst)

Hook: #8 Daiichi 1530
Thread: Fluorescent orange UTC 140
Tail: White 5 mm Booby foam, split
Body: Blushing sunburst orange Jelly Fritz
Underbody: Mirage Opal Mylar

Slush Jelly Blob (Beadhead)

Hook: #8-10 Daiichi 1120
Thread: 8/0 or UTC 70, color to match body
Tail: Pearl Krinkle Mirror Flash
Body: Safety orange, shocking pink, apricot, blushing sunburst, prawn, marshmallow pink Slush Jelly Fritz
Eyes: Gold tungsten

CHAPTER TAKEAWAYS

- It is important to understand what makes a good stillwater fly pattern, whether you buy or tie your flies.
- There are four important pattern elements to any fly: size, shape, color, and behavior.
- When trout are feeding selectively, shape is arguably the most important pattern consideration.
- Search image is an important factor trout use to measure prey characteristics.
- Try using a fly one size larger than the food item the trout are feeding upon to stand out in the crowd while appealing to the trout's naturally greedy, predatory nature.
- As most aquatic insects peak during the spring through early summer, use larger patterns in the spring and early summer, and smaller patterns toward the latter part of the season and into the fall.
- Fly behavior is a twofold process consisting of the materials used in the fly and the presentation techniques we use to bring the fly to life. Successful stillwater fly patterns must be both mobile and translucent.

- A number of variables influence pattern color and how trout see it, including presentation depth, available light, and water clarity.
- There are three basic fly categories: suggestive, imitative, and attractor.
- Suggestive flies possess characteristics common to a number of food sources—traits that appeal to a trout's naturally opportunistic nature.
- Presentation trumps pattern every time. The best pattern in the world won't work if it isn't presented at the right depth or moved in such a way to convince trout it is worth eating.
- Suggestive flies are excellent options when trout aren't focused on a particular food item, as searching flies, and to draw fish to a team of flies.
- Imitative flies are the best choice when trout are targeting a specific food item or stage. Chironomids are the best example of the match-the-hatch philosophy behind imitative flies.
- Attractor patterns trigger a predominantly non-feeding response from a trout through curiosity, territoriality, or aggression.
- Attractor flies can be used in an imitative fashion when trout are focused on tiny zooplankton.
- As with suggestive patterns, attractor patterns work well in a team of flies to attract fish from a distance.
- Avoid removing an attractor or suggestive fly in a team of flies if it is not hooking fish. Often these flies attract fish from a distance to smaller imitative flies on your team. Removing them could result in fewer fish caught.
- Weighted flies can negatively affect sinking line presentations by accelerating the sink rate, throwing your countdown out of balance.
- Be careful weighting curved shank hooks. A weighted curved shank hook concentrates the mass at the apex of the curve, causing the fly to roll over inverted.
- To maintain a slender profile, use one size smaller beads than most bead-to-hook size charts recommend for chironomid pupa and larva patterns.
- Due to the horizontal nature in which they suspend, balanced flies outperform traditional beadhead flies under a strike indicator.
- Balanced flies are also excellent flies to use with cast and retrieve presentations due, in part, to their jig-like action.
- If you aren't catching fish, think DRP (depth, retrieve, pattern) before changing your fly. Depth, presentation, and retrieve speed are more important in many instances than fly pattern.
- In my experience, slit-foam or slit-silicone fly boxes hold flies best.

INDEX

A

about: the fishing expertise of Phil Rowley, ix–x
accessories
  binoculars, 17, 35
  black electrical tape, 25
  bobber stops, 28–30, 37, 210, 229
  clear nail polish, 26
  clothes peg, 23
  depth locator, 24, 229
  first aid kit, 35
  flashlight and headlamp, 22
  floatant and desiccant, 33, 218, 244–46
  gloves and hand warmers, 35–36
  hemostat (forceps), 21
  kit bag, 17
  knot-tying tool, 32, 75
  landing nets, 15–16
  leader mud, 33, 244
  nippers and cutters, 22
  permanent markers, 229
  polarized sunglasses, 18
  sampling equipment, 19–20
  split shot, 27, 32, 227, 230–33
  sunscreen, 17, 35
  superglue, 26
  swivels, 26–28
  thermometers and Deptherms, 34–35, 37, 169–70, 172, 192
  throat pump, 19, 105, 148, 157, 188–91
  tippet rings, 31, 68, 82, 85, 226–27, 265
  tungsten putty, 27, 28, 32
  UV knot resin, 34, 76–77, 210
aeropneustic respiration, 109, 151
Albright knot, 77
algae/algae concentrations, 93–94, 132, 144, 180, 309
algal blooms, 89, 91, 100, 104, 283
American Angler (magazine), vii
anchors/anchoring
  anchor locks, 51–52
  anchor ropes, 53
  styles and weight requirements, 54–55
  See also watercraft
ants, 162–63
aquatic food sources
  about: characteristics of, 105–07
  about: trout digestion rate, 107–08
  availability, physiology and life cycle, 108–10
  backswimmers, 153–55
  caddisflies/sedges, 145–49
  Chaoborus, 113–18, 157, 165, 279–80
  chironomids, 111–18
  crayfish, 158–60
  damselflies, 128–32
  dragonflies, 132–37

forage fish (baitfish), 122–25
leeches, 125–28
mayflies, 137–44
scuds/shrimp, 118–22
snails, 160–61
water boatmen, 149–52
zooplankton, 155–57
See also match-the-hatch; terrestrial insects
atmospheric pressure, 174–76
attractors/attractor flies
benefits and use, 93, 100, 108, 189, 199, 201, 203, 243, 257, 276–78
color and size, 157, 283–84
as droppers, 78
matching the hatch, 287
presentation tactics, 269–70, 285–86
triggering a response, 278–82, 312

B

backswimmers, 153–55
balanced flies, 314–17
bank fishing, 38–39
barometric pressure, 174–76, 199
bass, fly fishing for, xviii, 89, 277, 315, 317
bathymetric maps, 182–83, 185, 187–88, 193
beetles, 163
belly boats (float tubes), 40–43, 58–59
benefits of lakes over moving waters
aim of this book to clarify, xi
avoiding the crowds, xiii
challenge of "matching the hatch," xv–xvi
larger fish size, xvi–xvii
no annual runoff, xii
offering a relaxed pace, xiv
variety of different species, xvii–xviii
binoculars, 17, 35, 188
birds/bird activity, 35, 115–16, 186, 273–74
black electrical tape, 25
blood knot, 73
bloodworms, 111–12, 114, 115, 117, 273, 284. *See also* chironomids
blue-green algae, 100
boats. *See* watercraft
bobber stops, 28–30, 37, 210, 229
Booby and Blob flies, 157, 201, 203, 243–44, 269–70, 285–87, 308, 312, 325–27, 330–31
buoyant attractors, 280, 285–87
buoyant flies, 12, 136, 152, 243–44, 263, 269–70, 308. *See also* non-buoyant flies

C

caddisflies/sedges, 145–49
Callibaetis. *See* mayflies
canoes and kayaks, 47
cassette (cartridge-style) reels, 6
catch-and-release, 12, 64, 216, 224
See also reviving and releasing fish
Chaoborus (phantom midges/glass worms), 113–18, 157, 165, 279–80
chapter takeways
attractor techniques, 288
equipment: accessories, 37
equipment: rods, reels, and lines, 14
figuring out what trout eat, 165–66
finding trout in lakes, 192–93
floating line techniques: dries and emergers, 257–58
floating line techniques: strike indicators and long leader nymphing, 237–38
floating line techniques: targeting sighted fish, 257–58
lake types, zones, and seasonal fluctuation, 104
leaders, knots, and droppers, 85–86
loch style (drifting) techniques, 304
stillwater flies, 331–32
stillwater presentation and retrieves, 211

subsurface (sinking line) techniques, 275
watercraft, anchoring and fishing from, 60–61
chironomids, vii, xvi, 109–18, 128, 133, 165, 174, 184, 188–89, 229, 239, 273–74, 285, 306, . *See also* bloodworms
clear intermediate lines, 6–7, 10, 13, 14, 129, 142, 152, 263–65, 268, 270
clear nail polish, 26
clear-tip lines (aka midge-tip), 6, 10, 79, 129, 142, 152, 243, 270, 303
clinch knot, 68
clothes peg, 23
cold weather, warming accessories, 35–36
competition fishing, 12, 277–78, 290, 293, 295, 301, 312
Corkies, indicators, 219–20
countdown, 12, 261–62, 264, 275, 332
Crawford, Jim, 327
crayfish, 158–60
Crowley Lake, CA, 226
Cruncher (fly), 251

D

damselflies, 128–32
dangling
about: the technique of, 270–71
how to find fish when, 273–74
leaders, 271–72
setting the depth, 229, 272–73
using a hang marker, 210
using bobber stoppers, 30
density-compensated sinking lines, 7–8, 12, 14, 264, 268, 271–72
depth locator, 24, 229, 238, 272
Deptherms. *See* thermometers and Deptherms
double anchoring, 48, 54–55, 61
double surgeon's knot, 74
dragonflies, 132–37
drift boats, 47–48, 291–93
drifting. *See* loch style (drifting) fishing
drogues (sea anchors), 295–300
drop-offs, 35, 38–39, 60, 97, 169, 175, 177–83, 188, 249, 274
droppers
benefits and use, 78
position/terminology, 79
rigging, methods for, 80–83
spacing and tag length, 79
tangles, reducing, 84–85
DRP (depth, retrieve, pattern), 317–18, 332
dry dropper, indicators, 218
dry flies and emergers
floating line technique, 9, 212
leader selection, 63, 224
Loch-style fishing with, 290, 303
using floatants and desiccants, 244–46
using yarn indicators, 218–19
See also stillwater flies; surface-feeding/rising trout

E

electrical tape, black, 25
electronic sounders, 24, 34–35, 53, 94, 157, 169–70, 174, 181–83, 186–87, 227
equipment. *See* accessories; fly lines; fly reels; fly rods
European Fly Fishing Team, x, 312
eutrophic lakes, 90–91, 96, 99

F

FAB flies, 157, 201, 203, 269, 285–86, 308, 312, 331
fan casting, 208, 211, 304
fast-sinking lines. *See* sinking lines
Fat Albert (fly), 277
fiberglass boats, 293
fighting butt (up-lock reel seat), 5
figure eight retrieve, 211
first aid kit, 35
fishing diary/journal, 192
flashlights and headlamps, 22

flat-bottom jon boats, 48–49, 292–93
flies. *See* stillwater flies
floatants and desiccants, 33, 218, 244–46
floating lines
about: selection/choice of, 8–9, 212–13
line color, 188
rod position with, 211
targeting rising/surface-feeding fish, 239–52, 257–58
targeting sighted fish, 252–58
when to use indicators or fish naked, 235–36, 289, 313
wind and surface-chop effects, 259, 268
wind drifting, 206–07, 211
See also indicators; indicator-style leaders; naked-technique leaders
float tubes (belly boats), 40–43, 58–59
Fly Fishing Team USA, x
fly lines
about: selection and style, 6
changing lines on the water, 23
density-compensation, 7–8, 12, 14, 264, 268, 271–72
integrated lines, 6, 12
line colors, 12
line core options, 7, 12, 14
See also clear-tip lines; floating lines; hover lines; sinking lines; sweep lines
Fly Patterns for Stillwaters (Rowley), vii
fly reels, 5–6
fly rods
choices and selection, 1–2, 14, 300–301
controlling and landing fish, 5
length and amount of hang, 5, 210, 300
length and casting distance, 2–4
length and mending, 4, 207
length and presentation control, 4
line cores and, 7
line weight and density, 266, 301
rod tip "fishing position," 195–97, 272
up-locking reel seat (fighting butt), 5
forage fish (baitfish), 122–25
foul hooking, 28
full-sinking lines. *See* sinking lines

G

Galloup, Kelly, 277
Gerbrandt, Glen, 325
global positioning system (GPS), 170, 181, 187
gloves and hand warmers, 35–36
Google Maps / Google Earth, 182–83, 185, 193
grasshoppers, 164
Gulley, Ernie, 184, 226

H

hand twist retrieve, 121, 131, 136, 151, 160, 163, 197, 199–200, 205–06, 209, 243, 250, 266, 268, 272, 285, 303
hand weave retrieve, 211
hang, 5, 66, 152, 188, 199, 207, 209–10
hang (line) markers, 28–30, 71, 210–11
Hebgen Lake, MT, 239
hemostat (forceps), 21
Henry's Lake, ID, ix–x, 49, 210
hooks, hook style, hook size, 114–15, 127, 130–31, 136, 142, 151, 154, 159, 161, 244, 313–17, 332
hook-set, 5, 195–96, 211, 233, 252
hover lines, 6, 8, 10–11, 63, 129, 142, 152, 263–65, 268, 270

I

ice-off, 96–98, 112, 149, 152, 168–69
ice-on (freeze-up), 168, 174, 205.142
imitative flies, 311–12, 323–24
indicators, types of
benefits and use, 212–17
choosing the right indicator, 222–23

Corkies, 219–20
dry dropper, 218
Quick Release, 220–22
Thingamabobber and Air-Lock balloon-style, 220
yarn, 218–19
indicator-style leaders
benefits and use, 223–24
deep-water leaders, 225–27
hybrid low-stretch leader, 227
standard leaders, 224
technique for setting depth, 227–29
techniques for casting, 236–37
use an indicator or go naked?, 235–36
See also naked-technique leaders
inducing a take
animating the fly in stillwater, 194
fan casting, 208
positioning the rod and hand, 195–97
the retrieve, about the types of, 199–204
the retrieve, elements of, 198–99
the retrieve, incorporating the hang, 208–11
the retrieve, with an indicator, 205–06
wind drifting, 206–07
insects, as food sources. *See* aquatic food sources; terrestrial insects
Instagram, 305
integrated lines, 6, 12
isotherms, 98

J

jon boats, 48–49, 292–93

K

Kamloops, BC, 312
kit bag, 17
knots: categories/types, 65–66
knots, primary
clinch knot, 68
nonslip loop knot, 66–67
perfection loop, 68–69
triple surgeon's knot, 70–71
knots, secondary
Albright knot, 77
blood knot, 73
double surgeon's knot, 74
nail knot, 75–76
uni knot, 71–72
knot-tying tool, 32, 75

L

Lago Strobel, Argentina (aka Jurassic Lake), xvi, 119, 216, 218
Lake Davis, CA, 178
lakes. *See* stillwater fishing
lakes, benefits over moving waters
aim of this book to clarify, xi
avoiding the crowds, xiii
challenge of "matching the hatch," xv–xvi
larger fish size, xvi–xvii
no annual runoff, xii
offering a relaxed pace, xiv
variety of different species, xvii–xviii
lakes, seasons
characteristics of, 95
effects on trout behavior, 174
fall, 102–03
spring, 97–99
summer, 99–101
winter, 95–97
lakes, structures/features
about: identifying, 182–83
drop-offs, 35, 38–39, 60, 97, 169, 175, 177–83, 188, 249, 274
points, 38–39, 60, 169, 175, 177–78, 180, 182–83, 188, 290
shoals, 10, 38–39, 89–90, 92–93, 95, 97, 178–79, 181–85, 256–57, 268, 274, 278, 299, 303
sunken islands and humps, 92, 177, 180–83, 249
weed beds, 129, 173, 177–78, 180–81, 183–85, 205, 268
lakes, types
classification, 87–89

eutrophic lakes, 90–91, 96, 99
mesotrophic lakes, 90
oligotrophic lakes, 89–90
lakes, zones
defined/described, 92
isotherms, 98
limnetic zone, 04, 93, 98–99, 157
littoral zone, 92–93, 94, 98–99
profundal zone, 94, 99–100
thermocline, 93–94, 99, 101–02, 157
lake stratification, 94–97, 100, 104, 174
See also seasonal turnover
landing nets, 15–16
Lasha, Paul, 324
leader mud, 33, 244
leaders
purpose and selection, 62–63
storage, 63–64
using tippets, 64
See also indicator-style leaders; naked-technique leaders
leeches, 108, 125–28, 165, 184, 325
licensing and regulations, 45, 47, 78, 216, 219, 244
light refraction, 252–54
limnetic (epilimnion) zone, 04, 93, 98–99, 157
lines. *See* fly lines
littoral zone (shoal), 92–93, 94, 98–99
loch style (drifting) fishing
benefits and growth in popularity, 289–91
boats, about the types of, 291–93
boat seats and thwart boards, 293–95
drogues (sea anchors), 295–300
presentation techniques, 301–03
rod and line selection, 300–301
setting up the drift, 303
lunar phases, 176

M

matching-the-hatch, xv–xvi, 276, 283, 285, 311, 332
mayflies, 137–44
McBride, Jerry, 284, 314, 323
mending, xiv, 4, 9, 207
mesotrophic lakes, 90
Mikulak, Art, 328
minnows. *See* forage fish
Modern Streamers (Galloup), 277
Montana Fly Company, 318
Morenski, Bob, 329

N

nail knot, 75–76
naked-technique leaders
about: elements and construction of, 229–31
basic 20-foot naked leader, 231–32
leader length vs. depth chart, 232
sink time and weight, 232–33
techniques for casting, 236–37
the retrieve and recognizing takes, 233–35
when to fish naked, 235–36
See also indicator-style leaders
nippers and cutters, 22
non-buoyant flies, 78, 269, 287
non-density-compensated sinking lines, 8, 12, 268
nonslip loop knot, 66–67

O

oligotrophic lakes, 89–90
oxygen level
lake zones and, 92, 98, 102
stillwater food sources and, 109, 117, 157, 184
water temperature and, 192, 270
See also seasonal turnover

P

parasites, 120–21
perfection loop knot, 68–69
permanent markers, 229
Pheasant Tail (fly), 157, 251, 319
phytoplankton, 100, 157
Pierce, Clarke, 329

pike and muskie, fly fishing for, xviii, 21, 203, 277
pinch strip retrieve, 197, 202, 205–06, 233, 272, 285
points, 38–39, 60, 169, 175, 177–78, 180, 182–83, 188, 290
polarized sunglasses, 18
pontoon boats, 43–46, 293
profundal (hypolimnion) zone, 94, 99–100
Pyramid Lake, NV, 25, 89, 222

Q

Quick Release, indicators, 220–22

R

Randall, Jason, 306
reels, 5–6
regulations and licensing, 45, 47, 78, 216–17, 219, 244
the retrieve
  animating the fly in stillwater, 194
  elements of, 198–99
  fan casting and, 208
  incorporating the hang, 208–11
  rod and hand positioning, 195–97
  wind drifting and, 206–07
the retrieve, types of
  about: choosing the retrieve, 199
  figure eight retrieve, 211
  hand twist retrieve, 121, 131, 136, 151, 160, 163, 197, 199–200, 205–06, 209, 243, 250, 266, 268, 272, 285, 303
  hand weave retrieve, 211
  pinch strip retrieve, 197, 202, 205–06, 233, 272, 285
  rolly polly retrieve, 203–04
  static retrieve, 205
  strip retrieve, 121, 148, 188, 201, 205–06
  strip-pause retrieve, 11, 148, 285–86, 317
  upwind retrieve, 206
  using an indicator, 205–06
  when is it time to change?, 317
reviving and releasing the fish, 46, 169, 191
Rickards, Denny, 310, 322
rising trout. *See* surface-feeding/rising trout
rods. *See* fly rods
roll cast, 3, 9, 39, 209, 216, 224, 227, 237, 238, 266
rolly polly retrieve, 203–04
Rosenbauer, Tom, ix–x
Royal Coachman (fly), 277
Royal Wulff (fly), 277
Rule of 12s, 261–62, 264, 275
runoff, rivers and stream, xii

S

sampling equipment, 19–20
scuds/shrimp, 118–22
sea anchors (drogues), 295–300
seasonal turnover
  about: the condition of, xii
  lake zones and, 92–94
  seasonal characteristics, 95–103
  water chemistry and oxygen levels, 270
  water temperature and, 174
seats and thwart boards, 293–95
shallow-water fishing, 10, 104, 119, 154, 270
shoals, 10, 38–39, 89–90, 92–93, 95, 97, 178–79, 181–85, 256–57, 268, 274, 278, 299, 303
shoreline fishing, 38–39
sight fishing
  about: light refraction and, 252–54
  being able to spot the fish, 254–55
  interpreting the trout's mood and actions, 256
  noise discipline and, 256–57
  See also surface-feeding/rising trout

sinking lines
about: features and selection, 6–8, 259–65
casting, 266
dangling, 270–74
fast-sinking lines, 2, 10, 23–24, 63, 93–94, 136, 224, 270–71, 285, 301
fishing buoyant flies, 269–70
full-sinking lines, 10, 11–12, 79, 152
line color, 12, 188
line cores, 12, 14
reducing tangles, 266–67
sink rate, 12, 261–63, 313
slow-sinking lines, 8, 10, 93, 268, 301, 313
snails, 160–61
Solunar Tables, 176
split shot, 27, 32, 227, 230–33
spring kill, 99, 104, 179
static retrieve, 205
stillwater fishing, compared to rivers and streams
aim of this book to clarify, xi
avoiding the crowds, xiii
challenge of "matching the hatch," xv–xvi
larger fish size, xvi–xvii
no annual runoff, xii
offering a relaxed pace, xiv
variety of different species, xvii–xviii
stillwater fishing, finding trout
about: understanding the needs of trout, 166–67
keeping a fishing diary, 192
understanding the food sources, 183–84
use your power of observation, 184–88
using a throat pump, 188–91
See also inducing a take
stillwater fishing, trout comfort factors
defined/described, 167–68
lunar phases, 176
seasonal changes, 174
water temperature, 168–74
weather changes, 174–76
stillwater fishing, trout protection factors
about: defining, 177
algae concentrations, 180
light, shadows and cloud cover, 178–79
underwater structures, 180–81
weed beds, 181
wind and water surface texture, 177–78
stillwater flies
availability of information, 305–06
patterns, categories, 310–12
patterns, key elements, 306–09
patterns, my favorite, 321–31
patterns, river and stream crossover, 319–21
storage boxes, 318–19
when to change patterns, 317–18
See also buoyant flies; dry flies and emergers; weighted flies
stillwater food sources. *See* aquatic food sources; terrestrial insects
strap-on anchoring system, 59, 61
strike indicators. *See* indicators
strip retrieve, 121, 148, 188, 201, 205–06
strip-pause retrieve, 11, 148, 285–86, 317
suggestive flies, 310–11, 321–23
sunken islands and humps, 92, 177, 180–83, 249
sunscreen, 17, 35
superglue, 26
surface-feeding/rising trout
fishing for, 239–41
leaders and the presentation, 242–44
reading the rise, 246–49
responding to the rise, 249–52
See also dry flies and emergers; sight fishing
sweep lines, 6, 12, 14, 152, 300
swing tipping, 302–03
swivels, 26–28

T

tangles, reducing
  casting into the wind, 206
  casting with indicators, 216, 218–19, 236–37
  casting with the wind, 290
  droppers and, 78–80, 82, 84–85
  fishing with two in the boat, 303
  leaders and, 11, 62, 224, 227, 230–31
  rod length, 2–3
  sinking lines, 11–12, 259, 266–68
  swivels and, 27
terrestrial insects
  about: feeding on, 161–62
  ants, 162–63
  beetles, 163
  grasshoppers, 164
thermocline (metalimnion), 93–94, 99, 101–02, 157
thermometers and Deptherms, 34–35, 37, 169–70, 172, 192
Thingamabobber and Air-Lock balloon-style, indicators, 220
throat pump, 19, 105, 148, 157, 188–91
tippet rings, 31, 68, 82, 85, 226–27, 265
triple surgeon's knot, 70–71
trolling, 11, 42, 259, 263–64
Trout Sense (Randall), 306
tungsten beads/tungsten powder, 7–8
tungsten putty, 27, 28, 32
turnover. *See* seasonal turnover
"Two Fish Rule," 187

U

ultraviolet light (UV), 18, 284
uni knot, 71–72
unweighted flies, 212, 248, 251, 263, 313
up-lock reel seat (fighting butt), 5
upwind retrieve, 206
U-shaped floats, 59
UV knot resin, 34, 76–77, 210

V

vision
  overcoming surface glare, 25, 37, 85
  polarized sunglasses and, 18, 254
  what can a trout see?, 252–54

W

waking flies, 148, 244, 270, 285
walleye, fly fishing for, xviii, 315, 317
washing line, 154, 218, 244, 269–70, 275, 280
water boatmen, 149–52
water chemistry, 270
  See also oxygen level
water clarity, 93–94, 98–99, 178, 192, 265, 270, 283, 308–09
water density, 262
water pH, 89
water temperature
  algae effects, 180
  aquatic insect hatch and activity, 134, 145
  crayfish activity and, 159
  depth locators and indicators, 229, 235
  forage fish behavior and, 124
  lake zones and, 92–94
  line selection and, 7, 11, 262–63
  maintaining records, 192
  oxygen levels and, 104, 117
  seasonal fluctuations, 95, 99–100, 102–03, 174
  seasonal turnover and, 174
  thermometers and Deptherms, 34–35
  trout behavior and, 167–74, 199, 205, 211
  trout metabolism and, 107, 165
  underwater features and, 181
  wader selection and, 42
  zooplankton levels, 147
watercraft
  about: categories and selection, 39, 49
  boats, 46–51

canoes and kayaks, 47
drift boats, 47–48, 291–93
drogues (sea anchors), 295–300
fiberglass boats, 293
flat-bottom jon boats, 48–49, 292–93
float tubes (belly boats), 40–43, 293
pontoon boats, 43–46, 293
seats and thwart boards, 293–95
wooden clinker boats, 291–93
watercraft, anchoring
anchor locks, 51–52
anchor ropes, 53
anchor ropes, fish entangling with, 58, 61, 299
anchor styles and weight requirements, 54–55
anchoring into the wind, 55–57
anchoring perpendicular to the wind, 57–58
double anchoring, 48, 54–55, 61
float tubes, 58–59
strap-on anchoring system, 59, 61
U-shaped floats, 59
weather, effect on trout behavior, 174–76
weed beds, 129, 173, 177–78, 180–81, 183–85, 205, 268
weighted flies, 9, 45, 93, 213, 229, 263, 313–17, 332
See also unweighted flies
wind drifting, 4, 10, 18, 161, 177, 199, 205–07, 233, 249, 259, 268, 271–72, 287, 302
winterkill, 96–97, 99–100, 104, 174
wooden clinker boats, 291–93
Woolly Bugger (fly), 127, 310, 321
World Fly Fishing Championship, 312

Y

yarn, indicators, 218–19
YouTube, 183, 274, 305

Z

zooplankton, 155–57